J.T.

J.T. J.T. J.T. J.T. J.T. J.T. J.T. J.T. J.T. J.T.
J.T. J.T. J.T. J.T. J.T. J.T. J.T. J.T. J.T. J.T.
J.T. J.T. J.T. J.T. J.T. J.T. J.T. J.T. J.T. J.T.
J.T. J.T. J.T. J.T. J.T. J.T. J.T. J.T. J.T. J.T.
J.T. J.T. J.T. J.T. J.T. J.T. J.T. J.T. J.T. J.T.
J.T. J.T. J.T. J.T. J.T. J.T. J.T. J.T. J.T. J.T.
J.T. J.T. J.T. J.T. J.T. J.T. J.T. J.T. J.T. J.T.
J.T. J.T. J.T. J.T. J.T. J.T. J.T. J.T. J.T. J.T.
J.T. J.T. J.T. J.T. J.T. J.T. J.T. J.T. J.T. J.T.
J.T. J.T. J.T. J.T. J.T. J.T. J.T. J.T. J.T. J.T.
J.T. J.T. J.T. J.T. J.T. J.T. J.T. J.T. J.T. J.T.
J.T. J.T. J.T. J.T. J.T. J.T. J.T. J.T. J.T. J.T.
J.T. J.T. J.T. J.T. J.T. J.T. J.T. J.T. J.T. J.T.
J.T. J.T. J.T. J.T. J.T. J.T. J.T. J.T. J.T. J.T.
J.T. J.T. J.T. J.T. J.T. J.T. J.T. J.T. J.T. J.T.
J.T. J.T. J.T. J.T. J.T. J.T. J.T. J.T. J.T. J.T.
J.T. J.T. J.T. J.T. J.T. J.T. J.T. J.T. J.T. J.T.
J.T. J.T. J.T. J.T. J.T. J.T. J.T. J.T. J.T. J.T.
J.T. J.T. J.T. J.T. J.T. J.T. J.T. J.T. J.T. J.T.

Jan Tschichold

Master Typographer
His Life, Work & Legacy

Cees W. de Jong
Alston W. Purvis
Martijn F. Le Coultre
Richard B. Doubleday
Hans Reichardt

Thames & Hudson

J.T.

First published in the
United Kingdom in 2008
by Thames & Hudson Ltd,
181A High Holborn,
London WC1V 7QX

www.thamesandhudson.com

First published in 2008 in
hardcover in the United States of
America by Thames & Hudson Inc.,
500 Fifth Avenue, New York,
New York 10110

thamesandhudsonusa.com

ORIGINAL EDITION
© 2008 VK Projects, Laren
THIS EDITION
© 2008 Thames & Hudson Ltd,
London

All Rights Reserved. No part of this
publication may be reproduced or
transmitted in any form or by any
means, electronic or mechanical,
including photocopy, recording
or any other information storage
and retrieval system, without prior
permission in writing from the
publisher.

British Library Cataloguing-in-
Publication Data
A catalogue record for this book is
available from the British Library

Library of Congress Catalog Card
Number: 2008900149

ISBN 978-0-500-51398-9

Printed and bound in China

EDITING & DESIGN
Cees W. de Jong, Laren

DESIGN & LAYOUT
Corine Teuben, Utrecht

ESSAYS
Martijn F. Le Coultre, Laren
Alston W. Purvis, Boston
Richard B. Doubleday, Boston
Hans Reichardt, Frankfurt
Cees W. de Jong, Laren

TRANSLATION
Roz & Hans Vatter-Buck,
Doe-eye, Lasserre

PREPRESS
BFC, Amersfoort
Colourset, Amsterdam

Table of Contents

13
Introduction
Cees W. de Jong

23
Tschichold and the New Typography
Alston W. Purvis

155
Tschichold and Poster Design
Martijn F. Le Coultre

257
Resurgence of Classical Design
Richard B. Doubleday

299
Perfectly Legible and Readable
Hans Reichardt & Cees W. de Jong

343
Index of Names

347
Selected Literature & Source List

351
Illustration Credits

1902 »

Johannes Tzschichhold was born in April 1902, the son of Franz Tzschichhold and Maria Zapff. His father was a lettering artist and sign painter in Leipzig.

He followed classes in calligraphy, wood engraving, etching, and bookbinding under Walter Tiemann from 1919 to 1921 and Hermann Delitsch from 1921 to 1923 at the Leipzig Staatliche Akademie für graphische Künste und Buchgewerbe (Academy for Graphic Arts and Book Production).

1919 »

He also followed classes with the type designer Heinrich Wieynck at the Kunstgewerbeschule (College for Applied Arts) in Dresden.

In addition to his formal training, he diligently studied Edward Johnston's book *Writing & Illuminating & Lettering* and Rudolf von Larisch's *Unterricht in ornamentaler Schrift* (Instruction in Ornamental Writing).

After completing his formal training, he first worked as a traditional calligrapher, designing advertisements mainly for the Leipzig trade fairs. He also taught an evening course in calligraphy at the Leipzig Academy.

1923 »

He began working as a freelance typographic designer and calligrapher for the printer Fischer & Wittig and the publisher Insel-Verlag, both based in Leipzig.

Seeing the Russian Revolution as a possibility for a new beginning, he openly demonstrated his interest in Russian design by changing his name to Iwan (Ivan) Tschichold.

1902–1974

1926 »

On March 31, 1926, Jan Tschichold married Maria Mathilda Edith Kramer. Edith was trained as a journalist.

Paul Renner, the designer of the typeface Futura, first made contact with Tschichold in 1926 when they were both accused of being "Bolsheviks" in the journals *Zeitschrift für Deutschlands Buchdrucker* (Journal for the Printers of Germany) and *Schweizer graphische Mitteilungen* (Swiss Graphic Notes).

In June 1926, Renner arranged for Tschichold to teach typography and calligraphy at the Munich Grafische Berufsschule (Vocational School for Graphic Arts) where Renner had been appointed to build a new faculty and curriculum.

After Tschichold assumed this post, Renner and some of his other colleagues persuaded him to drop the name Iwan for obvious political reasons, and it was then that he took on the name Jan, based on his given name Johannes.

Between 1926 and 1929, Tschichold produced a "universal alphabet" similar to one designed by Herbert Bayer in 1925. Other fonts designed by Tschichold include Transito in 1931, Saskia in 1931–1932, and Zeus in 1931.

1927 »

The Meisterschule für Deutschlands Buchdrucker (Master School for Germany's Printers) opened on February 1, 1927. Established largely through the efforts of Renner, this was a parallel school in Munich where Tschichold and Trump would also teach.

The first child of Jan and Edith Tschichold was born on June 10, 1927 and died after only six months.

Jan Tschichold

In August 1923, he visited the first Bauhaus exhibition in Weimar. Afterwards he incorporated Bauhaus functionalist and Russian constructivist design theories into his own work, along with the visionary and theoretical ideas of the Dutch De Stijl movement.

At the age of twenty-three, Tschichold quickly became the uncompromising voice and guiding force of what would be known as *Die neue Typographie*, or the New Typography.

László Moholy-Nagy was the first to use the term *Die neue Typographie* in the catalog for the 1923 Bauhaus exhibition.

1925 »

Two years after the Bauhaus exhibition, Tschichold was invited to work as guest editor for the October 1925 issue of the German printing trade journal *Typographische Mitteilungen* (Typographic Notes), for which he wrote and designed a 24-page insert entitled *elementare typographie*.

Printed in red and black, it featured samples of avant-garde typography including work by El Lissitzky and Kurt Schwitters. Lissitzky was delighted to have been included, and this resulted in a lasting friendship between him and Tschichold.

Essentially, the basics of the New Typography were clarity and form derived from functional needs. Tschichold preferred photography for illustrations because of its exact and objective nature, and he made it an additional element in the New Typography, especially in his poster designs.

1928 »

Tschichold's first book, *Die neue Typographie*, published in 1928, became one of the most important documents of modernist graphic design. In it, Tschichold further refined, codified, and articulated the design concepts of the New Typography for the printing trade.

Many advocates of the New Typography belonged to the Ring neuer Werbegestalter (Ring of New Advertising Designers), which eventually included 25 members. Founded by Kurt Schwitters in 1928, the main purpose of this association was to promote the work of its members.

In the summer, Tschichold visited Paris, where he met Piet Mondrian among others.

1929 »

In 1929, Georg Trump, designer of the slab serif typeface called City, also joined Renner's staff. Like Renner and Tschichold, Trump had a traditional training before embracing modernist typography.

In addition to Schwitters, its members included Tschichold, Willi Baumeister, Max Burchartz, Walter Dexel, Hans Leistikow, Robert Michel, Georg Trump, César Domela, Friedrich Vordemberge-Gildewart, Piet Zwart, and Paul Schuitema.

Peter, son of Jan and Edith Tschichold was born on January 4, 1929.

Master Typographer

1931 »

Between 1928 and 1931, the Ring sponsored meetings and design conferences and arranged 22 European exhibitions, one of the most important taking place in Amsterdam in 1931.

Several of these exhibitions also included designers who were not associated with the Ring, including Theo van Doesburg, the principal practitioner and promoter of De Stijl in the Netherlands, the Czech constructivist Karel Teige, and the Bauhaus designers Herbert Bayer and László Moholy-Nagy.

Between 1927 and 1933, Tschichold traveled throughout Germany, Austria, Czechoslovakia, Switzerland, and France in connection with publications, lectures, and exhibitions on the themes of the New Typography and type design. In 1935, Tschichold visited London and Denmark for lectures, with a follow-up visit to London in 1937.

1933 »

In January 1933, Tschichold submitted his resignation to the Munich Meisterschule to assume a teaching position at the Höhere Graphische Fachschule der Stadt Berlin (Berlin Higher Vocational School for Graphic Arts), where Trump had become director.

After visiting Berlin, he changed his mind and decided that he would rather stay in Munich.

After the Nazi victory in the March 5 elections of 1933, both Tschichold and his wife Edith were arrested, having been labeled "cultural Bolsheviks." Shortly after his arrest, Tschichold was removed from his teaching post at the Meisterschule, having been accused of advocating "un-German" typography.

Edith Tschichold was released a few days later, and Tschichold himself was set free after being held for six weeks in "protective custody."

1959 »

In *Typography USA*, Tschichold wrote: "In the light of my present knowledge, it was a juvenile opinion to consider the sans serif as the most suitable or even the most contemporary typeface. A typeface has first to be legible, nay, readable, and a sans serif is certainly not the most legible typeface when set in quantity, let alone readable…. Good typography has to be perfectly legible and, as such, the result of intelligent planning. The classical typefaces such as Garamond, Janson, Baskerville, and Bell are undoubtedly the most legible."

He then returned to the traditional and symmetrical typography that he had so vehemently rejected a decade earlier.

Many of the designers who had enthusiastically embraced the New Typography were angered by his reversal. Tschichold's most vehement detractor was Max Bill, an industrial designer, painter, sculptor, architect, and ultimately graphic designer. He had wholeheartedly embraced the principles of the New Typography, and now its most prominent spokesman had, in his eyes, rejected all that he had believed in. For this he was unforgiving.

Tschichold himself wrote: "In time, typographical things, in my eyes, took on a very different aspect, and to my astonishment I detected the most shocking parallels between the teachings of *Die neue Typographie* and National Socialism and fascism. Obvious similarities consist in the ruthless restriction of typefaces, a parallel to Goebbels's infamous *Gleichschaltung* [enforced political conformity], and the more or less militaristic arrangement of lines."

He now believed that typographers should embrace humanist ideals and use the wisdom and achievements of past typographers and the entire heritage of graphic design as sources of inspiration.

His Life, Work & Legacy

The couple immediately left Munich with their four-year-old son and went to Basel.

A few weeks later, Renner was also arrested and forced to resign from his teaching post.

With the backing of Dr. Hermann Kienzle, then Director of the Basel Allgemeine Gewerbeschule (School of Arts and Crafts) in Switzerland, Tschichold obtained a teaching post there and received design assignments from the publisher and printer Benno Schwabe.

1935 »

Widely read and very influential, Tschichold's most important book *Typographische Gestaltung* (Typographic Design) was published in 1935. It was also issued in Danish, Swedish, and Dutch editions.

In around 1936, he made his first visit to Berzona, in the Italian-speaking canton of Ticino, where he would built a house in 1946.

1942 »

Shortly before the outbreak of World War II, Tschichold began to reconsider and eventually reject the principles of the New Typography as well as the exclusive use of sans serif typefaces.

In 1942, Jan Tschichold was granted Swiss nationality by the canton of Basel.

1947 »

From 1947 to 1949, Tschichold worked for Penguin Books in London.

He established a fixed set of typographic standards, the Penguin Composition Rules.

Between 1950 and 1954, he was an independent typographer in Basel.

1966 »

As a typeface designer, Tschichold produced the complete type family Sabon in 1966–1967. Released in 1967, it was jointly commissioned by Linotype, Monotype, and Stempel. The roman is based on a Garamond and the italic on a Granjon typeface. The name Sabon, taken from a type founder in Frankfurt who produced Garamond types, was proposed by Stanley Morison.

1967 »

From 1955 until his retirement in 1967, he took commissions as a typographer for Hoffmann–La Roche in Basel.

In 1967, Tschichold visited the United States of America.

1974 »

An English edition of *Typographische Gestaltung* was published in 1967 under the title *Asymmetric Typography*, translated by Ruari McLean

Until his death at Berzona near Locarno in August 1974, Tschichold continued to work as a designer and writer in Switzerland.

1986 »

In his groundbreaking work as the leading propagandist of the New Typography his contributions to modernist graphic design are both lasting and manifold; in later years he played an important role in a carefully nuanced revival of traditional typography.

Edith Tschichold died in 1986 in the vicinity of Locarno.

Introduction

Cees W. de Jong

Introduction

Edith Tschichold, ca. 1926
(photo: Kurt Schwitters)

Jan Tschichold, ca. 1926
(photo: Kurt Schwitters)

J.T.

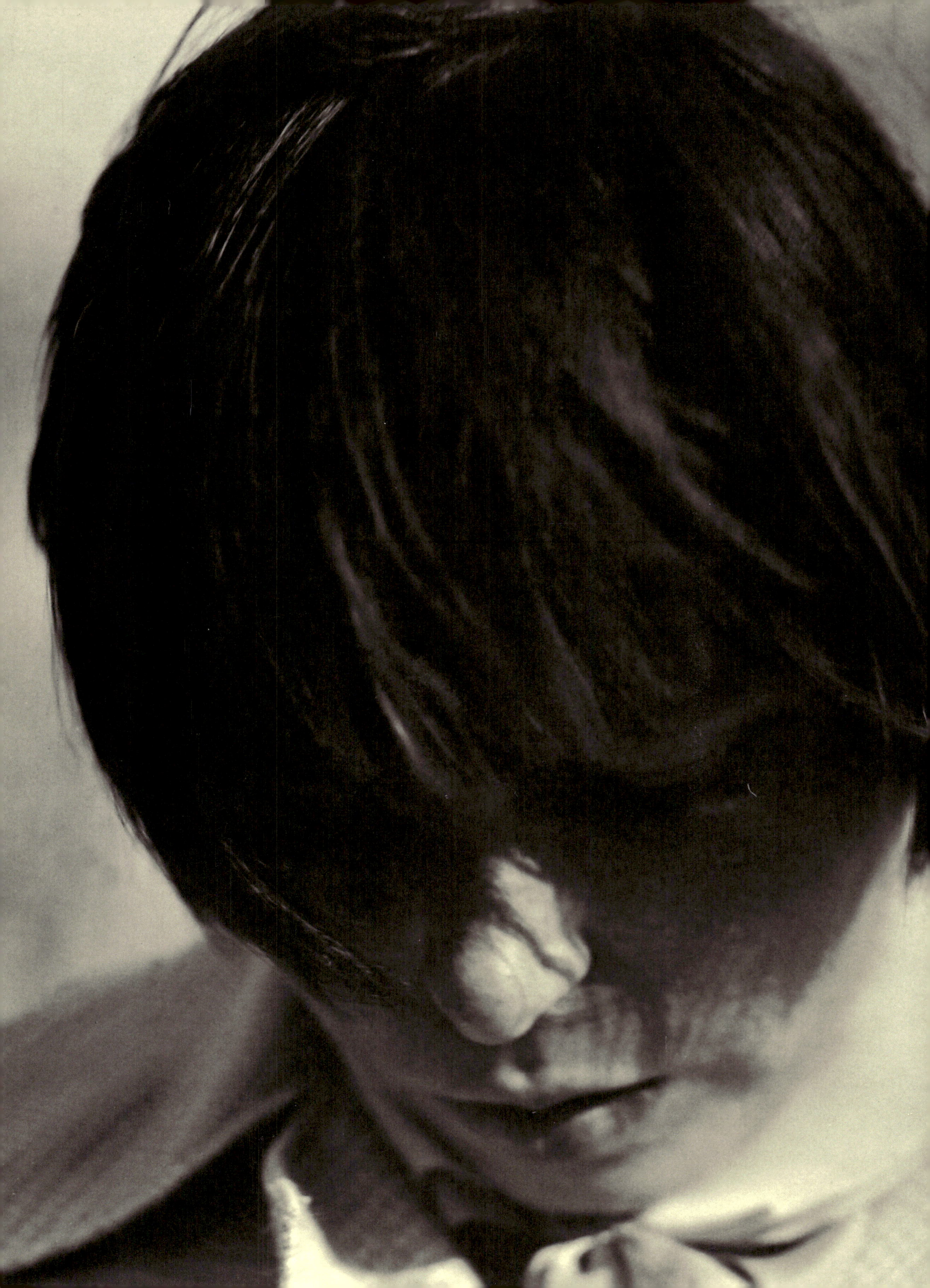

Introduction

Edith Tschichold, ca. 1931
(photo: Lucia Moholy)

Edith Tschichold, ca. 1928
(photo: Aenne Biermann, no. 2761)

Introduction

Jan Tschichold believed that typographers should learn to embrace humanist ideals and use the wisdom and achievements of past typographers and the entire heritage of graphic design as sources of inspiration.

In 1925 Tschichold published a special issue of *Typographische Mitteilungen* entitled *elementare typographie*, in which he first formulated his efforts to create a new typography: "Out of all typefaces available, grotesque or block faces are the nearest to what the new typography needs, because they are simple in design and easy to read. But there is no reason why other easy-to-read typefaces should not be used. The perfect typeface does not yet exist." Bauhaus leader László Moholy-Nagy responded in *Bauhausheft* 7 in 1926: "Since all existing grotesque book styles lack basic style, grotesque still has to be created." At the same time, Paul Renner was working on his design for a new grotesque style based on constructivist principles. His 1924 design Futura was based on simple basic forms such as the circle, triangle, and square, but Renner's experience with books and typography prevented him from casting aside tradition in favor of a new dogma. The first samples of the new style made their appearance in 1925.

Ever since he first formulated his efforts to create a new typography in 1925, Tschichold has inspired typographers and designers around the world. He was trained in Leipzig and started his career there as a traditional calligrapher, designing advertisements mainly for the Leipzig trade fairs. Between 1927 and 1937, Tschichold traveled through Germany, Austria, Czechoslovakia, Switzerland, France, the United Kingdom, and Denmark to present his publications, lectures, and exhibitions on the themes of the New Typography (*Die neue Typographie*) and type design. Tschichold belonged to the Ring neuer Werbegestalter (Ring of New Advertising Designers), which was initiated by Kurt Schwitters in 1928. Its other members included Schwitters, Willi Baumeister, Max Burchartz, Walter Dexel, Hans Leistikow, Robert Michel, Georg Trump, Friedrich Vordemberge-Gildewart, César Domela, Piet Zwart, and Paul Schuitema. Because of his international contacts, Tschichold was very well informed about what was happening in the world of typography, design, and art.

"In the light of my present knowledge, it was a juvenile opinion to consider the sans serif as the most suitable or even the most contemporary typeface."

Jan Tschichold

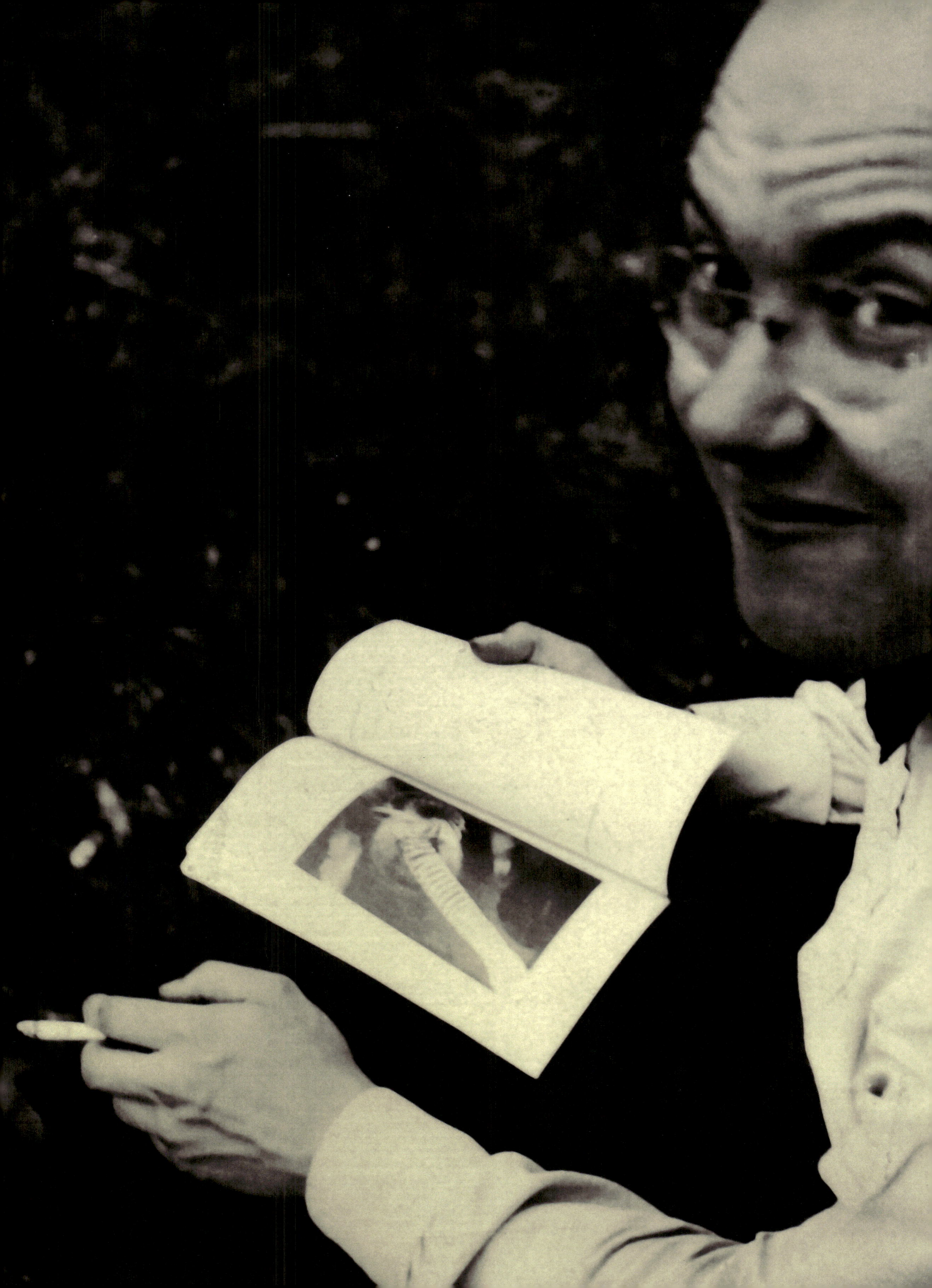

Introduction

After the Nazi victory in the March 5 elections of 1933, both Tschichold and his wife Edith were arrested, having been labeled "cultural Bolsheviks". Shortly after his arrest, Tschichold was removed from his teaching post at the Meisterschule, and accused of advocating "un-German" typography. In 1959 Tschichold wrote: "In the light of my present knowledge, it was a juvenile opinion to consider the sans serif as the most suitable or even the most contemporary typeface. A typeface has first to be legible, nay, readable, and a sans serif is certainly not the most legible typeface when set in quantity, let alone readable. …Good typography has to be perfectly legible and, as such, the result of intelligent planning. …The classical typefaces such as Garamond, Janson, Baskerville, and Bell are undoubtedly the most legible. In time, typographical matters, in my eyes, took on a very different aspect, and to my astonishment I detected most shocking parallels between the teachings of *Die neue Typographie* and National Socialism and fascism. Obvious similarities consist in the ruthless restriction of typefaces, a parallel to Goebbels's infamous *Gleichschaltung* (enforced political conformity) and the more or less militaristic arrangement of lines."

In 1967 Jan Tschichold released the complete type family Sabon, which he had produced in 1966–1967. The roman is based on a Garamond and the italic on a Granjon typeface. The name Sabon, taken from a type founder in Frankfurt who produced Garamond types, was proposed by Stanley Morison. With Sabon, Tschichold returned to the traditional and symmetrical typography that he had so vehemently rejected a decade earlier. And so in the end, the humanist ideals and the wisdom and achievements of past typographers and the entire heritage of graphic design became his own sources of inspiration.

Cees W. de Jong

Jan Tschichold in Basel, Switzerland, ca. 1930. In his hand he is holding *Champs délicieux*, the 1922 portfolio of photograms by Man Ray. Photo: Hilde Horn (estate)

Tschichold and the New Typography

Alston W. Purvis

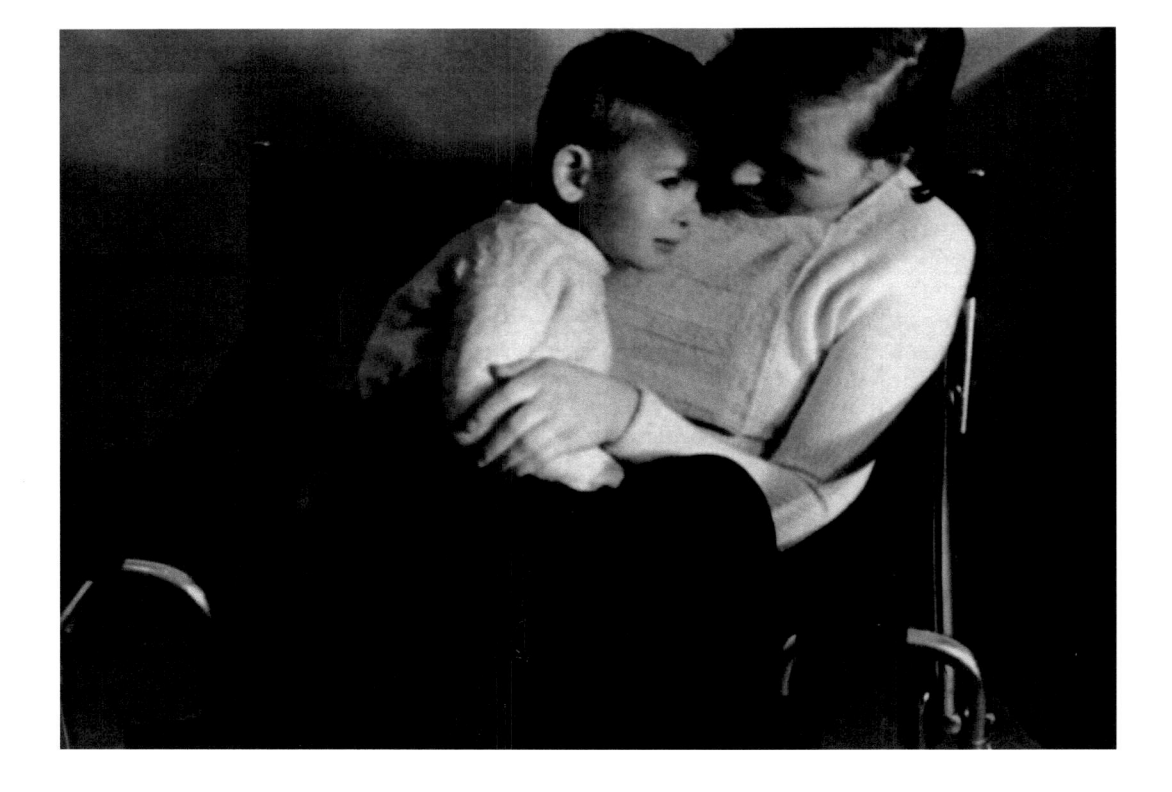

Edith and Peter Tschichold,
at home in Munich, ca. 1932

Jan and Edith Tschichold with
their son Peter, Munich 1929
(photo: Eduard Wasow)

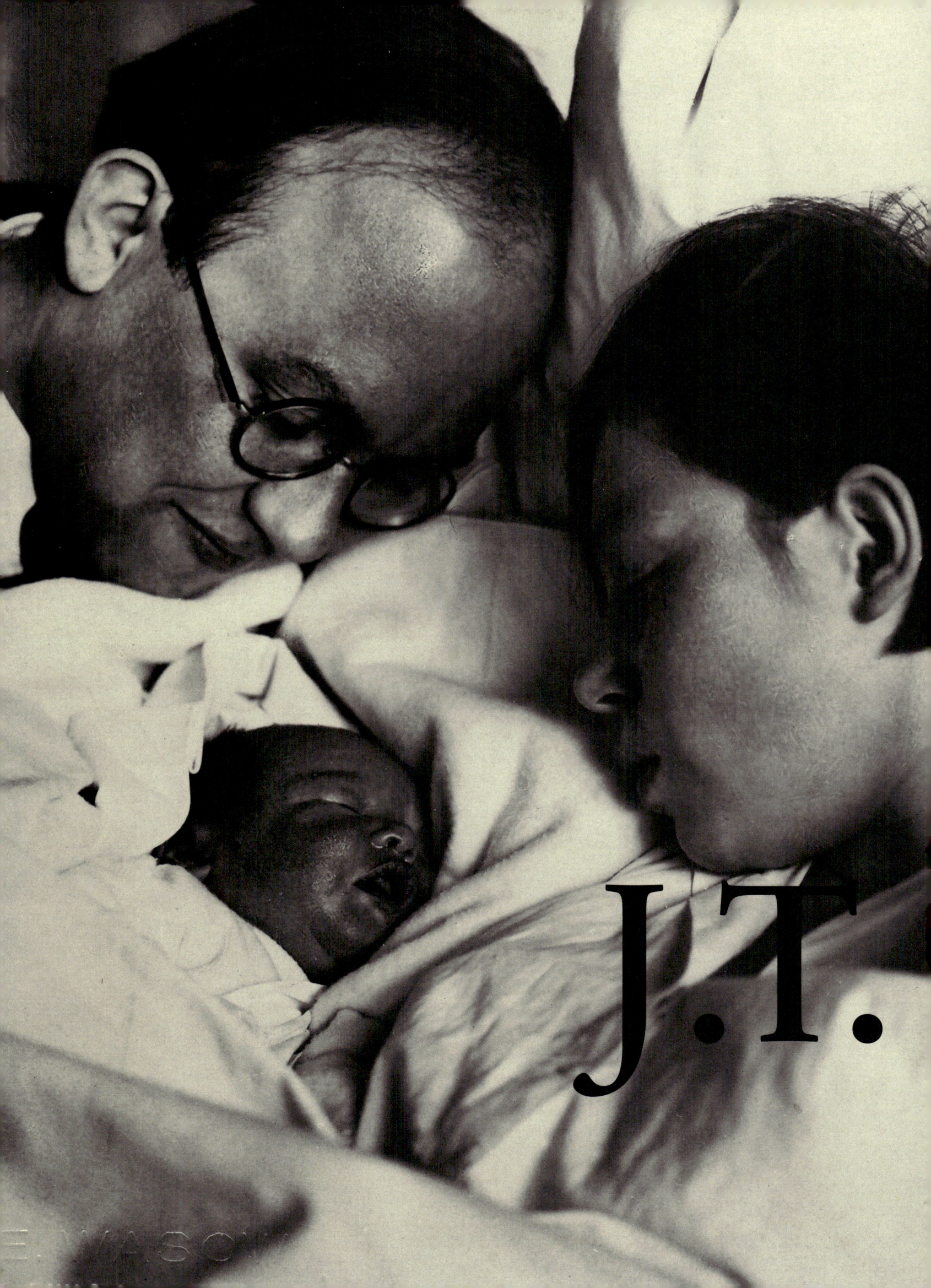

J.T.

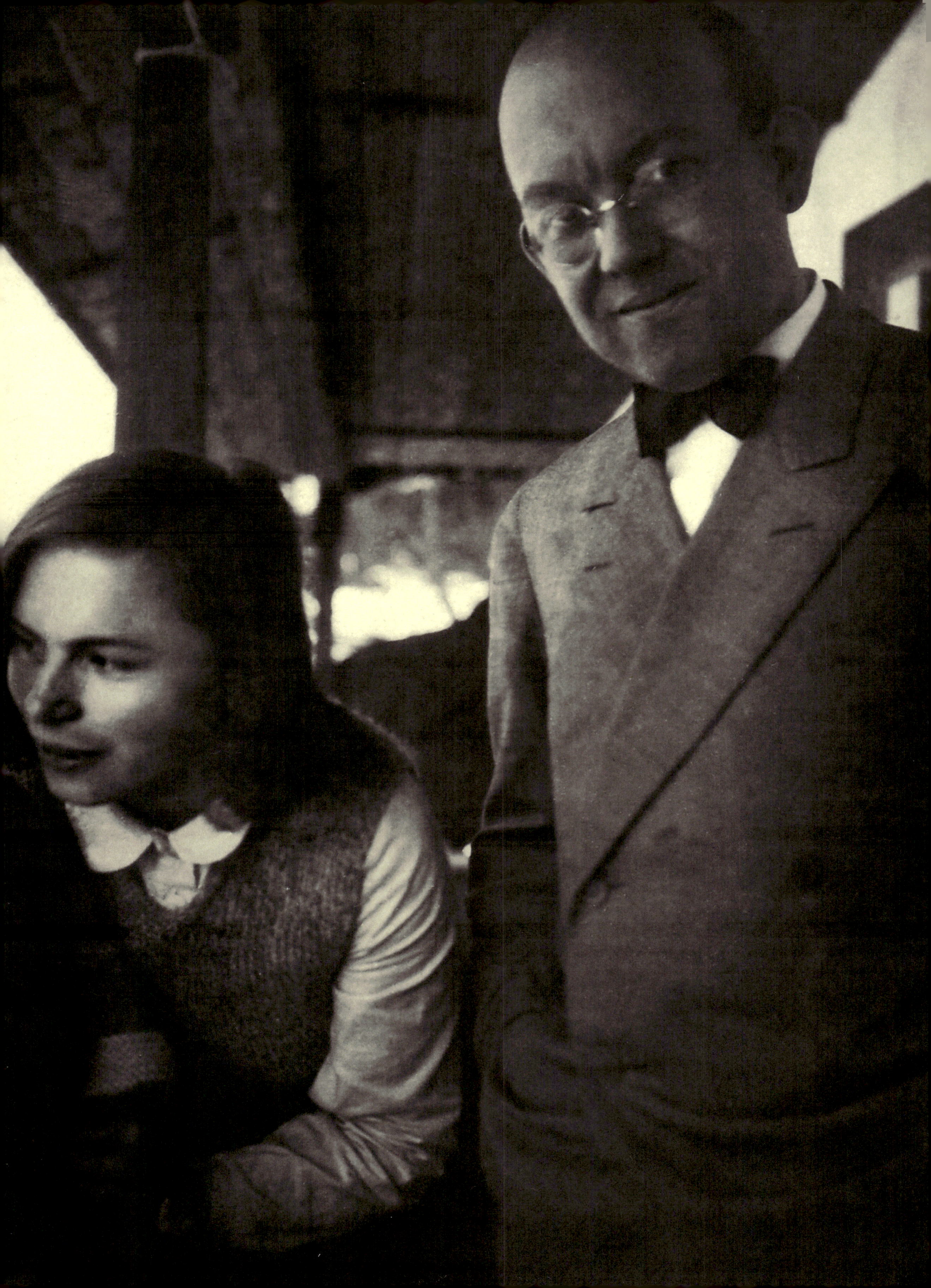

Jan and Edith Tschichold, ca. 1930

Peter Tschichold, at home in Basel,
ca. 1934

Tschichold and the New Typography

As the son of a Leipzig lettering artist and sign painter, Jan Tschichold acquired an early affinity for calligraphy and the skills of both contemporary and past writing masters. During Tschichold's formative years, Leipzig was a major publishing, printing, and type-manufacturing center in Germany. The town also had a printing museum in the Buchgewerbehaus (Book Industry Building), where Tschichold gained much of his early knowledge and appreciation of classical typography.[1]

Although his parents wanted Tschichold to be educated as a professional art teacher, he succeeded in persuading them to allow him to be trained as a "lettering artist."[2] It would have been hard for Tschichold's father to refuse his son's request, since "lettering artist" was a profession related to his own. Thus, Tschichold would become one of the few modernist typographers with experience in a field other than painting and architecture. From 1919 to 1921 he studied with Walter Tiemann (1876–1951), director of the Staatliche Akademie für graphische Künste und Buchgewerbe (Academy for Graphic Arts and Book Production); while there, he also took courses in printmaking and bookbinding, and learned calligraphy from Hermann Delitsch (1869–1937). In addition to his formal training, Tschichold diligently read the books *Writing & Illuminating & Lettering* by Edward Johnston (1872–1944), and *Unterricht in ornamentaler Schrift* (Instruction in Ornamental Writing) by Rudolf von Larisch (1856–1934). These two books greatly contributed to his understanding of letterspacing, wordspacing, and leading.[3] A 1922 exhibition in Leipzig of the work of Rudolf Koch (1876–1934) and his students would prove to be an additional source of inspiration.[4]

After completing his studies, Tschichold first found work designing calligraphic advertisements, mainly for the Leipzig trade fairs; in addition, he worked as Delitsch's assistant in teaching an evening course in calligraphy at the Leipzig Academy from 1921 to 1923. In 1923 he began working in Leipzig as a freelance typographer and calligrapher for the printer Fischer & Wittig and the publisher Insel-Verlag. He also produced work for the Warsaw publishing house Philobiblon as well as advertisements and printed material for various other clients.

Cover of *elementare typographie* by Jan Tschichold, special insert for *Typographische Mitteilungen*, 1925, 30 x 22.5 cm

typographische mitteilungen

zeitschrift des bildungsverbandes der deutschen buchdrucker leipzig • oktoberheft 1925

sonderheft

elementare typographie

natan altman
otto baumberger
herbert bayer
max burchartz
el lissitzky
ladislaus moholy-nagy
molnár f. farkas
johannes molzahn
kurt schwitters
mart stam
ivan tschichold

ELEMENTARE TYPOGRAPHIE   198
IWAN TSCHICHOLD

1. Die neue Typographie ist zweckbetont.
2. Zweck jeder Typographie ist Mitteilung (deren Mittel sie darstellt). Die Mitteilung muss in kürzester, einfachster, eindringlichster Form erscheinen.
3. Um Typographie sozialen Zwecken dienstbar zu machen, bedarf es der *inneren* (den Inhalt anordnenden) und *äußeren* (die Mittel der Typographie in Beziehung zueinander setzenden) Organisation des verwendeten Materials.
4. *Innere Organisation* ist Beschränkung auf die elementaren Mittel der Typographie: Schrift, Zahlen, Zeichen, Linien des Setzkastens und der Setzmaschine.
   Zu den elementaren Mitteln neuer Typographie gehört in der heutigen, auf Optik eingestellten Welt auch das exakte Bild: die Photographie.
   Elementare Schriftform ist die **Groteskschrift** aller Variationen: mager — halbfett — **fett** — schmal bis breit.
   Schriften, die bestimmten Stilarten angehören oder beschränkt-nationalen Charakter tragen (𝔊𝔬𝔱𝔦𝔰𝔠𝔥, Fraktur, Kirchenslavisch) sind nicht elementar gestaltet und beschränken zum Teil die internationale Verständigungsmöglichkeit. Die Mediäval-Antiqua ist die der Mehrzahl der heute Lebenden geläufigste Form der Druckschrift. Im (fortlaufenden) Werksatz besitzt sie heute noch, ohne eigentlich elementar gestaltet zu sein, vor vielen Groteskschriften den Vorzug besserer Lesbarkeit.
   Solange noch keine, auch im Werksatz gut lesbare elementare Form geschaffen ist, ist zweckmässig eine unpersönliche, sachliche, möglichst wenig aufdringliche Form der Mediäval-Antiqua (also eine solche, in der ein zeitlicher oder persönlicher Charakter möglichst wenig zum Ausdruck kommt) der Grotesk vorzuziehen.
   Eine ausserordentliche Ersparnis würde durch die ausschliessliche Verwendung des kleinen Alphabets unter Ausschaltung *aller* Grossbuchstaben erreicht, eine Schreibweise, die von allen Neuerern der Schrift als unsre Zukunftsschrift empfohlen wird. Vgl. das Buch »Sprache und Schrift« von Dr. Porstmann, Beuth-Verlag, G. m. b. H., Berlin SW 19, Beuthstrasse 8. Preis Mark 5.25. — durch kleinschreibung verliert unsre schrift nichts, wird aber leichter lesbar, leichter lernbar, wesentlich wirtschaftlicher. warum für einen laut, z. b. a zwei zeichen A und a? ein laut ein zeichen. warum zwei alfabete für ein wort, warum die doppelte menge zeichen, wenn die hälfte dasselbe erreicht?

DIE MODENSCHAU
findet heute und morgen (Donnerstag und Freitag) nachmittags und abends im „Intimen-Theater" statt.
Beginn der Vorführungen: 4 und 6½ Uhr. Eintritt: 3½ und 6 Uhr.

Erste Berliner Mannequins führen neueste Schöpfungen der besten Häuser zum Herbst und Winter vor:
Schlichte Kleider
Nachmittags-Tee und Abendtoiletten
Pelzverbrämte Mäntel und Kostüme
Pelze und Pelzjacken
Straßen- und Abend-Hüte
Schuhwerk der Firma F. W. Böhmer, Bongardstr. 12

Die künstlerische Leitung übernahm Hans Tobar.
Zur Unterhaltung wirken erste Kräfte mit.
Neue Gesellschaftstänze tanzen S. Noack, Berlin, Klubmeister des deutschen Klubs für Tanzsport und seine Partnerin.
Musik von beiden Kapellen des Intimen-Theaters.

baruch
BOCHUM, BONGARD- UND KORTUMSTR.-ECKE

Die logische Gliederung des Druckwerks wird durch Anwendung stark unterschiedlicher Grade und Formen ohne Rücksicht auf die bisherigen ästhetischen Gesichtspunkten optisch wahrnehmbar gestaltet.
Auch die unbedruckten Teile des Papiers sind ebenso wie die gedruckten Formen Mittel der Gestaltung.

5. *Äussere Organisation* ist die Gestaltung stärkster Gegensätze (Simultanität) durch Anwendung gegensätzlicher Formen, Grade und Stärken (die im Werte ihrer Inhalte begründet sein müssen) und der Schaffung der Beziehung dieser positiven (farbigen) Formwerte zu den negativen (weissen) Formwerten des unbedruckten Papiers.
6. Elementare typographische Gestaltung ist die Schaffung der logischen und optischen Beziehung der durch die Aufgabe gegebenen Buchstaben, Wörter, Satzteile.
7. Um die Eindringlichkeit, das Sensationelle neuer Typographie zu steigern, können, zugleich als Mittel innerer Organisation, auch vertikale und schräge Zeilenrichtungen angewendet werden.
8. Elementare Gestaltung schliesst die Anwendung jedes *Ornaments* (auch der ornamentalen Linie, z.B. der fettfeinen) aus. Die Anwendung von Linien und an sich elementaren Formen (Quadraten, Kreisen, Dreiecken) muss zwingend in der Gesamtkonstruktion begründet sein.
   Die *dekorativ-kunstgewerblich-spekulative Verwendung* an sich elementarer Formen ist nicht gleichbedeutend mit elementarer Gestaltung.
9. Der Anordnung neuer Typographie sollten in Zukunft die normierten (DIN-)Papierformate des Normenausschusses der Deutschen Industrie (NDI) zugrunde gelegt werden, die allein eine alle typographischen Gestaltungen umfassende Organisation des Druckwesens ermöglichen. (*Literatur:* Dr. Porstmann, »Die Dinformate und ihre Einführung in die Praxis«, Selbstverlag Dinorm, Berlin NW 7, Sommerstrasse 4a. Mark 3.—.)
   Insbesondere sollte das Format DIN A 4 (210:297 mm) allen Geschäfts- und andern Briefen zugrunde gelegt werden. Der Geschäftsbrief an sich ist ebenfalls genormt worden: DIN 676, Geschäftsbrief, zu beziehen direkt vom Beuth-Verlag, G. m. b. H., Berlin SW 19, Beuthstrasse 8, Mark 0,40. Das DINblatt »Papierformate« trägt die Nummer 476. — Die DINformate sind erst seit kurzem in der Praxis eingeführt. In diesem Heft ist nur eine Arbeit, der bewusst ein DINformat zugrunde gelegt ist.
10. Elementare Gestaltung ist auch in der Typographie nie absolut oder endgültig, da sich der Begriff elementarer Gestaltung mit der Wandlung der Elemente (durch Erfindungen, die neue Elemente typographischer Gestaltung schaffen — wie z. B. die Photographie) notwendig ebenfalls ständig wandelt.

200

DIE SPAR-DEKADE
fängt Montag morgen an.

Sparen muß und möchte heut ein jeder. Was eine Spar-Dekade bei uns für Sie bedeutet, das sagt Ihnen unser großes Inserat am Montag, das sagen Ihnen am Sonntag unsere Schaufenster.

baruch
BOCHUM, Bongard- und Kortumstraßen-Ecke

Pages 198 and 200 of *elementare typographie* by Jan Tschichold, special insert for *Typographische Mitteilungen*, 1925, 30 x 22.5 cm

Tschichold and the Bauhaus Before moving to Dessau, the Staatliches Bauhaus was located in Weimar from 1919 until 1925. It further expanded on the ideas of the Deutscher Werkbund, an association established in 1907, in which architects, painters, craftspeople, artisans, and designers united to work with industry to create housing and well-designed products for the growing middle classes. The major Werkbund exhibition in Cologne ended with the outbreak of World War I in the summer of 1914, and the exhibition hall was converted into an emergency hospital. Afterwards, headed by Walter Adolf Gropius (1883–1969), the Bauhaus became a center of progressive ideas where students were encouraged to arrive at their own creative solutions and discover new approaches made possible by new technology.

In August 1923, Tschichold visited the first Bauhaus exhibition in nearby Weimar. There he was introduced to the work of the architects Gropius and Ludwig Mies van der Rohe (1886–1969), the painters Oskar Schlemmer (1888–1943) and Wassily Kandinsky (1866–1944), and the Hungarian constructivist designer, photographer, and former law student László Moholy-Nagy (1895–1946). For Tschichold, the Bauhaus exhibition proved to be an epiphany in his life. Soon afterwards he would also be captivated by the work of the Dutch graphic designer Piet Zwart (1885–1977), the Russian Suprematist painter Kazimir Malevich (1878–1935), and the Russian constructivists El Lissitzky (1890–1941) and Alexander Rodchenko (1891–1956). He soon began to assimilate into his own work the functionalist design concepts of the Bauhaus and the Russian constructivists, as well as the visionary and theoretical ideas of the Dutch De Stijl movement.

Moholy-Nagy's interest in both typography and photography generated experiments in the unification of these two fields at the Bauhaus. He saw graphic design as gravitating toward a combination of these two media, referring to the integration of word and image as *Typophoto* and "the new visual literature." In 1923 he wrote that, through photography's intrinsic objectivity, the viewer was no longer dependent on the interpretation of a third party. It is noteworthy that the 1923 Bauhaus exhibition was held during the severe economic crisis in Germany when inflation was at its height; to keep up with the decreasing currency values, new banknotes had to be printed almost overnight. With this exhibition, the Bauhaus was audacious in openly proclaiming something so radically new in such uncertain times. Perhaps, though, this was one of the reasons why the Bauhaus found such an enthusiastic acceptance among the intelligentsia of its day; it boldly suggested a radical renewal that was far preferable to the discredited past.

After returning to Leipzig, Tschichold ordered through the Bauhaus some pieces of tubular furniture by the Hungarian designer Marcel Breuer (1902–1981), and later, furniture designed by Mies van der Rohe. He soon began an extensive correspondence with many of the pivotal avant-garde figures of the time. Among others, these included Lissitsky, Kurt Schwitters (1887–1948), Josef Albers (1888–1976), Willi Baumeister (1889–1955), Herbert Bayer (1900–1985), Max Bill (1908–1994), Walter Dexel (1890–1973), and Moholy-Nagy. Others included Piet Mondrian (1872–1944), Ben Nicholson (1894–1982), Rodchenko, Gustav Klutsis (1895–1938), Schlemmer, Ladislav Sutnar 1897–1976), Friedrich Vordemberge-Gildewart (1899–1962), Malevich, and the Dutch constructivists Piet Zwart and Paul Schuitema (1897–1973).

Through Moholy-Nagy, Tschichold was introduced to El Lissitzky. The latter spoke German, and the meeting engendered a long and productive friendship between the two kindred spirits. It is significant that at the beginning of 1923, Johannes (or Iohannes) Tzschichhold changed his name to Iwan (or Ivan) Tschichold, in order to express his optimism over the cultural developments inspired by the Russian Revolution. Other figures associated with the European avant-garde also went through name changes. For example, the Surrealist photographer Emmanuel Radnitzky (1890–1976) assumed the name Man Ray, and the French designer A.M. Cassandre (1901–1968) was actually born Adolphe Jean Marie Mouron. Later, the American graphic designer Paul Rand (1914–1996) would discard his original name, Peretz Rosenbaum, early in his career.

Even before his encounter with the Bauhaus, Tschichold had shown an interest in progressive European art movements. In 1921 he subscribed to the German edition of the Dutch monthly *Wendingen*, published under the auspices of the Amsterdam-based architects and artists' association Architectura et Amicitia. Designed and, until 1924, edited by the architect and visionary Hendrikus Theodorus Wijdeveld (1885–1987), it was distinguished by its square-format Japanese binding and its covers designed by different artists (including El Lissitzky in 1922). In addition, existing typesetting material was used like building blocks to construct the page ornaments and display letters. There is little evidence that this magazine had any effect upon Tschichold's typography, except possibly in the construction of flat printed areas built up from rectangular typesetting ornaments.

Wendingen's Dutch competitor was *De Stijl*, a monthly published by the artists' group of the same name, with the Dutch architect Theo van Doesburg (1883–1931) as its driving force. The De Stijl group was excluded from participation in the 1925 Art Deco exhibition in Paris, which had originally been planned to take place in 1922. The modern developments surrounding the Bauhaus were also absent; Germany was excluded because of French bitterness over the Great War. Austria, with its important representatives of the Vienna Secession, was only reluctantly admitted later.

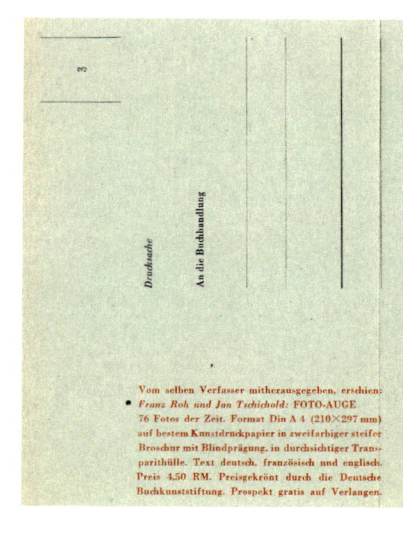

Order form for *Eine Stunde Druckgestaltung* by Jan Tschichold, 1930. Akademischer Verlag Dr. Fritz Wedekind & Co., Stuttgart

JAN TSCHICHOLD:

EINE STUNDE DRUCKGESTALTUNG

Grundbegriffe der Neuen Typografie in Bildbeispielen für Drucksachenhersteller und -verbraucher

In many aspects, the Bauhaus and De Stijl had related objectives. By the end of 1920, van Doesburg was in contact with the Bauhaus, and in 1921 he moved to Weimar. Although he expected to be offered a teaching position, van Doesburg was never accepted as a colleague by most of the Bauhaus associates. Gropius in particular considered van Doesburg far too inflexible in his use of geometry and repudiation of individualism, attitudes which were in sharp contrast to those of the Bauhaus. Also, unlike van Doesburg, Gropius was against promoting a unified Bauhaus style or imposing one on the Bauhaus students. Van Doesburg's rejection was also a result of his often patronizing and contentious manner. However, he persisted: he made his home available as a meeting place for some of the Bauhaus students and faculty, and enthusiastically and defiantly began giving his own De Stijl courses in the studio of Karl Peter Röhl (1895–1975), a Bauhaus student. Van Doesburg's condescending attitude is evident in a letter he wrote to De Stijl member Antony Kok (1882–1969) in January 1921: "In Weimar I have turned everything upside down. This is the acclaimed academy with the most modern teachers! Each evening I have talked to the students and spread the toxin of the new spirit. De Stijl will soon rematerialize in an even more radical shape. I have mountains of strength and now know that our ideas will prevail over everything and everyone."[5]

German book printers were also making strides in improving the quality of their products. In Leipzig, where the Deutsche Buchdruckerverband (Association of German Book printers) had its own publishing house with a printing facility, delegates to the Bildungsverband der Deutschen Buchdrucker (Educational Federation of German Book Printers) decided on August 29, 1924 to establish the Büchergilde Gutenberg (Gutenberg Book Guild). The purpose of this non-profit organization was "to claim full rights of participation in literary matters on the part of workers and the realm of labor and to recognize as its sole guiding principle the conscientious satisfaction of the intellectual needs of the workers." Two months later, Der Bücherkreis (The Book Circle) was established with intentions similar to those of the Büchergilde but more closely allied with politics, and in particular with the Social Democratic Party of Germany (SPD).

A principal distinction between the Büchergilde and Der Bücherkreis lay in the design and preparation for printing. The use of the word *Gilde* (guild) indicated more of a craft orientation. For over two decades the monthly printing trade journal of the Bildungsverband der Deutschen Buchdrucker had been published under the title *Typographische Mitteilungen* (Typographic Notes), and it devoted ample space to discussing the desirability of renewal in typography and book design. Many of those associated with the magazine saw the use of Gothic and Fraktur (blackletter) types as an obstacle to reaching new readers and to adequately getting advertising messages across, arguing that Roman typefaces should be used universally. Some even went a step further by advocating the

Cover of *Eine Stunde Druckgestaltung* (A Lesson in Printing Design) by Jan Tschichold, 1930. Akademischer Verlag Dr. Fritz Wedekind & Co., Stuttgart sole use of sans serif typefaces and the abandonment of capital letters for nouns, the latter being a standard characteristic of German texts. This practice, called *kleinschreiben* (small writing), was, for example, adopted by Bayer and Tschichold who, in their own drive for renewal, wanted to dispense with capital letters altogether. Because *kleinschreiben* was associated with modernism and socialist or even communist (Bolshevik) ideas, the practice was not without political danger. Bayer, working in a government-affiliated school, sought to avoid the problem by having the excuse "I write everything in small letters, thus I save time" printed on his letterhead. For the rest, Bayer was quite alert to shifts in the political winds. Of the Bauhaus staff, he was one of the last for whom the authorities made it impossible to work in Nazi Germany. He did not emigrate to the United States until 1938, whereas Moholy-Nagy, for example, who had never hidden his leftist sympathies, left Germany as soon as power changed hands in 1933, settling in Chicago in 1937, via Paris, Amsterdam, and London.

Two years after the 1923 Bauhaus exhibition, Tschichold was invited to serve as guest editor for the October 1925 issue of the printing trade journal *Typographische Mitteilungen*, for which he designed a twenty-four-page *Sonderheft* (special issue) insert entitled *elementare typographie*. Originally intended as a Bauhaus special edition, this issue of *typographische mitteilungen* (the name of the journal being set in lowercase letters on this occasion) was entirely devoted to *Die neue Typografie* (the New Typography)—a term that was then being used by Tschichold and others working in this manner. Printed in red and black, the *Sonderheft* helped to clarify, demonstrate, and display the principles of the New Typography for professional printers, typesetters, and typographers. In addition to Tschichold's own typography, it presented work by the avant-garde designers Max Burchartz (1887–1961), Johannes Molzahn (1892–1965), Schwitters, Moholy Nagy, Lissitzky, Bayer, and the Swiss poster designer Otto Baumberger (1889–1961). These images were accompanied by Tschichold's own articulate comments and observations.

Other texts included "typo-photo" by Moholy Nagy; "die reklame" (advertising) by Lissitsky and the Dutch architect, urban planner, and chair designer Mart Stam (1899–1986); and "elementare gesichtpunkte" (Elementary Perspectives) by the Russian painter, sculptor, typographer, and teacher Natan Altman (1889–1970). It is less known that the *Beiblatt* (supplemental sheet) "*Das Schiff*" (The Ship) in the *Sonderheft* included a text about *Neues Bauen* (New Housing), by the Berlin architect and art critic Adolf Behne (1885–1948), so one can assume that Tschichold and Behne were in contact by this time. Although Tschichold was fully aware of van Doesburg and De Stijl, it is notable that he omitted this Dutch group. Lissitzky was delighted to have been included, and this helped to solidify the friendship between him and Tschichold.

Pages 10–11, "Standard Paper Formats," from *Eine Stunde Druckgestaltung* (A Lesson in Printing Design) by Jan Tschichold, 1930. Akademischer Verlag Dr. Fritz Wedekind & Co., Stuttgart.

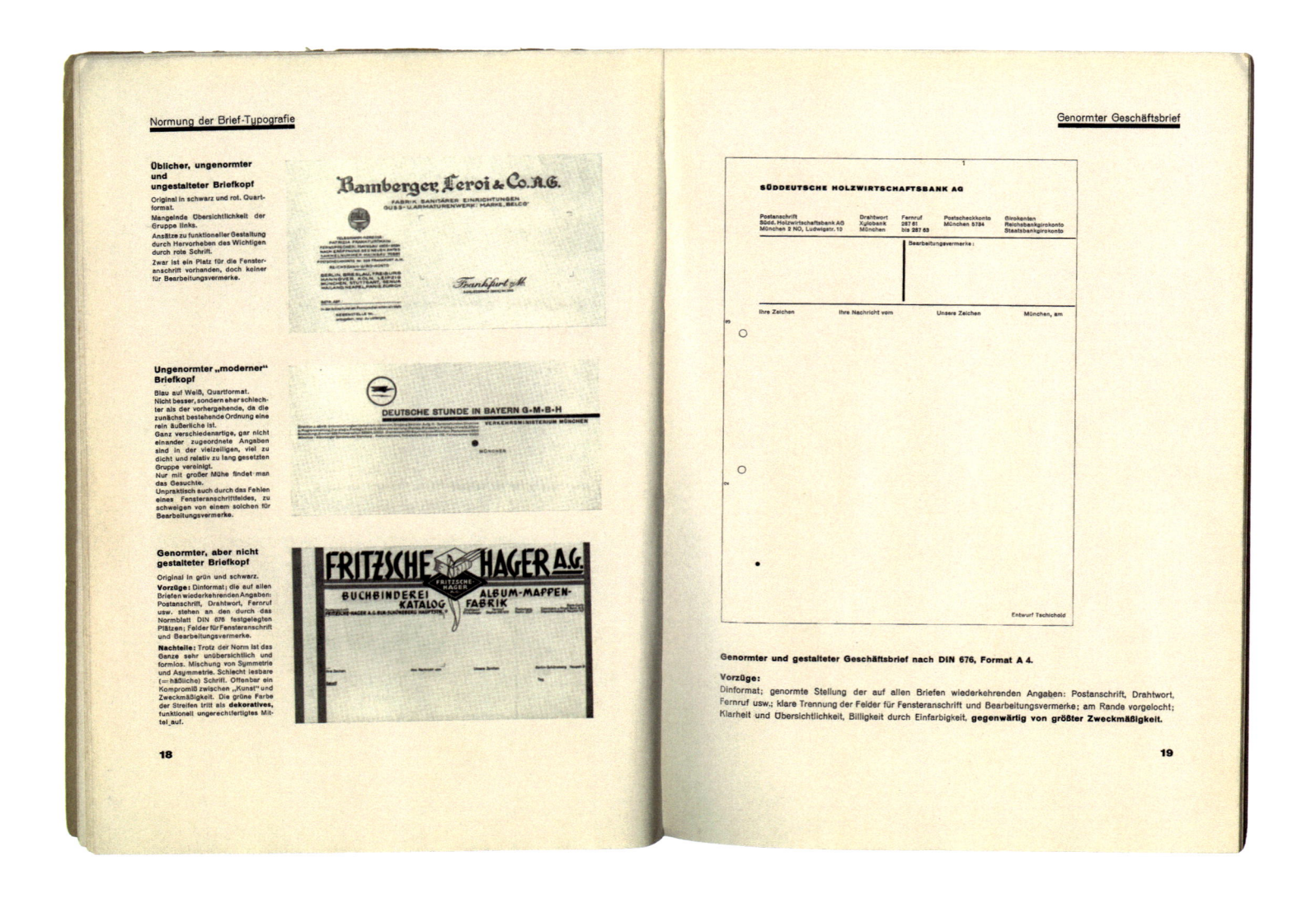

Pages 18–19, "Rules for Letter Typography." from *Eine Stunde Druckgestaltung* (A Lesson in Printing Design) by Jan Tschichold, 1930. Akademischer Verlag Dr. Fritz Wedekind & Co., Stuttgart

Since most German typography was still symmetrical, with medieval Textura being the most popular typeface, *elementare typographie* caused quite a sensation and engendered much enthusiasm and controversy among a wide audience. At the age of twenty-three, Tschichold had become the leading spokesman and guiding force of what would be known as the New Typography.

For Tschichold, *elementare typographie* was, in effect, a manifesto for the New Typography. Because the magazine was distributed in an edition of 20,000 to printers and typographers, Tschichold's name became immediately known throughout German-speaking Europe. He illustrated his article "die neue gestaltung" (The New Design) with images from El Lissitzky's "Mär von zwei Quadraten" (Fairytale of Two Squares), from the *De Stijl* issue of 1922, and maintained: "The art of the future will transcend the frontiers of that which until now has been denominated as 'art' and is likely to use FILM and PHOTOGRAPHY to an ever-increasing extent." He presented ten premises to state his objectives, the first four being the most relevant:

1 The purpose of the New Typography is functionality.

2 The purpose of any typography is communication (the means of which are visualized). This communication has to appear in the shortest, simplest and most compelling form.

3 For typography to serve social purposes, the inner form of the material employed must arrange the content whereas the outer form must establish a relationship between the different typographic means.

4 Inner organization means using as few basic constituents as possible: typefaces, numbers, signs, lines from the type cases, and the typesetter. In the modern world focused on optics, the precise picture, i.e. photography, must be considered as a basic constituent of the New Typography.

"My dear Tschichold, bravo, bravo," Lissitzky responded from Moscow in a letter dated October 22, 1925: "With all my heart I congratulate you on the beautiful brochure *elementare typographie*. To me it is a physical pleasure to hold a publication of such quality in my hands, fingers, eyes. All my nerve antennae extend and the whole motor speeds up. And in the end this is what counts—to overcome inertia."[6] It was also well received at the Bauhaus by Moholy-Nagy and Gropius. Others, such as the German constructivist Dexel, reacted more critically. He took issue with the fact that some German designers had been omitted, precisely those whom he considered to be leaders in the field of new typography. "For example Schlemmer, Baumeister, Röhl, my own humble self and some others. Furthermore, it is to misrepresent history if Moholy is named whereas van Doesburg and the entire De Stijl group are left out."[7]

In general, Tschichold's *Sonderheft* made a major impression on the field of advertising design. However, the June 1926 issue of *Die Reklame* (Advertising), the magazine of the Verband Deutscher Reklamefachleute (Association of German Advertising Professionals), devoted a major article to the New Typography without mentioning the *Sonderheft*. In another professional journal, *Die Gebrauchsgraphik* (Applied Graphics), the supplement was also scarcely cited. This came as no surprise, since Tschichold's views were in contrast to the decorative approach of the Bund Deutscher Gebrauchsgraphiker (Association of German Functional Designers), which *Die Gebrauchsgraphik* represented. Nor, in 1927, did *Die Deutsche Werbegraphik* (German Advertising Design), a book written by Walter Schubert refer to Tschichold's new approach. The *Sonderheft* did, however, engender some commissions for Tschichold, among them designing the publicity for Lasar Galpern's Schule für Tanzkultur (School of Dance) in Leipzig.

A department of printing and advertising ("Druck und Reklame") was started at the Bauhaus in 1925, and two years later the former Bauhaus student Bayer became its head. On March 10, 1927, Bayer wrote to Tschichold: "With the beginning of the new semester I will be teaching a proper advertising class; typography will be dealt with as a separate subject." In 1925, Tschichold proposed that he and Bayer produce a book on advertising and typography, but he soon learned that it could only deal with work produced at the Bauhaus. Eventually, this was published as *Buch und Werbekunst* (Book and Advertisement Art) in 1926 as a special issue of the journal *Offset-, Buch- und Werbekunst* (Art in Offset Printing, Book Production, and Advertising), with many images by Bauhaus designers.

Moholy-Nagy, the leading exponent of progressive typography at the Bauhaus, had first used the term "new typography" in the 1923 Bauhaus exhibition catalog. "Die neue Typographie" was the title of Moholy-Nagy's essay in the catalog, in which he emphasized the use of contrast and clarity, viewpoints that he and Tschichold held in common. Tschichold in turn chose it as the title for his first book, *Die neue Typographie*, published in the spring of 1928. This groundbreaking book remains one of the most important documents of modernist graphic design. Here Tschichold further refined, codified, and articulated the design concepts of the New Typography for the printing trade and vigorously advocated the new ideas. Distributed across all of Europe, *Die neue Typographie*, was his magnum opus and a pioneering work in both content and design. Ruari McLean (1917–2006) began an English translation and revision of *Die neue Typographie* in 1967 and allowed his draft to be used for research at the St. Bride Printing Library in London. The Berlin publisher Brinkmann & Bose issued a facsimile edition in 1987, and, using McLean's translation, an English edition was published by the University of California Press in 1995.

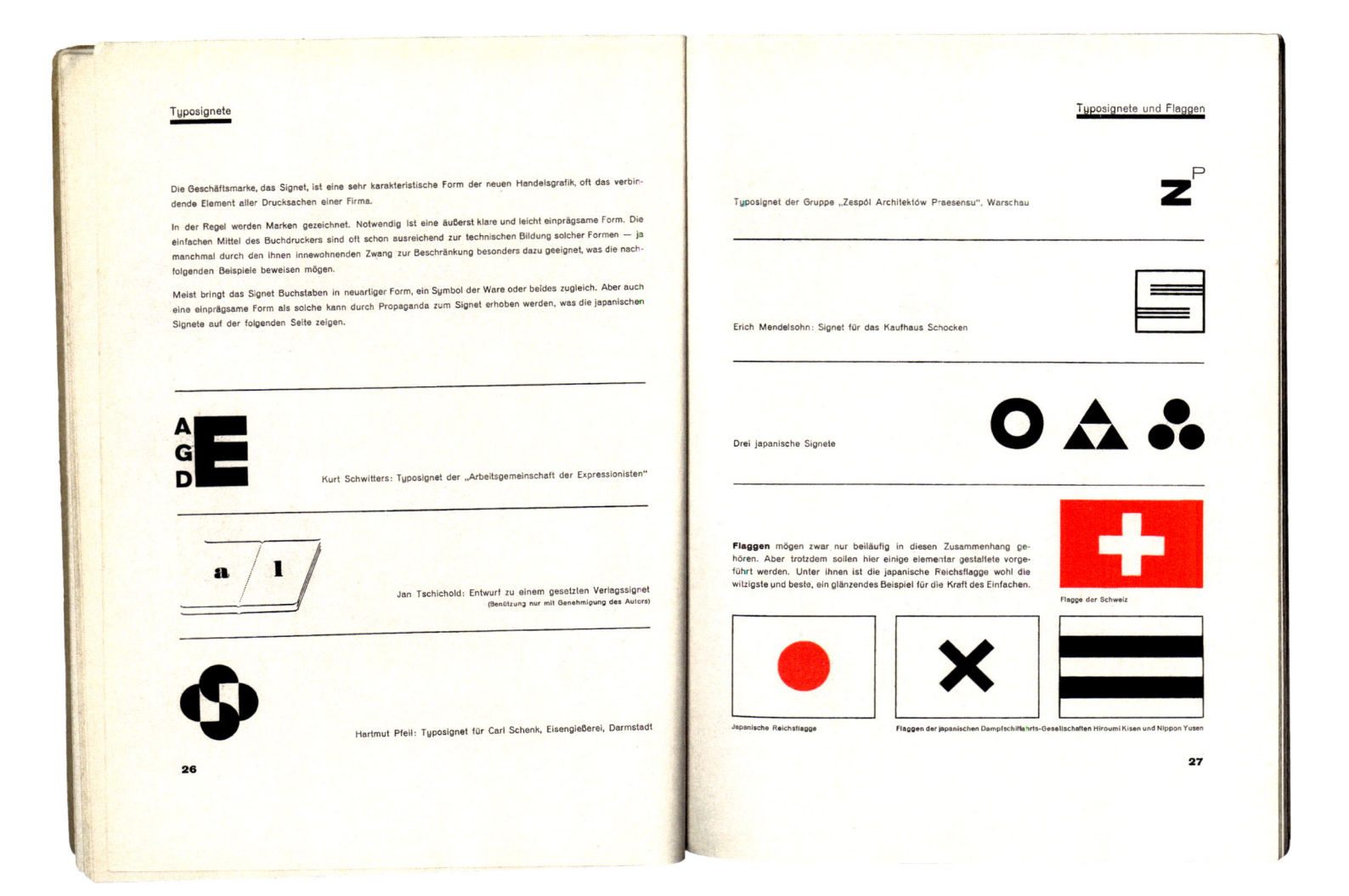

Pages 26–27, "Typographical Symbols and Flags," from *Eine Stunde Druckgestaltung* (A Lesson in Printing Design) by Jan Tschichold, 1930. Akademischer Verlag Dr. Fritz Wedekind & Co., Stuttgart

Pages 28–29, "Advertising Photography," from *Eine Stunde Druckgestaltung* (A Lesson in Printing Design) by Jan Tschichold, 1930. Akademischer Verlag Dr. Fritz Wedekind & Co., Stuttgart

It was intended as a textbook for graphic designers, printers, typesetters, and typographers and a sequel to the 1925 *elementare typographie* special edition. While neither discarding beauty nor regarding it as an end in itself, the spirit of the New Typography was clarity, with form functionally derived from the text. Tschichold stressed the importance of machine composition and its impact on the design and printing processes, while rejecting typographic symmetry because of its rigid structure unrelated to content. He contended that the New Typography should emit a dynamic energy and imply movement as well as balance, and he advocated the asymmetrical placement of contrasting elements with flush left headlines in irregular lengths. In addition, he proposed layouts based on horizontal and vertical underlying grids with spatial intervals and empty spaces employed as design components. As introduced by Lissitsky in *The Isms of Art*, he recommended the use of rules, bars, and rectangles to enhance structure, balance, and stress. He disparaged what he deemed archaic and "degenerate" typefaces and stated that type should be reduced to elemental forms in controlled variations of weight. According to him, sans serif type fulfilled these requirements. Not only were sans serif typefaces (then referred to as Grotesque faces) unembellished in design, but with four distinct weights and corresponding italics they were more complete type families than traditional fonts. Because of its accuracy and objectivity, photography was the preferred illustration medium. These precepts, he believed, accurately reflected the spirit, character, essence, and visual awareness of the machine age. Stressing a functional and simple approach, he maintained that the objective of New Typography should be clarity in communication, with form derived from functional needs, and information delivered in the most direct and effective manner possible.

After an introduction using examples by modernist painters, Tschichold explained in *Die neue Typographie* that things can and must be done differently. He supported his premises with samples of his own work and that of individuals such as Zwart and Filippo Marinetti (1876–1944). In spite of Marinetti's fascist affiliations (in 1934 he was appointed Mussolini's Minister of Culture), Tschichold was still able to recognize his importance to avant-garde typography. Although 5,000 copies were printed, the book quickly sold out and was used as a textbook at the Bauhaus, even though the Bauhaus received less coverage than it had in the *Sonderheft*. The design of *Die neue Typographie* did not fully reflect its content, and perhaps since it was an official publication of the Bildungsverband der Deutschen Buchdrucker in Berlin, Tschichold felt restrained from using lowercase letters throughout. His accompanying brochure for *Die neue Typographie* superbly displays in a single page the principles of the New Typography with its emphasis on rational design and functional communication.

In fifteen pages Tschichold summarily relegated typography between 1450 to 1914 to the dustbin. In a commentary written on the occasion of the Leipzig *Internationale Buchkunstausstellung* (International Exhibition of Book Art) in 1927, he continued his criticism of previous typography: "Book 'art'? When the Englishman William Morris, founding father of the Arts and Crafts movement, turned to the designing of books round the year 1890, he laid the floor for the book art that reached its heyday in 1914 and whose evolution today must be seen as completed.... For today we know that Morris fought on the wrong front. Through his principal rejection of any kind of machine work, he barred the way to what is the natural development and became responsible for the kind of tawdry, expensive arts-and-crafts products nowadays on sale in shops catering to the rich."

From 1927 until 1933 Tschichold traveled in Germany, Austria, Czechoslovakia, Switzerland, and France, promoting the New Typography with publications, lectures, and exhibitions. However, the New Typography was never an overwhelming force during the Weimar Republic or in the rest of Europe. The majority of publications and advertisements during that time proved this. Also, it must be noted that Tschichold's conversion to the New Typography was neither immediate nor unconditional. In spite of his adherence to the New Typography after 1923, Tschichold did not entirely abandon traditional book design, especially in his work for Insel-Verlag in Leipzig, one of his earliest clients. Until 1933 a number of these designs still displayed the symmetry, decorative ornaments, and both the serif and Fraktur (blackletter) typefaces that he had rejected. Since his name was not credited in the more traditional designs, it is clear that he considered them lesser achievements than his work reflecting the New Typography.[8] A poetry edition for which Tschichold designed the binding was selected as one of the best-designed books of the year, but he was not credited, indicating he might have considered it to be more pedestrian work. Perhaps he was also cautious about compromising his drive for the New Typography.

Since 1925 the painter, typographer, designer, and type designer Paul Renner (1878–1956) had been teaching at the Kunstgewerbeschule (College for Applied Arts) in Frankfurt am Main. Renner sent Tschichold the first sketches for his sans serif typeface Futura. Although Tschichold felt some letters were too abstract to be easily read, he was most enthusiastic. Futura was issued by the Bauersche Gießerei in Frankfurt in 1927 and soon became the most popular typeface for those involved with innovative typography. However, there were competitors: Bayer developed Bayer-Type, Schwitters was working on a "*neue plastische Systemschrift*" (a new plastic system type), which he used in his 1927 *Opel-Tag* poster, and new sans serif typefaces were also being explored in other countries.

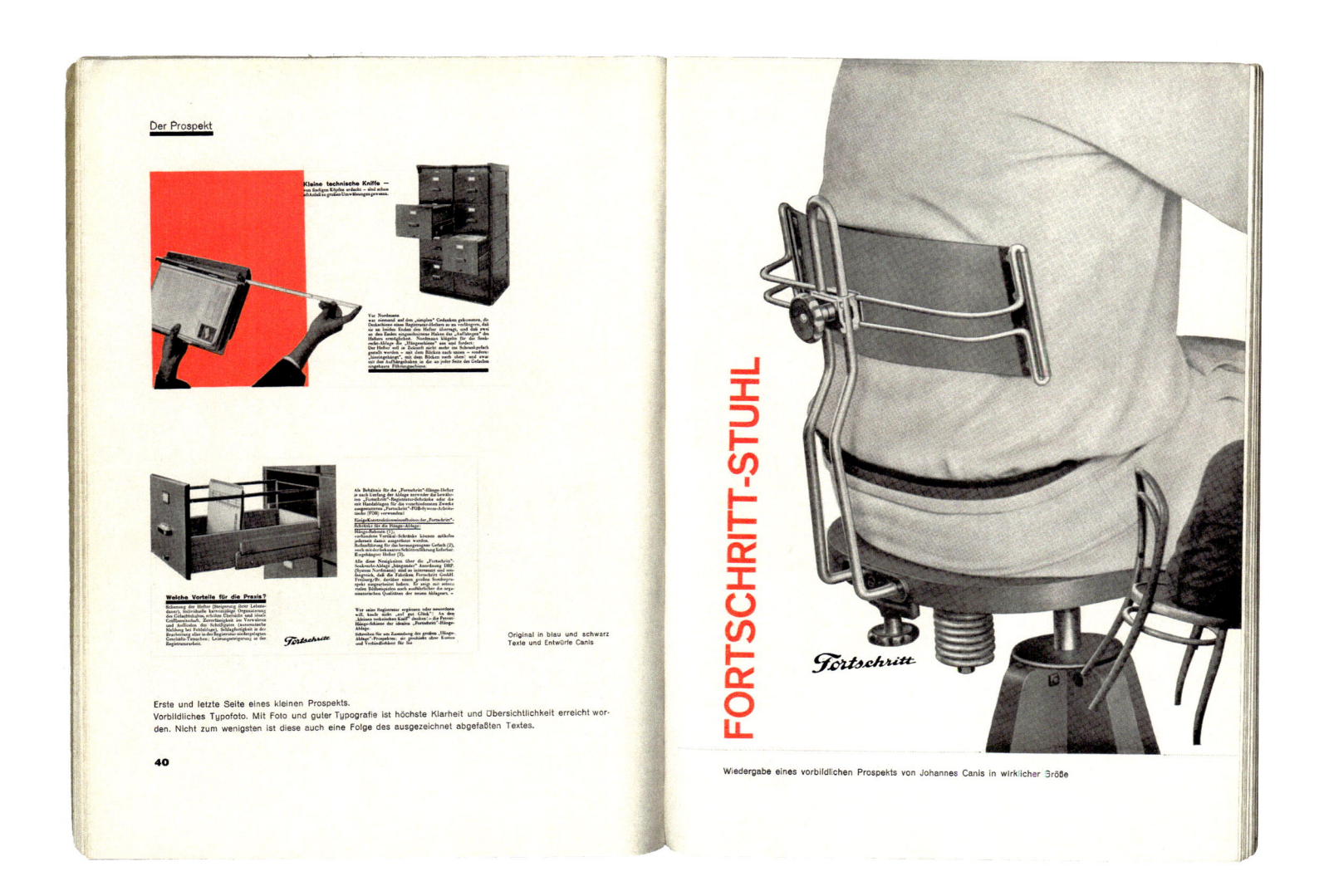

Pages 40–41, "The Catalogue,"
from *Eine Stunde Druckgestaltung*
(A Lesson in Printing Design) by
Jan Tschichold, 1930. Akademischer
Verlag Dr. Fritz Wedekind & Co.,
Stuttgart

Pages 48–49, "The Photographic Poster," from *Eine Stunde Druckgestaltung* (A Lesson in Printing Design) by Jan Tschichold, 1930. Akademischer Verlag Dr. Fritz Wedekind & Co., Stuttgart

Twenty-four years older than Tschichold, Renner belonged to another generation, and, having worked for years as a traditional book designer, he was a much less enthusiastic exponent of the New Typography.[9] However, in June 1926 Renner arranged for Tschichold to receive a temporary assignment to teach typography and calligraphy at the Tagesfachschule für die graphischen Berufe (Vocational School for Graphic Arts) in Munich, where Renner had recently been appointed to set up a new faculty and curriculum. After Tschichold assumed this post, Renner and some of his other colleagues persuaded him to drop the name Iwan for obvious political reasons, and it was then that he took on the name Jan, based on his given name Johannes, while retaining the new spelling of his surname, Tschichold. In 1929 Georg Trump (1896–1985), designer of the slab serif typeface called City, also joined Renner's staff. Like Renner and Tschichold, Trump had a traditional training before embracing modernist typography. The Meisterschule für Deutschlands Buchdrucker (Master School for Germany's Printers) was opened on February 1, 1927. Established largely through the efforts of Renner, this was a parallel school in Munich where Tschichold and Trump would also teach.

Tschichold was an exceptionally prolific and skilled writer. Most of his books are of a didactic nature, and he produced several books specifically intended for use in education. These included *Schriftschreiben für Setzer* in 1931 (Lettering and Calligraphy for Typesetters) and *Typographische Entwurfstechnik* (Typographical Design Methods) in 1932. The first of these two volumes, a calligraphy textbook, makes it clear that Tschichold retained an admiration for the lettering of the past. The summer of 1930 saw the publication of *Eine Stunde Druckgestaltung* (A Lesson in Printing Design), a textbook with examples, and a successor to *Die neue Typographie*. *Eine Stunde Druckgestaltung* received international attention, and the Dutch professional journal *De Reclame* reviewed it extensively in its October 1931 issue.

Tschichold was not the only one to publish his aesthetic concepts in book form. In 1929 his friends Werner Graeff (1901–1978) and Hans Richter (1888–1976) organized a large-scale Werkbund exhibition in Stuttgart, called *Film und Foto*. To accompany this exhibition (for which Tschichold designed smaller printed pieces but not the poster, which was apparently done by Richter and Graeff themselves), they published the books *Es kommt der neue Fotograf!* (Here Comes the New Photographer!) and *Filmgegner von heute—Filmfreunde von morgen* (Enemies of Film Today—Friends of Film Tomorrow). The book on photography would become a classic. Together with Franz Roh (1890–1965), Tschichold then wrote *Foto-Auge* (Photo-Eye, 1929), a collection of 76 applications for modern photography. In order to promote the photographers involved, their addresses were listed at the back of the book. Then, in 1930 Tschichold and Roh began a series of monographs on contemporary photography under the collective title *Fototek*. Unfortunately, only the first two parts, on Moholy-Nagy and Aenne Biermann (1898–1933), were ever published. Obviously, Tschichold provided the design of the publication and the promotional materials for *Fototek*, as he had also done for *Foto-Auge*.

Tschichold had been introduced to Roh by the graphic designer and photographer Hilde Horn. Both Horn and Roh lived in Munich. Horn had studied at the Bauhaus in Weimar under Moholy-Nagy from 1925 to 1926, and it was Moholy-Nagy who had introduced Tschichold to Horn. During one of their Bauhaus outings, Moholy-Nagy had made a series of photographic studies in which Hilde Horn featured. One of those studies was later published by Roh and Tschichold in their first volume of *Fototek*, dedicated to the works of Moholy-Nagy. Probably also through Tschichold, another version was published in *Arts et Métiers Graphiques* (1930, XVI, p. 69).

By 1930, Tschichold had begun to distance himself from advertising design. Beginning in 1930 he welcomed the opportunity to become the main designer of books for the socialist book club and publisher Der Bücherkreis, at that time directed by Karl Schröder, a well-known member of the KAPD (German Communist Party). Founded in 1924 by the SDP (Socialist Democratic Party), Der Bücherkreis often gave him far more freedom to design the total book: layout and typography, binding, and book jacket. Here he was able to apply the principles of the New Typography without the usual restraints of other publishers. According to Tschichold, a book had to be designed as an entity, assembled from "typeface, picture, cover, binding, paper, etc." From 1930 he would design close to 25 books for Der Bücherkreis until he left for Switzerland in 1933.

While writing *Die neue Typographie* in 1927 and 1928, Tschichold maintained close contacts with designers throughout Europe. For example, from Zwart he was given the addresses of Sybold van Ravesteyn (1889–1983) and other Dutch artists. During the summers of 1928 and 1930 he visited Paris where he made or renewed contacts with the painters Piet Mondrian and Michel Seuphor (1901–1999), and designers such as Jean Carlu (1900–1997) and Cassandre. In *Publicité*, published in late 1928, Cassandre included Tschichold's work. This issue was number 12 in the series *L'art international d'aujourd'hui*, and included 49 reproductions, of which at least four were designs by Tschichold and three by Zwart, whom Tschichold had recommended to Cassandre.

At the end of 1927 a group comprised of many members of the typographic avant-garde decided to establish their own organization, the Gruppe radikaler Reklamegestalter in Deutschland (the Group of Radical Advertising Designers), to advance their ideas through exhibitions and publications. These included Trump, Burchartz, Baumeister, Tschichold, Dexel, Friedrich Vordemberge-Gildewart (1899–1962), the Dutch designer and painter César Domela (1900–1992), then living and working

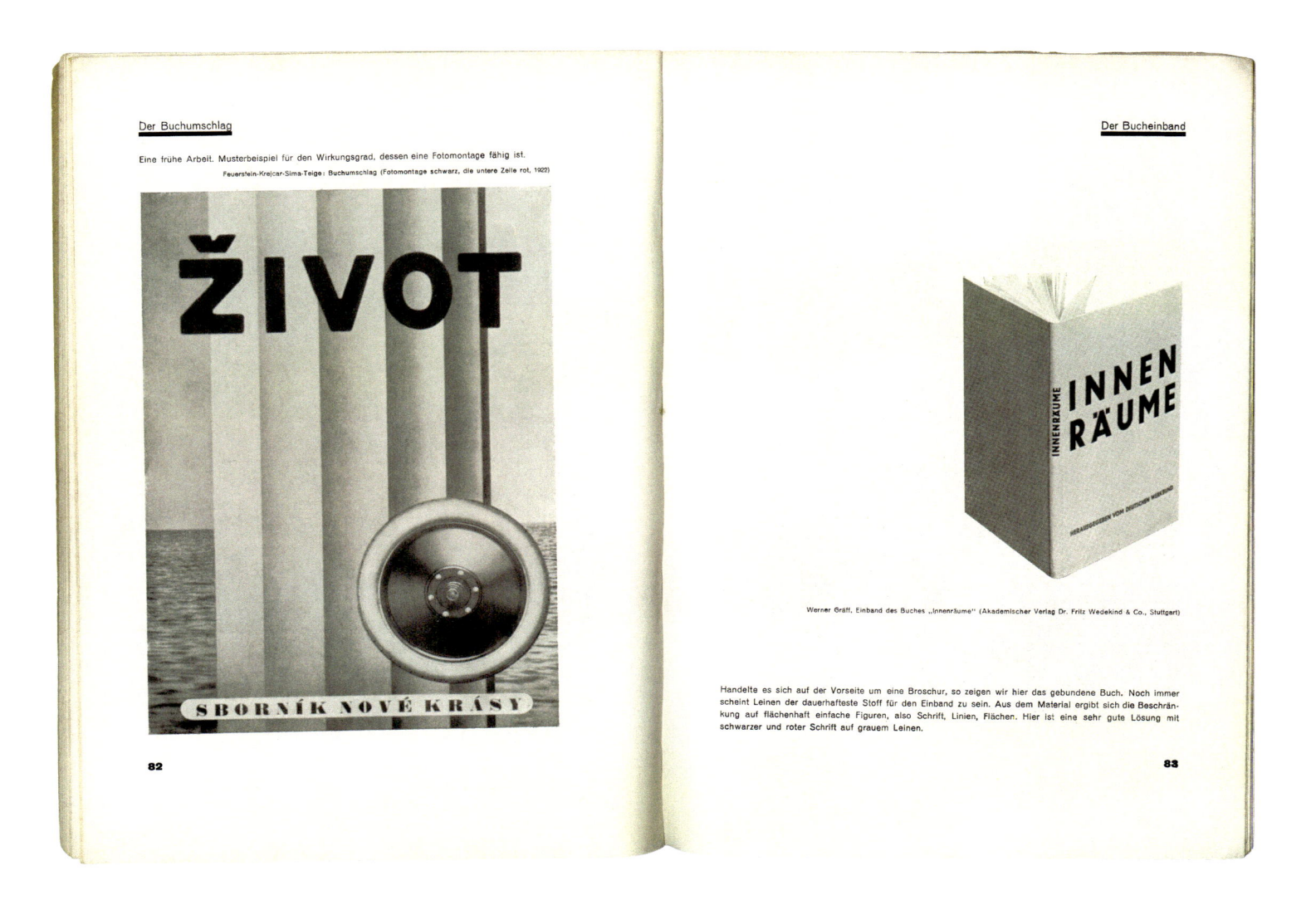

Pages 82–83, "The Book Cover,"
from *Eine Stunde Druckgestaltung*
(A Lesson in Printing Design) by
Jan Tschichold, 1930. Akademischer
Verlag Dr. Fritz Wedekind & Co.,
Stuttgart

Hilde Horn during a Bauhaus excursion, ca. 1925–1926, photographs by Lázsló Moholy-Nagy. Private collection, formerly estate Hilde Horn/Jan Tschichold

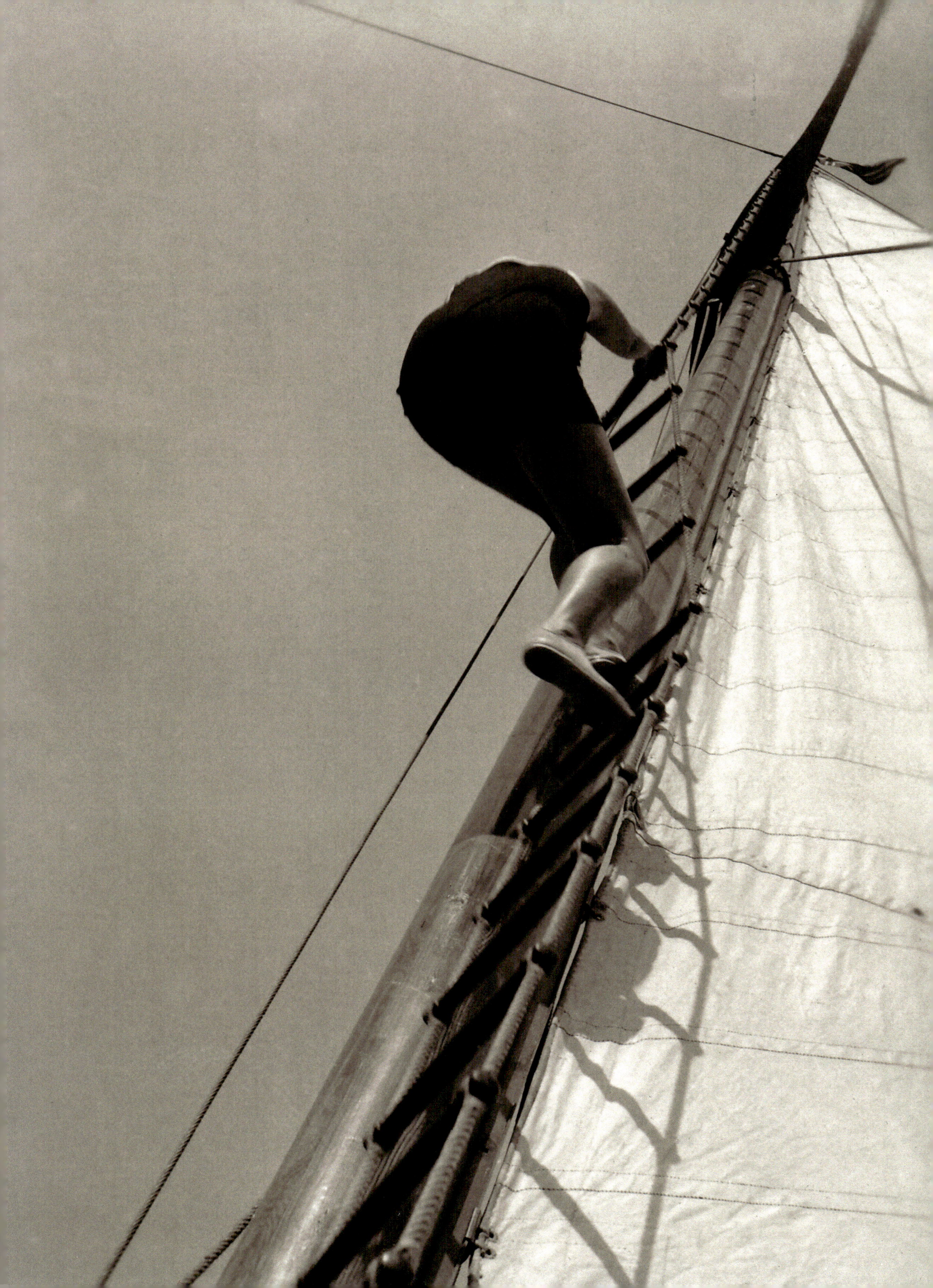

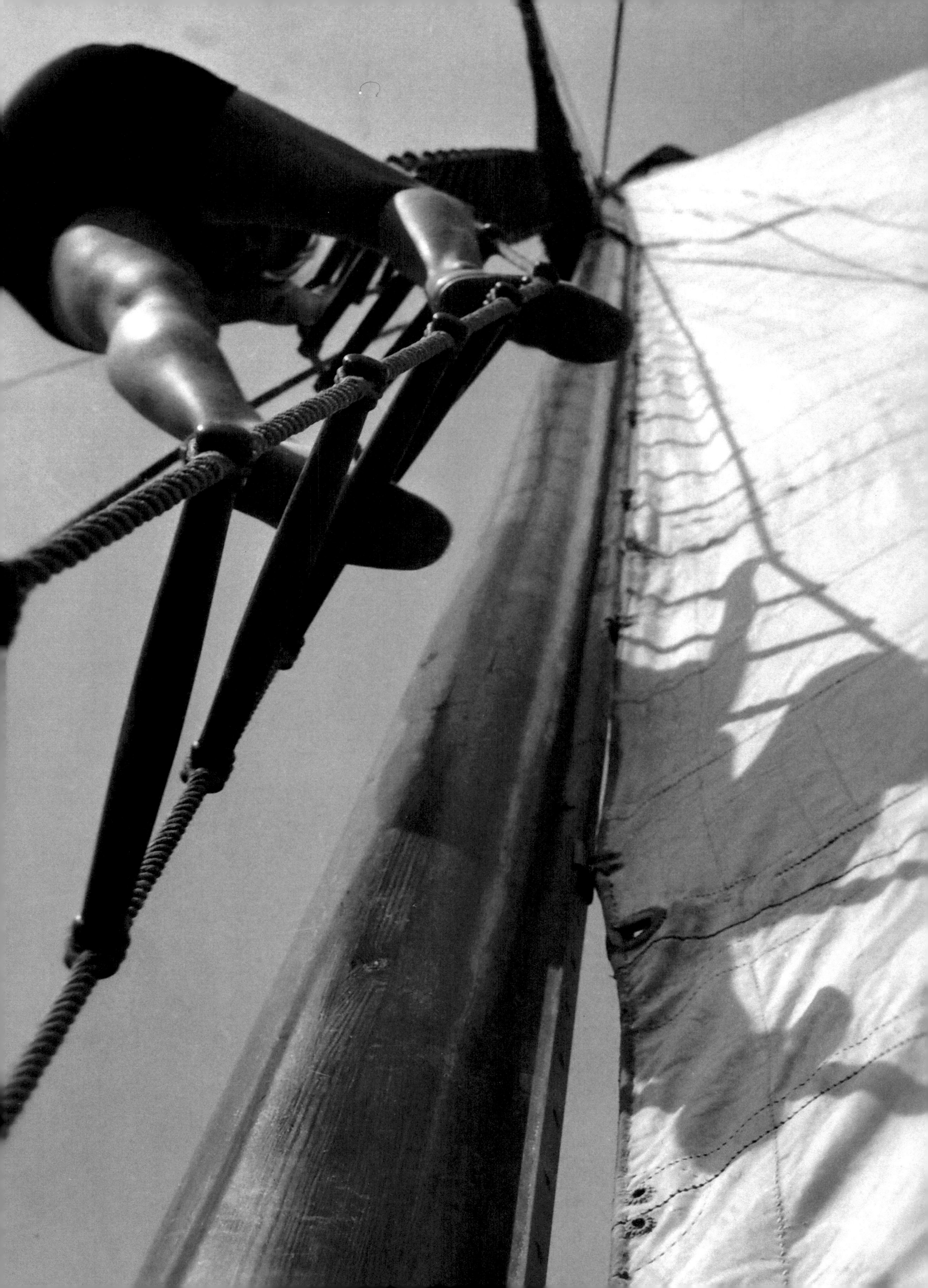

Hilde Horn during a Bauhaus excursion, ca. 1925–1926, photographs by Lázsló Moholy-Nagy. Private collection, formerly estate Hilde Horn/Jan Tschichold a strikingly new type face something quite different which will please your customer:

TRANSITO

Page from a type specimen book for Transito, 1931, issued by Lettergieterij Amsterdam, designed by Jan Tschichold, 27.3 x 19.8 cm in Germany, and Schwitters, the latter being the president and driving force behind the organization. Most of the founding members were painters who had mastered typography and advertising design by themselves. Only Trump and Tschichold had any professional knowledge of typography and printing. In early 1928 the association was officially founded under the name of the Ring neue Werbegestalter (Ring of New Advertising Designers) and would eventually have twenty-five associates. Its main purpose was to promote the work of its members. Even though the association's preferred typeface was Futura, Renner never joined. Shared perspectives included the use of sans serif type, bold rules, primary colors, and machine-based production. Like Tschichold, in typography they favored decisive contrasts and strong use of color, stressing clarity in communication. While embracing many of Tschichold's concepts, they absorbed the principles of the New Typography while retaining their own individual approaches. To a large extent it was through the Ring that Tschichold's ideas were disseminated throughout Europe.

From 1928 until 1931 the "Ring" sponsored meetings and design conferences and arranged 22 European exhibitions, one of the most important but also the last being in Amsterdam in 1931. At times, these exhibitions included designers who were not associated with the Ring such as van Doesburg in the Netherlands, the Czech constructivist Karel Teige (1900–1951), and the Bauhaus designers Bayer and Moholy-Nagy. In 1929 Zwart and Schuitema were the first two members from abroad to join the group, Tschichold having met Schuitema through Zwart. Together Zwart and Schuitema organized the Ring exhibition in December 1928. Hans Leistikow (1892–1962), John Heartfield (Helmut Herzfeld) (1891–1968), Graeff, Richter, and Molzahn became members as well. Candidates for membership had to be proposed by a current member and, after presenting examples of their work, elected by a majority vote. From the outset Tschichold intended to expand the group beyond Germany. Thus, he wrote on November 30, 1927 in a letter to Zwart: "Here in Germany we have founded an association of radical designers—intention: to represent our interests in exhibitions etc.—(Schwitters, Dexel, Burchartz, Baumeister [sic] for example, but we will accept no nominal members). I have proposed to invite our friends in spirit from other countries, that is people like you, Kassák, Teige, Lissitzky. Well, you will be hearing from us." Although Tschichold had corresponded with him and was aware of his work, the Dutch maverick H. N. Werkman (1882–1945) was not included. However, Werkman's typography was always outside of the European mainstream, and joining any group or movement was never one of his goals. Although proposed as a new member, van Doesburg characteristically declined.

In 1930 the members of the Ring publicized themselves in the book titled *Gefesselter Blick* (The Captured Gaze). This provided biographical information on Ring members, together with examples of their work. Tschichold profiled himself as "advertising designer, teacher at the German school for master printers in Munich," and stated: "In my advertising designs I strive for a maximum of purpose and I try to connect single elements harmonically—to design."

In April 1930, a combined exhibition was held in the Gewerbemuseum in Basel. With posters from Tschichold's extensive collection of modern graphic design, the exhibition was supplemented with work from Ring members and French posters from the collection of the Paris architect and communist Roger Ginsburger (1901–1980). In the exhibition catalog, designed by Tschichold, Schwitters wrote: "The Ring of New Advertising Designers was founded in the year 1928 and aimed to be a ring of all advertisement designers. It is incomplete [the Ring then had twelve members!], but then again what on earth is complete anyway? Advertising designers are people advertising by means of designing printed matter or rather, those not merely compiling printed matter, but designing it. Those are beautiful words. One could venture to state that for them, advertising and designing are synonyms. The advertising directly generates the design, and vice versa. Advertising and design have formed a union. Advertising design. It all sounds very simple and, like everything that looks simple, is a very intricate matter."

Gefesselter Blick did not provide the anticipated stimulus. In Germany the political and economic tide was against the designers of the New Typography. On March 28, 1931, Schwitters wrote to Tschichold: "I believe our Ring no longer exists." Yet that year there would still be exhibitions taking place in Stockholm, Essen, and Amsterdam. The material from this last exhibition would remain in the Netherlands with Schuitema.[10]

Tschichold felt a special kinship with Zwart and wrote to him saying that they worked in a similar manner. He assumed that opposition to innovation was as great in the Netherlands as it was in Germany. After receiving from Zwart an NKF (Nederlandsche Kabelfabriek) catalog, Tschichold wrote to him on June 13, 1928: "Splendid... it is wonderful that when working for this firm you feel your work is being duly respected and is receiving support. In general, I suspect you will have to cope, just like us here, with much opposition." However, in 1931–1932, Zwart and Schuitema received commissions from the Dutch PTT (Post, Telephone and Telegraph), a tangible indication of official acknowledgment. The cinema intrigued both men, and Tschichold sent Zwart many of the film posters that he designed for the Phoebus-Palast cinema in Munich. Zwart in turn sent Tschichold examples of his own work and advertisements for the NKF. The typography of the latter designs would to some extent influence Tschichold's 1927 posters for the Phoebus-Palast.

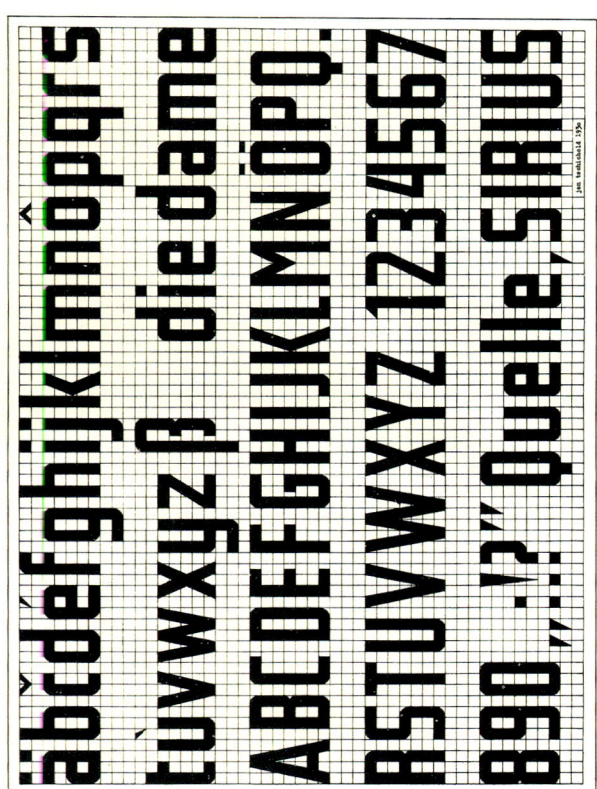

Page 239 from the magazine
Buch- und Werbekunst, vol. 7, 1930,
featuring the article 'Das neue
Plakat" (The New Poster) by
Jan Tschichold, type design
by Jan Tschichold, 31.5 x 23.5 cm

Cover from type specimen of Transito, 1931, issued by Lettergieterij Amsterdam, 27.3 x 19.8 cm

To proliferate his ideas on the New Typography, Tschichold frequently published in periodicals, including *Die Form*, the journal of the Deutscher Werkbund, for which he offered to redesign the cover. For the June 1930 issue of the British magazine *Commercial Art*, Tschichold wrote a major article on the New Typography titled "A New Life in Print," and he also provided an important contribution to the French magazine *Arts et Métiers Graphiques* (no. 19, September 1930), a publication closely associated with A. M. Cassandre and his circle. Other articles by Tschichold were published in the Polish journal *Europa* and the Czech periodical *VS Výtvarné snahy*.

Although the Nazis did not come to power in Bavaria until 1933, their influence was felt in Munich long before. In circles around Tschichold, people spoke of the *Hitlerei*—a derogatory term that left no room for misunderstanding what the speaker thought of the Nazi leader, his followers, and their methods. Edith Tschichold remembered how in the Borstei, the apartment complex where the Tschicholds lived in Munich, they saw ever more residents walking around in SA and SS uniforms. It was clear that the climate no longer afforded any room for the Tschicholds to work in Munich. Trump, who had come to the Meisterschule in Munich from Bielefeld in 1929, had accepted a post at the new Höhere Graphische Fachschule der Stadt Berlin (Berlin Higher Vocational School for Graphic Arts). In 1932 Tschichold had submitted his resignation from his Munich post to join the faculty at Trump's new school in Berlin in the summer of 1933. In January 1933, an announcement appeared in *Gebrauchsgraphik*: "Jan Tschichold, who teaches at the Munich Meisterschule für Deutschlands Buchdrucker and who has made contributions of high merit to the development of contemporary typography, has been offered the headmaster's post at the Department of Typography of the Höhere Graphische Fachschule der Stadt Berlin, which has been reorganized by Professor Trump. Tschichold's appointment will be a considerable gain, both for the school, which was able to thrive despite unfavorable conditions in the course of the year, as well as for the graphic industry of Berlin."

However, because of the Nazi accession to power, things turned out differently. When the Tschicholds moved to the Borstei in Munich, there had already been some controversy. Their Bauhaus furniture contrasted with the architecture of the Borstei, and journalists came to take photos and ran a newspaper interview.[11] Moreover, the Tschicholds had no curtains, and therefore were regarded as "different." Years later it was learned that the neighbours across the street and the cleaning woman had been asked to keep an eye on them. In early 1933, while the Nazis were consolidating their grip on power, six SA men arrived on the doorstep with drawn pistols to arrest Tschichold who was away on a lecture tour. Still, they did not go away empty-handed. After two searches, a number of items, including a collection of children's books in Russian, were "confiscated for the Fighting League for

Pages from type specimen of Transito, 1931, issued by Lettergieterij Amsterdam, 27.3 x 19.8 cm

Culture." The Bauhaus furniture and the painting by Mondrian were left untouched. When, several days later, they had been unable to arrest Tschichold, Edith was taken into custody on March 14. Tschichold voluntarily turned himself in the next day in order to get his wife released and was then held in *Schutzhaft* (protective custody) without any official charge or legal process. By calling on acquaintances, Edith attempted to get him freed, but neither she nor their friends had contacts with Nazi party members. Renner, fully conscious of his own precarious position, did not wish to act on Tschichold's behalf. Like Tschichold, he was suspected by the Nazis of being a *Kulturbolschewist* (cultural Bolshevik). Fortunately Tschichold was freed under a general amnesty. According to Edith, his first words upon his release were: "I will not stay in this country for one minute longer than I have to." Immediately after his arrest, Tschichold was fired from his job at the Meisterschule, and the appointment in Berlin, where the situation was of course no better, had become unthinkable. On July 28, 1933 the Tschicholds left Germany for Switzerland.

The Tschicholds were able to go to Basel because their friend Hermann Kienzle, the director of the Gewerbemuseum in Basel, had found a half-day a week's work for Tschichold with the printer and publisher Benno Schwabe. Tschichold was also able to teach typography two hours a week at the Gewerbeschule (Vocational School). Later he would work as a book designer for the publishers Birkhäuser and Holbein. However, the combined incomes were too small to support a family. In a 1935 letter to Vordemberge-Gildewart in Hanover, Tschichold complained about this, but received the following answer: "My dear Tschichold, hello, what is the matter with you? I was not too pleased by your last two letters.... With all your cares and troubles: just think of us! Not a single commission in sight. And this in addition to all the 'other' things. Difficulties—we have known them all the way, that's why we're avant-garde."[12]

Widely read and very influential, one of Tschichold's most important books was *Typographische Gestaltung* (Typographic Design), published in 1935 after Tschichold had moved to Switzerland. There were also Danish and Swedish editions in 1937, and in 1938 a Dutch edition was published by Franz Duwaer (1911–1944), the heroic Amsterdam printer who was executed by the Nazis in 1944. Also, an English translation by Ruari McLean was published in 1967 under the title *Asymmetric Typography*, without including much of the original illustration material. Although in *Typographische Gestaltung*, Tschichold continued to promote the New Typography, at the beginning of the book (perhaps as a portent), he acknowledged that symmetrical typography did have at least some merit. Reflecting his growing preference of modern typefaces, the text for *Typographische Gestaltung* was set in Bodoni, and script and Egyptian faces were used for headings.

Transito

moderne letter
voor slagregels

LETTERGIETERIJ
'AMSTERDAM'
VOORH. N. TETTERODE

compagnie des lampes
PARIS • 41 RUE DE LA BOÉTIE • PARIS

DOOR
NEDERLAND
MET **8** DAAGSCHE
Abonnementskaarten

NEDERLANDSCHE SPOORWEGEN

1ste klasse f 29.—
2de klasse f 22.50
3de klasse f 16.—
verkrijgbaar van 1 Maart
tot en met 15 September

Inlichtingen worden verstrekt aan
de Stations en de informatiebureaux
der Nederlandsche Spoorwegen

't Seizoen vangt aan bij
KOCH

Weer is het bijna winter en komt de Mode in het middelpunt Uwer belangstelling te staan. Gij denkt aan den killen wintertijd met zijn lange avonden, aan sneeuw en ijs maar ook.... aan de naderende feestdagen. Nu dwalen Uw blikken langs de helder verlichte etalages; gij zoekt iets moois, iets nieuws, een heerlijk koesterende bontmantel, een warme huisjapon, een prachtig, slank avondtoilet. Beperk U echter niet tot de etalages, maar treed binnen in onze ruime winkels. We verlangen er naar, U onze uitgebreide collecties te laten zien. We hebben er veel zorg aan besteed en zijn er van overtuigd, dat U slagen zult zoo wel bij ons als bij onze filialen in:
DEN HAAG, KNEUTERDIJK 122
AMSTERDAM, KALVERSTRAAT 18
GRONINGEN, HEERESTRAAT 5-7
UTRECHT, OUDE GRACHT 23-25

H. C. KOCH & ZOON
HOOGSTRAAT 21, ROTTERDAM

TRANSITO — ONTWERP: J. TSCHICHOLD

Platwerk
SNELPERS

Het Binden
DRUKKERS

Onze Fabriek
LETTERBORD

LETTERGIETERIJ „AMSTERDAM" VOORH. N. TETTERODE

TRANSITO — ONTWERP: J. TSCHICHOLD

Gereedschappen
DE COPIEERPERS

Een nieuwe Serie voor
HET RECLAME WERK

Stofvrij is ons Houtwerk
HARDE STERKE SPECIE 243

Wij bieden U de eerste kwaliteit
BEZICHTIGT U ONZE FABRIEKEN

1 2 3 4 5 6 7 8 9 0

LETTERGIETERIJ „AMSTERDAM" VOORH. N. TETTERODE

SADDIER
ET ses FILS
MEUBLES DÉCORATION
29-31 RUE DES BOULETS, TÉL. 22345
PARIS

ils réalisent eux-mêmes
les intérieurs qu'ils créent

Kerstgeschenken

die met zorg zijn gekozen uit een keur van de „Allan"
artikelen, behouden lang hun waarde. Linnen en
katoen damasten tafellakens, servetten en ontbijt-
stellen zijn een welkom geschenk. In onze magazijnen
vindt Ge voorts nog velerlei, dat als Kerstgeschenk
bijzonder geschikt is, wij noemen U bijvoorbeeld
tafelkleeden, tafelloopers, pull-overs, handschoenen,
Zakdoeken, Eau de Cologne, zeep en snuisterijen.

ALLAN GROOTE MARKT 16, ROTTERDAM

In *Typographische Gestaltung*, Tschichold further elaborated on the use of photography as a design component: "Photography has its own rules which are based on the same principles as those of the New Typography.... As well as normal photography, there are variations which can play a part in the new typography. For example photograms (photography without a camera, a technique developed and made new by Moholy-Nagy and Man Ray), negative photography, double exposures and other combinations (e.g. the outstanding self-portrait of Lissitsky), and photomontage. Any or all could be used in the service of graphic expression."[13]

Shortly before the beginning of World War II, Tschichold began to reconsider and ultimately discard the principles of the New Typography. Regarding the supremacy of sans serif typefaces, he wrote in 1959 to *Typography USA*, a seminar sponsored by the Type Directors Club of New York City: "In the light of my present knowledge, it was a juvenile opinion to consider the sans serif as the most suitable or even the most contemporary typeface. A typeface has first to be legible, nay, readable, and a sans serif is certainly not the most legible typeface when set in quantity, let alone readable.... Good typography has to be perfectly legible and, as such, the result of intelligent planning. The classical typefaces such as Garamond, Janson, Baskerville and Bell are undoubtedly the most legible."[14]

He then reverted to the traditional and symmetrical typography he had so fervently rejected almost two decades earlier. Since the New Typography had been a response to the disorder in European typography during the early twenties, perhaps Tschichold now felt that further progress was no longer necessary or possible and that he had gone as far as he could in exploring the new frontiers. Also, most of his work in Switzerland consisted of book designs, and his more conservative clients were not overly receptive to the New Typography.

Many designers who had fervently embraced the New Typography were bewildered and even wounded by his reversal. Tschichold's most vehement detractor was Max Bill (1908–1994), a Swiss industrial designer, painter, sculptor, architect, and ultimately graphic designer who had returned to Zurich in 1929 after two years at the Bauhaus in Dessau. Discouraged by the difficulty of finding work as an architect, he began to design advertisements and, greatly inspired by Tschichold, soon developed into a master typographer. After having wholeheartedly embraced the principles of the New Typography, its most prominent spokesman had, in his eyes, rejected all that he had believed in. This he could neither ignore nor pardon.

Tschichold had also begun to equate the New Typography with fascism, so his reversal was related to political as well as design factors. This he explained in the same 1959 letter to *Typography USA*: "A

Pages from type specimen of Transito, 1931, issued by Lettergieterij Amsterdam, 27.3 x 19.8 cm few years after the New Typography, Hitler came. I was accused of creating 'un-German' typography and art, and so I preferred to leave Germany. Since 1933 I have lived in Basel, Switzerland. In the very first years I tried to develop what I had called the New Typography. In 1935 I wrote another textbook, *Typographische Gestaltung*, which is much more prudent than *Die neue Typographie* and is still a useful book! In time, typographical things, in my eyes, took on a very different aspect, and to my astonishment I detected most shocking parallels between the teachings of *Die neue Typographie* and National Socialism and fascism. Obvious similarities consist in the ruthless restriction of typefaces, a parallel to Goebbels's infamous *gleichschaltung* (political alignment), and the more or less militaristic arrangement of lines. Because I did not want to be guilty of spreading the very ideas that had compelled me to leave Germany, I thought over again what a typographer should do." [17] He added that the New Typography also did not "allow for the human desire for variety. It has an entirely militaristic attitude." [15]

He continued by saying: "The aim of typography must not be expression, least of all self-expression, but perfect communication achieved by skill. Taking over working principles from previous times or other typographers is not wrong but sensible...."[16] Tschichold now believed that typographers should embrace humanist ideals and utilize the wisdom and achievements of past typographers and the entire heritage of graphic design as sources of inspiration. Although he continued to consider the New Typography appropriate for fields such as advertising and perhaps for some publications having to do with contemporary art and architecture, he found it inappropriate for most scholarly and literary publications.

Much of the creative impetus in graphic design during the first part of the 20th century was connected to art movements such as Futurism, De Stijl, Dada, and the Bauhaus. However, these movements were to a large extent confined to small circles removed from the broad spectrum of society. On the other hand, Tschichold strove to make his new graphic design concepts accessible to printers, typesetters, and designers involved with ordinary design assignments. Tschichold's visual language made use of minimalist forms while seeking optimal results. Even though he saw utilitarianism and modernism as being closely related, he sought an artistic quality closely tied to the materials used in production. A highly developed awareness of graphic style and principles and an innate perfectionism resulted in efficient yet elegant designs.

In the United States, Alexey Brodovitch (1898–1971), the Art Director of *Harper's Bazaar* who revolutionized American magazine design, was one of many graphic designers who openly acknowledged a debt to Tschichold. The great American graphic designer Paul Rand was introduced to Tschichold

galerie vernier

LUC. ALBERT MOREAU
LES DEUX FEES (LITHO)

exposition permanente

eaux-fortes, lithographies et bois de:
coubine, dubreuil, dufresne
dufy, dérain, hermine-david
marie laurencin, l. a. moreau
matisse, jean puy, vlaminck

24-28 rue jacques-callot (rue de seine) vi.

AMSTERDAM
DEN HAAG
ROTTERDAM

N.V. HOUTHANDEL V.H. G. KEY

NIJMEGEN
WEURTSCHEWEG 118
TEL 630 EN 2652

■ THE PALLADIUM ■
LIFE
MAURICE COWAN'S REVUE
PROGRAMME

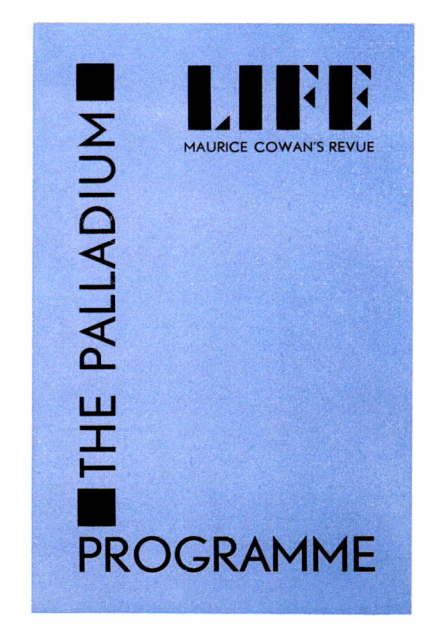

Pages from type specimen of Transito, 1931, issued by Lettergieterij Amsterdam, 27.3 × 19.8 cm

TRANSITO
TRANSITO
TRANSITO
TRANSITO
TRANSITO
TRANSITO
TRANSITO
Transito
Transito

EEN MODERNE LETTER VOOR SLAGREGELS

Transito
Transito
Transito
Transito
Transito
Transito
Transito
Transito

LETTERGIETERIJ "AMSTERDAM" VOORHEEN N. TETTERODE

J. TSCHICHOLD

de bekende voorganger van de moderne, "zakelijk" genoemde typografie, ontwierp voor ons de

Transito

die ondanks haar eenvoud toch een zekere elegance bezit. Zij wordt gegoten in zeven corpsen

LETTERGIETERIJ "AMSTERDAM"
VOORHEEN
N. TETTERODE

GEDRUKT OP PAPIER VAN DE
N.V. DE HOLLANDSCHE PAPIER INDUSTRIE, E. DE VRIES & Co., AMSTERDAM

Transito
TRANSITO

by the article titled "A New Life in Print" in the July 1930 issue of the British journal *Commercial Art*. A translation of Tschichold's introduction to *Die neue Typographie*, this article greatly inspired Rand and made him aware of modernist graphic designers such as Zwart, Schwitters, Lissitsky, Burchartz, Sutnar, Dexel, and Moholy-Nagy. In his pioneering work as the leading advocate of the New Typography, Tschichold made a contribution to modernist graphic design that is both enduring and omnipresent. Through his writing and typographic innovations, he not only disseminated the principles of the New Typography but also the concepts of Russian constructivism and the Bauhaus throughout Europe and North America. His influence on contemporary graphic design continues to be immeasurable.

NOTES

1. Christopher Burke, *Active Literature: Jan Tschichold and New Typography*, London: Hyphen Press, 2007, p. 16
2. Burke, *Active Literature*, p. 19.
3. Richard B. Doubleday, *Jan Tschichold, Designer: The Penguin Years*, New Castle, DE: Oak Knoll Press; London: Lund Humphries, 2006.
4. Burke, *Active Literature*, p. 19.
5. Theo van Doesburg, letter to Antony Kok, 1921.
6. El Lissitzky, letter to Tschichold, October 1925.
7. Card from Dexel dated December 4, 1925. The letters from Lissitzky and Dexel are to be found in the Jan and Edith Tschichold Papers, Getty Institute, Los Angeles.
8. Christopher Burke, *Paul Renner: The Art of Typography*, London: Hyphen Press, p. 201.
9. Burke, *Paul Renner*, p. 66.
10. The smaller materials are presently in the Gemeentemuseum, The Hague.
11. The source unfortunately cannot be traced.
12. Letter dated March 28, 1935, in answer to a letter of March 17, 1935, Jan and Edith Tschichold Papers, Getty Institute, Los Angeles.
13. Jan Tschichold, *Typographische Gestaltung*, Basel, 1935; trans. Ruari McLean as *Asymmetric Typography*, London: Faber and Faber, 1967, p. 85.
14. Edward M. Gottschall, *Typographic Communications Today*, Cambridge/London: The MIT Press, 1989, p. 43.
15. Gottschall, p. 43.
16. Gottschall, p. 43.

Foldout from type specimen of Transito, 1931, issued by Lettergieterij Amsterdam, 54.6 x 39.6 cm

SASKIA

Cover from type specimen of Saskia, issued by Lettergieterij Amsterdam, designed by Jan Tschichold, 1931-1932. 27.3 x 19.8 cm

Pages from type specimen of Saskia, issued by Lettergieterij Amsterdam, designed by Jan Tschichold, 1931-1932. 27.3 x 19.8 cm

Als Rembrandt, der Sohn des Müllers vom Rhein, auf der Höhe seines Lebens stand, nahm er sich ein anmutiges junges Mädchen, die Saskia, zum Weibe. Aus manchen seiner Bilder spricht das Glück dieser Ehe in unverhohlener Lebensfreude zu uns. Rembrandt hat das Bild seiner jungen Frau andrucksstark in Radierungen der Mit- und Nachwelt übermittelt. Wie in den zarten und doch sicheren Strichen dieser Letzteren Anmut und Eleganz sich vereinen mit dem in ernster Arbeit errungenen Können des Meisters, so ist es auch dem Münchener Graphiker Jan Tschichold gelungen, in seiner Schraasschrift eine Type voll Zartheit und doch voll ernster Sachlichkeit auf das Papier zu werfen. Gemildert ist in der Schrift allerdings etwas das Helldunkel Rembrandts, das er in seinen Radierungen zur höchsten Vollendung entwickelt, zu einer ausgeglichenen milden Tönung, und wie leichtfüßige schlanke Rehe durchs Gelände eilen, so gleiten hier die Buchstaben über das Papier, dem Auge ein Wohlgefallen. Wer eindrucksvoll und doch voll Milde und Ruhe dem Leser begegnen will, dem sagt diese Schrift, was er erstrebt. Sie ruft in dem Leser jene zarte Stimmung hervor, die wohl manche Anzeige im Herzen von Verwandten und Freunden erzeugen möchte. Aber auch wer in Klarheit und Reinheit der Form zum Leser sprechen will, der findet in dieser Schrift, das, was er sucht. Nichts ist verschnörkelt, nichts barock, und doch tritt in der Schrift eine Eigenart voll Reiz, Vornehmheit und Eleganz zutage, die sie weit erhebt über alles Hergebrachte und Alltägliche.

SCHELTER & GIESECKE AG . SCHRIFTGIESSEREI . LEIPZIG

SASKIA
SCHELTER & GIESECKE AG . SCHRIFTGIESSEREI . LEIPZIG

Die Entwicklungsgeschichte des Leipziger Buchdrucks ist sehr eng mit dem steigenden Erfolg der Leipziger Messen als Büchermarkt verbunden

SASKIA
SCHELTER & GIESECKE AG . SCHRIFTGIESSEREI . LEIPZIG

Aa Bb Cc Dd Ee Ff Gg Hh Ii Jj Kk
Ll Mm Nn Oo Pp Qq Rr Ss ß Tt Uu Vv
Ww Xx Yy Zz Ää Öö Üü Æ æ Œ œ $ £
Áá Àà Çç Éé Îî Ññ Óó Òò Ûû Ýý Žž
1 2 3 4 5 6 7 8 9 0 & . , : ; - ' „ « () [ ] ! ? * † §

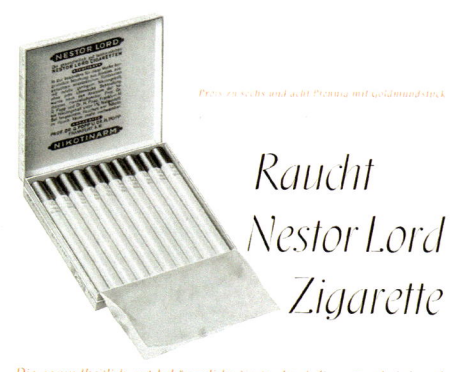

Pages from type specimen of Saskia, issued by Lettergieterij Amsterdam, designed by Jan Tschichold, 1931-1932. 27.3 x 19.8 cm

SASKIA
SCHELTER & GIESECKE AG · SCHRIFTGIESSEREI · LEIPZIG

Il focolare domestico era sempre ai miei occhi una figura rettorica, buona per incorniciarvi gli affetti più miti e sereni, come il raggio di luna per baciare le chiome bionde; ma sorridevo allorquando sentivo dirmi che il fuoco del camino è quasi un amico. Sembravami in verità un amico troppo necessario, a volte uggioso

SASKIA
SCHELTER & GIESECKE AG · SCHRIFTGIESSEREI · LEIPZIG

In den vorm van een boeiend verhaal wijst de schrijver op den nood der tijden en op het geneesmiddel, dat de opgeschroeide menschheid noodig heeft: de hernieuwing van den band met het Onzienlijke en daarvan als gevolg een geest van welgezindheid

HAPAG
HAMBURG-AMERIKA LINIE · HAMBURG

Vertretungen der Hamburg-Amerika Linie in sämtlichen größeren Städten Europas und der überseeischen Länder

Die Hamburg-Amerika Linie wurde in dem Jahre 1847 unter der Firma »Hamburg-Amerikanische Packetfahrt-Actien Gesellschaft« gegründet. Aus den Anfangsbuchstaben der offiziellen Firmenbezeichnung hat man das Wort »Hapag« geprägt, das zum in der ganzen Welt bekannten Kennwort für die Hamburg-Amerika Linie und ihre Schiffe geworden ist. Die Gesellschaft verfügt heute bei einer Gesamttonnage von mehr als einer Million Bruttoregistertonnen über 178 Seedampfer, die nach allen Teilen der Welt fahren. In den mehr als 84 Jahren ihres Bestehens war die Hamburg-Amerika Linie auf Vervollkommnung ihrer transatlantischen Passagierdienste stets bedacht

HAMBURG · AMERIKA LINIE

Cover of a brochure for the Meisterschule für Deutschlands Buchdrucker by Jan Tschichold, ca. 1927, 30 x 21 cm

Program sticker for the Phoebus-Palast cinema by Jan Tschichold, 1927, 5.5 x 9.3 cm

Pages 2 and 3 of a Phoebus-Palast program, 1927

Cover and page 4 of a promotional brochure for the Meisterschule by Jan Tschichold, ca. 1927, photos by Eduard Wasow, 30 x 21 cm

Meisterschule

für Deutschlands Buchdrucker Schule der Stadt München und des Deutschen Buchdrucker-Vereins EV

Leitung: Oberstudiendirektor Paul Renner
Typografie: Professor Trump, Tschichold
Lehrer für Satz: Käufer
Lehrer für Druck: Schwemer

Als Beilage für das »Archiv für Buchgewerbe und Gebrauchsgraphik« gesetzt und gedruckt von Schülern der Meisterschule für Deutschlands Buchdrucker in München

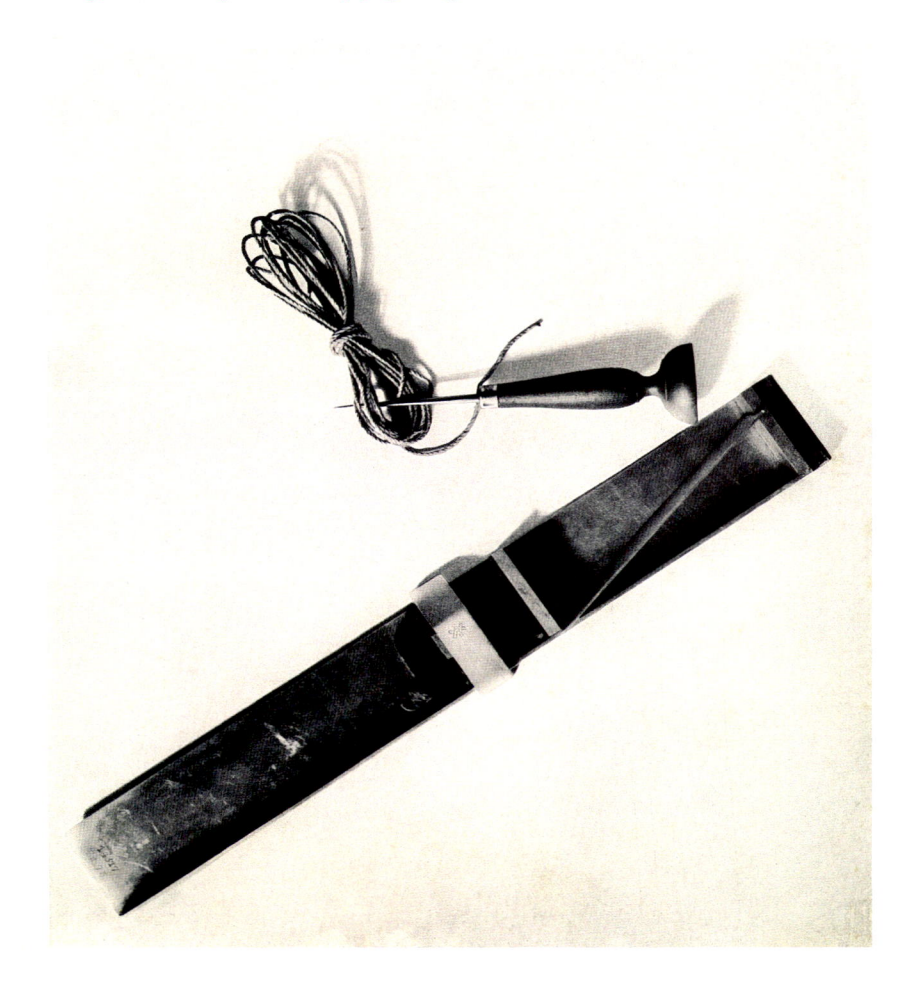

Cover of promotional brochure for the Meisterschule, supplement for *Deutsche Drucker* by Jan Tschichold, 1931, 31 x 23.5 cm

Sportpolitische Rundschau, magazine cover by Jan Tschichold, 1928, 31 x 23.7 cm. The same cover design was reused every month but with a different sports photo each time.

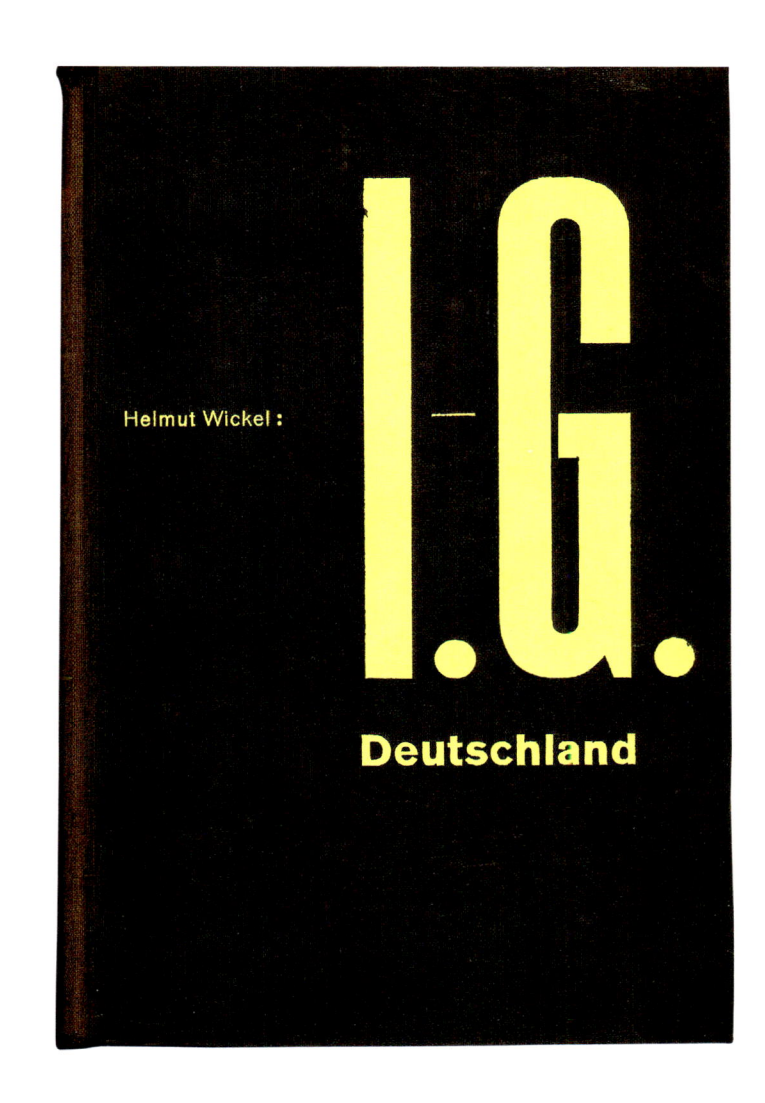

Das lustige Buch (The Funny Book), cloth book cover by Jan Tschichold, 1931, 19.2 x 12.8 cm. Verlag der Bücherkreis GmbH, Berlin

Helmut Wickel, *IG-Deutschland*, cloth book cover by Jan Tschichold, 1932, 22.5 x 14 cm. Verlag der Bücherkreis GmbH, Berlin

Letterhead for the publisher Der Bücherkreis (including logo) by Jan Tschichold, ca. 1930, 29.8 x 21.2 cm

Hilde Horn, ca. 1931
(photo: Grete Eckert, Munich)

Franz Roh, ca. 1927
(photo: Kurt Schwitters)

Invoice form for Eduard Wasow,
designed by Jan Tschichold,
ca. 1928, 21 x 14.5 cm

Eduard Wasow, ca. 1930
(photo: Hilde Horn estate)

Postcard advertising a lecture in Stuttgart by Jan Tschichold, 1927

Window card advertising an illustrated lecture by Jan Tschichold on *Die neue Typographie*, 1927, 15 x 20.8 cm

Window card advertising a lecture by Jan Tschichold on advertising and standard printing formats, 1930–1931, letterpress, 29.5 x 42.2 cm

Thomas Morus	16. Jahrhundert
Bellamy	19. Jahrhundert
Illing	20. Jahrhundert

Illing

uto-polis

Werner Illing

utopolis

Phantastischer Zukunftsroman

„Ein Zukunftsgemälde einer freien Gemeinschaft Utopien mit der Hauptstadt Utopolis. Von erfinderischer Phantasie mit allen technisch-mechanischen Fortschrittsmöglichkeiten ausgestattet • In vielem ist das Buch Gegenwartssatire am Stoff einer imaginär erschauten Zukunft. Illing hat Phantasie, einen einfachen, bildhaft genauen, unprätentiösen Stil und als Bestes eine gute, tatwillige Gesinnung." Die Literatur.

In Ganzleinen gebunden 4.30 RM

Werner Illing **utopolis**
Roman

Ein Schiffbruch verschlägt Hein und Karl in das Land der freien Arbeitergenossenschaft von Utopien, die nahezu die vollkommene sozialistische Gemeinschaft verwirklicht hat. Sie erleben hier am praktischen Beispiel, wie weit selbst der organisierte europäische Proletarier noch mit der Anschauung und Denkweise der bürgerlichen Welt verbunden ist. Als der Arbeiterstaat durch den verbrecherischen Anschlag einer kleinen Kapitalistengruppe in höchste Gefahr gerät, gelingt es Karl, einen wesentlichen Beitrag zur Rettung beizusteuern.

Der Verfasser hat es vermieden, seine Utopie mit lehrhaften theoretischen Ausführungen zu belasten. Die Handlung ist abenteuerlich-spannend und hält sich bewußt innerhalb der Grenzen des Möglichen. Nur so gelang es, aus dem Wunschbild einer denkbaren Zukunft die Gegenwart satirisch und kritisch herauszuspiegeln. Der Roman ist mit einem Humor geschrieben, der das Buch in den Vordergrund des literarischen Interesses rückt.

». . . eine einfache, aber eindringlich gefaßte Gesellschaftssatire voll des großen Atems der Menschlichkeit.« »La Nouvelle Revue Critique«, Paris

». . . Dem Verfasser kommt es darauf an, dem Leser den Gegensatz zwischen kapitalistischer Gegenwart und einer möglichen besseren und schöneren Zukunft zum Bewußtsein zu bringen. Und wir entnehmen dem Buch die Nutzanwendung: das Zukunftsbild, das uns der Dichter entwirft, braucht keine Utopie zu sein. Freilich müssen wir darum kämpfen.«
»Arbeiter-Jugend«, Berlin

Werner Illing, *Utopolis*, dust jacket by Jan Tschichold, 1930, 19.2 x 24 cm. Verlag der Bücherkreis GmbH, Berlin

**Lettre d'une jolie femme
à un monsieur passéiste**

ÈÈÈÈÈÈÈèèèèèèèèèèèèèèèèèèèèèèèèèèèèèè
+ baisers + — × + + caresses + fraîcheur
beauté élégance 3000 frs. par mois
+ — + — × + — + bague rubis 8000
vaniteeeeeeeeeeee + 6000 frs. chaus-
sures Demain chez
toi Je suis serieuse
dévouée Tendresses

CH Al Rrrrrr R

nicht ausgeglichen
ausgeglichen

Die **richtige Weite** ist ziemlich genau bestimmbar: Die Versalien sollen so weit auseinanderstehen, daß die Senkrechten der weiten Buchstaben H, N noch gegenüber den Flächenräumen zwischen den Staben zusammenstehen.

NICHT AUSGEGLICHEN (durchaus unzulässig)

AUSEINANDERGEZOGEN

SCHLECHT AUSGEGLICHEN

CH, AU, LI zu weit; HL, GE, GL, HEN zu eng

RICHTIG AUSGEGLICHEN

Es genügt nicht, sich bloß nach der Regel zu richten, daß die Räume zwischen den Buchstaben gleich sein müssen. Im Worte HUHN sind sie gleich, doch ist das Wort schwerer lesbar als das ausgeglichene. Die Flächen in den Buchstaben müssen durch genügendes Ausgleichen unauffällig gemacht werden. Erst dann wird das Wort lesbar.

falsch: **HUHN**   richtig: **HUHN**   zu weit: **HUHN**

Ein O darf nicht als Loch erscheinen, sondern muß in seiner Wirkung neutralisiert werden:

falsch: **OHNE**   richtig: **OHNE**   zu weit: **OHNE**

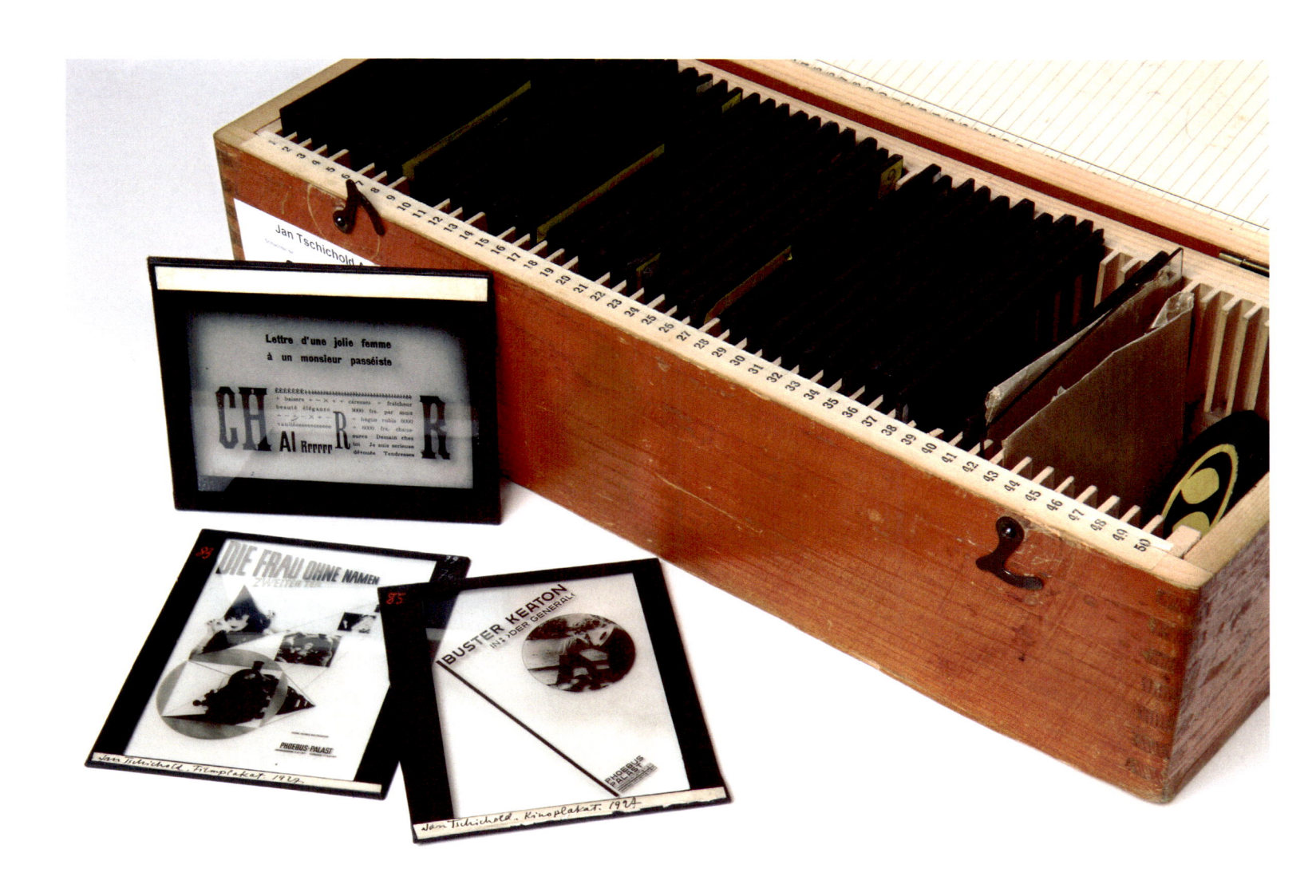

Lantern slide used by Jan Tschichold,
ca. 1930, showing Marinetti's poem
"Chèèèr," from the book *Les mots en
liberté futuristes*, 1919

Lantern slide used by Jan Tschichold
ca. 1930, showing kerning variations

Case of lantern slides used by Jan
Tschichold betwzen 1926 and 1935

83

Graphisches Kabinett exhibitions 1928–1930

May 1928: 100 drawings by Vincent van Gogh.
June 1928: Self-portraits by contemporary artists.
July 1928: Emil Nolde, paintings from the years 1910 to 1926.
August 1928: Otto Pankok, graphic prints; photographs by Aenne Biermann; photographs by A. Renger-Patzsch, Bad Harzburg.
August to mid-September 1928: Paintings by Hans Reichel.
Mid-September to mid-October 1928: Max Beckmann, paintings from the years 1910 to 1928.
Mid-October to end of November 1928: *Verre églomisé* paintings from the last two centuries.
November 22 to end of December 1928: Vincent van Gogh, 35 unknown paintings from private collections.
January 1929: Otto Mueller, recent paintings.
February 17 to end of March 1929: August Macke.
From April 10, 1929: The German landscape in contemporary drawings and watercolors.
June 1929: M. Kogan, drawings with red chalk.

May 28 to mid-June 1928: Miniature paintings from Persia and India.
July 8 to mid-August 1929: Konrad Westermayer.
From August 25th, 1929: French graphic art: from Ingres to Picasso.
October 24 to November 17, 1929: Max Beckmann, paintings, pastels, drawings.
November 1929: Photos and photocollages by Moholy-Nagy.
December 17, 1929 to January 15, 1930: The paths of abstract painting.
January 24 to February 10, 1930: Posters of the avant-garde: from the Jan Tschichold collection.
February to end of March 1930: Stages in the graphic work of Max Beckmann.
From November 5, 1930: The drawings of Alfred Kubin.

Graphisches Kabinett window card by Jan Tschichold, 1929, 29.5 x 41.8 cm

The Max Beckmann exhibition
at the Graphisches Kabinett,
Briennerstraße 10, ca. 1928
(photo: Eduard Wasow)

gewerbemuseum basel

neue
werbegraphik

30. märz bis 27. april 1930

"New Advertising Graphics", catalog cover by Jan Tschichold, 1930, 21 x 14.8 cm. His collection of avant-garde posters was included in this exhibition.

Letter from Jan Tschichold to the Kunstgewerbemuseum in Hamburg, 1928. It is reported that the posters were being offered for sale for 1 *Reichsmark* a piece.

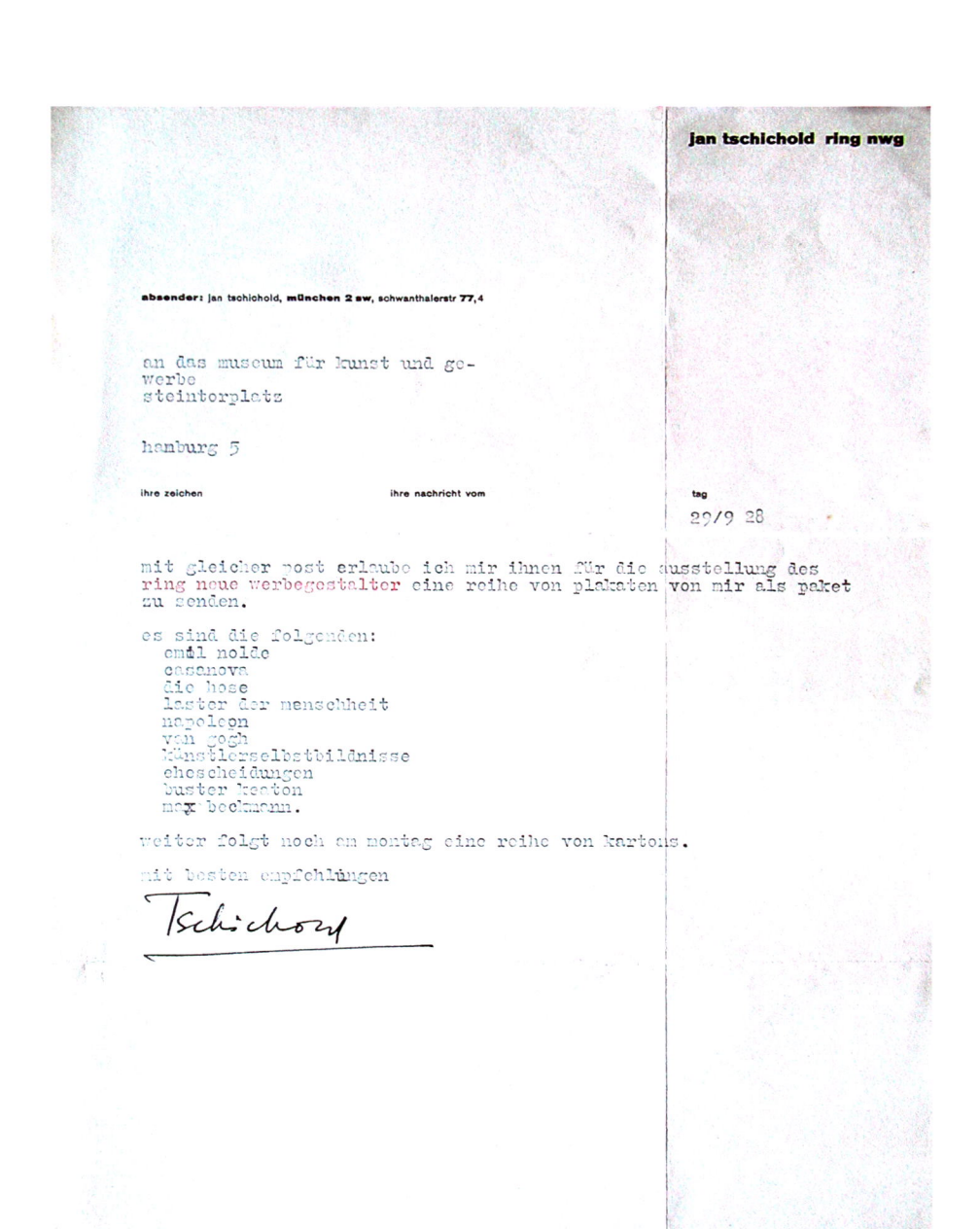

Die Form magazine, cover design by Jan Tschichold, ca. 1929, photocollage, watercolor, and pen, 26 x 18.4 cm

Commercial Art magazine, cover design by Jan Tschichold, 1931, pencil, 29.5 x 21 cm

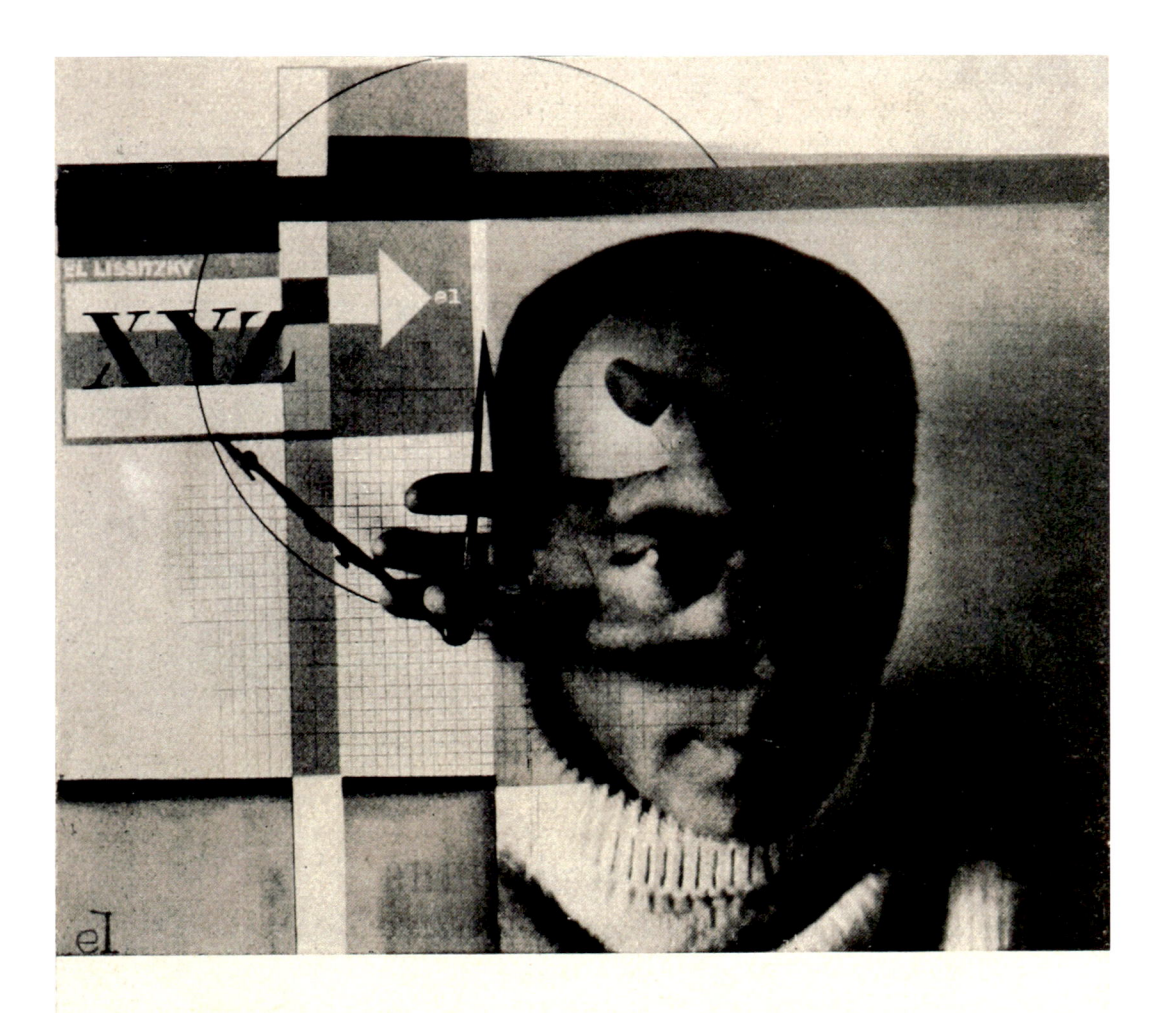

Advertising brochure for the book *Foto-Auge*, 1929, design by Jan Tschichold, photo by El Lissitzky, 13.5 x 10 cm

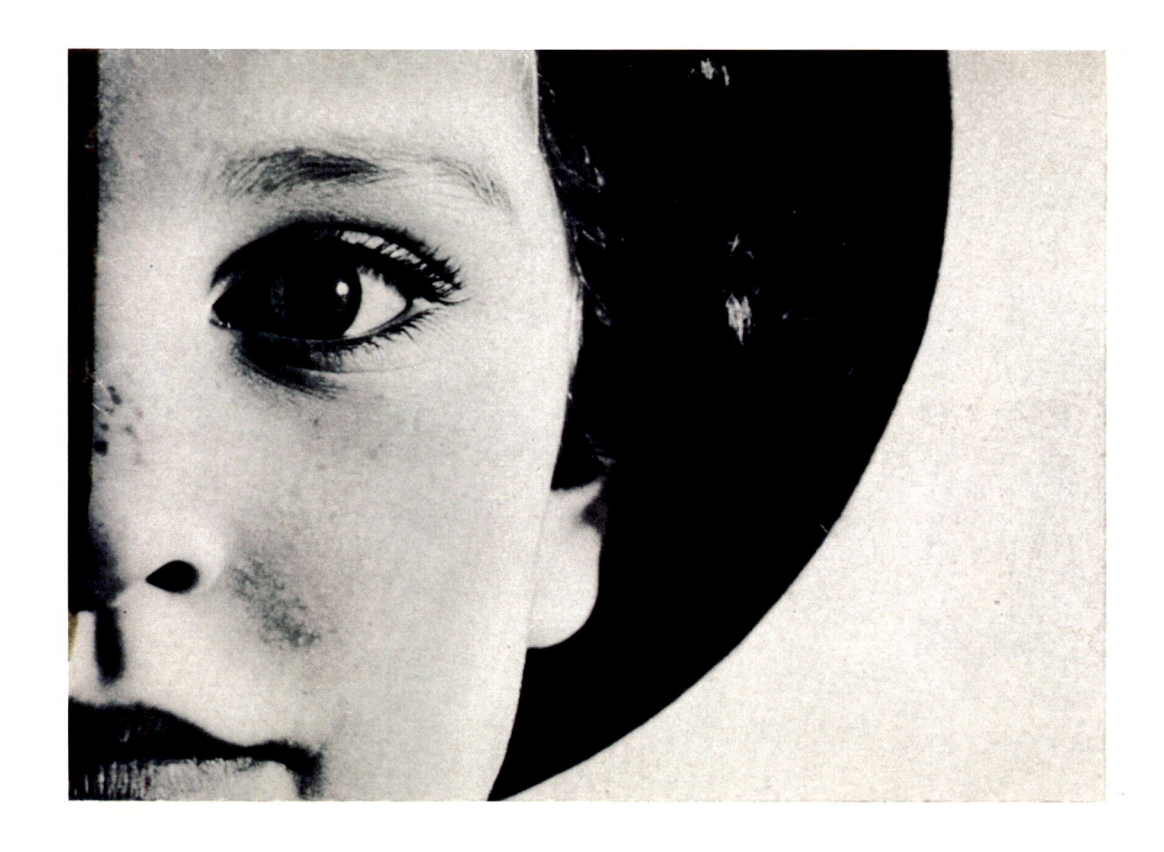

foto-auge
76 fotos der zeit   zusammengestellt von franz roh und jan tschichold

photo-eye
76 photos of the period   edited by franz roh and jan tschichold

œil et photo
76 photographies de notre temps   choisies par franz roh et jan tschichold

akademischer verlag dr. fritz wedekind & co, stuttgart, kasernenstraße 58

Advertising brochure for the Akademischer Verlag Dr. Fritz Wedekind & Co., designed by Jan Tschichold, 1929, photo by Max Burchartz, 19.5 x 13.5 cm

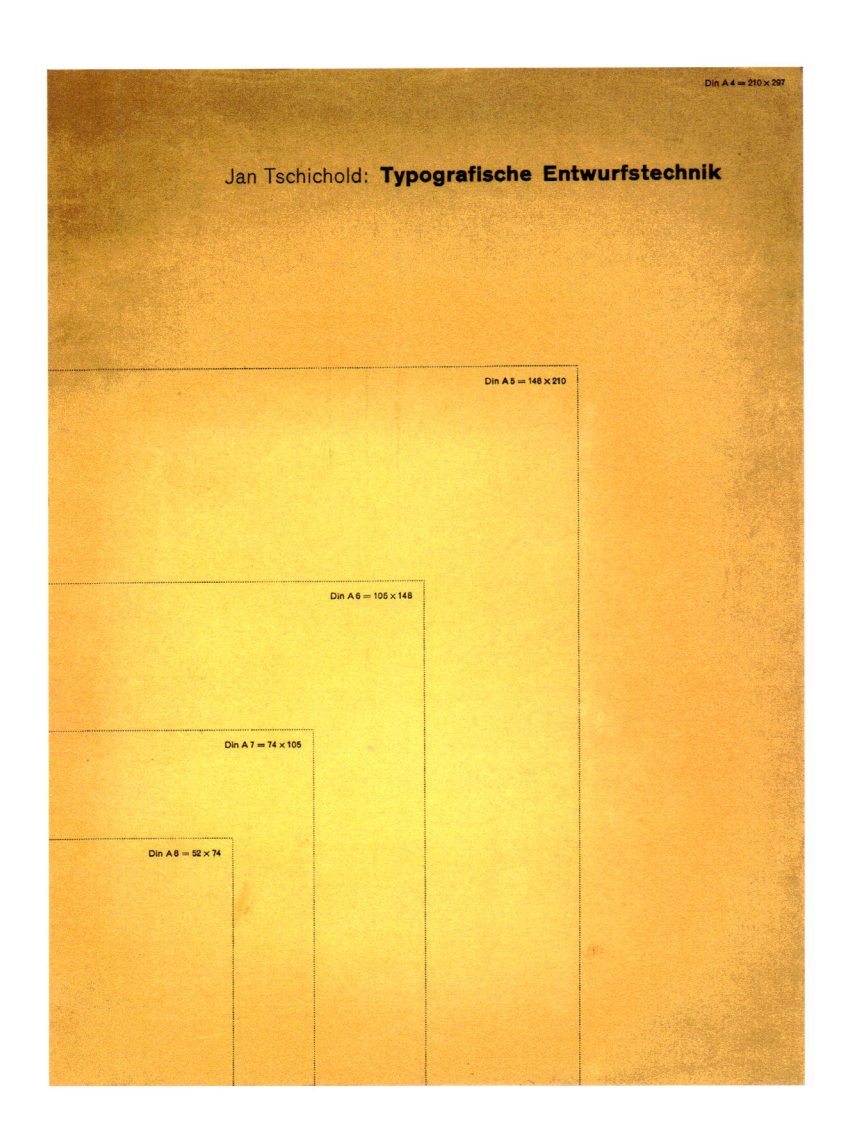

Cover of *Typografische Entwurfstechnik* (Typographical Design Methods) by Jan Tschichold, 1932, 29.7 x 21 cm

Cover of *Schriftschreiben für Setzer* (Lettering and Calligraphy for Typesetters) by Jan Tschichold, ca. 1931, 15 x 21 cm

Pages 1 and 4 of a Munich film festival program by Jan Tschichold, 1932, 21 x 30 cm

UHERTYPE AG, Glarus (Schweiz) Büro: Zürich, Talstraße 15

UHERTYPE

Lichtsetztechnik

für Akzidenzarbeiten in **Offset**, **Tiefdruck** und **Buchdruck**

abcdefghijklmnopqrsßtuv
wxyz äöü 1234567890
ABCDEFGHIJKLMNOP
QRSTUVWXYZÄÖÜ

*ABCDEFGHIJKLM
NOPQRSTUVWXY
ZÄÖÜ1234567890*

Uhertype

Cover of an advertising brochure for the Uhertype photo-typesetting system, design by Jan Tschichold, 1933, 29.8 x 21 cm

Sans serif specimen type, designed by Jan Tschichold for the pioneering photo-typesetting system Uhertype, 1933

abcdefghijklmnopqrsßtuv
wxyz äöü 123456789o
ABCDEFGHIJKLMNOP
QRSTUVWXYZÄÖÜ

abcdefghijklmnopqrsß
tuvwxyz äöü 12345678
ABCDEFGHIJKLMNO
PQRSTUVWXYZÄÖÜ

Uhertype

g g g g

abcdefghijklmnopqrsßtuv wxyz äöü 1234567890 ABCDEFGHIJKLMNOP QRSTUVWXYZÄÖÜ

ABCDEFGHIJKL MNOPQRSTUVW XYZÄÖÜ123456

Sans serif specimen type, designed by Jan Tschichold for the pioneering photo-typesetting system Uhertype, 1933

Tschichold's experiments with type for a new "phonetic" alphabet devised by Walter Porstmann (1886–1959), 1927

Envelope and pages of an advertising brochure for the Emil Gerasch print studio by Jan Tschichold, 1927, envelope: 17.5 x 24 cm, page size: 16.8 x 23.6 cm. The logo is not by Jan Tschichold.

JAN TSCHICHOLD
DIE NEUE TYPOGRAPHIE
EIN HANDBUCH FÜR ZEITGEMÄSS SCHAFFENDE

BERLIN 1928
VERLAG DES BILDUNGSVERBANDES DER DEUTSCHEN BUCHDRUCKER

VORZUGS-ANGEBOT

Im VERLAG DES BILDUNGSVERBANDES der Deutschen Buchdrucker,
Berlin SW 61, Dreibundstr. 5, erscheint demnächst:

JAN TSCHICHOLD
Lehrer an der Meisterschule für Deutschlands Buchdrucker in München

DIE NEUE TYPOGRAPHIE

**Handbuch für die gesamte Fachwelt
und die drucksachenverbrauchenden Kreise**

Das Problem der neuen gestaltenden Typographie hat eine lebhafte Diskussion bei allen Beteiligten hervorgerufen. Wir glauben dem Bedürfnis, die aufgeworfenen Fragen ausführlich behandelt zu sehen, zu entsprechen, wenn wir jetzt ein Handbuch der **NEUEN TYPOGRAPHIE** herausbringen.

Es kam dem Verfasser, einem ihrer bekanntesten Vertreter, in diesem Buche zunächst darauf an, den engen Zusammenhang der neuen Typographie mit dem **Gesamtkomplex heutigen Lebens** aufzuzeigen und zu beweisen, daß die neue Typographie ein ebenso notwendiger Ausdruck einer neuen Gesinnung ist wie die neue Baukunst und alles Neue, das mit unserer Zeit anbricht. Diese geschichtliche Notwendigkeit der neuen Typographie belegt weiterhin eine kritische Darstellung der **alten Typographie**. Die Entwicklung der **neuen Malerei**, die für alles Neue unserer Zeit geistig bahnbrechend gewesen ist, wird in einem reich illustrierten Aufsatz des Buches leicht faßlich dargestellt. Ein kurzer Abschnitt „**Zur Geschichte der neuen Typographie**" leitet zu dem wichtigsten Teile des Buches, den **Grundbegriffen der neuen Typographie** über. Diese werden klar herausgeschält, richtige und falsche Beispiele einander gegenübergestellt. Zwei weitere Artikel behandeln „**Photographie und Typographie**" und „**Neue Typographie und Normung**".

Der Hauptwert des Buches für den Praktiker besteht in dem zweiten Teil „**Typographische Hauptformen**" (siehe das nebenstehende Inhaltsverzeichnis). Es fehlte bisher an einem Werke, das wie dieses Buch die schon bei einfachen Satzaufgaben auftauchenden gestalterischen Fragen in gebührender Ausführlichkeit behandelte. Jeder Teilabschnitt enthält neben **allgemeinen typographischen Regeln** vor allem die Abbildungen aller in Betracht kommenden **Normblätter** des Deutschen Normenausschusses, alle andern (z. B. postalischen) **Vorschriften** und zahlreiche Beispiele, Gegenbeispiele und Schemen.

Für jeden Buchdrucker, insbesondere jeden Akzidenzsetzer, wird „Die neue Typographie" ein **unentbehrliches Handbuch** sein. Von nicht geringerer Bedeutung ist es für Reklamefachleute, Gebrauchsgraphiker, Kaufleute, Photographen, Architekten, Ingenieure und Schriftsteller, also für alle, die mit dem Buchdruck in Berührung kommen.

INHALT DES BUCHES

Werden und Wesen der neuen Typographie
Das neue Weltbild
Die alte Typographie (Rückblick und Kritik)
Die neue Kunst
Zur Geschichte der neuen Typographie
Die Grundbegriffe der neuen Typographie
Photographie und Typographie
Neue Typographie und Normung

Typographische Hauptformen
Das Typosignet
Der Geschäftsbrief
Der Halbbrief
Briefhüllen ohne Fenster
Fensterbriefhüllen
Die Postkarte
Die Postkarte mit Klappe
Die Geschäftskarte
Die Besuchskarte
Werbsachen (Karten, Blätter, Prospekte, Kataloge)
Das Typoplakat
Das Bildplakat
Schildformate, Tafeln und Rahmen
Inserate
Die Zeitschrift
Die Tageszeitung
Die illustrierte Zeitung
Tabellensatz
Das neue Buch

**Bibliographie
Verzeichnis der Abbildungen
Register**

typ. tschichold

Das Buch enthält über **125 Abbildungen**, von denen etwa ein Viertel **zweifarbig** gedruckt ist, und umfaßt gegen **200** Seiten auf gutem Kunstdruckpapier. Es erscheint im Format DIN A5 (148× 210 mm) und ist biegsam in Ganzleinen gebunden.

Preis bei Vorbestellung bis **1. Juni** 1928:   **5.**00 RM
durch den Buchhandel nur zum Preise von   **6.**50 RM

Bestellschein umstehend ➡

Title page and page spread for *Die neue Typographie* by Jan Tschichold, 1928, 21 x 28.4 cm

Publicity sheet for *Die neue Typographie* by Jan Tschichold, 1928

Cover and pages 6–7 and 18–19 of *Das Fahrten- und Abenteuerbuch* (The Travel and Adventure Book) by Colin Ross, design by Jan Tschichold, 1925. Verlag der Büchergilde Gutenberg, Leipzig

1 Kruppsche Zeche Hannover I und II

18

2 Friedrich-Alfred-Hütte, Rheinhausen

19

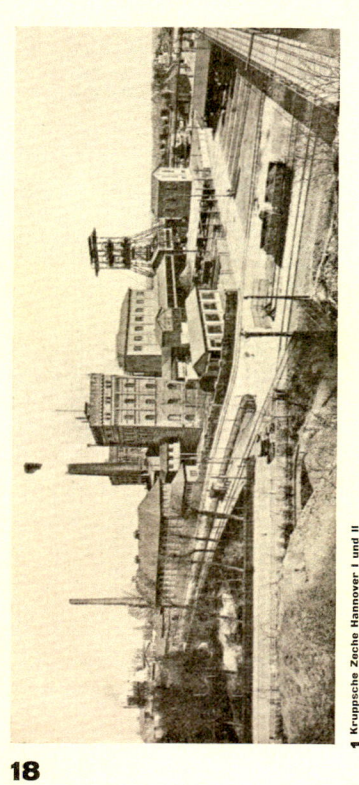

TYPOGRAPHIE UND EINBAND: IVAN TSCHICHOLD

INHALTSVERZEICHNIS

EINLEITUNG	9
I. DER INGENIEUR	
1 Kohlenzeche	15
2 Hochofenwerk	23
3 Vom fließenden Stahl	30
4 Walzwerk	37
5 Maschinenfabrik	43
II. DER KRIEGSBERICHTERSTATTER	
IM BALKANKRIEG	
6 Zurück mit der geschlagenen Armee	51
7 Der Ritt um die Depesche	56
8 Aus den Kämpfen um die Tschataldscha-Stellung	63
9 Der letzte Sieger	68
IM MEXIKANISCHEN REVOLUTIONSKRIEG	
10 Das Abenteuer beginnt	71
11 Zur Rebellenarmee	78
12 Vor Zacatecas	86
13 Finale	89
III. DER OFFIZIER	
14 Die Erstürmung von Badonviller	93
15 Ritt hinter der Front	99
16 Ave Maria	103
17 Kampf im Mais	108
18 Toten Mannes Ostern	113

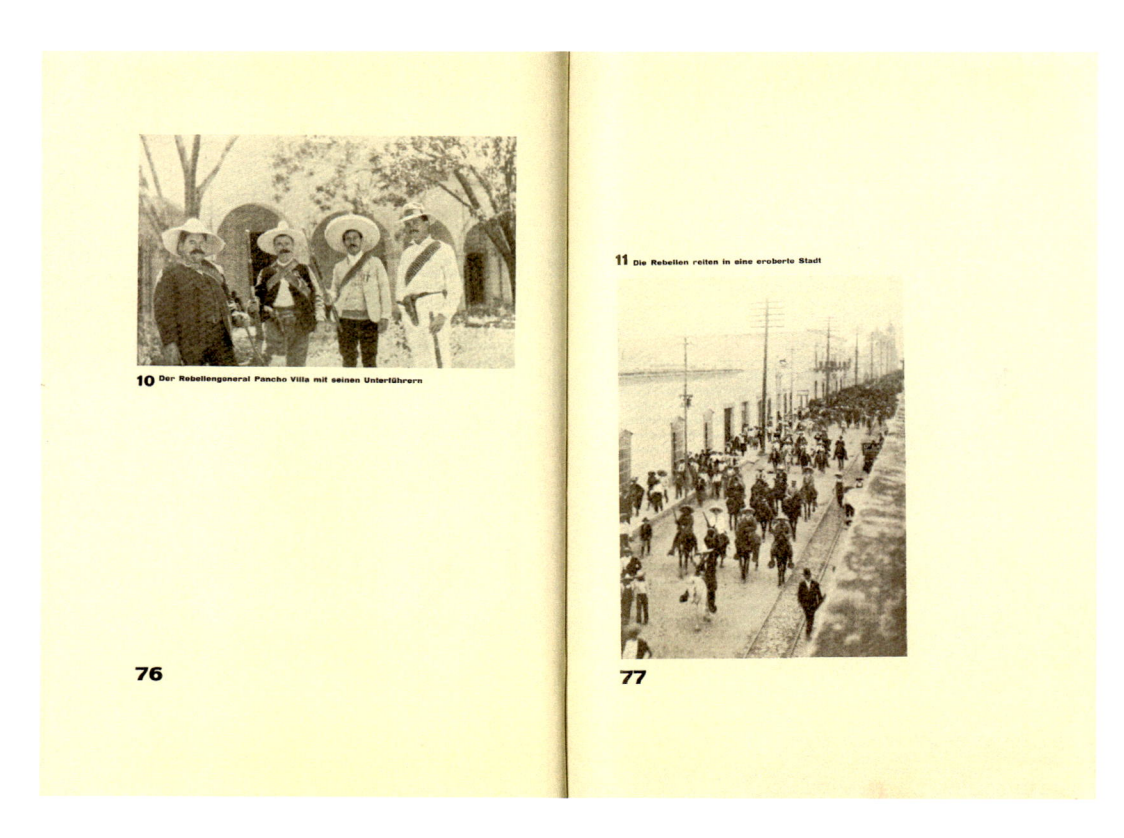

Pages 34–35 and 76–77 of *Das Fahrten- und Abenteuerbuch* (The Travel and Adventure Book) by Colin Ross, design by Jan Tschichold, 1925. Verlag der Büchergilde Gutenberg, Leipzig

Cover of *Der Dollar steigt* (The Dollar Is Rising) by Felix Scherret, design by Jan Tschichold, 1930. Verlag der Bücherkreis GmbH, Berlin

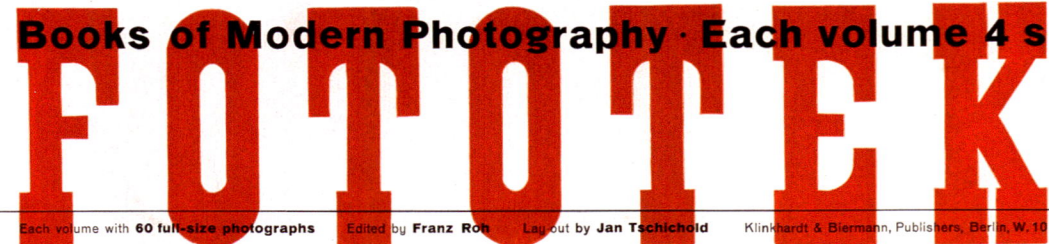

Window card advertising the *Fototek* book series, 1930, photo offset on board, "typo Tschichold," 50.9 x 32.4 cm, photos: László Moholy-Nagy, printer: F. Bruckmann AG, Munich

Cover of subscription form for the *Fototek* book series, 1930, design by Jan Tschichold, 25 x 17.5 cm. The cover image shows Oskar Schlemmer.

FOTOTEK

Bibliothèque de la photographie nouvelle,   publiée par Franz Roh

Klinkhardt & Biermann Editeurs   **Berlin W 10**

Proof of spine and cover for *Fototek 1*, 1930, design by Jan Tschichold, 27.4 x 20 cm, photogram by László Moholy-Nagy. Klinkhardt & Biermann, Berlin

Moholy-Nagy

L. Moholy-Nagy
60 Fotos
60 photos
60 photographies

1 Fototek 1 Klinkhardt & Biermann Verlag-Publishers-Editeurs Berlin W 10

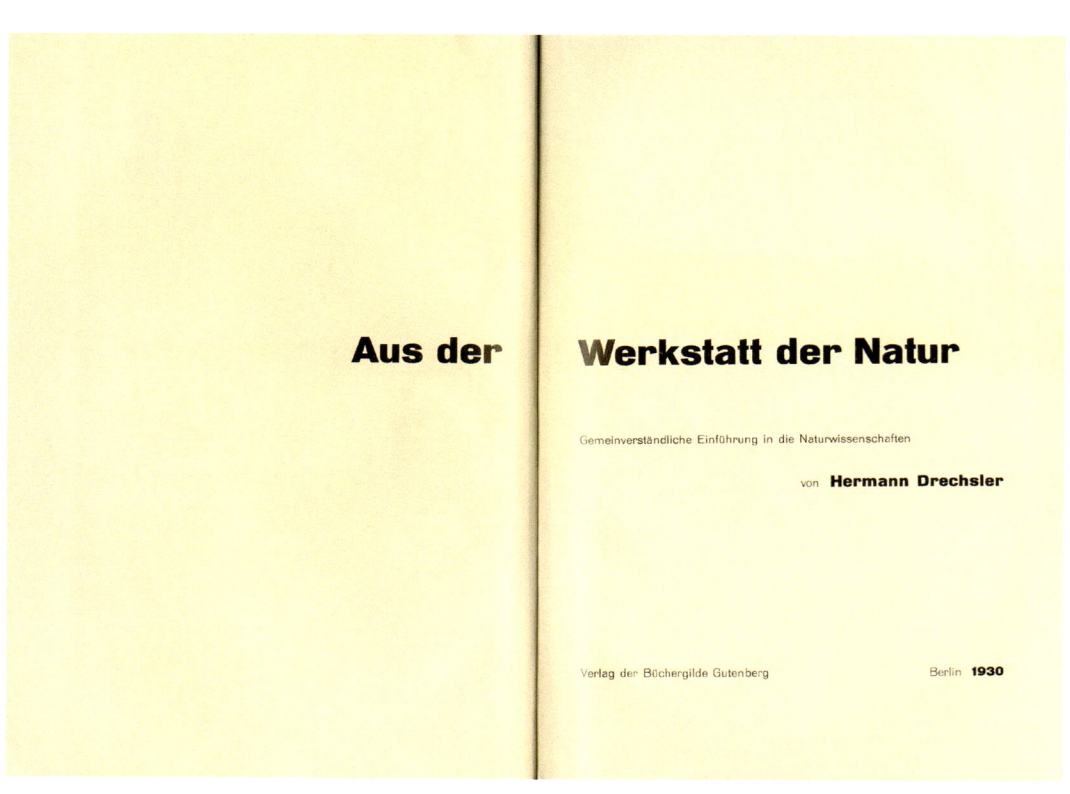

Cover and pages 4–5, 12–13, and 36–37 of *Aus der Werkstatt der Natur* (From the Workshop of Nature) by Hermann Drechsler, 1930, design by Jan Tschichold. Verlag der Büchergilde Gutenberg, Berlin

Einführung

Wenn wir als Laien vor dem ewigen Walten und Gestalten, dem Leben und Weben draußen in der Natur stehen, dann fühlt wohl mancher Einsichtige die ganze Unzulänglichkeit unseres Wissens, die ganze Verkehrtheit unseres Bildungswesens, unserer Erziehung. Mindestens acht lange Jahre hat jeder Deutsche die Schulbank gedrückt, hat sich mit Sprachen und mathematischen Formeln gequält, hat Bibelsprüche und Gesangbuchverse zu Hunderten in sich aufgenommen. Auch Naturgeschichte hat er gehabt. So an die vierhundert Stunden. Aber wenn es gut geht, kann er draußen in der Natur mit Mühe und Not die Buche von der Birke unterscheiden. Bei der Tanne und der Fichte fällt ihm die Artbestimmung schon schwer, und wenn er tiefer hineinsteigt, steht er vor einer unbekannten Welt. Da kennt er keine Blume außer der Gänseblume, keinen Vogel außer dem Spatz, außer dem Kohlweißling keinen Schmetterling beim Namen.

Das ist fürwahr ein geradezu beschämender Zustand, ein geradezu vernichtendes Urteil über unser gesamtes Bildungswesen; ein Leerlauf unserer ganzen Erziehung!

Dabei kommt sich der Städter furchtbar klug vor. Mit welcher Überheblichkeit sieht er auf das Landvolk herab! Wie turmhoch erhaben dünkt sich mancher Akademiker über dem, der nur die Volksschule zu besuchen in der Lage war! Und wieviel Unwissenheit wälzt mancher dieser Akademiker mit herum! So ein verknöchertes Juristengehirn beherrscht oft genug neben dem eingepaukten Spezialwissen kaum das Abc der Naturerkenntnis.

Ein Jurist in hoher Staatsstellung, mit dem ich mich über wissenschaftliche Fragen unterhielt, hatte keine Ahnung davon, daß unser Kochsalz entweder als Steinsalz oder als Sole gefördert wird. Er glaubte vielmehr, daß alles Salz aus dem Meerwasser gewonnen würde!

Eines Tages betrat ich das Arbeitszimmer eines Juristen. Am Fenster tummelten sich zahlreiche Stubenfliegen, darunter auch einige Schmeißfliegen. Von mir befragt, glaubte der Herr Regierungsrat – o heilige Einfalt! –, es seien wohl einige alte Fliegen, die ihre Jungen ausführten! Der Mann ist mittlerweile in eine wichtige Staatsstellung aufgerückt.

Das ist kein Einzelfall. Mit wenigen Ausnahmen trifft man auch unter den sogenannten Gebildeten so viel Scheinbildung, so viel Unwissenheit, so viel aufgeblasene Hohlheit, daß man darüber erschrecken kann. Über mitunter ganz einfache Vorgänge in der Natur wissen oft selbst Lehrer keinen Bescheid, von den anderen gar nicht zu reden.

Es ist an der Zeit, unser Wissen vom Werden, vom Sein und Vergehen in der Natur zu erweitern. Dabei brauchen wir uns nicht in dickbändige Werke zu vertiefen oder in verstaubten Naturalienkabinetten herumzukriechen. Die Natur schrieb ihre Geschichte vom Werden und Vergehen selbst, und wer in diesem Buch zu lesen versteht, wird bald sehend werden. Andererseits wird sich auch jeder, der nicht mit Blindheit geschlagen ist, leicht in die uns umgebende Gegenwart hineinarbeiten, wenn er nur ein wenig Interesse für das zwar etwas komplizierte, aber außerordentlich lehrreiche Leben draußen in der Natur hat. Unsere gute Mutter Erde macht es uns so leicht, sie zu verstehen, wenn wir uns als gelehrige Schüler in ihre Werkstatt begeben. Wir müssen nur hellen Blick und offenes Ohr mitbringen, dann verstehen wir bald die Sprache der uns umgebenden Natur, dann können wir auch bald in ihrem großen Lehrbuch vom Werden und Vergehen lesen, das sie selbst unermüdlich Seite um Seite schrieb, wie eine gute Mutter, die vorsorglich auf vergilbendem Papier ihrem Kinde gute Lehren und Lebensregeln hinterläßt.

Es ist ganz gleich, wo wir stehen: Überall können wir der Stimme der Natur lauschen. Wenn wir nachts auf freier Höhe stehen und das Heer der Sterne

Von der Tätigkeit des Wassertropfens, von Wind und Wetter

Im vorigen Kapitel haben wir gesehen, wie die herrschenden Urgewalten die Erdrinde zusammenfalteten und zu Gebirgen emporstauten. Nun wollen wir betrachten, welche Kräfte die Zerstörung der Gebirge bewirken, wir wollen der Natur bei ihrer Arbeit zusehen.

Bei der Zerstörung der Gebirge, die sich vor unseren Augen vollzieht, spielen Naturereignisse nur eine untergeordnete Rolle, denn Katastrophen, die in wenigen Minuten Millionen von Steinmassen loslösen und zu Tal bringen, sind glücklicherweise verhältnismäßig selten. Bei der Zerstörung der Gebirge kommt vielmehr, wie wir später sehen werden, vor allen Dingen die Kleinarbeit des Wassertropfens in Betracht.

17 Felssturz bei Matt (Bergbahn Schwanden-Elm, Kanton Glarus)

Bei dem Bergsturz von Elm im Kanton Glarus gingen am 11. September 1881 zehn Millionen Kubikmeter Gestein zu Tal, 90 Hektar Land bedeckend. Von diesem Naturereignis sieht man nicht mehr viel, photographische Aufnahmen geben keinen Begriff vom Umfang der Katastrophe.

Das Material war ein schwarzblauer, leicht verwitternder Schiefer. Man hat diese Geröllmassen an ihrer Oberfläche eingeebnet, zum Teil geschieht das heute noch, und wieder zu Wiesenland gemacht. Alte Einwohner von Elm können sich noch sehr gut des gräßlichen Unglücks erinnern. Mit unbeschreiblichem Krachen, das alle Einwohner förmlich betäubte, sei die Wand südlich des Ortes, in der Schieferbau betrieben wurde, plötzlich zu Tal gegangen. Eine schwarze Staubwolke habe das ganze Tal stundenlang in tiefste Finsternis gehüllt und das Atmen schier unmöglich gemacht. Als die Unversehrten sich hervorwagten, war die Hälfte der Wiesen und Weiden und 83 Gebäude verschüttet. 115 Menschen wurden getötet und ruhen heute noch unter den Trümmern. Der Sernft, dem aus der Tschingelschlucht hervorbrechenden Wildwasser, wurde der Weg verlegt, sie mußte sich durch die Trümmer hindurch ein neues Bett bahnen.

Unterhalb Elm, bei dem Dorfe *Matt* (1000 Meter Höhe) ist erst kürzlich ein Felssturz niedergegangen, der ein gutanschauliches Bild gibt (Abbildung 17). Derartige kleinere Felsstürze sind im Gebirge nicht selten, weshalb man auch

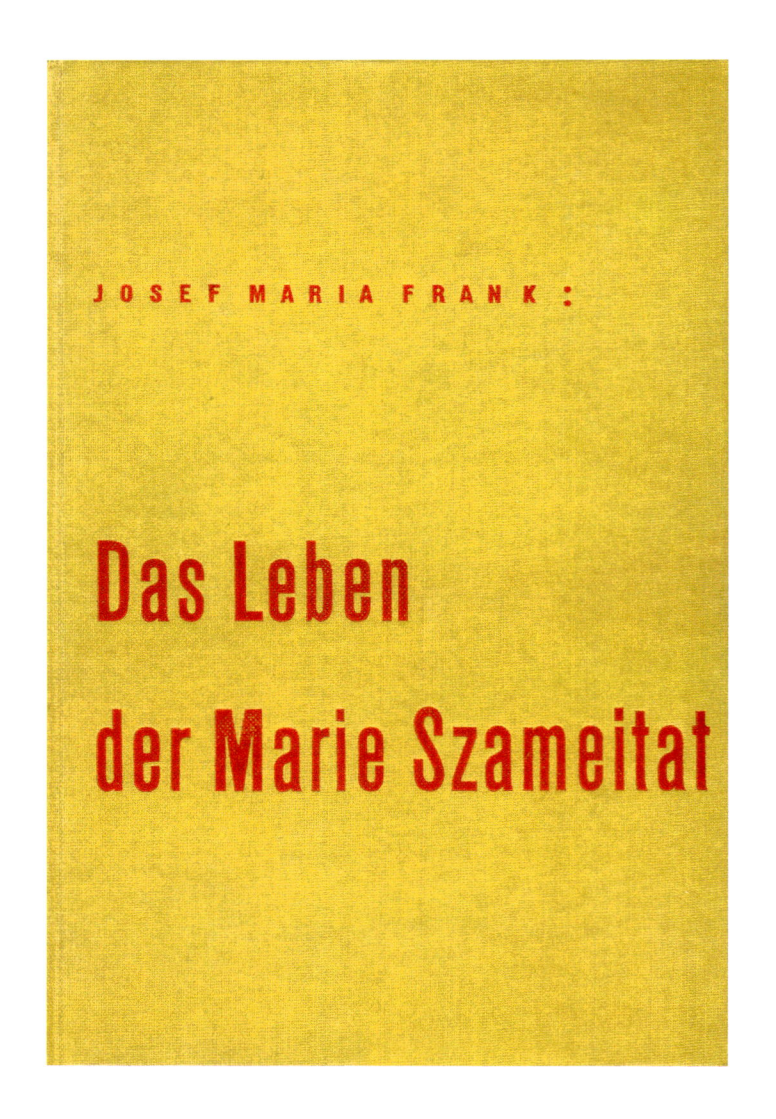

Pages 106–107 of *Aus der Werkstatt der Natur* (From the Workshop of Nature) by Hermann Drechsler, 1930, design by Jan Tschichold. Verlag der Büchergilde Gutenberg, Berlin

Cover of *Das leben der Marie Szameitat* (The Life of Marie Szameitat) by Josef Maria Frank, 1930, design by Jan Tschichold. Verlag der Bücherkreis GmbH, Berlin

Cover and pages 6–7 of *Hausierer* (Pedlar) by Franz Jung, 1931, design by Jan Tschichold. Verlag der Bücherkreis GmbH, Berlin

Dmitrij Tschetwerikov

Die Rebellion des Ingenieurs Karinski

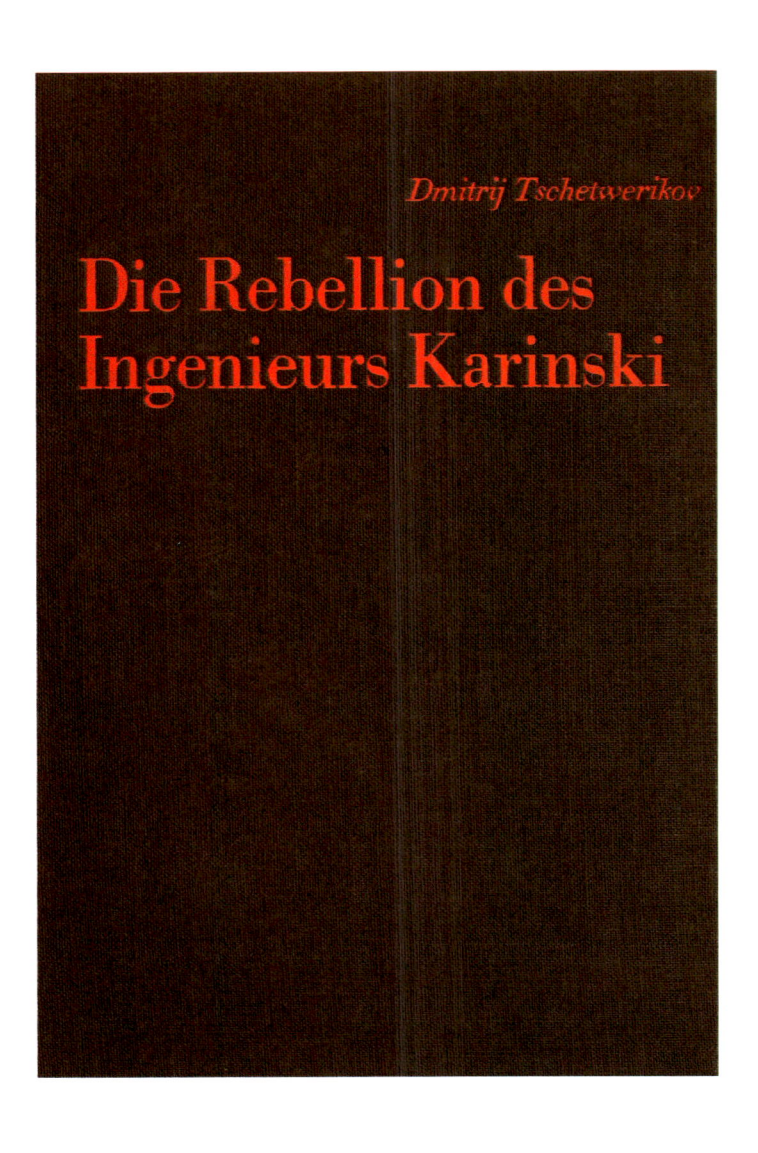

Autorisierte Übersetzung von Nina Stein
Alle Rechte, insbesondere die des Nachdrucks, der Übersetzung, der Verfilmung und der Radioübertragung, vorbehalten

Copyright 1931 by Der Bücherkreis GmbH, Berlin SW 61
Einbandentwurf und Typographie: Jan Tschichold, München
Satz u. Druck: Fränkische Verlagsanstalt & Buchdruckerei GmbH, Nürnberg
Buchbinderarbeiten: Vorwärts Buchdruckerei, Berlin SW 68, Lindenstraße 3

VORBEMERKUNGEN

Ort und Zeit der Handlung: *Leningrad und Moskau, etwa 1925 bis 1928*
Handelnde Personen:

Pável Konstantinowitsch Karinski (Pawlúschka, Páwlik)	Ingenieur
Natálja Alexándrowna (Natáscha)	seine Frau
Dárja Spiridónowna	seine Schwiegermutter
Njúscha	Dienstmädchen bei Karinski
Grigórij Iwánowitsch Tichanówitsch	Techniker
Ludmílla Viktorowna (Ljud)	seine Frau
Pólja	ihre Tante
Rudakóv	Vorgesetzter von Karinski
Michaíl Micháilowitsch Drápkin	Dienstkollege von Karinski
Larissa Petrówna	seine Frau
Pelagéjuschka	Dienstmädchen bei Drapkin
Lichótin	Funktionär der Kommunistischen Partei
Olga Filátowna	seine erste Frau
Sója Witáljewna	seine zweite Frau
Nina (Ninotschka)	ihre Tochter
Alexander Wassíljewitsch	zweiter Mann von Sója
Surjagínzewa	Leiterin einer Fabrik
Kláwdia	Jungkommunistin
Arkádij Timoféjewitsch Swétschnikov	Kunstmaler
Semjón Safrónov	Bauer
Márja	seine Frau
Aníssja	junge Bäuerin
Feklúnjka	Bauernmädchen
Nastásja	Bauernfrau
Oríschka	Bauernfrau

Die Namen sind mit Akzenten versehen, damit sie richtig ausgesprochen werden.
Die Übersetzerin
Berlin, Januar 1931.

7

| 1 |

 Pawel Karinski wachte in der Nacht auf. Er hörte die Uhr einmal schlagen. Es war halb, aber die volle Stundenzahl wußte er nicht.
 Er lauschte. Das Uhrpendel brummte geruhsam, es war, als schlürfe die Zeit auf weichen Pantoffeln durch die Zimmer — an der Schlaflosigkeit des Alters leidend, hüstelnd in der Erwartung des Morgentees.
 Pawel Karinski dachte schläfrig:
 Es wird wohl halbfünf, vielleicht sogar schon halbsechs sein.
 Vor dem Fenster raschelten die unablässig fallenden Schneeflocken, es zog vom Fenster her, und kalte, würzige Schneeluft drang herein.
 Schneesturm, dachte Karinski träge. Es war so angenehm zu wissen, daß man das Gehalt eines Spezialisten bezog, eine schöne Wohnung hatte, zu spüren, daß die Öfen geheizt waren, daß man in einem weichen Bett lag, in dem man sich so schön räkeln konnte.
 Neben ihm schlief seine Frau, und es erfüllte ihn mit Zärtlichkeit, daß sie so ruhig atmete und sogar wie ein kleines Kind mit der Nase schnaufte.

Cover and pages 6–7 and 8–9 of *Die Rebellion des Ingenieurs Karinski* (The Rebellion of Karinski the Engineer) by Dmitrij Tschetwerikov, 1931, design by Jan Tschichold. Verlag der Bücherkreis GmbH, Berlin

Cover and pages 4–5, 102–103, and 142–143 of *Reise ins asiatische Tuwa* (Journey to Tuva, Central Asia) by Otto Manchen-Helfen, 1931, design by Jan Tschichold. Verlag der Bücherkreis GmbH, Berlin

Lächeln bei, hielt den Blick gesenkt, drehte den Rosenkranz durch die Finger und wollte durchaus nicht erzählen, wie er zu seiner Erfindung gekommen war. Ich wurde bewirtet mit Gebäck, Ziegeltee und Tsampa. Von allen Geheimnissen Tibets war mir immer das geheimnisvollste gewesen, wie es die Tibeter fertig brächten, Tsampa zu essen. Das Rezept ist einfach: man verrührt in Tee Butter, Salz und Mehl zu einem dicken Brei. Nachdem ich einmal versucht hatte, mir selber Tsampa aus Tee, Salz, Grieß und gezuckerter Kondensmilch zu bereiten (es war zur Inflationszeit), war ich von der Unüberbrückbarkeit der Rassengegensätze auf kulinarischem Gebiet fest überzeugt. Jetzt weiß ich, daß man zu Tsampa fette Milchhaut nehmen muß, geröstete Hirse oder Gerstenmehl und dreißig Kilometer im Sattel gesessen sein muß, um Tsampa herrlich zu finden.

Das Gespräch kam auf Tibet. Der Lama wehrte erschrocken ab, als ich fragte, ob das Kloster noch Beziehungen zu Lhassa habe. (Er wußte offenbar, daß ich mit Nazow bekannt war.) Ich wollte dem freundlichen alten Manne keine Unannehmlichkeiten bereiten und ließ das Thema fallen. Es mag sein, daß jetzt direkte Beziehungen zum Oberhaupt der lamaistischen Kirche nicht mehr bestehen. Doch gehen immer noch Pilger nach Urga in die Mongolei und mongolische Lama nach Tibet, so daß zumindest über die Mongolei Tuwa und Tibet verbunden sind. Unter den Bildern und Statuen von Göttern stand auf dem Altar des Mönches auch ein Bild des Dalai-Lama. Es ist mir, solange ich in Tuwa war, nicht gelungen, den Lama zu sehen, der der »tibetische schlechthin heißt. Mein Uebersetzer hatte ihn im Tannu-olagebirge getroffen; im tiefsten Winter saß der riesige Mann halbnackt im Schnee und las seine heiligen Sutren. Die Tuwiner verehren ihn scheu. Er reist unbegreiflich schnell, heilt heute abend einen Kranken und ist morgen früh hundertfünfzig Kilometer weit in einem anderen Lager, erwirbt in wenigen Wochen gewaltige Herden und verschenkt sie an arme Hirten. Er spricht Russisch, war in den ersten Revolutionsjahren in Moskau, niemand weiß, was er dort gemacht hat, und ist höchstwahrscheinlich ein Agent des Dalai-Lama. Tibet ist englische Einflußsphäre! In dem Kloster lebt auch ein Mönch, der jahrelang in Sikkim und Ladakh gelebt hat. Die Scheu Lobsans, von dem Alphabet zu sprechen, erklärt sich wohl daher; der Mann,

Kemtschigol spielt für den Photographen „Diktieren"

Kontinents verliert es sich fast. Die Tuwiner sind ein kleines Volk. Wem »die Erde kein Völkermuseum« ist, braucht sich um sie keinen Deut zu kümmern. Aber Tuwa, dieser verlorene Winkel Innerasiens, hat ganz eminente Bedeutung für die Erkenntnis des Wesens Sowjetrußlands.

Sowjetrußland ist den einen die Erfüllung alles dessen, wofür die sozialistische Arbeiterbewegung seit Jahrzehnten kämpft. Es ist ein ganz neuer, ein ganz anderer Staat, ein sozialistischer Staat. Seine Außenpolitik hat nichts, kann nichts gemein haben mit der hinterlistigen, zynischen Außenpolitik der imperialistischen Mächte. So die einen. Die anderen sehen in der Außenpolitik der Sowjets die geradlinige Fortsetzung der Politik, die der Zarismus betrieben hat. Andere Phrasen, andere Methoden, die gleichen Ziele. Grattez le bolchevik et vous trouverez le russe. Was ist die Wahrheit? Man wird nicht erwarten dürfen, die ganze Wahrheit in Tuwa zu finden. Aber ein Stück, vielleicht ein sehr wichtiges Stück, ist in Tuwa zu finden.

Die Russen kamen mit Tuwa zuerst zu Beginn des 17. Jahrhunderts in Berührung. Sie suchten damals einen Bundesgenossen in ihrem schweren Kampf mit den Kirgisen und glaubten ihn in dem Altan Chan, dem Herrscher im Kemtschikgebiet, zu finden. 1616 kamen die ersten Gesandten des Tomsker Wojewoden an seinen Hof. Sie konnten ebensowenig wie die folgenden ihr Ziel erreichen. Denn der Altan Chan wollte wieder die Russen ausnutzen als Helfer gegen seine Feinde, die Oiraten. Das Bündnis, mit dem der eine den anderen zu betrügen hoffte, kam nicht zustande. Die Verhandlungen gingen hin und her, ein Ergebnis hatten sie nicht. Die Russen kamen auch nicht, wie sie erwartet hatten, über den Altan Chan in Verbindung mit China. Der Hof in Peking dachte nicht daran, durch einen Barbaren mit anderen Barbaren zu unterhandeln.

Eine Folge hatten allerdings diese frühen Beziehungen Moskaus zu Tuwa doch. 1914, als Rußland das Land annektierte, berief es sich darauf, daß die Altan Chane stets in dem Zaren ihren Oberherrn gesehen hätten. Es soll sogar der Altan Chan Lousan dem Zaren feierlich den Untertaneneid geschworen haben. Diese »Untertanen« behandelten die Gesandten ihres

Gegenüber: Tuwinische Kavallerie

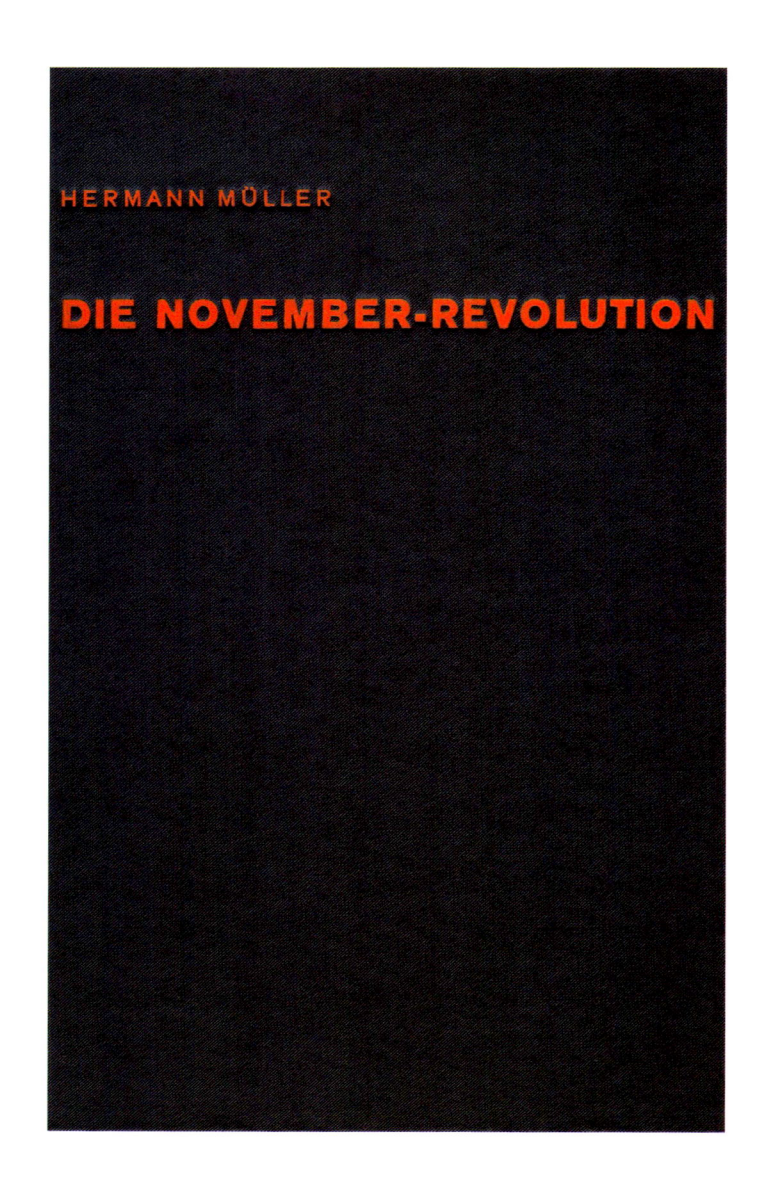

Cover of *Die November-Revolution* (The November Revolution) by Hermann Muller, 1931, design by Jan Tschichold. Verlag der Bücherkreis GmbH, Berlin

Cover and pages 8–9 of *Herz in Flammen* (Heart in Flames) by Berta Selinger, 1932, design by Jan Tschichold. Verlag der Bücherkreis GmbH, Berlin

DER SIEG

Ein Buch vom Sport

Herausgegeben von **Günter Mamlok** und **Sergius Sax**
320 Seiten Umfang   **422** herrliche Bilder

Die besten Sportschriftsteller schrieben einen packenden Text
Die mitreißende Chronik unvergeßlicher Siege aus allen Sportarten

Geleitwort von Staatssekretär a. D. Dr. **Lewald**

Reichsmark **4.**80

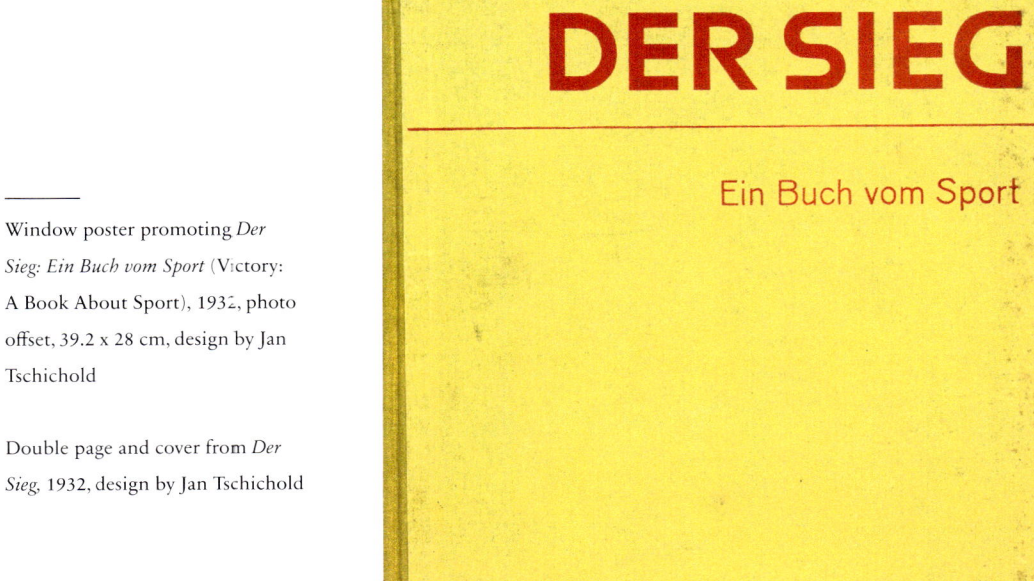

Window poster promoting *Der Sieg: Ein Buch vom Sport* (Victory: A Book About Sport), 1932, photo offset, 39.2 x 28 cm, design by Jan Tschichold

Double page and cover from *Der Sieg*, 1932, design by Jan Tschichold

FRANCESCO F. NITTI:
FLUCHT

Autorisierte Übersetzung von Dr. Gertrud Müller
Einband und Schutzumschlag von Jan Tschichold, München
Druck von Mänicke & Jahn A.-G., Rudolstadt
Alle Rechte, besonders das des Abdrucks, vorbehalten

VORWORT

Nur wenig Abenteuer sind so interessant wie dieses. Denn hier ist Wahrheit, seltsamer als alle Dichtung, Erlebnis, das in diesem Zeitalter der Freiheit politischen Denkens und Handelns unglaubhaft erscheint.

Es ist die einfache, ohne jeden literarischen Anspruch erzählte Geschichte von drei jungen Menschen, die ihrer politischen Gesinnung wegen, ohne Untersuchung ihres Falles, ja sogar ohne jedes Verhör, nach Lipari, einer kleinen Insel bei Sizilien, verschickt und dort in grausamer und demütigender Gefangenschaft gehalten wurden. Es ist die Erzählung von ihrer, in ihrer Tollkühnheit ans Unwahrscheinliche grenzenden Flucht von dieser Insel der Schmerzen, von Italiens „Teufelsinsel", zu der heute niemand mehr freien Zutritt hat. Etwa sechshundert Leute der faschistischen Regierung überwachen dort Tag und Nacht etwa fünfhundert Verbannte. Schwerbewaffnete Kriegsschiffe, mit

In dieser von religiösem Geiste erfüllten Atmosphäre, in dieser christlichen Luft, mit dem Beispiel meiner Eltern vor Augen, wuchs ich heran in Abneigung und Widerwillen gegen jede Form der Gewalt. Und gleichzeitig mit dieser Ablehnung aller Gewalt und brutalen Kraft lehrte mich die protestantische Religion den Respekt und die Liebe zur Freiheit des Individuums. Der Protestantismus, der sich unmittelbar an den individuellen Geist wendet, ist eine vorbildliche Schule der Freiheit. Er lehrte mich, daß man sich in acht nehmen muß vor allzu absoluten Behauptungen und vor politischen oder sozialen Dogmen; in seiner Atmosphäre erwuchs in mir der glühende Wunsch nach Freiheit für alle, Große und Kleine, die Freiheit als wichtigste Basis alles menschlichen Fortschrittes und aller Zivilisation.

Unser Familienleben war ganz durchwoben mit Erinnerungen und Traditionen aller Zeiten, wo es um Freiheit und Unabhängigkeit unseres Vaterlandes ging. Mein Urgroßvater, Francesco Nitti, berühmter Arzt und Chirurg, wurde Jahre hindurch von den Bourbonen verfolgt. Er verband eine starke Intelligenz mit einer asketischen Seele. Heute noch werden seine Gesänge in den Kirchen unserer Ländereien gesungen. Als die Parteigänger der Bourbonen der liberalen Bewegung die Reaktion entgegenstellten, starb er eines grausamen Todes. Noch vor seinen Henkern rief er: Es lebe die Freiheit! Unser altes, an Erinnerungen so reiches Familien-

23

Cover and pages 4–5 and 22–23 of *Flucht* (Flight) by Francesco F. Nitti, ca. 1932, design by Jan Tschichold. Muller & I. Kiepenheuer GmbH, Potsdam.

Cover and pages 8–9 of *Mensch unterm Hammer* (Man under the Hammer) by Josef Lenhard, 1932, design by Jan Tschichold. Verlag der Bücherkreis GmbH, Berlin

Cover of *Mit Kamera und Schreibmaschine durch Europa* (With a Camera and Typewriter Through Europe) by Erich Grisar, 1932, design by Jan Tschichold. Verlag der Bücherkreis GmbH, Berlin

Motiv auf Marken

ONBEWOONBAAR VERKLAARDE WONING

Die Stadtverwaltung von Amsterdam läßt fast alle Kellerwohnungen durch Unbewohnbarerklärung enteignen

Mit Kamera und Schreibmaschine durch Europa

Bilder und Berichte von Erich Grisar

Verlag Der Bücherkreis GmbH, Berlin SW 61   1932

Frauen auf einer Ziegelei

Frauen auf der Lampenstube einer Zeche

geschmückt, die den Kampf der Arbeiter und den Sieg der arbeitenden Klasse symbolisch darstellen. Außerdem hängen hier die Bildnisse aller führenden Genossen der Internationale.

In Quaregnon ist auch die Brotfabrik der Cooperative, die das Brot für die Bewohner der benachbarten Orte liefert. Außerdem hat die Cooperative im Borinage eigene Werke für die Herstellung von Arbeitsschuhen und Arbeitskleidern, Seife, Schuhpolitur, Schokolade und Konfitüren und eine eigene Brauerei, in der neben dem Bier auch das Mineralwasser, das in den Volkshäusern ausgeschenkt wird, hergestellt wird.

Mit großem Stolz führen mich einige Genossen durch das neue Lagerhaus, das 1929 in einer Länge von 60 Metern und einer Breite von 30 Metern bei einer Höhe von drei Etagen und zwei gleichgroßen Kellergeschossen neben dem alten Schuppen errichtet worden ist, der vorden das Lager der Cooperative barg.

Die Verbilligung der Lebenshaltung, wie sie durch die cooperativen Einrichtungen der organisierten Arbeiterschaft zweifellos gewährleistet wird, kann natürlich die niedrigen Löhne, die im Borinage gezahlt werden, nicht wettmachen, und selbst die dürftige Existenz, die die Mehrzahl der Bewohner dieses Gebietes führen, wäre noch in Frage gestellt, wenn nicht die Frau in so großem Maße, wie es kaum in einem anderen Lande Europas der Fall ist, mit in das Erwerbsleben einbezogen wäre. Schon, wenn man die belgische Grenze überschreitet, sieht man vom Zuge aus, daß fast alle Bahnwärterhäuschen und Blockstationen der belgischen Eisenbahn von Frauen besetzt sind. Die meisten Frauen werden jedoch nicht von der Eisenbahn, sondern in den Fabriken und Gruben des Borinage beschäftigt. Ganze Extrazüge mit jungen Mädchen und Frauen verlassen jeden Morgen die Stadt Mons, in deren Nähe einige große Seidenfabriken sich befinden, wo die Frauen zu Tausenden beschäftigt werden. Viele Frauen finden ihr Brot auf den Gruben des Reviers, und wenn auch keine Frau mehr, wie zu der Zeit, da Zola seinen Roman »Germinal« schrieb, unter Tage beschäftigt wird, über Tage gibt es kaum eine Arbeit, die nicht auch von Frauen getan wird. Die meisten Frauen kann man auf den riesigen Schlackenhalden des Reviers beobachten, wo sie wie die Ameisen an den bröckelnden Hängen herumklettern und die noch brauchbaren Kohlestückchen aus dem Abraum heraussuchen. Da diese Arbeit sehr schmutzig ist und lange Kleider bei ihr hinderlich sind, so sieht man die Frauen und Mädchen meist in Männerhosen herumlaufen, die so oft geflickt sind, daß man den Stoff, aus dem sie ursprünglich gemacht wurden, nicht mehr erkennen kann.

37

Pages 4–5, 36–37, 72–73, and 120–121 of *Mit Kamera und Schreibmaschine durch Europa* (With a Camera and Typewriter Through Europe) by Erich Grisar, 1932, design by Jan Tschichold. Verlag der Bücherkreis GmbH, Berlin

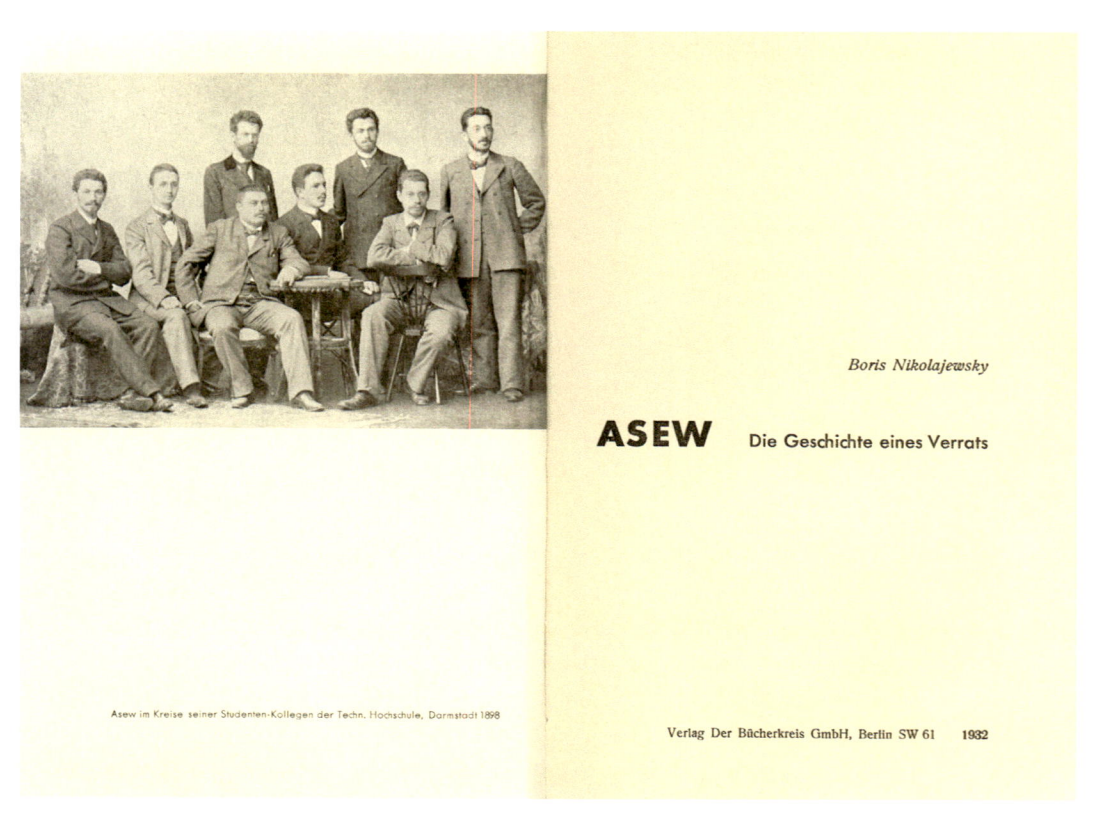

Cover and pages 2–3, 14–15, and 192–193 of *Asew. Die Geschichte eines Verrats* (Asew: the Story of a Betrayal) by Boris Nikolajewsky, 1932, design by Jan Tschichold. Verlag der Bücherkreis GmbH, Berlin

Gründer der sozialrevolutionären Partei Rußlands (von links nach rechts):
V. Tschernoff, F. Wolchowsky, N. Tschaikowsky, E. Lazarew und L. Schischko

bewegliche Burzew — in seiner Kleidung und in seinen Gesten der typische russische „Nihilist" von früher — war äußerst erregt. Er fuchtelte mit den Armen, sprang auf, setzte sich wieder hin, unterbrach sich selber, kam immer wieder auf bestimmte Einzelheiten zurück, die ihm besonders wichtig erschienen — und schaute die ganze Zeit Lopuchin gierig in die Augen, um die Wirkung seiner Worte aus ihnen abzulesen. Lopuchins Gesicht verriet nur ein ständig steigendes Interesse. Aber als Burzew über die Organisierung des Attentats auf Plehwe zu sprechen begann, verließ ihn seine Kaltblütigkeit. „Ganz fassungslos" — so berichtete Burzew später — „fragte er mich:
Sind Sie davon völlig überzeugt, daß dieser Agent von den Vorbereitungen zu der Ermordung Plehwes wußte?"
„Er wußte es nicht nur" — erwiderte Burzew —, „er war es ja, der dieses Attentat organisierte."
Und er begann ihm ausführlich und mit allen Einzelheiten zu erzählen.
Burzews Bericht war klar, genau; er enthielt zahlreiche glaubwürdige Einzelheiten — und trotzdem konnte der Verstand sich nur schwer mit dem Gehörten abfinden.
Nach Plehwes Tod begann eine schwere Zeit für Lopuchin. Der neue Minister des Innern, Fürst Swjatopolk-Mirski, war ihm zwar gutgesinnt, aber seine eigene Stellung war sehr unsicher; die reaktionäre Hofclique intrigierte gegen ihn, wobei sie in ihren Angriffen vor allem auf die Fehler und Mängel in der Tätigkeit des Polizei-Departements hinwies. Dieses Netz von Intrigen wurde hauptsächlich von Ratschkowski gesponnen — einem angesehenen höheren Beamten der Geheimpolizei, der einflußreiche Verbindungen am Zarenhof besaß. Zwei Jahre vorher hatte Plehwe ihn unter völliger Mißachtung seiner früheren Verdienste kurzerhand entlassen — und Lopuchin hatte noch seinerseits Salz auf die Wunde gestreut. Zu Plehwes Lebzeiten war Ratschkowski machtlos, obwohl er gegen ihn zu intrigieren versuchte. Jetzt aber war die Zeit gekommen, wo sich für die erlittene Unbill rächen konnte. Die Technik des Polizeiwesens kannte er besser als Lopuchin — und seine wohlgezielten Angriffe trafen diesen schmerzhaft. Der Ausgang des Kampfes wurde durch die Ermordung des Großfürsten Sergius, des Onkels und einflußreichsten Ratgebers des Zaren, entschieden. Als das Telegramm mit der Nachricht über diese Ermordung in Petersburg eintraf, eilte der Petersburger Generalgouverneur Trepoff, der damals ein Günst-

---

einer politischen Demonstration aus. Im Einvernehmen mit ihm reichten die monarchistischen Mitglieder der Duma eine Anfrage ein, in der sie die Regierung um Auskunft über die „Verschwörung gegen den Zaren" ersuchten, da die darüber zirkulierenden Gerüchte sie in große Unruhe versetzt hätten. Stolypin beantwortete sofort die Anfrage und nutzte in demagogischer Weise alle für ihn günstigen Momente aus. Das Ergebnis war, daß eine monarchistische Entschließung angenommen wurde.
Dies war zweifellos ein großer Sieg für Stolypin. Aber wenn er gehofft hatte, die monarchistische Stimmung im Lande zu heben, so mußte er eine schwere Enttäuschung erleben: Der Versuch der monarchistischen Organisationen, einen „Entrüstungssturm" im Lande zu inszenieren, erlitt ein vollkommenes Fiasko. Die Nachricht, daß auf das Leben des „vergötterten Monarchen" ein Attentat geplant war, wurde bestenfalls mit geringschätziger Gleichgültigkeit aufgenommen. Mitunter merkte man aber auch aufrichtiges Bedauern, daß es den Terroristen nicht gelungen war, ihre Pläne zu verwirklichen. In politischer Beziehung war dieses Ergebnis sehr wichtig: Wenn man vorher — vor dem monarchistischen Lärm wegen der „Verschwörung gegen den Zaren" — befürchten konnte, ein Anschlag auf den Zaren werde zu einer Wiederauflebung der monarchistischen Stimmungen führen, so waren diese Befürchtungen jetzt grundlos geworden. Im Bewußtsein der Massen war die Ermordung des Zaren bereits im voraus gerechtfertigt.
Von den Verhafteten wurden 18 Personen vor das Kriegsgericht gestellt. Ende August fand die Verhandlung statt. Das Urteil war im voraus bestimmt. Naumoff zog vor Gericht den größten Teil seiner Aussagen zurück. Den anderen Angeklagten half das aber nur wenig, und er selbst gab sich dadurch dem Tode preis, denn man nahm sein Verhalten zum Vorwand, um das Versprechen, ihm das Leben zu schenken, nicht einzuhalten*). Er wurde zusammen mit Nikitenko und Ssinjawski, einem früheren Studenten, zum Tode verurteilt. Die Hinrichtung wurde am 3. September 1907 vollstreckt. Die anderen Angeklagten wurden zu Zuchthausstrafen und zur Verbannung verurteilt.

*) Wenn früher über die wahren Gründe der Hinrichtung Naumoffs Zweifel bestehen konnten, so sind sie nach der Veröffentlichung der Erinnerungen General Spiridowitschs beseitigt worden. Aus dieser Veröffentlichung geht unzweifelhaft hervor, daß Naumoff begnadigt worden wäre, wenn er sich bereit gefunden hätte, vor Gericht gegen die anderen Angeklagten auszusagen. (Siehe A. Spiridovitch: „Les dernières années de la Cour de Tzarskoïe Selo." Paris 1929, p. 172.)

Vera Figner

Herm. Lopatin, Vorsitz. des Gerichts

P. Krapotkin

Wl. Burzew, der Asew entlarvte

Ehrengericht gegen Burzew

Cover, picture section and pages 40–41 of *Die Roten Lanzen* (The Red Lances) by Arturo Uslar-Pietri, 1932, design by Jan Tschichold. Verlag der Bücherkreis GmbH, Berlin

Bilderanhang

Caracas, die Hauptstadt Venezuelas

empfinden, fühlte sich der Gatte durch diesen Aufzug tief beleidigt. Fernandos Eltern lebten fortan noch mehr voneinander geschieden. Bald danach starb die Mutter eines plötzlichen Todes; ihre Kinder sahen sie nur noch auf dem Totenbett. Ohne Blumenschmuck lag sie in dem Gewand jener Pilgerschaft da, beschienen von dem gelben Licht einer ungewöhnlich großen Kerze.

Das Verhältnis der Kinder zu ihrem Vater wurde nun noch kühler und förmlicher. Man kleidete sie stets in Schwarz. In der lebenstrotzenden, fruchtbaren Natur, zwischen den rohen Sklaven, neben dem unzugänglichen Vater erschienen sie in ihrer Trauertracht als starker Gegensatz zu ihrer Umgebung. Damals begann sie eine alte Sklavin, die ihrer Mutter gehört hatte, zu begleiten. Sie führte sie zu Spaziergängen aus, erzählte ihnen Familiengeschichten und erfüllte ihren Geist mit phantastischen, furchterregenden Negerlegenden.

III

Bis zum Alter von 16 Jahren blieb Fernando bei Vater und Schwester in ›El Altar‹. In reifendem Leibe ein unentschlossener, zager Geist. Mußte er eine Entscheidung treffen, so hörte er hundert verschiedene Stimmen. Er konnte niemals unmittelbar nach einem einzigen Gedanken handeln. Als er ins siebzehnte Jahr ging, beschloß Don Santiago, ihn in die Hauptstadt zu schicken, damit er dort nach seinen Neigungen studiere. Er schrieb an einen alten Freund, Don Bernardo Lazola, einen Beamten des Domkapitels in Caracas, ob er ihn für die Zeit seiner Ausbildung gegen angemessene Entschädigung in seinem Hause aufnehmen würde. Lazola antwortete zustimmend. Nach schmerzlichem Abschied von seiner Schwester verließ Fernando in Begleitung des Vaters ›El Altar‹.

Bis Caracas war es ein Ritt von mehreren Tagen. Sie übernachteten auf den Haciendas ihrer Freunde, wo sie gastfrei aufgenommen wurden. Vom Ufer des Guaire aus

Cover of *Russland vor der Sturm* (Russia before the Storm) by Semjon Rosenfeld, 1933, design by Jan Tschichold. Verlag der Bücherkreis GmbH, Berlin

"The New Typography, in its concern to satisfy the needs of our own period and to make sure that every single piece of printing is in harmony with the present...."

Jan Tschichold

Typographische Gestaltung

Ein neues Buch von *Jan Tschichold*
über zeitgemäße typographische Formgebung
und über Randgebiete
(Photographie, Photomontage, neue Malerei)
mit vielen originalgroßen
und verkleinerten Nachbildungen
teils in mehreren Farben
und auf verschiedenfarbigen Papieren

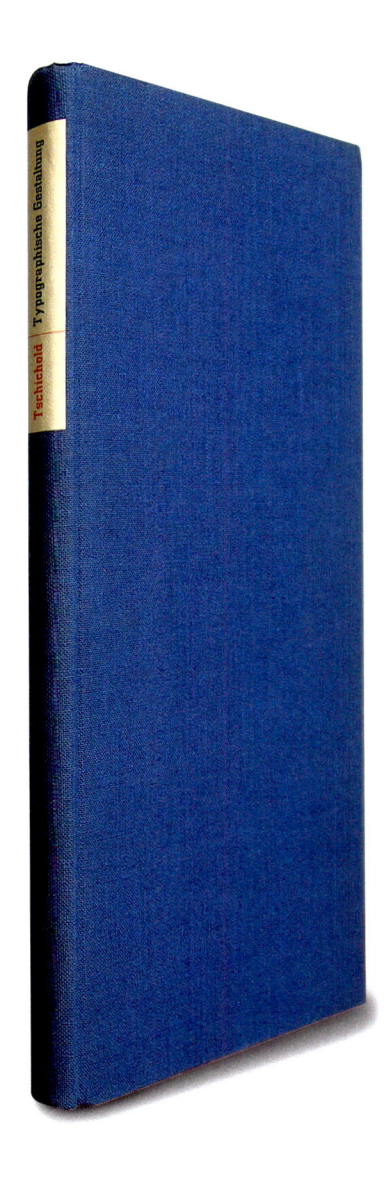

Cover, spine, and pages 4–5 of *Typografische Gestaltung* (Typographic Design) by Jan Tschichold, 1935. Benno Schwabe & Co., Basel

Pages 14–15, 16–17, 30–31, 40–41 of *Typografische Gestaltung* by Jan Tschichold, 1935. Benno Schwabe & Co., Basel

Bodoni als besseren Ersatz die fette Bodoni). Dann können etwa die Walbaumfraktur mit der fetten Hänelfraktur, ferner eine Egyptienne, eine Anglaise oder eine moderne Schreibschrift folgen. Schmal laufende Schriften braucht man kaum. Sie werden viel zu häufig grundlos gebraucht.

Sind bestehende Schriften zu ergänzen, so sollen Neuanschaffungen nicht auf gut Glück oder auf naive Kundenwünsche hin, sondern ebenfalls planmäßig erfolgen. Man baue bestehende Familien, soweit sie nicht modischen Charakter getragen haben, mit Kursiv und Halbfetter in allen Graden aus. Niemals sollte man neben einer Grotesk eine andere Grotesk als Fette oder Kursiv, also zur Ergänzung, gebrauchen. Man muß entweder die alte Grotesk wegwerfen und eine neue Familie kaufen, oder aber die alte nachbestellen und mit weiteren Garnituren, mager und fett etwa, ergänzen. Nichts ist für ein geschultes Auge peinlicher, als Akzidenzgrotesk mit Futura oder andere Zusammenstellungen von Grotesken verschiedenen Schnittes nebeneinander zu sehen.

Längere Zeit hat die Frage der allgemeinen Kleinschrift die Gemüter bewegt. Sicher wäre der Verlust der Großbuchstaben in Wirklichkeit ein großer wirtschaftlicher und ästhetischer Gewinn. Wirtschaftlich, da die Versalien auf vielen graphischen Gebieten die Produktion erschweren, ästhetisch, da in der jetzigen barocken Schreibweise der deutschen Sprache die Versalien das Schriftbild der Antiqua stören. Denn Gemeine und Versalien sind eigentlich zwei einander fremde, zumindest ferne Schriften. Die gegenwärtigen Verhältnisse erlauben uns jedoch nicht, die Lösung der etwas untergeordneten Frage zu befördern. Man hat hin und wieder die Möglichkeit, eine Arbeit klein geschrieben zu setzen, und soll sich daran freuen. Vielleicht wird bald die ‹gemilderte› Kleinschreibung (nur Satzanfänge und Eigennamen groß) eingeführt, die gewiß ein Fortschritt wäre. Diese Reform hat die meisten Aussichten auf Erfolg. Die vom Schreibenden vor einigen Jahren angeregte und vom früheren Bildungsverband der Deutschen Buchdrucker durchgeführte Rundfrage unter tausenden von Fachleuten und Laien ergab, daß ungefähr 50% der Abstimmenden für gemilderte, etwa 25% für absolute Kleinschreibung und nur etwa 25% für die geltende Rechtschreibung eintraten. Doch ist nicht anzunehmen, daß zur Zeit die Rechtschreibung der deutschen Sprache neu geregelt werden könne. Wir müssen uns auf einzelne Realisationen beschränken.

Gegenüber: *Umschlag eines Bücherkatalogs, verkleinert*

Katalog 88

Kunst und verwandte Gebiete

Perspektive
Festlichkeiten
Architektur
Ornamentik
Gartenbau
Festungsbau
Kostümbücher
Kunsttheorie

Jacques Rosenthal, Buch- und Kunstantiquariat, München

Durchschuß, Zeilenfall und Gruppenbildung

So wie der Abstand zwischen den Wörtern erkennbar größer sein muß als der Zwischenraum zwischen den Buchstaben, muß auch der sichtbare Abstand zwischen den Zeilen größer oder doch nicht kleiner sein als der Ausschluß zwischen den Wörtern. *Guter Satz muß also durchschossen sein.* (Ausnahmen bilden nur die gotischen Schriften, Fraktur- und die meisten Mediäval-Antiqua-Schriften.) Kompresser Satz erscheint uns unklar. Besonders die Grotesk gewinnt durch kräftigen Durchschuß, während sie kompreß gesetzt schwer lesbar ist. 8-Punkt-Grotesk sieht zum Beispiel mit 3-Punkt-Durchschuß am besten aus. Der Durchschuß richtet sich dazu nach dem umgebenden Weiß und nach der angestrebten Grauwirkung.

Der Zeilenfall von Überschriften, kleineren Bemerkungen und Ähnlichem richtet sich in erster Linie nach den *Sprech- und Sinngruppen,* wobei die nachfolgende Zeile unter dem Ausgangspunkt der ersten beginnt. Die Formregeln über den axialen Zeilenfall gelten für die neue Typographie nicht. Die erste Zeile darf ebenso gut länger wie kürzer als die zweite sein. Trennungen sind zu vermeiden. Blocksatzartige Wirkungen, die gelegentlich zufällig entstehen, beseitige man durch leichte Änderungen des Ausschlusses in einer Zeile. Sie sind unerwünscht und auf keinen Fall anzustreben.

Bei der Untereinanderordnung gleichwertiger, aber verschieden langer Zeilen (wie bei *Aufzählungen*) ist es nicht freigestellt, die Zeilen entweder links oder rechts anzurücken. Derartige Zeilen müssen gedichtsatzartig links an einer Linie beginnen. Das Gegenteil ist falsch. Unsere Schrift ist nämlich rechtsläufig; wir kehren mit dem Auge am leichtesten zu dem Ausgangspunkt der gelesenen Zeile zurück. Beginnt die neue Zeile nicht unter ihm, so empfinden wir das als Störung, die gehäuft besonders unangenehm ist.

Nicht alle Schriften laufen wie die unsrige: so lasen die Türken bis vor kurzem waagrecht von rechts nach links; die Chinesen und Japaner (die beide dieselbe Bilderschrift benutzen) lesen abwärts und von rechts nach links, können aber ihre Bildzeichen, deren jedes einen Begriff bezeichnet, in Ausnahmefällen auch von rechts nach links waagrecht anordnen.

Wir sind weder Türken noch Chinesen und haben keine Freiheit, Zeilen der erwähnten Art so oder so anzuordnen. Es ist durchaus kein Zufall, daß Gedicht-

---

Auf den nachfolgenden zwei Seiten: *Erste und vierte Seite eines Zirkulars. Originalgröße. Klischee: Meisterschule für Deutschlands Buchdrucker, München. Futura der Bauerschen Gießerei, Frankfurt am Main.*

bild und schrift

wettbewerb des kreises münchen im bildungsverband der deutschen buchdrucker die unserm Geschmack nahe stehen und von denen sich Varianten in vielen Druckereien vorfinden. Fügt man zu einem Satze eine fremde Auszeichnungsschrift, so wird man auf den Inhalt des Textes Rücksicht nehmen und ungeeignete Charaktere vermeiden. Trotzdem besteht keine Notwendigkeit, die Auswahl der Type überall dem Inhalt in literarischer Weise anzuschneiden.

Schattierte und überhaupt unflächige Buchstaben widersprechen der Flächengestaltung der neuen Typographie. Hier liegt die Grenze, die der Anwendung von satzfremden Titelschriften in der neuen Typographie gezogen werden muß.

Normung

Eine weitgreifende Normung der häufigsten Drucksachen wäre ein großer Gewinn für Besteller, Drucker, Papiererzeuger und Verbraucher. Zumindest wäre zu wünschen, daß die Anwendung der *genormten Papierformate* noch weiter fortschreite. In den meisten Fällen ist es unnötig, ein persönliches Format zu wählen. Die Auswahl der Normgrößen ist reich genug, und entspricht fast allen Bedürfnissen. Einzige wichtige Ausnahme sind die Buchgrößen für Romane und ähnliche Bücher, die man in der Hand statt auf dem Tisch liest; für diesen Zweck ist das Normformat A 5 zu breit. Sonst aber lassen sich fast alle Drucksachen auf den Normformaten herstellen, die in der Schweiz, in Deutschland, der Tschechoslowakei und Polen die gleichen sind. Die wichtigsten Normformate und ihre Anwendungsgebiete gehen aus der nachfolgenden Übersicht hervor:

Formulare und Drucksachen:

A 4   210×297 mm: Briefe, Rechnungen, Lieferscheine, Drucksachen und Formulare aller Art, Vorschriften, Preislisten, Kataloge, Zeitschriften, Notizblöcke, Zeichnungen, Normblätter usw.

A 5   148×210 mm: Halbbriefe, Rechnungen, Lieferscheine, Drucksachen und Formulare aller Art, Vorschriften, Preislisten, Kataloge, Blöcke, Karteikarten usw.

A 6   105×148 mm: Postkarten, Karteikarten, Drucksachen, Formulare aller Art, Paketadressen, verschiedene Karten

A 7   74×105 mm: Karten, Klebmarken usw.

Gegenüber: Obere Hälfte eines Normbriefs nach Din 676 (Deutsche Norm). Adreßfeld links.

Briefumschläge:

C 4   229×324 mm: für Bogen A 4 ungefalzt
C 5   162×229 mm: für Bogen A 4 einmal gefalzt
              für Bogen A 5 ungefalzt
C⁶/₈ 114×224 mm: für Bogen A 4 zweimal quergefalzt
C 6   114×162 mm: für Bogen A 4 zweimal gefalzt
              für Bogen A 5 einmal gefalzt
              für Bogen A 6 ungefalzt
C 7   81×114 mm: für Karten A 7

Außer dem Normblatt «Papierformate» (Schweiz: SNV 10120, Deutschland: DIN 476) existiert eine ganze Reihe weitere Normen, die die buchgewerbliche Produktion angehen. Vor allem verdient das Normblatt über «Geschäftsbriefe» (Schweiz SNV 10131, Deutschland DIN 676) Beachtung.

Die *schweizerischen* Normblätter SNV 10131 *Geschäftsbriefe* und SNV 10130 *Erläuterungen dazu* sind bei allen Postbureaux der Schweiz zusammen für 10 Rappen zu haben. Dort bekommt man auch die Merkblätter *Briefumschläge und Adressen* und *Drucksachen in Kartenform* umsonst, die überall Beachtung finden sollten.

Vom VSM-Normenbureau, Zürich, Lavaterstraße 11, können folgende Normblätter bezogen werden: SNV 10120 *Papierformate*; SNV 10121 *Papierformate, Anwendung*; SNV 10122 *Hüllformate*; SNV 10125 *Briefumschläge, Formate*; SNV 66100 *Korrekturzeichen*.

Die wichtigsten deutschen buchgewerblichen Normen sind auf den Seiten 23 und 24 meines Buches «Typographische Entwurfstechnik» (Stuttgart 1932) ausführlich zitiert.

Die Akzidenzarbeit

Typographie heißt mehr als «mit Typen schreiben»; denn man rechnet eine mit der Schreibmaschine hergestellte Mitteilung nicht zu den typographischen Arbeiten, obwohl auch sie aus einer Art von Typen zusammengesetzt ist. Das Gedruckte soll nicht nur besser als das Geschriebene lesbar, sondern von idealer Lesbarkeit sein.

Gegenüber: Erste und dritte Seite einer Einladung

Gestaltung des Flächenraums

Alle Typographie ist flächige Gestaltung. Die richtige Verteilung der Zeilen und Gruppen ist eine ebenso wichtige Arbeit wie die Bildung sinnrichtiger und optisch wirksamer Kontraste und steht mit dieser in inniger Verbindung. Da heute die Schrift nackt auftritt und nicht durch Ornamente übertönt werden kann, sind wir für die Wirkung der Schrift nicht nur als Wort und Zeile, sondern auch als Teil der Flächengestalt besonders empfindlich geworden. Natürlich werden Schriftgrößen und Garnituren zunächst durch den Inhalt bestimmt. Doch haben wir fast immer einigen Spielraum, einen Grad größer oder kleiner zu wählen oder auf ähnliche Weise den graphischen Ausdruck dieser und jener Zeile zu verändern. Wir können auch eine Zeile statt nach links ganz oder nur weiter nach rechts stellen. Hier beginnt die eigentlich gestaltende Arbeit, die Ordnung der Formwerte.

Jeder Formwert lebt nur dank seiner Umgebung. Die gleiche Zeile wirkt ganz anders in einer großen und in einer kleinen Fläche. In jedem der Fälle können wir die gleiche Zeile überzeugend stellen; doch werden ihre Stellung und der graphische Ausdruck des Ganzen wahrscheinlich sehr verschieden sein. Daraus geht hervor, daß ein bestimmter Formwert in einer bestimmten Situation einen bestimmten Platz verlangt, der ihm gemäß ist. Gelingt es uns, diese Plätze zu finden, so nennen wir die Arbeit vollendet.

Daß sich nun immer mehrere Möglichkeiten zeigen, wenn mehrere Elemente zu ordnen sind, belegen die nachfolgenden sechs abstrakten Ordnungen. Die erste ist eine schematische, ungeistige Scheinordnung: die drei Elemente stehen in Reih und Glied untereinander. In den anderen Beispielen bestehen zwischen den Elementen Spannungen. Das zweite Beispiel (oben rechts) zeigt eine geometrische, waagrecht-senkrechte Ordnung. Im dritten Bild folgen Linie und Quadrat weiter den Richtungen der Begrenzung, doch sind ihre Beziehungen zueinander nicht mehr so geometrisch fest, wie im zweiten Beispiel. Linie und Kreis sind im vierten wieder stärker gebunden; das Quadrat steht in Opposition zu den Begrenzungslinien. Im fünften Beispiel wenden sich Quadrat und Linie gemeinsam gegen die Richtungen der Grenzen, und im letzten schlagen beide jede für sich eine fremde Richtung ein. Der Kreis ist immer indifferent und ruhend. In keinem der Beispiele außer dem ersten ist die Lage der Elemente zufällig; jedes Bild stellt für sich eine mögliche Ordnung dar. Jedesmal sind die Lage der Teile, ihre Beziehungen zueinander und die Intervalle notwendig und nicht zufällig.

Im gleichen Sinne muß man nach dem richtigen Platz der Teile einer Satzarbeit suchen. Doch haben wir es dort nicht von vornherein mit drei Elementen zu tun, sondern müssen diese in der Regel erst durch Ballung bilden; erst dann können wir die entstandenen Gruppen auf der Fläche ordnen.

Schon früher haben wir dargelegt, daß *drei Gruppen* die Regel bilden sollen. Bei ihrer Ordnung im Raum ist darauf zu achten, wie wir lesen. Der Ablauf der

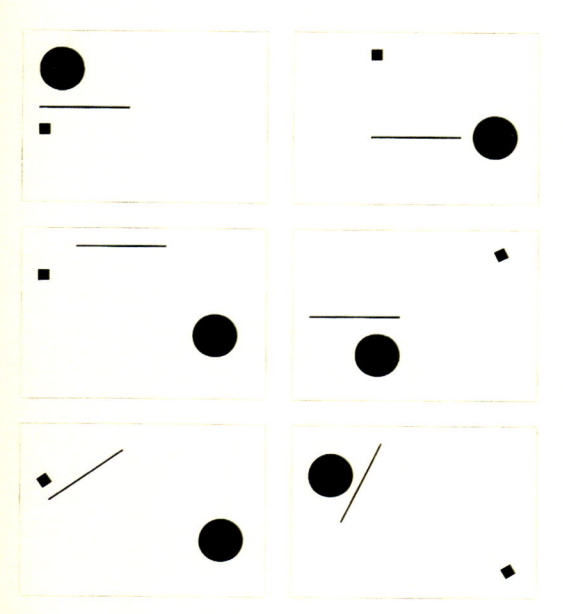

Farben

Wenn wir in einer Drucksache ein Wort in roter Farbe erscheinen lassen, so wünschen wir, daß es aus der übrigen schwarzen Schrift heraustrete. Rot hat die Eigenschaft, auf uns zuzueilen. Gelb wirkt ähnlich aggressiv. Blau tritt eigentlich zurück, doch wirkt es als bunte Farbe lebhafter als Schwarz. In diesem Sinne angewandt, dienen die Farben der *Hervorhebung des Wichtigen*.

Sie können auch zur *Unterscheidung* und Kennzeichnung verschiedener Prospekte, verschiedener Teile eines Buches oder zu ähnlichen Zwecken benutzt werden.

Endlich können farbige Zeilen und Linien in der Symphonie der Teile eines Satzes einen *Klang* bilden, dem keine so greifbare Funktion wie die deutliche Hervorhebung oder die zu unterscheidende Farbe zukommt. Alle Farben, auch Schwarz, sollen stets auf das zu bedruckende Papier und untereinander abgestimmt sein. Hierüber kann man schwer schreiben; es gehört ein geübtes Gefühl dazu, Farbklänge zu bilden und anzuwenden.

Reine Farben sind zwar ursprünglich sehr schön, können aber gedruckt abscheulich aussehen. Eine Farbfläche wirkt farbig ganz anders als Schrift, die mit derselben Farbe gedruckt wurde. Man darf auch nicht übersehen, daß schon verschieden große Flächen von gleicher Farbe optisch verschieden wirken.

Große Nähe oder lebhafte Gegensätze sind die beiden Hauptmöglichkeiten, zwei verschiedene bunte Farben in eine Beziehung zu setzen. Die neue Typographie arbeitet ebenso gerne mit lebhaften, manchmal ungebrochenen Farben, wie mit ›unbunten‹ Tönen, etwa Grau, Sepiabraun und Schwarz.

Im Schriftsatz sollten zweifarbig gesetzte Zeilen möglichst nie vorkommen, da auch ein aufmerksamer Drucker die zweite Farbe nicht immer genau eindrucken kann. Es stört sehr, wenn sie nicht genau Linie hält. Fast immer lassen sich derartige Spielereien durch Verwendung halbfetter schwarzer statt farbiger Schrift vermeiden.

Je sparsamer und seltener die zweite Farbe auftritt, umso kostbarer wirkt sie. Wenn man sie im oberen Teil einer Arbeit als Schrift erscheinen und unten etwa als Linie noch einmal anklingen läßt, so sieht das schöner aus, als wenn sie die ganze Arbeit in kleinen Flecken durchzieht. Auch hier steigert Beschränkung die Klarheit des Ganzen.

Gegenüber: *Vierte Seite eines Dankschreibens*. Originalgröße.

Für die anläßlich unserer Geschäftsübernahme und unserer Vermählung

dargebrachten vielen Glückwünsche und Geschenke danken wir, zugleich

im Namen beider Eltern, auf das herzlichste

Charles Seetzen und Frau Friedel Seetzen-Meyer

Zürich, den 26. März 1935

Pages 54–55, 56–57, 64–65, 74–75 of *Typografische Gestaltung* by Jan Tschichold, 1935. Benno Schwabe & Co., Basel

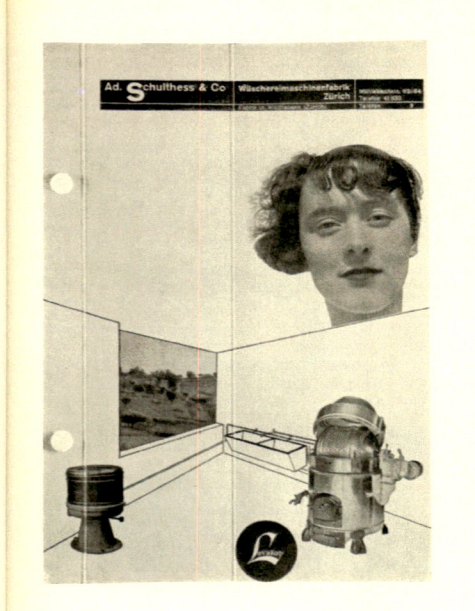

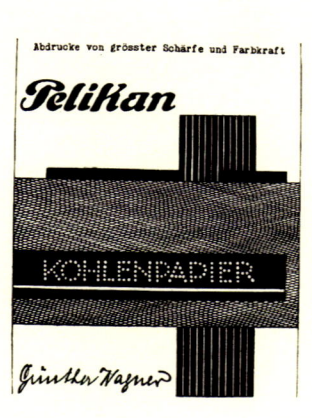

Pages 78–79, 80–81, 82–83, and 94–95 of *Typografische Gestaltung* by Jan Tschichold, 1935. Benno Schwabe & Co., Basel

Typographische Elemente: Linien, Flächen, Felder, Streifen, Kreise, Punkte, Dreiecke, Pfeile, Raster u. ä.

Rhythmus und Glanz geben. Nicht die absolute Gewalt der Kontraste gibt den Ausschlag, sondern ihre überzeugende Spannung.

Notwendig setzen diese Empfindungen das ‹abstrakte› Sehen voraus, das auch den Erscheinungswert an sich wahrnimmt und nicht nur seine rohe Brauchbarkeit. Das Kunstwerk entsteht doch, wo es uns gelingt, ein längst bekanntes Material so zu gestalten, daß es uns ganz neu erscheint. Dieses neue Sehen ist für uns von der konkreten Malerei vorbereitet worden. Sie vermittelt uns das Empfinden für die neue Formenwelt. Es ist auch in anderen Zeiten und Kulturgebieten zu erkennen, etwa in den vorgotischen Miniaturen oder im japanischen Holzschnitt, deren Formen auch unseren Absichten verwandt sind. Am reinsten aber verkörpert sich das neue Sehen in der neuen Kunst, die zugleich Grundlage und Spitze der neuen Gestaltung ist.

Die konkrete Kunst

Nicht wenige Leser dieses Buches werden von vornherein bestreiten, daß zwischen Malerei und Typographie überhaupt Beziehungen beständen. Solange man an die gegenständliche Malerei denkt, ist das auch richtig. Wenn auch die Gebiete optischer Gestaltung aus derselben Zeitspanne niemals ganz beziehungslos sind, so wäre es doch übertrieben, von lebhaften Beziehungen zwischen der gegenständlichen Malerei und der früheren Typographie zu sprechen. Die ältere Typographie ist viel stärker an die Fassadenarchitektur der Renaissance und der von ihr abhängigen Stilperioden a.o.s. an deren Malerei gebunden. Das soll nicht heißen, daß sich früher der Setzer etwa bemühte, mit einem gesetzten Buchtitel den Eindruck einer Kirchenfassade zu erwecken; so wörtlich sind die gegen-

seitigen Beziehungen nicht zu nehmen. Doch ist die innere Verwandtschaft zwischen Renaissancefassaden und dem üblichen Buchtitel unverkennbar.

Heute besteht ebenfalls eine Verwandtschaft zwischen Typographie und neuer Architektur. Jedoch ist die Typographie heute nicht von der Architektur abhängig, sondern beide von der neuen Malerei, die ihnen die Modellformen der Gestaltung geliefert hat. Die neue Malerei, worunter hier die gegenstandslose oder konkrete Malerei verstanden wird, entstand vor der neuen Architektur; diese ist ohne jene nicht denkbar.

Meistens nennt man die gegenstandslose Malerei abstrakt. Doch handelt es sich hier gar nicht um Abstraktionen, sondern um Konkretes; denn eine Linie, ein Kreis, eine Fläche bedeuten in dieser Malerei nur sich selbst, während sie in der gegenständlichen Malerei für etwas anderes stehen. Es wäre darum eher möglich, die gegenständliche Malerei abstrakt zu nennen. Auch der Ausdruck ‹absolute Malerei› ist anfechtbar. Mit vollem Recht daher hat Theo van Doesburg und die Gruppe AC den Ausdruck ‹konkrete Malerei› für diese Malerei aufgestellt (1930), und wir wollen ihn auch im Nachfolgenden anwenden.

Inserat ‹Négatif›

Gegenüber: **Herbert Bayer**: *Umschlag eines Prospekts.* Um 1928. Originalgröße.

98 Das neue Buch

Ein Buch über Typographie kann nicht geschlossen werden, ohne daß auch über das Buch als Aufgabe gesprochen wird. Ein gut gemachtes Buch ist ein Beweis großen Könnens, da es eine Menge von Fachproblemen aufrollt, die so gelöst werden müssen, daß das Ganze eine selbstverständlich scheinende Einheit ergibt.

Ursprünglich war das gedruckte Buch eine Nachahmung des geschriebenen; und erst allmählich befreite sich die Typographie von Formvorstellungen, die vom geschriebenen Kodex herkamen. Die Beschränkung auf eine Farbe und auf reinen Schriftsatz waren bedeutende Fortschritte, die nur langsam erobert wurden. Die eigentlichen Väter des modernen Buches sind die Meister des klassizistischen Satzes: Didot, Bodoni und Göschen. Sie entwickelten um die Wende des 18. Jahrhunderts einen Buchtyp, der in seiner Vollkommenheit nur mit den Wiegendrucken verglichen werden kann. Dieser Typ ist so gut, daß auch die meisten gut gedruckten Bücher der Gegenwart ihm folgen. Daraus schließen viele, daß die typographische Gestalt des Buches für alle Zukunft gefunden und jede Bemühung um Änderungen umsonst oder verfehlt sei.

Vergleichen wir den Buchanfang einer Inkunabel mit der Titelei eines üblichen Romans der Gegenwart, so finden wir gewaltige Unterschiede. Ebenso wird jeder feiner Empfindende den üblichen Buchtitel von heute als mehr oder weniger altmodisch ansehen. Ich bin überzeugt, daß die typographischen Bemühungen der Gegenwart nicht vor dem Buche halt machen werden. Denn es ist nicht einzusehen, warum unsere Zeit, die so viele Neuerungen hervorbringt, nicht auch dem Buche ihren Stempel aufdrücken sollte. Sie tut es oft, aber selten richtig: entweder beweist das Buch nur die oberflächlichste, ungenügende Kenntnis der klassischen Satzregeln, oder es ist von einem Spezialisten gemacht, der diese genau studiert hat. Auch der zweite Fall ist nicht sehr rühmlich; beweist er doch eine gewisse künstlerische Unfruchtbarkeit, die heute sonst selten ist. Mithin kommt es darauf an, daß wir ein Buch unserer Zeit mit unseren Mitteln gestalten lernen und uns nicht länger an das klassische Schema binden lassen. (Es ist hier nicht etwa nur von buchartigen Drucksachen die Rede, sondern ausdrücklich auch von Werken der hohen Literatur.)

Indessen gibt es vieles, das richtig ist und bleiben wird. So ist das *Buchformat des Romans* keine willkürliche, sondern eine eminent praktische Größe, die auch

Gegenüber: **El Lissitzky:** *Photoplakat* (Photogramm). 1924.

Pages 98–99 and two pages of advertisements from *Typografische Gestaltung* by Jan Tschichold, 1935. Benno Schwabe & Co., Basel

Page 55 of *Typografische vormgeving* (Dutch edition of *Typografische Gestaltung*) by Jan Tschichold, 1938. N.V. vh. J.F. Duwaer & Zonen, Amsterdam

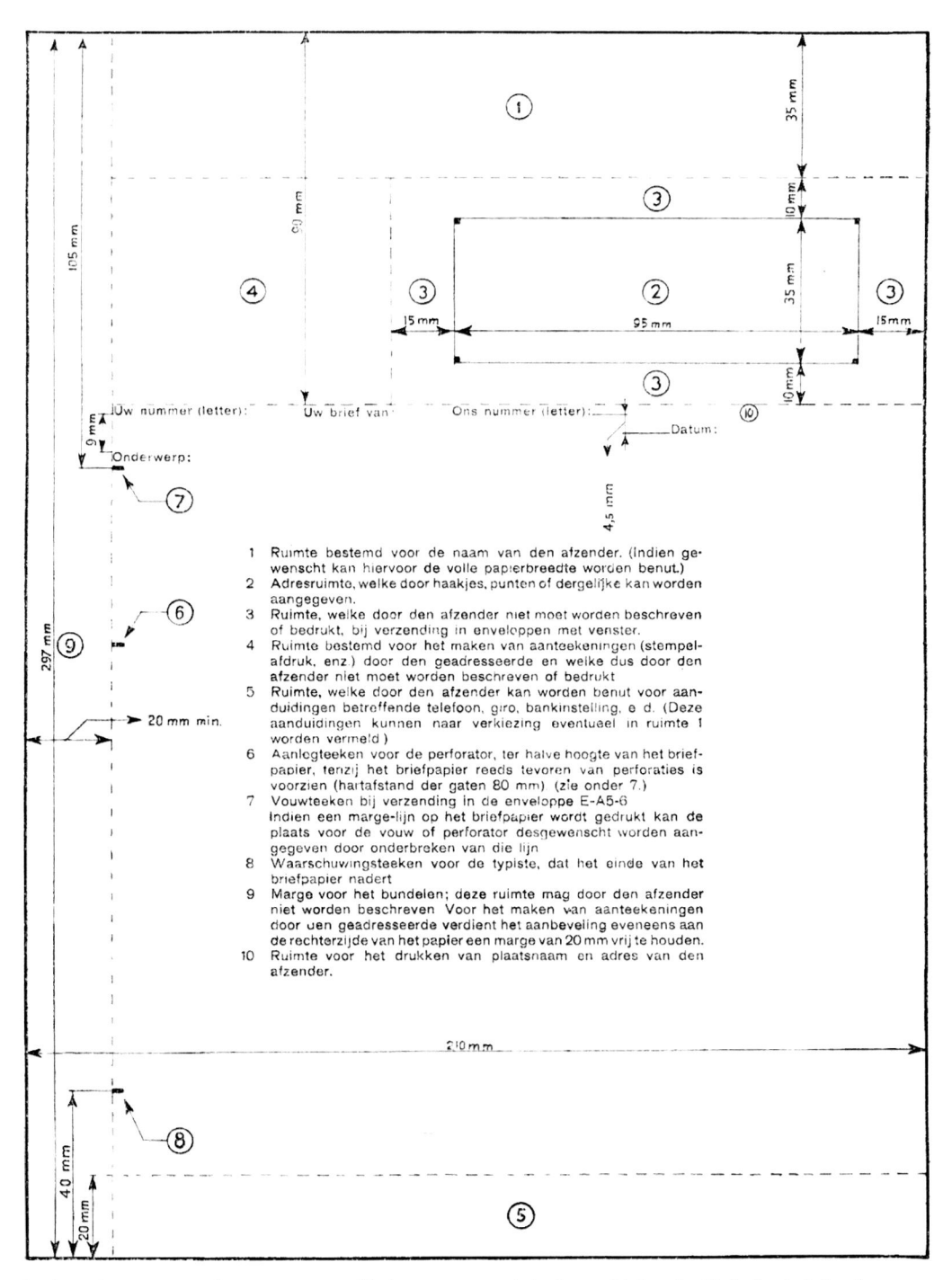

1. Ruimte bestemd voor de naam van den afzender. (Indien gewenscht kan hiervoor de volle papierbreedte worden benut.)
2. Adresruimte, welke door haakjes, punten of dergelijke kan worden aangegeven.
3. Ruimte, welke door den afzender niet moet worden beschreven of bedrukt, bij verzending in enveloppen met venster.
4. Ruimte bestemd voor het maken van aanteekeningen (stempelafdruk, enz.) door den geadresseerde en welke dus door den afzender niet moet worden beschreven of bedrukt
5. Ruimte, welke door den afzender kan worden benut voor aanduidingen betreffende telefoon, giro, bankinstelling, e.d. (Deze aanduidingen kunnen naar verkiezing eventueel in ruimte 1 worden vermeld.)
6. Aanlegteeken voor de perforator, ter halve hoogte van het briefpapier, tenzij het briefpapier reeds tevoren van perforaties is voorzien (hartafstand der gaten 80 mm) (zie onder 7.)
7. Vouwteeken bij verzending in de enveloppe E-A5-6
 Indien een marge-lijn op het briefpapier wordt gedrukt kan de plaats voor de vouw of perforator desgewenscht worden aangegeven door onderbreken van die lijn
8. Waarschuwingsteeken voor de typiste, dat het einde van het briefpapier nadert
9. Marge voor het bundelen; deze ruimte mag door den afzender niet worden beschreven. Voor het maken van aanteekeningen door den geadresseerde verdient het aanbeveling eveneens aan de rechterzijde van het papier een marge van 20 mm vrij te houden.
10. Ruimte voor het drukken van plaatsnaam en adres van den afzender.

Eenheidsformaat A 4. *Ontwerp* vastgesteld door een commissie, ingesteld door het Nederlandsch Instituut voor Efficiency, in samenwerking met de Hoofdcommissie voor de Normalisatie in Nederland. *De indeeling is voorloopig en moet nog definitief worden vastgesteld.*

Cover of *Typografische vormgeving* (Dutch edition of *Typografische Gestaltung*) by Jan Tschichold, 1938. N.V. vh. J.F. Duwaer & Zonen, Amsterdam

Dit boek wil een nieuw typografisch inzicht ingang doen vinden

Typografische vormgeving

Jan Tschichold

● Een nieuwe typografische traditie is de wensch van vele boekdrukkers. Natuurlijk eischen de groote veranderingen in de zet- en druktechniek van de laatste jaren een aangepaste typografische vormgeving. Hierover en over de noodzakelijkheid verantwoord te werken, zooals de oude boekdrukkers, handelt dit boek. De schrijver heeft de vormgeving in den nieuwen typografischen stijl gedurende een reeks van jaren reeds overwegend beïnvloed.

Jan Tschichold

Typografische vormgeving

N.V. vh. J. F. Duwaer & Zonen   Amsterdam   1938

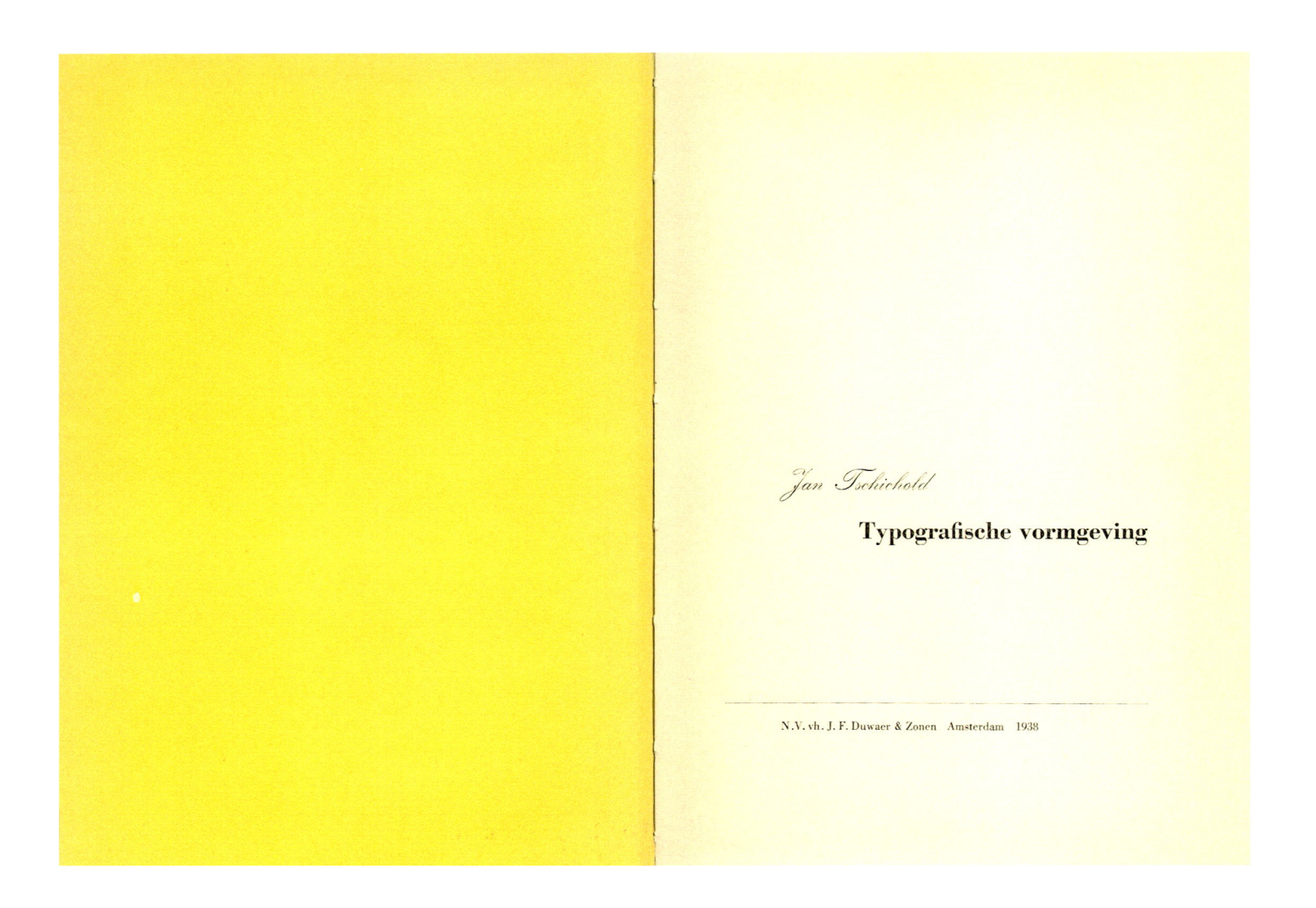

Pages 4–5, 14–15, and 18–19 of *Typografische vormgeving* (Dutch edition of *Typografische Gestaltung*) by Jan Tschichold, 1938. N.V. vh. J.F. Duwaer & Zonen, Amsterdam

Titel van Giambattista Bodoni. Sterk verkleind.

aan de studie van hun drukken en aan de aansluitende leerboeken van Henri Fournier (Traité de la typographie, Paris 1825) en M. Brun (Manuel pratique de la typographie française, Paris 1825) veel wetenswaardigs, niet over het wat, maar over het hoe. Iedere druk van deze meesters is een kunstwerk, waarvan de oudere stijl ons niet blind mag doen zijn voor de zuivere typografische eigenschappen en verdiensten. Daarom reproduceeren wij twee werken van Bodoni en bevelen deze aan in de aandachtige studie van den lezer.

Bij Bodoni en Didot dient het bij gelegenheid verwijden of vernauwen der regels in kapitalen geenszins enkel daartoe om bepaalde « fraaie » lengten der regels te verkrijgen, maar ook tot het vormen van verschillende, lichtere en donkere groepen, die in het geheel van de bladzijde van beteekenis zijn. Hun navolgers waren in het spatieeren van zulke woorden gewetenloozer en ten slotte werd deze technische mogelijkheid misbruikt, om in ieder geval bepaalde woordenregellengten te maken. Men vereenigde op dezelfde bladzijde wijd gespatieerde en zeer nauw gezette regels. Dit *spatieeren als middel bij een smaakvolle vorm-*

14

Beginpagina's van nevenstaanden titel. Sterk verkleind.

geving is een betreurenswaardige erfenis van de 19de eeuw, die wij niet aanvaarden mogen. Het verstoort rhythmisch het woordbeeld, wekt een onverantwoorde onrust en is daarmede in tegenspraak met functioneele typografie. (Ook het spatieeren als middel tot accentueeren in een loopenden zin moet vermeden worden; hierover nader in het hoofdstuk « Accentueeren in den zetregel ».)

De voor ons allen als vanzelfsprekend geworden rationeele indeeling van den titeltekst maakt het den zetter des te moeilijker mooie regelindeelingen en den vaasachtigen vorm van den titel te verkrijgen. Een verkeerd begrepen normaliseering van den vorm was het doel van alle moeiten.

De 19de eeuw bracht met de uitvinding van den steendruk en naast het ontstaan van eenige waardevolle lettertypen een overdaad van fantasie-letters, die gedurende langen tijd het uiterlijk van typografische werkstukken bepaalden. Uiteindelijk beschikte men over een schier eindelooze hoeveelheid lettertypen (waarvan vele slechts in één corps), maar over geen mogelijkheid meer om deze in de orde van het werk op te nemen.

15

---

zijn binnen het kader van de oude typografische wetten niet toelaatbaar. Deze vorderen een betrekkelijk gelijkmatig grijs van het geheel; halfvette en zelfs vette typen, die allereerst een duidelijke verdeeling vergemakkelijken, golden als leelijk. Ook moet de regel in het midden uitgevuld zijn: dit is echter een zetwijze, die maar zelden werkelijk de beste vorm is en niet steeds een duidelijk, gemakkelijk te begrijpen aanzien biedt. Zij streeft daarbij naar een vrijwel gelijksoortig uiterlijk van alle drukwerken, die toch naar aard en doel verschillend zijn en dus om verschillende vormgevingen vragen. Daarom beantwoorden de regels van de oude typografie geenszins aan onze wenschen ten opzichte van een doelmatige vormgeving. De mogelijkheden van een *onsymmetrischen bouw* zijn voor vele doeleinden geëigender en passen zich gemakkelijker aan aan de practische en esthetische behoeften van den modernen mensch.

Het arbeidstempo van den tegenwoordigen tijd verlangt ook van de *techniek* der typografie, dat deze zich aanpast. Wij kunnen heden aan een briefhoofd of een ander smoutwerk slechts een gering gedeelte van den tijd besteden, dien men bijvoorbeeld in de negentiger jaren daaraan geven kon. Daarom hebben wij nieuwe wetten noodig, die eenvoudiger zijn dan de oude en die toch een zeer goede vormgeving waarborgen. Het aantal dezer wetten moet verminderd worden en de nieuwe moeten, ondanks hun eenvoud, meer mogelijkheden dan de oude bieden. Zij moeten met de techniek van het *machinezetten*, die thans gedeeltelijk het smoutwerk overneemt, volkomen harmonieeren, aangezien het oude handzetsel en het moderne machinezetsel moeten samenwerken en ongelijksoortige zetregels het werk onsamenhangend konden maken. De te volgen regels moeten in wezen veroorloven, dat smoutwerk volledig op de machine gezet kan worden. (Schrijver dezes behoort geenszins onvoorwaardelijk tot de verheerlijkers van het machinezetsel; hij is ervan overtuigd, dat het werkelijk feilloos handzetsel in zijn grafische kwaliteiten wel nimmer geheel door machinaal zetsel vervangen kan worden; de fijnste onderscheidingen immers van het beeld van den letter en in het uitvullen zijn voorloopig bij machinezetsel onbereikbaar. Het zij toegegeven, dat dit wellicht niet zeer belangrijk is. Maar een ieder poogt toch een overigens erkende mogelijk-

Vervolg zie bls. 24

Nevenstaande en volgende bladzijden: *Omslag en eerste pagina's van een tentoonstellingscatalogus.* Ware grootte. Typografie: Jan Tschichold. Proeve van een nieuwe bladspiegel. Een harmonieerend geheel van titel met tekst (register aan de zijkanten en beneden). De tekst geheel uit 8 punts gezet, de accentueering uit de cursief en halfvet: hoofdjes vet. Lettertype: Futura. Voor iedere interpunctie een vliesspatie.

18

Gewerbemuseum Basel

Ausstellung

Fünftausend Jahre Schrift

Die Schrift, ihre Entwicklung, Technik und Anwendung

14. Juni bis 19. Juli 1936

Pages 34–35, 40–41, 54–55, and 56–57 of *Typografische vormgeving* (Dutch edition of *Typografische Gestaltung*) by Jan Tschichold, 1938. N.V. vh. J.F. Duwaer & Zonen, Amsterdam

Normalisatie

De sterke toename van het papierverbruik en de moderne fabrikagemethoden hebben een behoefte doen ontstaan aan beperking van de groote verscheidenheid in de formaten, waarvan de afmetingen grootendeels gebaseerd zijn op de oorspronkelijke wijze van papiermaken, n.l. met handschepvormen, en waartusschen onderling weinig verband bestaat.

De normalisatie, die in verschillende landen op dit gebied is ter hand genomen, streefde naar de opstelling van een beperkte reeks formaten met regelmatige opklimming, die toch voldoende keuze laat voor de meest voorkomende toepassingen.

Door internationaal overleg is bereikt, dat er in 14 landen overeenstemming bestaat tusschen de betreffende normalen, t.w. in België, Duitschland, Finland, Hongarije, Japan, Nederland, Noorwegen, Oostenrijk, Polen, Roemenië, Rusland, Tsjecho-Slowakije, Zweden en Zwitserland.

De z.g. eenheidsformaten kenmerken zich door hun gelijkvormigheid, de breedte verhoudt zich tot de hoogte steeds als $1 : \sqrt{2}$, de eenige verhouding, waarbij het in de lengte gehalveerde formaat gelijkvormig blijft aan het formaat, waarvan is uitgegaan. Als grondformaat A0 is genomen een oppervlak van 1 m² (841×1189 mm), waaruit door opvolgende halveering de kleinere formaten zonder papierverlies worden verkregen. Het voordeel van de aanname van een grondformaat ter grootte van 1 m² is, dat de afgeleide formaten steeds een gemakkelijk te herleiden gedeelte van een m² aangeven en daar de machinale papieren alle naar een m² gewicht worden vervaardigd, is dit systeem van voordeel voor de omrekening dezer gewichten uitgedrukt in grammen, op riemgewichten in kg of per 1000 vel.

Bij opvolgende halveering van het formaat A0 ontstaat het formaat $A4 = 210 \times 297$ mm, dat het midden houdt tusschen het z.g. folio en kwarto-formaat en bestemd is om deze beide formaten te vervangen. Het kan gebruikt worden voor brieven, rekeningen, tijdschriften, catalogi, schrijfblocs, teekeningen, en alle soorten van drukwerken en formulieren, vooral indien deze bestemd zijn om als bijlagen met een brief te worden verzonden.

De halveering van het grondformaat A0 geeft telkens sprongen in de lengte en breedte van 40 %, waardoor de keuze tamelijk beperkt is. Daarom is naast de A-reeks nog aangenomen een B-reeks, waarvan de afmetingen midden evenredig zijn tusschen twee opvolgende afmetingen van de A-reeks. De opklimming wordt daardoor teruggebracht tot 20 %. Ook deze sprongen zouden nog bij uitzondering practische bezwaren bij de toepassing kunnen opleveren. Vandaar, dat nog

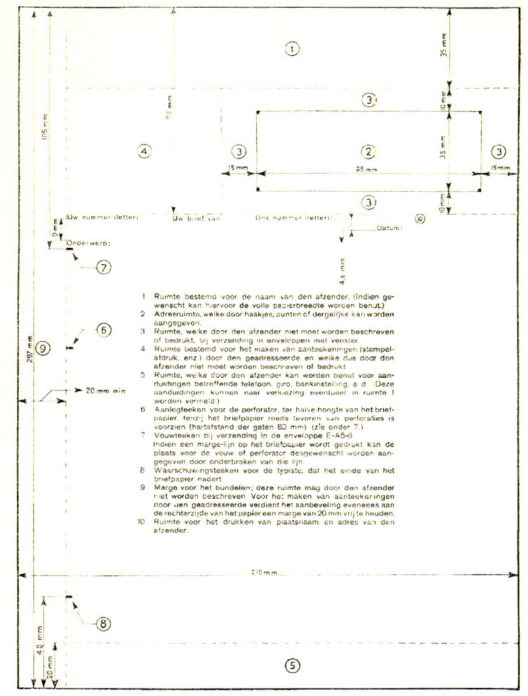

Eenheidsformaat A 4. *Ontwerp* vastgesteld door een commissie, ingesteld door het Nederlandsch Instituut voor Efficiency, in samenwerking met de Hoofdcommissie voor de Normalisatie in Nederland. *De indeeling is voorloopig en moet nog definitief worden vastgesteld.*

2 intercalaire hulpreeksen zijn toegevoegd, n.l. de C en D reeksen, waardoor opklimmingen tot 10 % gereduceerd worden. Met de 4 grondformaten A0, B0, C0 en D0 en opvolgende halveeringen, waartoe dus bij de fabrikage met vier rolbreedten wordt volstaan, moet practisch aan elke behoefte kunnen worden voldaan.

De tot stand gebrachte normalisatie beoogde in de eerste plaats bevordering van een economische *fabrikage* van papier, doordat met enkele rolbreedten wordt volstaan en de machines dus geregeld en volbenut kunnen loopen.

Voor den *handel* en de drukkerijen bieden de genormaliseerde formaten het uitzicht op verkleining van den papiervoorraad, waardoor minder renteloos kapitaal verloren gaat, bovendien kunnen drukpersen, aangepast aan de internationaal vastgestelde normen, hun vol rendement opleveren.

Voor den *papiergebruiker* opent zich het uitzicht op lagere papierprijzen, maar deze normalisatie heeft vooral het voordeel, dat orde en regelmaat is gebracht in de talrijke in gebruik zijnde formulieren en drukwerken, waarvan de centrale aanschaffing wordt bevorderd, terwijl overzichtelijkheid in administratie en archief toenemen, temeer daar de normalisatie der formaten leidde tot die van verschillende opbergmiddelen, zooals enveloppen, mappen, brievenhouders, kaarten en kasten.

Al deze voordeelen kunnen echter eerst bij algemeene toepassing der eenheidsformaten ten volle tot hun recht komen. De Regeering is hierin voorgegaan. Bij Kon. Besluit van 31 Jan. 1927 werd zij voor alle rijksinstellingen bindend verklaard. De lagere publiekrechtelijke lichamen, zooals provinciën en gemeenten, zijn geleidelijk gevolgd, evenals het Indische Gouvernement. Verder werd in de nieuwe zegelwet 1936 de afwijkende afmetingen van zegelpapier in overeenstemming gebracht met de eenheidsformaten. Ook vele industrieele ondernemingen passen reeds de eenheidsformaten toe voor hun talrijke formulieren en geschriften en ondervinden daarvan de voordeelen in administratie en archief.

Al kan dus met voldoening worden geconstateerd dat deze veld wint, van een algemeene toepassing mag nog lang niet worden gesproken en zeker niet in zulk een mate, dat daarvan bezuiniging bij de papierfabrikage of in den papierhandel wordt gevoeld.

Het ware inderdaad te wenschen, dat van de zijde van de industrie, den handel, de drukkerijen en den boekhandel meer dan tot nu toe werd gedaan om het gebruik van eenheidsformaten te bevorderen door deze zooveel mogelijk bij hun afnemers aan te bevelen. Immers, alleen door een algemeene vraag kan worden verwacht, dat de eenheidsformaten snel veld winnen en dat zij de oude formaten geheel zullen verdringen.

Hieronder volgt een opgave van de normaalbladen, die door de Hoofdcommissie voor de Normalisatie in Nederland op dit gebied zijn vastgesteld. Zij zijn verkrijgbaar bij het Centraal Normalisatie Bureau, Willem Witsenplein 6, 's-Gravenhage, en door tusschenkomst van den boekhandel.

N 381 Eenheidsformaten van papier
N 382 (Idem) Aanbevolen toepassingen
N 383 Papiergewichten van eenheidsformaten
N 538 Enveloppen voor eenheidsformaten volgens de A-reeks
N 539 (Idem) Volgens de B en C reeks
N 629 Liniaturen van onbedrukt schrijfpapier
N 633 Eenheidsformaten van papier; maximum afsneden
N 690 Mappen en brievenhouders
N 781 Formaten voor kaartsystemen
N 379 Formaten voor teekeningen
N 632 Correctieteekens voor drukproeven
N 782 Tijdschriften; titelafkortingen
N 783 (Idem) Titelvoet

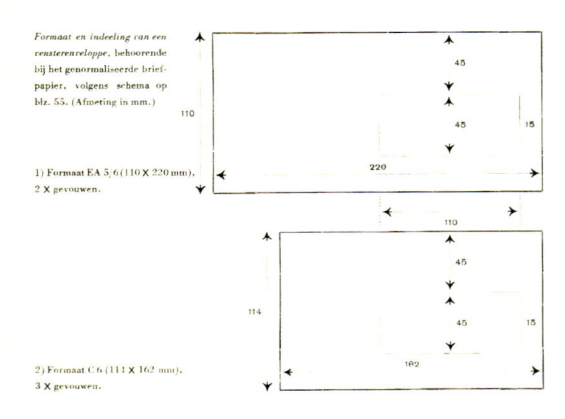

Formaat en indeeling van een vensterenveloppe, behoorende bij het genormaliseerde briefpapier, volgens schema op blz. 55. (Afmeting in mm.)

1) Formaat EA 5/6 (110×220 mm), 2 × gevouwen.

2) Formaat C 6 (114×162 mm), 3 × gevouwen.

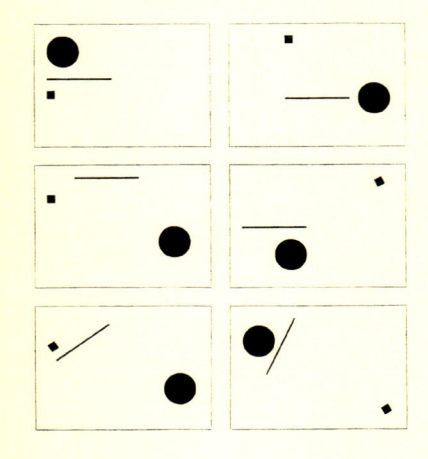

Pages 66–67, 76–77, 78–79, and 80–81 of *Typografische vormgeving* (Dutch edition of *Typografische Gestaltung*) by Jan Tschichold, 1938. N.V. vh. J.F. Duwaer & Zonen, Amsterdam

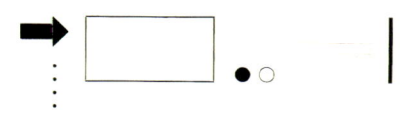

Typografisch materiaal: lijnen, vlakken, stroopen, cirkels, punten, driehoeken, pijlen, rasters e. d.

karakter geven. Niet de absolute dwang der contrasten bepaalt den uitslag, maar hun overtuigende onderlinge spanning.

Onvermijdelijk vooronderstellen deze mogelijkheden het « abstracte » zien ervan, dat bovendien de eigenlijke optische waarde schat en niet enkel de bloote bruikbaarheid. Het kunstwerk ontstaat immers, indien ons dit gelukt, met het dusdanig verwerken van het vanouds bekende materiaal zóó, dat het ons voorkomt geheel nieuw te zijn. Dit vernieuwde zien werd door de concrete schilderkunst voorbereid. Zij bracht ons het gevoel voor de nieuwe vormenwereld. Deze is ook in andere tijden en kultuurgebieden te herkennen, b. v. in de voor-gothische miniaturen of in Japansche houtsneden, waarvan de vormen verwant zijn aan onze inzichten. Het zuiverst belichaamt zich het nieuwe zien in de moderne kunst, die tegelijk grondslag en toppunt van de nieuwe vormgeving is.

De concrete kunst

Niet weinig lezers van dit boek zullen al direct bestrijden, dat er tusschen schilderkunst en typografie van eenige betrekking sprake kan zijn. Zoolang men denkt aan het voorwerpelijk schilderij, is dit ook juist. Zijn de gebieden van optische vormgeving uit den zelfden tijd nimmer zonder eenig verband, zoo zou het toch overdreven zijn te spreken van levendige verhoudingen tusschen de voorwerpelijke schilderkunst en de vroegere typografie. De oudere typografie is veel sterker aan de gevelarchitectuur der Renaissance en de daarvan afgeleide stijlperioden gebonden dan aan de gelijktijdige schilderkunst. Dit houdt nu weer niet in, dat vroeger de zetter poogde, met een gezetten boektitel den indruk van een kerkgevel te wekken; zoo woordelijk zijn de wederkeerige betrekkingen niet op te vatten.

Toch is de innerlijke verwantschap tusschen Renaissancegevels en boektitels uit dien tijd onmiskenbaar.

Heden bestaat eveneens een verband tusschen typografie en moderne architectuur. Toch is de hedendaagsche typografie niet afhankelijk van de architectuur, maar beide zijn zij het van de nieuwe schilderkunst, die het model geweest is voor de vormgeving. De moderne schilderkunst, waaronder hier de onvoorwerpelijke of concrete schilderkunst verstaan wordt, ontstond voor de nieuwe architectuur; deze is zonder de andere ondenkbaar.

Vaak noemt men de onvoorwerpelijke schilderkunst abstract. Toch gaat het hier niet om abstracties, maar om het concrete; want een lijn, een cirkel, een vlak beduiden in deze schilderkunst enkel zich zelf, terwijl zij in de voorwerpelijke schilderkunst aan iets anders ondergeschikt zijn. Het zou daarom eerder passend, de voorwerpelijke schilderkunst abstract te noemen. Ook de aanduiding « absolute schilderkunst » is aanvechtbaar. Met het volste recht heeft Theo van Doesburg en de Groep AC de benaming « concrete schilderkunst » voor deze schilderkunst gebezigd (1930). In 't hierna volgende zullen wij haar dan ook gebruiken.

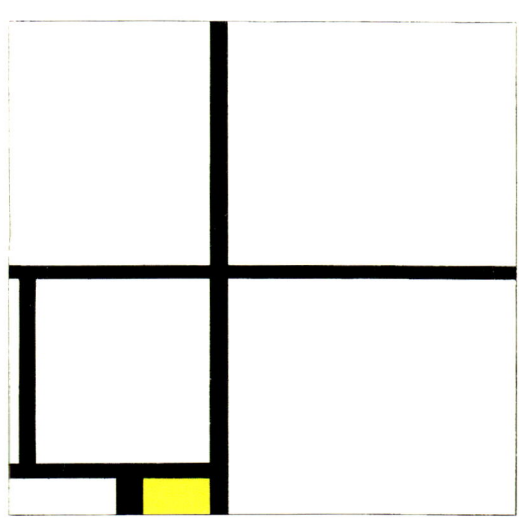

Advertentie (diapositief)

Piet Mondriaan: Compositie, 1930. Verzameling Jan Tschichold

Theo van Doesburg: Dessin arithmétique IV, 1930.

Hetgeen in een voorwerpelijke voorstelling boeit, is tweeledig. Veel menschen zien enkel één deel: het bloote voorwerp. Zij vinden het aangenaam, door een voorstelling herinnerd te worden aan een zonsondergang of een gebraden haas. Daarnaast biedt een goed schilderij nog iets anders, hetgeen de meeste menschen zich maar half, velen zelfs heelemaal niet bewust zijn: de onderlinge verhoudingen van kleuren en vormen, zooals de schilder deze geschikt heeft. Deze zintuigelijke en geestelijke waarden hebben met het voorwerpelijke maar zeer weinig te maken. Voor een goed schilder is het voorwerp betrekkelijk onbelangrijk; dit te schil-

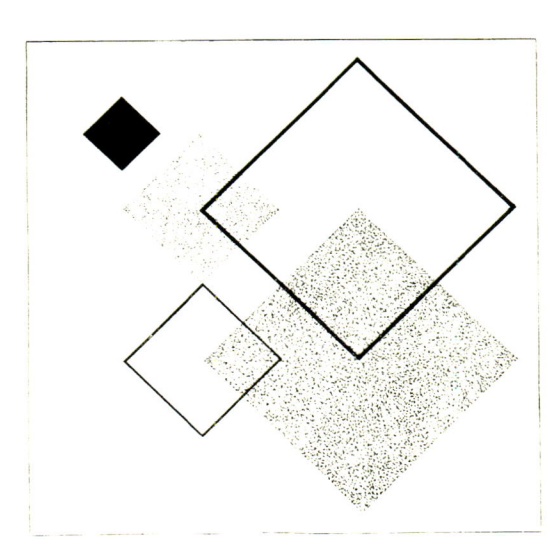

deren is voor hem veeleer aanleiding mooie kleur- en vormverhoudingen te scheppen.

Om de voorwerpen uit de wereld rond ons getrouw, « zooals wij ze zien », af te beelden, daartoe hebben wij den schilder niet meer beslist van noode. De fotograaf kan deze opgave beter en sneller oplossen. Verlangt men bovendien de kleur, dan kan een kleurenfotografie gemaakt worden.

Daarom moet men het afbeelden van voorwerpen overlaten aan den fotograaf. Want sedert de fotografie uitgevonden is, is het de taak van de schilderkunst zich uitsluitend van haar wettelijke middelen, kleuren en vormen op het vlak, te

El Lissitzky: *Proun 93 - Spiral*, Omstreeks 1922.

bedienen. Deze zullen in de concrete kunst niet meer, nabootsend, in dienst staan van naturalistische illusies, maar enkel zich zelf voorstellen. Sedert ongeveer 1910 heeft de nieuwe kunst een langen, belangrijken weg van de naturalistische illusie naar de *concretiseering* afgelegd, dien men kan nagaan in werken over kunstgeschiedenis. Wij spreken hier alleen over den huidigen stand van deze kunst, die eerst rond 1920 van algemeene bekendheid werd en sedert een beduidenden

Nevenstaand: L. Moholy-Nagy: *Constructie* (Emaille), 1922-1923.

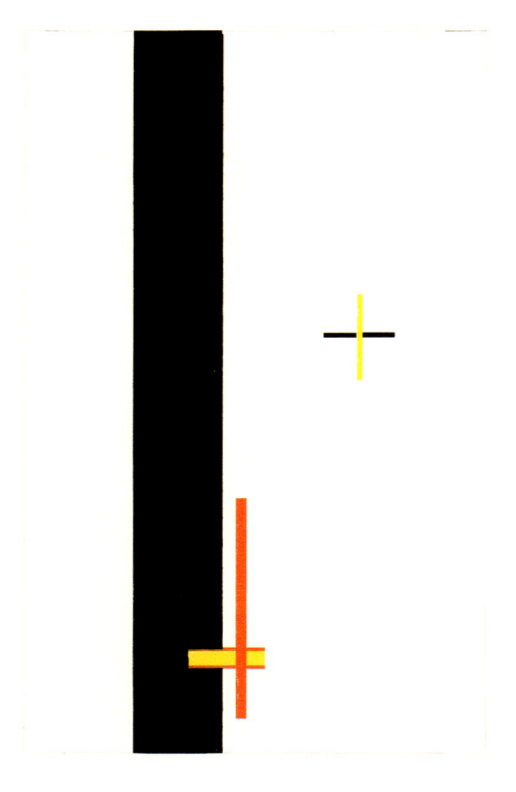

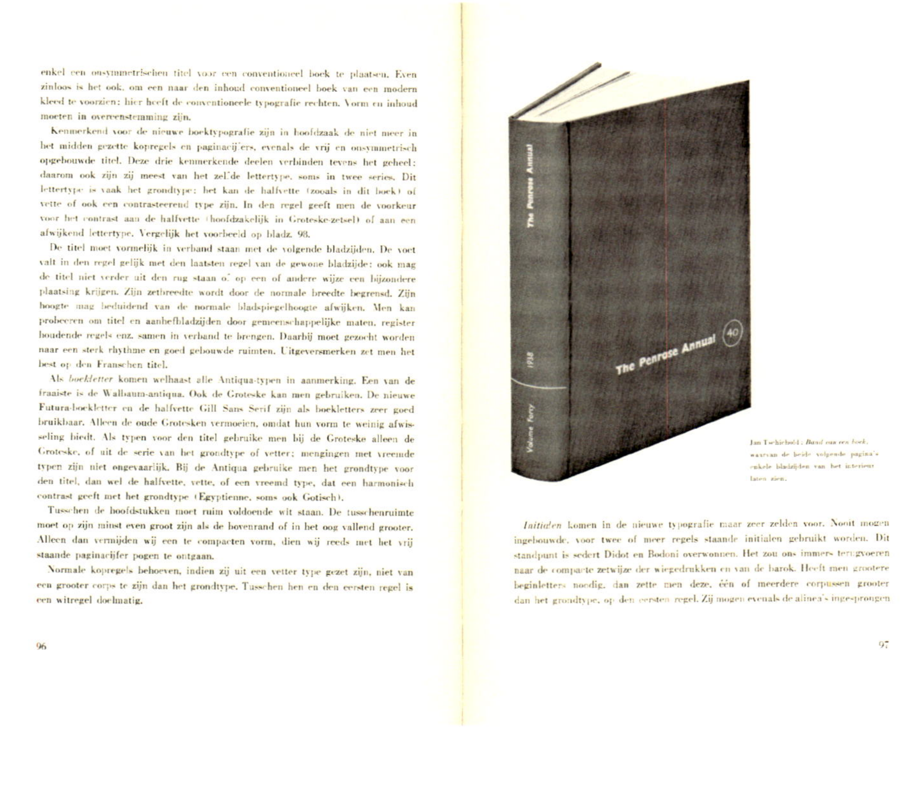

enkel een onsymmetrischen titel voor een conventioneel boek te plaatsen. Even zinloos is het ook, om een naar den inhoud conventioneel boek van een modern kleed te voorzien: hier heeft de conventioneele typografie rechten. Vorm en inhoud moeten in overeenstemming zijn.

Kenmerkend voor de nieuwe boektypografie zijn in hoofdzaak de niet meer in het midden gezette kopregels en paginacijfers, evenals de vrij en onsymmetrisch opgebouwde titel. Deze drie kenmerkende deelen verbinden tevens het geheel; daarom ook zijn zij meest van het zelfde lettertype, soms in twee series. Dit lettertype is vaak het grondtype; het kan de halfvette (zooals in dit boek) of vette of ook een contrasteerend type zijn. In den regel geeft men de voorkeur voor het contrast aan de halfvette (hoofdzakelijk in Groteske-zetsel) of aan een afwijkend lettertype. Vergelijk het voorbeeld op bladz. 98.

De titel moet vormelijk in verband staan met de volgende bladzijden. De voet valt in den regel gelijk met den laatsten regel van de gewone bladzijde; ook mag de titel niet verder uit den rug staan of op een of andere wijze een bijzondere plaatsing krijgen. Zijn zetbreedte wordt door de normale breedte begrensd. Zijn hoogte mag beduidend van de normale bladspiegelhoogte afwijken. Men kan probeeren om titel en aanhefbladzijden door gemeenschappelijke maten, register houdende regels enz. samen in verband te brengen. Daarbij moet gezocht worden naar een sterk rhythme en goed gebouwde ruimten. Uitgeversmerken zet men het best op den Franschen titel.

Als *boekletter* komen welhaast alle Antiqua-typen in aanmerking. Een van de fraaiste is de Walbaum-antiqua. Ook de Groteske kan men gebruiken. De nieuwe Futura-boekletter en de halfvette Gill Sans Serif zijn als boekletters zeer goed bruikbaar. Alleen de oude Grotesken vermoeien, omdat hun vorm te weinig afwisseling biedt. Als typen voor den titel gebruike men bij de Groteske alleen de Groteske, of uit de serie van het grondtype of vetter; mengingen met vreemde typen zijn niet ongevaarlijk. Bij de Antiqua gebruike men het grondtype voor den titel, dan wel de halfvette, vette, of een vreemd type, dat een harmonisch contrast geeft met het grondtype (Egyptienne, soms ook Gotisch).

Tusschen de hoofdstukken moet ruim voldoende wit staan. De tusschenruimte moet op zijn minst even groot zijn als de bovenrand of in het oog vallend grooter. Alleen dan vermijden wij een compacten vorm, dien wij reeds met het vrij staande paginacijfer pogen te ontgaan.

Normale kopregels behoeven, indien zij uit een vetter type gezet zijn, niet van een grooter corps te zijn dan het grondtype. Tusschen hen en den eersten regel is een witregel doelmatig.

Jan Tschichold: *Band van een boek*, waarvan de beide volgende pagina's enkele bladzijden van het achterinhoud laten zien.

Initialen komen in de nieuwe typografie maar zeer zelden voor. Nooit mogen ingebouwde, voor twee of meer regels staande initialen gebruikt worden. Dit standpunt is sedert Didot en Bodoni overwonnen. Het zou ons immers terugvoeren naar de compacte zetwijze der wiegedrukken en van de barok. Heeft men grootere beginletters noodig, dan zette men deze, één of meerdere corpussen grooter dan het grondtype, op den eersten regel. Zij mogen evenals de alinea's ingesprongen

Pages 82–83, 96–97, 98–99, and two pages of advertisements from *Typografische vormgeving* (Dutch edition of *Typografische Gestaltung*) by Jan Tschichold, 1938. N.V. vh. J.F. Duwaer & Zonen, Amsterdam

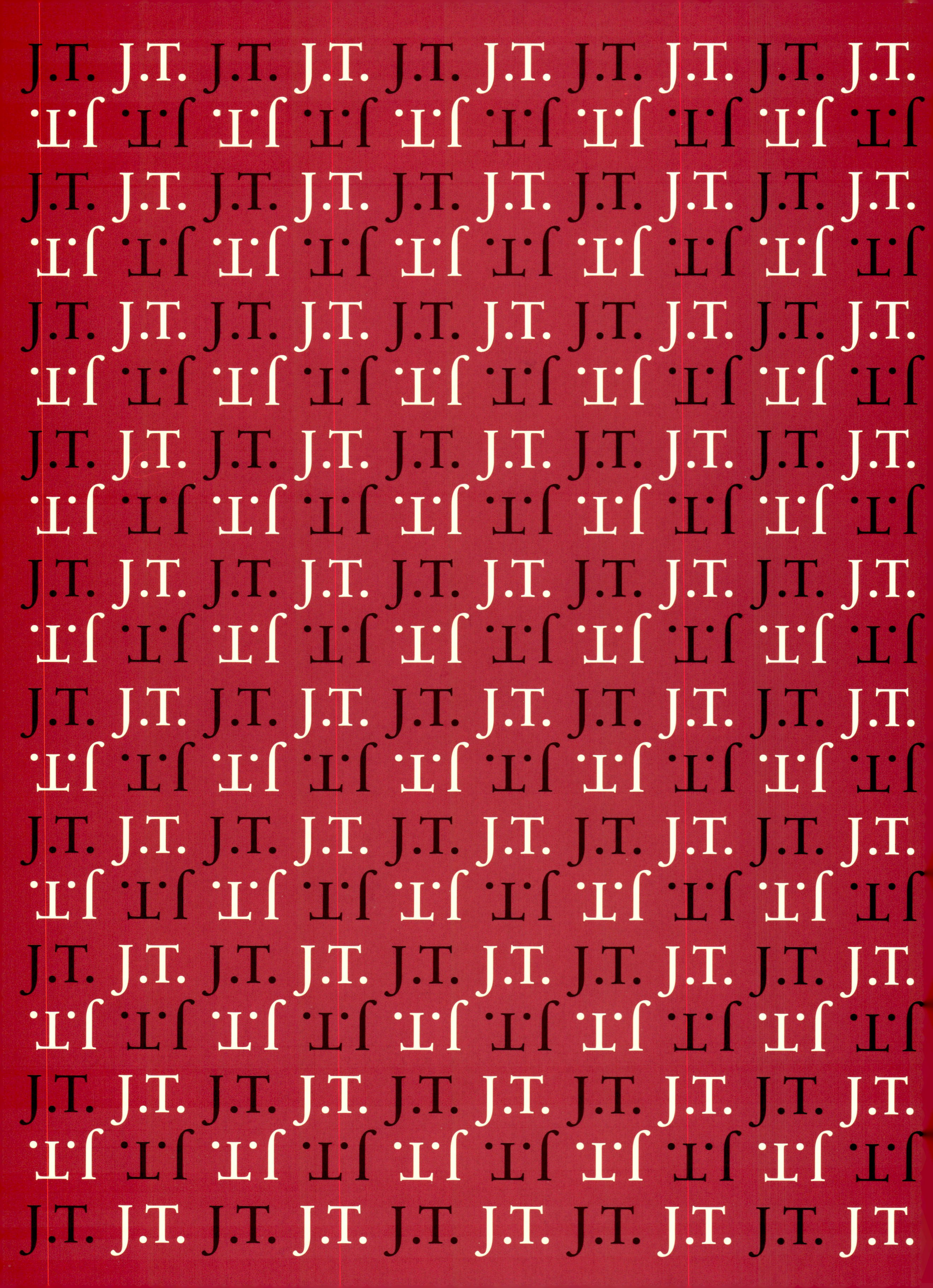

Tschichold and Poster Design

Martijn F. Le Coultre

An outing with El Lissitzky, Sophie Lissitzky-Küppers and their sons, ca. 1931

Official portrait of Jan Tschichold, ca. 1930 (photo: Eduard Wasow)

J.T.

Christmas with Kurt Schwitters,
his wife and son, ca. 1931

Outing with Werner Graeff and
Hans Richter, ca. 1930

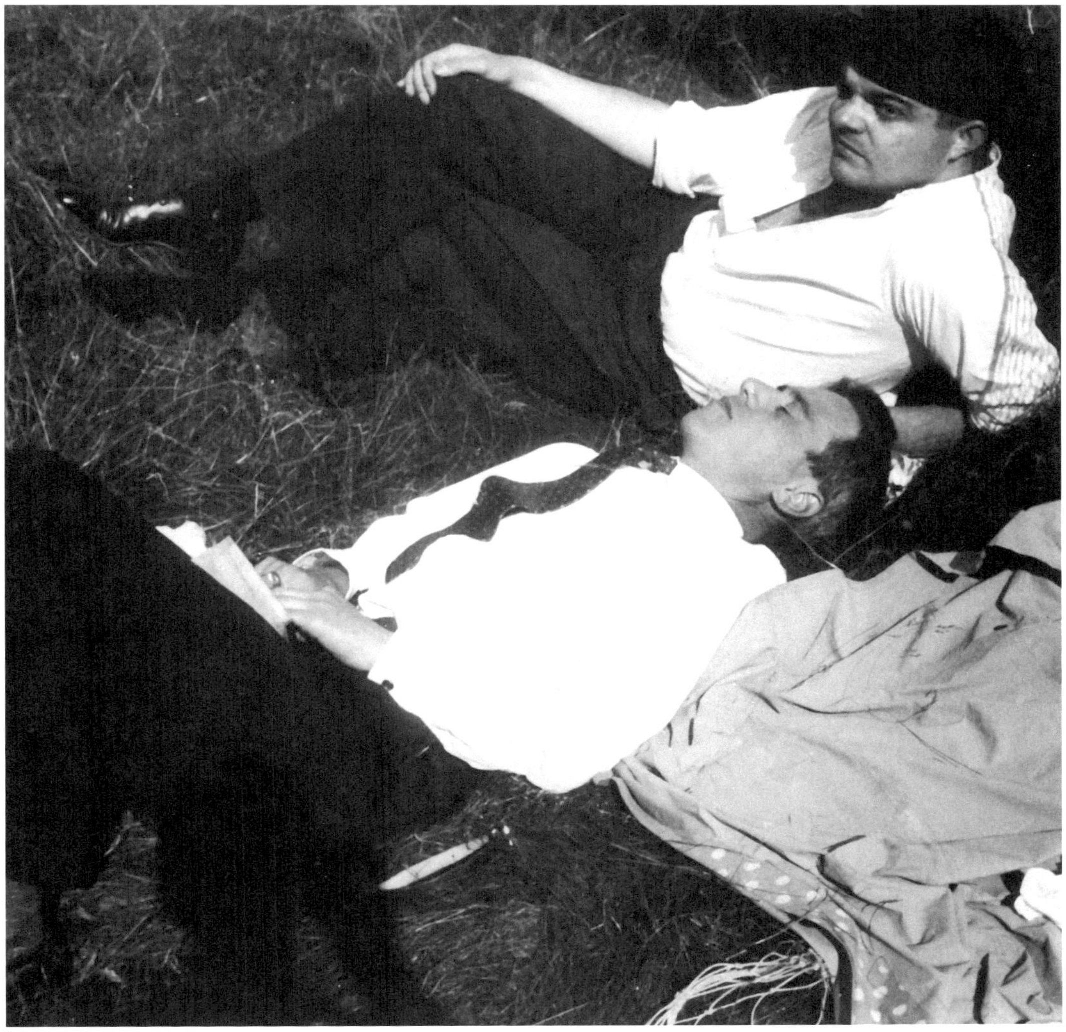

Tschichold and Poster Design

Posters by Jan Tschichold:
List of Collections and
Corresponding Abbreviations
Basler Plakatsammlung, Basel (BPS)
Bayerisches Hauptstaatsarchiv, Munich (BHSA)
Deutsches Plakatmuseum, Essen (DPM)
Deutsche Städte Medien GmbH, Munich (DSM)
Die Neue Sammlung, Munich (DNS)
Filmmuseum, Amsterdam (FMA)
Filmmuseum, Berlin (FMB)
Gemeentemuseum, The Hague (HGM)
Kunstbibliothek, Staatliche Museen zu Berlin – Preußischer Kulturbesitz, Berlin (KB)
Library of Congress, Washington DC (LoC)
Merrill C. Berman, Scarsdale, NY (MB)
Museum für Gestaltung, Zurich (MGZ)
Museum für Kunst und Gewerbe, Hamburg (MKG)
Museum of Modern Art, New York (MoMA)
Münchner Stadtmuseum, Munich (MSM)
Private collections (PC)
Ruki Matsumoto (RM)
Stedelijk Museum, Amsterdam (SMA)
Suntory Museum, Osaka (SMO)
Tama Art University Museum, Japan (TA)
Tschichold Estate, Switzerland and Leipzig (TE)

List of poster designers and
corresponding abbreviations
Carl Otto Müller (COM)
Hilde Horn (HH)
Jan Tschichold (JT)
Sametzki (S)
NS = not signed

In the summer of 1944, while the war against the fascist powers was at its height in Europe, an exhibition called "Art in Progress" was held at the Museum of Modern Art in New York, marking the institution's 15th anniversary. The catalog stated: "During the twenties, Rodchenko and the Russian suprematists introduced geometrical patterns in posters; these graphic and typographical potentialities were further explored by another Russian, El Lissitzky, by van Doesburg and the Dutch De Stijl group, of whom Mondrian was the foremost painter, and somewhat later by Jan Tschichold in Munich, Herbert Bayer and others in and around the Bauhaus, and Ladislav Sutnar in Prague." Sutnar had helped in assembling the exhibition's modern poster section. The exhibition included work by those who had gained a following in the world of graphic design. The United States proved a temporary refuge for some of them: Jean Carlu returned to France after the war to resume his graphic design career. Sutnar, from Czechoslovakia, who had been in New York in connection with the 1939 World's Fair when the war began, brought over his family from Europe after the war, to settle permanently in his new homeland.

Others, such as the Austrian-born Herbert Bayer and the Hungarian László Moholy-Nagy, had earlier fled the rising tide of Nazism and begun new lives in the United States. In Chicago, Moholy-Nagy continued the concept of the Bauhaus that had been closed on the orders of the Nazis in 1933, and became director of the New Bauhaus, from which the Institute of Design was to evolve. Bayer organized a large Bauhaus exhibition at the Museum of Modern Art in 1938, the year he emigrated from Berlin to the United States.

Not far from the Museum of Modern Art, at the A-D Gallery, 130 West 46th Street, as early as 1942 a number of designers had already organized a collective exhibition, presenting themselves as the "advance guard of advertising artists."[1] Apart from Bayer, Carlu, Moholy-Nagy, and Sutnar, the group showing its works included the Hungarian Gyorgy Kepes (1906–2001), Herbert Matter from Switzerland (1907–1984), and the Americans Paul Rand, Lester Beall (1903–1969), and Edward McKnight Kauffer (1890–1954). The Montana-born expatriate Kauffer had recently returned to the United States after living and working for twenty-five years in London.

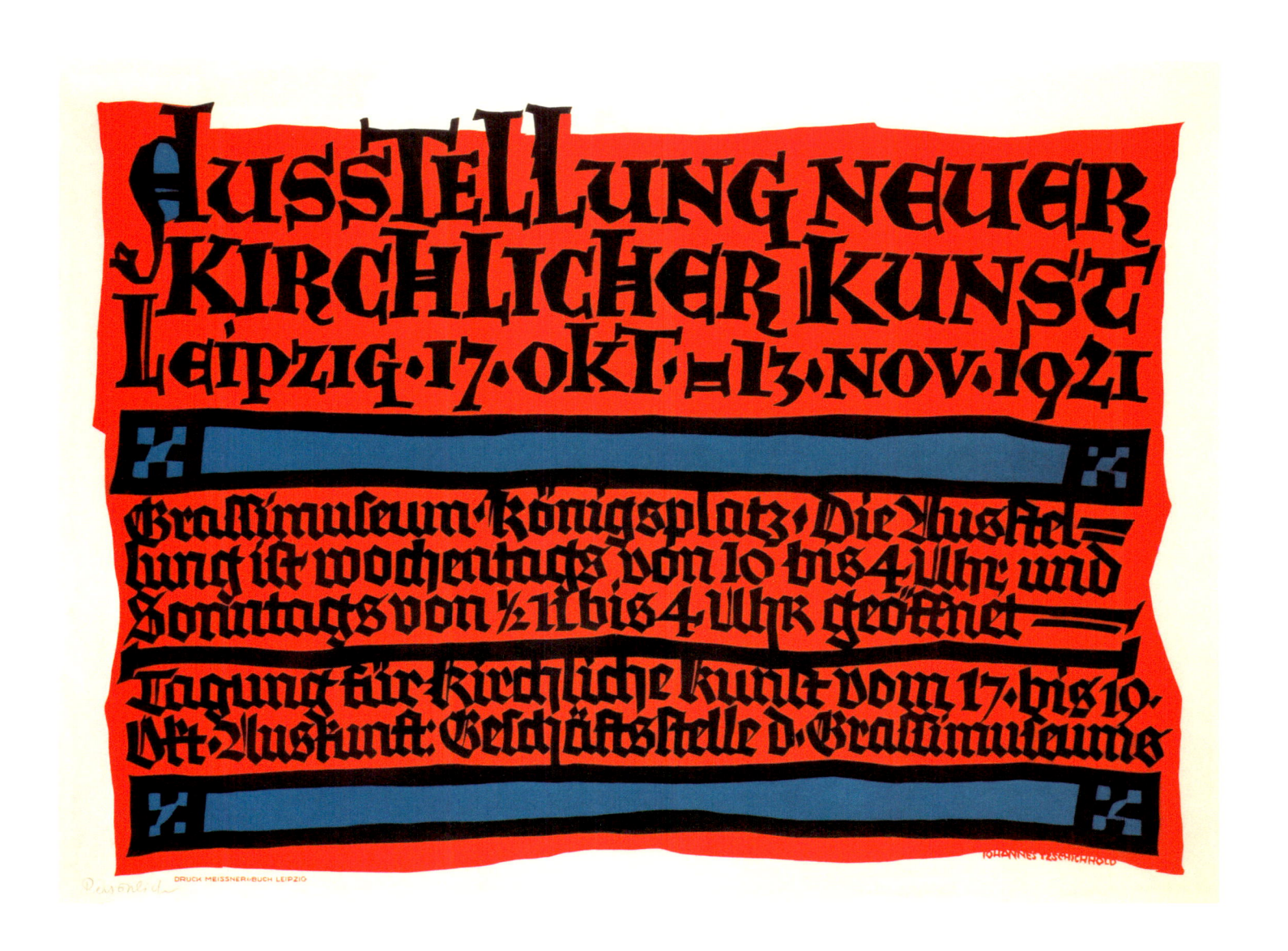

"Exhibition of New Religious Art," poster, 1921, lithograph, "Johannes Tzschichhold," 44.5 x 59.5 cm. Printed by Meissner & Buch, Leipzig

Advertising flyer for Leipzig Spring Fair, 1922, letterpress, NS, 31.5 x 24.5 cm, TE

"Exhibition of Graphic Works," poster for the Leipzig Academy for Graphic Arts and Book Production, 1919, linocut with collotype, 1 sheet, NS, 68 x 48.5 cm, MGZ

Ausstellung Graphischer Arbeiten

des Verbands d. Studierenden
a. d. Akademie für graph. Künste
u. Buchgewerbe / Leipzig
Wächterstraße 11

EINTRITT FREI · GEÖFFNET:
Alltags: 10–12^{30}, 2–3^{30}
Feiertags: 10–12^{30}

Window card for the Warsaw publisher Philobiblon, 1924, letterpress (uncut), "Jan Czychold," 37.7 x 37 cm, PC. There is also a good reprint of this poster, although it uses a poorer quality paper. A version with pencil annotations by Jan Tschichold on the copy is in the TE.

In the catalog for the exhibition "New Poster," organized in April 1937 by Alexey Brodovitch at the Franklin Institute in Philadelphia, the art critic Christian Brinton (1870–1942) stated: "We of today, poised upon the threshold of a new culture cycle, are creatures of wheels, wings, ether waves. Children of the Second Machine Age, we typify the characteristics of this particular era.... Modern man, the neo-Archimedian, is eye-minded.... Posters appeal ideally to the short-interval optic of the present age. With its sense of suggested motion, stimulating color impact, psychology of immediacy, avidity of the actual, modern poster epitomizes the essential spirit of this dynamic, high frequency existence of ours.... The successful creation and control of an authentically 'modern' style, a style based upon high-quality mass production by machine and constructively formulated principles of functional design, was convincingly initiated at the Paris Exposition des Arts Décoratifs of 1925." The work of the French designer A. M. Cassandre, working at that time in America, was specifically highlighted: "His is the true projectional imagination. Sheer poster magic." For decades Cassandre's 1937 poster for Ford was displayed at the Museum of Modern Art.

The Russian-born Alexey Brodovitch had come to America from France in 1930 and had swiftly risen to the post of art director of the trendsetting fashion magazine *Harper's Bazaar*. There he welcomed talent arriving from Europe, including Herbert Matter in 1935, and also gave commissions to Cassandre during the latter's stay in the United States. As a refugee from rising Nazism, Tschichold had moved from his German fatherland to Switzerland in 1933, but there is nothing to indicate he considered going to North America at that time (or later on, for that matter), as so many others did. Because of the war, it was only at the end of 1945 that Tschichold heard from his friend Sutnar that the 1944 exhibition had taken place at the Museum of Modern Art, but by then Tschichold had already turned away from modern design.

Much about what Tschichold accomplished emerges from the writings of his friends Ruari McLean and Werner Klemke (1917–94). However, his contributions to graphic design are largely illuminated only by anecdotes. One reason for this is that Tschichold later distanced himself from that period of his life when he had placed so much effort into spreading his ideas about New Typography. In those formative years he had invested most of his creative energy into propagating ideas which, in the political and economic atmosphere of that time, were considered utopian. The years between 1927 and 1933, in which Tschichold had firsthand experience with the stifling rise of Nazism in Munich, must have been a traumatic experience for him, about which he would have rather not been reminded. The new art that he and others associated with progressive ideas was made increasingly impossible by the Nazis, who soon declared it to be *entartet* (degenerate). Anyone probing deeper into Tschichold's personality will see a single-minded man who must have suffered from seeing his efforts at renewing the field of graphic design being frustrated, even undone. In many respects, Tschichold was the right man with the right ideas, but in the wrong place and at the wrong time. He was a great typographer and book designer, and it is in these fields that most has been written about him. His revamping of the Penguin pocket books between 1947 and 1949 is especially well known. With this text I hope to shed light on the lesser-known aspects of Tschichold's work, and his poster designs will serve as my leitmotif. Although an effort was made to recover all of his posters and related artwork, in the course of those turbulent times, some things were inevitably lost. Moreover, Tschichold did not preserve the occasional printed pieces he considered to be less successful or devoid of artistic value.

Tschichold continued to live in Leipzig from 1919 to 1925. In late 1925 he moved to Berlin where on March 31, 1926 he married Maria Mathilda Edith ('Edith') Kramer. Like he himself, his wife was a native of Leipzig; she was three years his junior and had trained as a journalist. In the summer of 1926 the young couple moved to Hofmarckstraße 39 in Planegg, near Munich, because Jan had obtained a temporary appointment as a teacher at the Tagesfachschule für die graphischen Berufe (Vocational School for Graphic Arts). Roughly half a year later he was installed as an instructor at the Meisterschule für Deutschlands Buchdrucker (Master School for Germany's Printers), opened on February 1, 1927 at Pranckhstraße in Munich.[2] Their first-born child, born on June 10, 1927, died after only six months. On March 1, 1928 the pair moved into rooms at Schwanthalerstraße 77/4 in Munich. They relocated once more in the city, on December 1, to a flat at Voitstraße 8/1, part of a recently built apartment complex called the Borstei. On January 4, 1929 their son Peter was born. Peter would eventually marry Liselotte Christine Friederike Link on April 6, 1962 in Basel, and the couple would subsequently present the Tschicholds with two grandchildren.

Lasar Galpern School of Dance, poster, 1925–1926, proof, NS, printer: Bär & Hermann, Leipzig, TE

Lasar Galpern School of Dance, poster, 1925–1926, proof on gray paper, NS, 51 x 33.8 cm, printer: Bär & Hermann, Leipzig, TE

Lasar Galpern School of Dance, postcard, 1925–1926, NS, 10.4 x 14.7 cm, TE

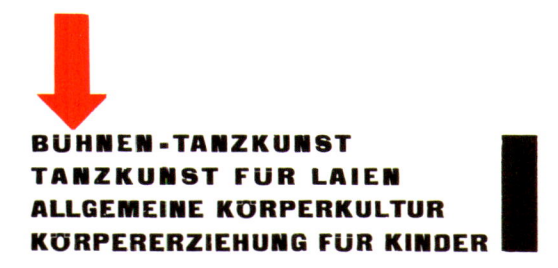

SCHULE FÜR TANZKULTUR

CHOREOGRAPHISCHE LEITUNG:
LASAR GALPERN

↓

BÜHNEN-TANZKUNST
TANZKUNST FÜR LAIEN
ALLGEMEINE KÖRPERKULTUR
KÖRPERERZIEHUNG FÜR KINDER

AUSKUNFT, ANMELDUNG: TÄGLICH 5–8 UHR
UFERSTRASSE 16, PART. RECHTS, AM ZOO

DRUCK VON BÄR & HERMANN IN LEIPZIG

SCHULE FÜR TANZKULTUR
LASAR GALPERN

BÜHNEN-TANZKUNST
TANZKUNST FÜR LAIEN
ALLGEMEINE KÖRPERKULTUR
KÖRPERERZIEHUNG FÜR KINDER

AUSKUNFT U. ANMELDUNG:
TÄGLICH VON 17 BIS 20 UHR
UFERSTR. 16 ● TELEF. 33333

DRUCK VON BÄR & HERMANN IN LEIPZIG

SCHULE FÜR
TANZKULTUR
LASAR GALPERN

BÜHNEN-TANZKUNST
TANZKUNST FÜR LAIEN
ALLGEMEINE KÖRPERKULTUR
KÖRPERERZIEHUNG F. KINDER

AUSKUNFT U. ANMELDUNG
TÄGLICH VON 17 BIS 20 UHR
UFERSTRASSE 16 · TEL. 11104

SCHULE FÜR TANZKULTUR
LASAR GALPERN

BÜHNEN-TANZKUNST
TANZKUNST FÜR LAIEN
ALLGEMEINE KÖRPERKULTUR
KÖRPERERZIEHUNG FÜR KINDER

DRUCK VON BÄR & HERMANN IN LEIPZIG

AUSKUNFT U. ANMELDUNG
TÄGLICH VON 17 BIS 20 UHR
UFERSTR. 16 · TELEFON 111 04

Lasar Galpern School of Dance, poster, 1925–1926, letterpress, NS, 44.4 x 29.5 cm, printer: Bär & Hermann, Leipzig, TE

THE WEIMAR REPUBLIC   Tschichold's life and work cannot be properly understood without seeing it in the context of events surrounding him, events which he observed and in which he participated. By the end of 1918, the Germans had lost the Great War, their empire had collapsed, and Kaiser Wilhelm II (1859–1941) had fled ingloriously to the neutral Netherlands, leaving behind a desperate nation. Inspired by the Russian Revolution of 1917, the communist Spartacists, under the leadership of Rosa Luxemburg (1870/71–1919) and Karl Liebknecht (1871–1919), tried to seize power in Berlin. With the government casting a blind eye, both were murdered by a right-wing paramilitary squad on January 15, 1919. Despite massive political unrest, the democratically elected government remained in control, and the period known as the Weimar Republic began.

In 1919 the Treaty of Versailles was imposed on Germany, forcing the country to pay massive reparations. The Ruhr, the northwest German industrial heartland, remained occupied by French troops for years. Runaway inflation forced further hardships on the population. In the years 1922 and 1923 the prices of the basic necessities of life rose to millions and then billions of marks, and the savings of many citizens were wiped out. The reintroduction of the gold mark at the end of 1923 heralded a cautious recovery that lasted until the international stock market collapse of 1929. The 1929 Depression produced massive unemployment and further political polarization and instability. One result of the manifold political and economic crises was the rise of the National Socialist German Workers Party (NSDAP) under the leadership of Adolf Hitler (1889–1945). Having slowly gathered numbers and momentum during the 1920s, the NSDAP experienced a breakthrough after the turn of the decade. In the presidential elections of 1932, a second round took place between three candidates: the president-in-office and World War I hero Paul von Hindenburg (1847–1934), Hitler, and Ernst Thälmann (1886–1944), the leader of the German Communist Party (KPD). Supported by the democratic parties who hoped to ward off Hitler, Hindenburg won the elections, although his differences with the NSDAP were minimal. In January 1933 Hindenburg appointed Hitler as Chancellor of the German Reich. On March 24, Hitler received far-reaching powers when the controversial Enabling Act was came into force, and the Weimar Republic was abolished.

EARLY GERMAN POSTER DESIGN Tschichold felt an affinity toward what was called the *Sachplakat* (object poster), developed by Lucian Bernhard (1883–1972). This approach can be seen as a forerunner of the photographic poster promoted by Tschichold. Indeed, Tschichold later used Bernhard's designs for Stiller (shoes) and Priester (matches) in his lectures. A *Sachplakat* limits itself to depicting the actual subject of the poster, and accompanies the illustration with only the most essential text.

From about 1910, two schools of poster design existed in Germany: the Berlin school, with the *Sachplakat* of Bernhard, and the Munich school, with the decorative posters of Ludwig Hohlwein (1874–1949). When Bernhard immigrated to America in 1923, Germany lost one of its important champions of the modern poster. Hohlwein, however, would continue to work in Munich as a poster designer for the entire first half of the 20th century and in the 1930s produced a series of posters for the Nazi movement. In addition to Hohlwein there was a group of poster designers who had come together as *die Sechs* (the Six), which later grew into the Neue Vereinigung Münchner Plakatkünstler (New Association of Munich Poster Painters). Members included Franz Paul Glass (1886–1967), Emil Preetorius (1883–1973), and Valentin Zietara (1883–1935). In 1932 Preetorius was appointed "scenic manager of the Bayreuth Festival," and taught at the Akademie der Künste (Academy of Arts) and at the Staatsschule für angewandte Kunst (State School for Applied Arts) in Munich. Together with Paul Renner he founded the Schule für Illustration und Buchgewerbe (School for Illustration and Book Design) in Munich in 1909.

For awarding official commissions, Germany (and other European countries) used poster design competitions with independent juries. Through advertisements in the press and professional magazines, artists were called upon to submit designs. The competitions took place anonymously, with the jury selecting winners who received sums of money as prizes. Generally, the first prize also included the actual printing of the work, although the jury often required the designer to make revisions. Some businesses also used design competitions to find new advertising talent. Others simply gave new artists a chance to prove themselves. The concept of a consistent house style, through which a single designer would define the public image of a business, was seldom known in those years. Peter Behrens (1868–1940), who for years was not only the architect for the Allgemeine Elektrizitätsgesellschaft (AEG, General Electricity Company) but also dealt with their posters, packaging, and other printed matter, was a rare exception.

BÜCHER AUS DEM INSEL-VERLAG

Poster for Insel-Verlag publishing house, ca. 1926, lithograph, "IT", 77.5 x 53.5 cm, TE

DIE BÜCHER DES
INSEL-VERLAGS

gehen nicht aus billiger Massenfabrikation hervor. Sie erstreben in Papier, Druck und Einband höchste Leistung. Sie wollen nicht blenden, sondern dauern.

Insel-Bücherei ⟨der Band 1 M⟩ · Vier Mark-Bücher · Bibliothek der Romane ⟨der Band 5 M⟩ · Briefbücher und Memoiren · Illustrierte und Kunstbücher · Goethe-Bücher · Deutsche Klassiker auf Dünndruckpapier · Gesamtausgaben von Balzac, Dickens, Dostojewski, Shakespeare, Tolstoi · Werke zeitgenössischer Dichter

VORRÄTIG IN DEN GUTEN BUCHHANDLUNGEN

Poster for Insel-Verlag publishing house, ca. 1926, lithograph, NS, 89.5 x 59.5 cm, PC. The logo was designed by Peter Behrens.

Modern posters that fulfilled Tschichold's later criteria did not exist in Germany. The situation in other countries was similar, although there were some experiments taking place. One early example was the 1915 poster for the Batavier Line, a steamship connection between Rotterdam and London, designed by the Dutch artist Bart van der Leck (1876–1958), one of the first members of De Stijl. There were also efforts in this direction by Bauhaus artists such as Moholy-Nagy, but these experiments were chiefly limited to occasional pieces produced within the Bauhaus itself. Both the Bauhaus and De Stijl lacked professionally trained typographers, and at the Bauhaus, only Bayer had acquired any such knowledge. Posters for exhibitions and lectures related to the Bauhaus or the Werkbund were close to being autonomous artworks, because the needs of clients or the limitations of mass printing did not need to be considered. The editions were usually small, and one could experiment at will, especially if students were available to help realize the design. In this way, the design process became part of the learning experience. The poster for the 1923 Bauhaus exhibition, designed by Bauhaus student Joost Schmidt (1893–1943) under the influence of Schlemmer, is a fine example.

Commercial posters intended to entice the public were rarely made by those of the avant-garde. Cassandre was one of the few who concentrated exclusively on the design of commercial posters and other commercial printing. There was also a great difference between designing posters and smaller presswork. Designers such as Piet Zwart and Paul Schuitema in the Netherlands skillfully used photography in advertisements and catalogs, but in their later photographic posters they were less successful in producing designs that could be clearly grasped from a distance. These posters often had a cluttered impression and seem to be heavily influenced by Tschichold and Russian designers such as Gustav Klutsis and the Stenberg brothers (Vladimir, 1899–1982, and Georgii, 1900–1933), with whom Zwart and Schuitema were acquainted. In their posters the Russians used photographs both as illustrations and points of focus through an ingenious application of montage. John Heartfield also skillfully used photographs and photomontage, but in his work the photographs never formed a stylistic unit with the text. For him, photography was chiefly a means of reaching the often illiterate masses through the eloquence of images.

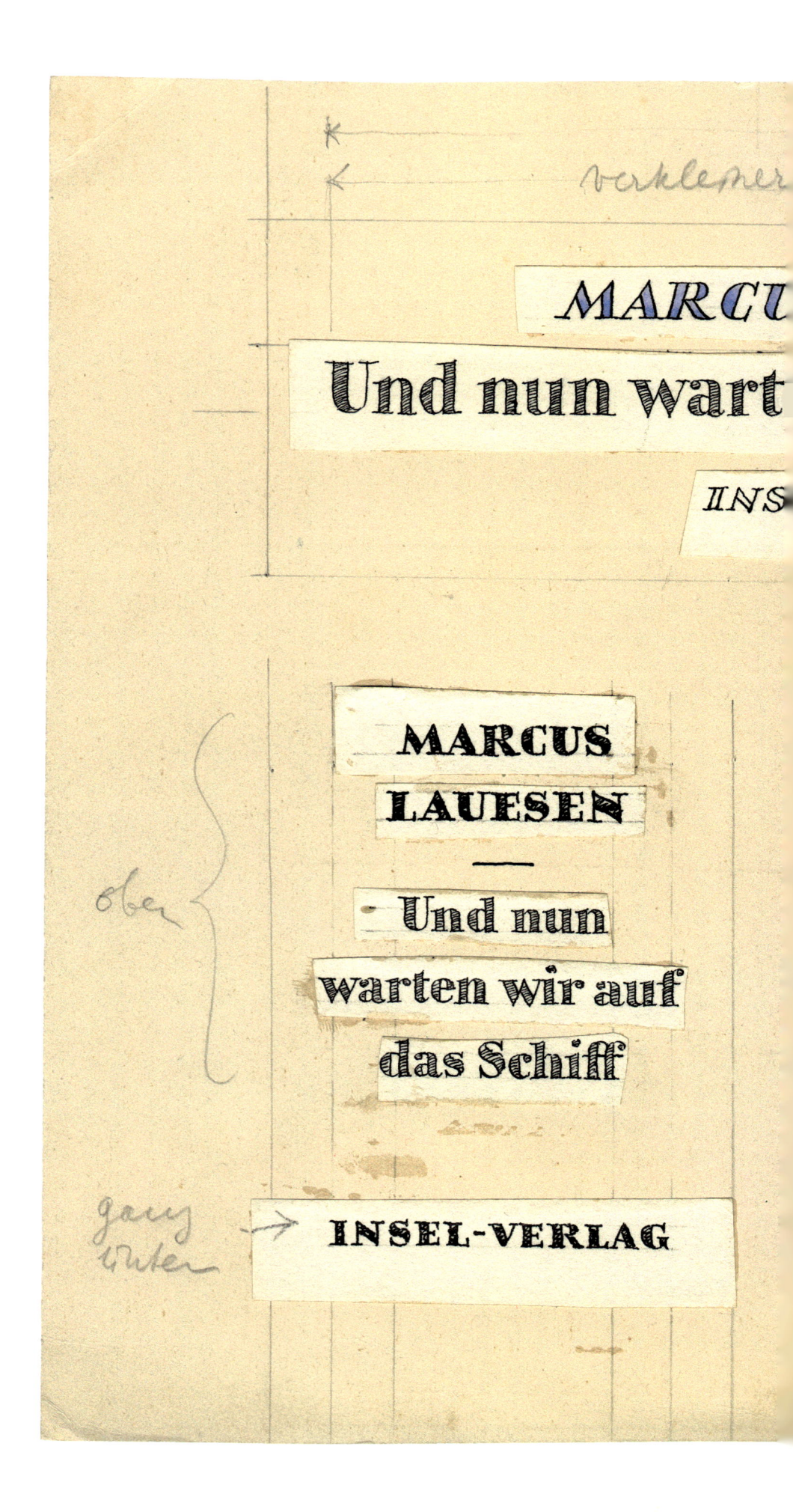

Marcus Lauesen, *Und nun warten wir auf das Schiff* (Waiting for the Ship) ca. 1926, cover design by Jan Tschichold. Insel-Verlag, Leipzig

LAUESEN

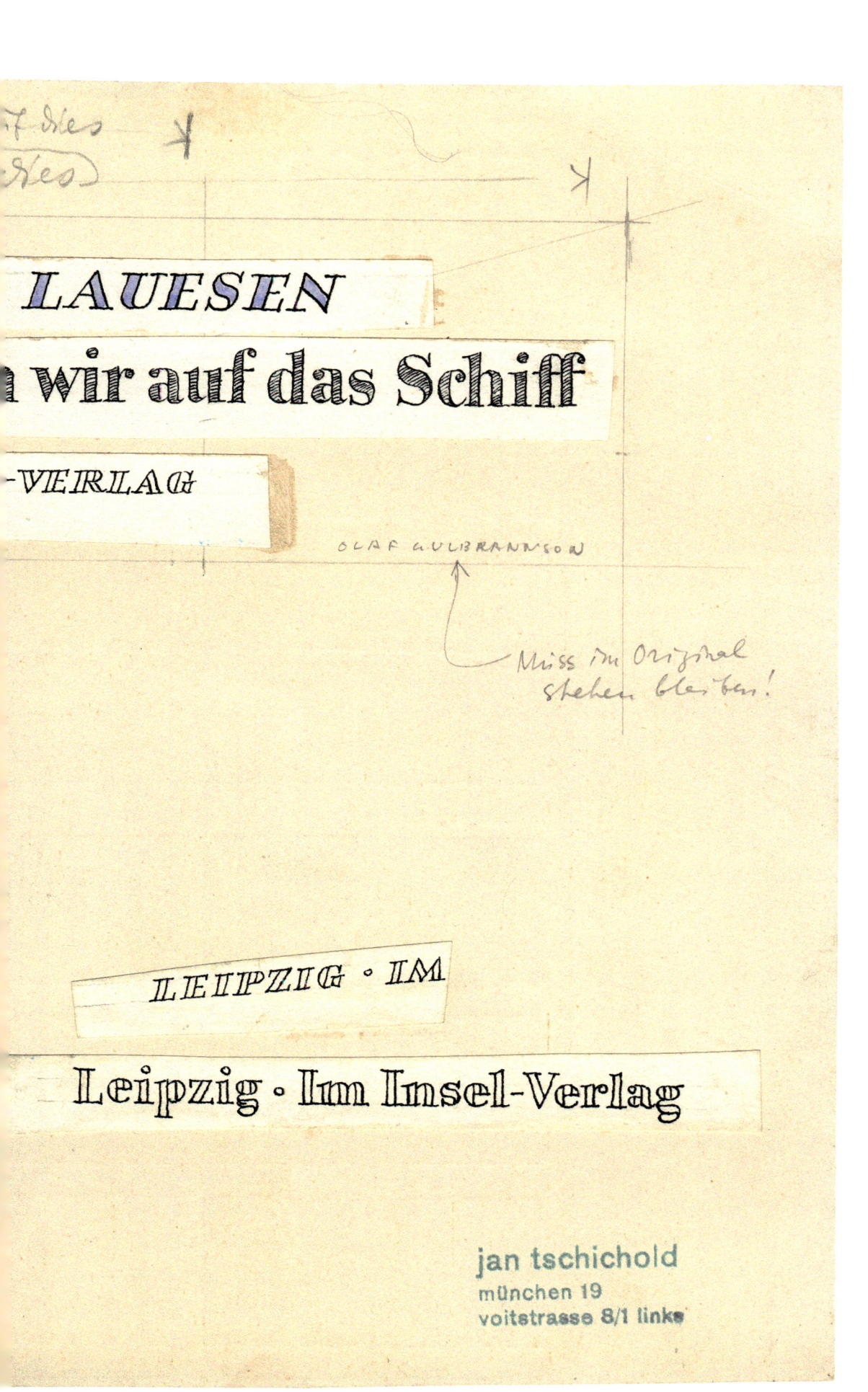

wir auf das Schiff

-VERLAG

OLAF GULBRANNSON

Muss im Original stehen bleiben!

LEIPZIG · IM

Leipzig · Im Insel-Verlag

jan tschichold
münchen 19
voitstrasse 8/1 links

"Good cheap books from Insel-Verlag," window poster, ca. 1926, lithograph, "IT", 42.3 x 57.5 cm, TE. The logo was designed by Peter Behrens.

"Good cheap books from Insel-Verlag," window poster, ca. 1926, NS, 41.5 x 57 cm, TE

Insel Almanac 1929, cover by Jan Tschichold, 1928, 18.1 x 12.1 cm. Insel-Verlag, Leipzig

Paul Renner, the designer of the typeface Futura, was already in touch with Tschichold in 1926 when they were both accused of being "Bolsheviks" in the journals *Zeitschrift für Deutschlands Buchdrucker* and *Schweizer Graphische Mitteilungen*. Seeing the Russian Revolution as a possibility for a new beginning, Tschichold had openly made his own interest in Russian design clear when he changed his name to Iwan (Ivan) in 1923. However, both he and Renner dismissed the allegations as the nonsense they obviously were.[3] In 1926 Renner was appointed director of the Grafische Berufsschule in Munich, of which the soon to be established Meisterschule für Deutschlands Buchdrucker was to be a part. At that time he asked Tschichold to succeed him at his post in Frankfurt. The Tschicholds were then living in Berlin where he had found little interest in his New Typography, so, attracted by an offer with a steady salary, Tschichold initially accepted the Frankfurt appointment.

"Divorce Statistics in Germany," poster for the *Ehe-Buch* (Marriage Book), 1926, "Tschichold. Planegg bei Munich," 84.3 x 59.2 cm, DIN format A1, PC/TE

STATISTIK DER
EHE SCHEIDUNGEN
IN DEUTSCHLAND:

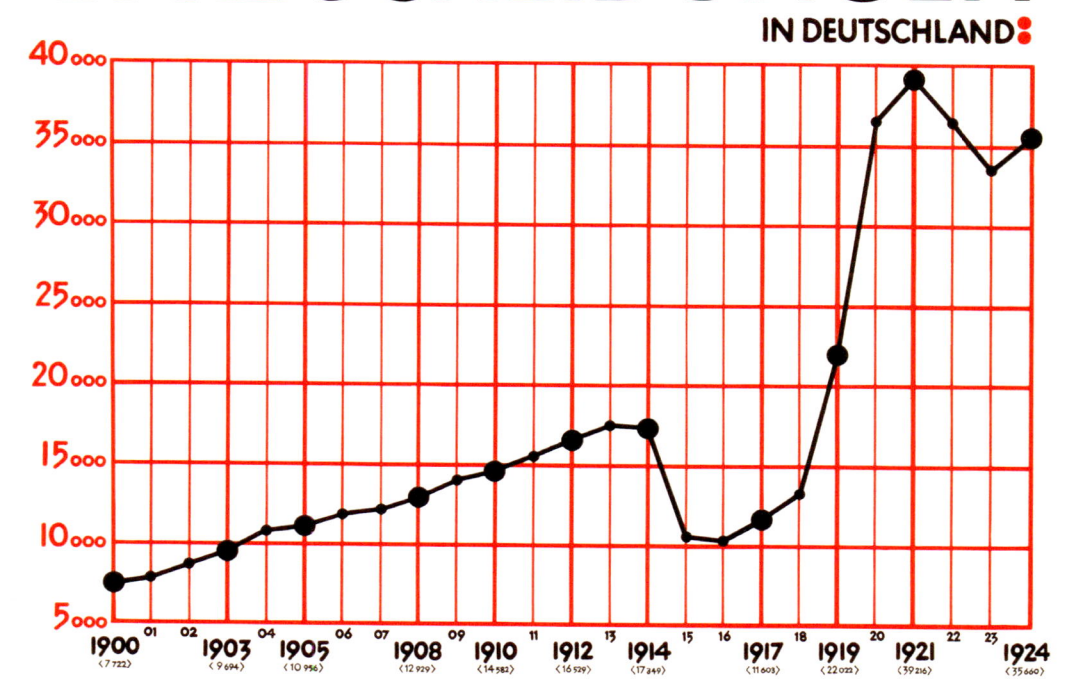

[Graph showing divorce statistics from 1900 to 1924, with values ranging from about 7,722 in 1900 to 35,660 in 1924, peaking around 1921 at 39,216]

1900	1903	1905	1908	1910	1912	1914	1917	1919	1921	1924
(7722)	(9694)	(10956)	(12929)	(14582)	(16529)	(17249)	(11603)	(22022)	(39216)	(35660)

IM EHE-BUCH

ZEIGEN 24 FÜHRENDE GEISTER DEN AUSWEG AUS DIESER KRISE ● JEDER WIRD IN DIESEM WERK AUF DEN TIEFEN SINN SEINER PERSÖNLICHEN FRAGE DIE ANTWORT UND EINEN RAT FINDEN

MITARBEITER: GRAF KEYSERLING (HERAUSGEBER UND MITARBEITER) ● THOMAS MANN ● RICARDA HUCH ● JACOB WASSERMANN ● HAVELOCK ELLIS ● RABINDRANATH TAGORE ● FÜRSTIN LICHNOWSKY ● A.W. NIEUWENHUIS ● LEO FROBENIUS ● ERNST KRETSCHMER ● BARONIN LEONIE UNGERN-STERNBERG ● RICHARD WILHELM ● BEATRICE HINKLE ● HANS VON HATTINGBERG ● MATHILDE VON KEMNITZ ● GRAF THUN-HOHENSTEIN ● MARTA KARLWEIS ● ALPHONS MAEDER ● LEO BAECK ● JOSEPH BERNHART ● PAUL ERNST ● ALFRED ADLER ● C.G. JUNG ● PAUL DAHLKE

NIELS KAMPMANN VERLAG CELLE

PREIS: HALBLEINEN: 12.50 GANZLEINEN: 15.00 HALBLEDER: 20.00

Poster for a lecture by Walter Gropius, 1926, letterpress on steel gray paper, "Tschichold, Pranckhstr. 2," 43.5 x 67.7 cm, printer: Kunst im Druck, Munich, BPS. The lecture in fact took place on July 22, 1926 and not on June 22 as printed.

Munich However, on further reflection, Renner decided that he wanted Tschichold as an instructor at his new Meisterschule, so the Tschicholds instead moved to Munich. For Tschichold this was preferable to Frankfurt: after all, the school in Munich was to become a Fachschule für Buchdrucker (Technical School for Printing), where he would have a chance to realize his ideas for New Typography. That the Bavarian capital was a conservative city did not deter him. "Munich has always been conservative and it will probably remain so. But the charms of Munich do not lie in politics or anywhere else but in the city itself. It is the people, it is the architecture. Politics did not concern us. That was but of secondary importance," Edith explained years later. Tschichold maintained contacts with Russian artists such as El Lissitzky and Klutsis; posters by the latter designer were pure propaganda for Soviet ideas. The German Communist Party also commissioned posters from artists such as Heartfield and Gebs (Max Gebhard, 1906–90), in which the use of photography was central. Anyone who collected and publicized these posters as examples of good, modern design risked incurring suspicions of favoring the political movements that issued them. Yet Tschichold was never a communist. His approach to these posters was entirely professional, and he could be accused of nothing more than being politically naive. Edith recalled: "Despite their being colleagues, there was no close contact with Renner; this was mainly due to the fact that Tschichold also kept in touch with Russian abstract artists." According to her, Renner visited them only a couple of times. Relations with colleagues such as Georg Trump, teacher at the Meisterschule in Munich from 1929 to 1931, and his successor Hermann Virl (1903–1958) were much better. These colleagues were more or less equals facing the same material problems caused by the financial crisis. Renner was the *Oberstudiendirektor* (principal) and as such was well paid, and furthermore he received income from his Futura typeface, which was enormously successful. According to Edith, politics were hardly discussed in the Tschichold household. The conversation at meetings with visiting artists such as Moholy-Nagy, Lissitzky, and even Schwitters revolved primarily around developments in the modern arts.

When Tschichold started in Munich, Renner gave him ample room to put his ideas into practice. In addition to teaching typesetting and "Typografisches Skizzieren" (Typographic Sketching) for one afternoon in the week, he designed all the print material for the school: letterhead, promotional posters, and registration forms, although there was also input from the students, particularly in the execution. It is not surprising that the school attracted commissions from firms and businesses that wanted something different from the work of Hohlwein, Glass, and other like-minded Munich designers. Apparently that is how contacts began with BMW, which at the time was celebrating its success in motorcycle racing, and with Berlin's Phoebus-Gesellschaft (Phoebus Society), which had opened a large cinema in Munich at the end of 1926.

TSCHICHOLD AND POSTER DESIGN

Films at the Phoebus-Palast 1926–1928	Advertisement by	Poster by	Collection
Dagfin (Dec. 23, 1926: opening of the theater)			
Der Student von Prag (Jan. 4, 1927)			
Die Sporck'schen Jäger (Jan. 13, 1927)			
Der Seeräuber (Jan. 18, 1927)			
Liebe (Jan. 27, 1927)			
Die Frau ohne Namen, Part I (Feb. 10, 1927)	JT	JT	
Die Frau ohne Namen, Part II (Feb. 17, 1927)	JT		
Die Sünde am Kinde (Feb. 23, 1927)	JT	JT	
Iwan der Schreckliche (Mar. 1, 1927)	JT	JT	
Das edle Blut (Mar. 10, 1927)	HH	JT	
Kiki (Mar. 22, 1927)		JT	
Prinz Louis Ferdinand (Apr. 4, 1927)	JT	JT	
Laster der Menschheit (Apr. 12, 1927)		JT	
Die Lady ohne Schleier (Apr. 23, 1927)		JT	
Der General (Apr. 28, 1927)		JT	
Nacht der Liebe (May 6, 1927)		JT	
Kabarett (May 12, 1927)	HH		
Die 3 Niemandskinder (May 18, 1927)	HH	JT	
Entfesselte Elemente (May 24, 1927)	HH	JT	
Nju: eine unverstandene Frau (Jun. 4, 1927)	HH	JT	
Man spielt nicht mit der Liebe (Jun. 10, 1927)		JT	
Das Meer (Jun. 17, 1927)		JT	
Der Bettelpoet (Jun. 23, 1927)	JT	JT	
Der Mann mit der Peitsche (Jun. 30, 1927)	HH		
Die Mühle von Sanssouci (Jul. 8, 1927)			
Mittelholzers Afrikaflug (Jul. 14, 1927)	HH	JT	
Danton (Jul. 19, 1927)	HH	S	DSM
Ihr Spielzeug (Jul. 28, 1927)			
Die Lindenwirtin am Rhein (Aug. 2, 1927)		JT	
Ein schwerer Fall (Aug. 9, 1927)	HH	JT	
Primanerliebe (Aug. 16, 1927)			
Piquedame (Aug. 23, 1927)		JT	
Gehetzte Frauen (Aug. 30, 1927)	HH	JT	
Rivalen (Sep. 6, 1927)	HH		
Die Hose (Sep. 14, 1927)	HH	JT	
Die Vorbestraften (Sep. 21, 1927)	HH		
Svengali (Sep. 28, 1927)	HH		
Der Meister von Nürnberg (Oct. 5, 1927)			
Die Kameliendame (Oct. 14, 1927)	HH	JT	
Der Student, Buster Keaton (Oct. 21, 1927)			
Orient-Express (Oct. 28, 1927)	HH	JT	
Casanova (Nov. 4, 1927)		JT	
Der Anwalt des Herzens (Nov. 19, 1927)		JT	
Violantha (Nov. 25, 1927)		JT	
König Harlekin (Dec. 3, 1927)	HH	JT	
Napoleon (Dec. 8, 1927)		JT	
Leichte Kavallerie (Dec. 20, 1927)		COM	RM
Der Gaucho, Douglas Fairbanks (Dec. 25, 1927)		COM	RM
Sonnenaufgang (Dec. 30, 1927)		COM	

182

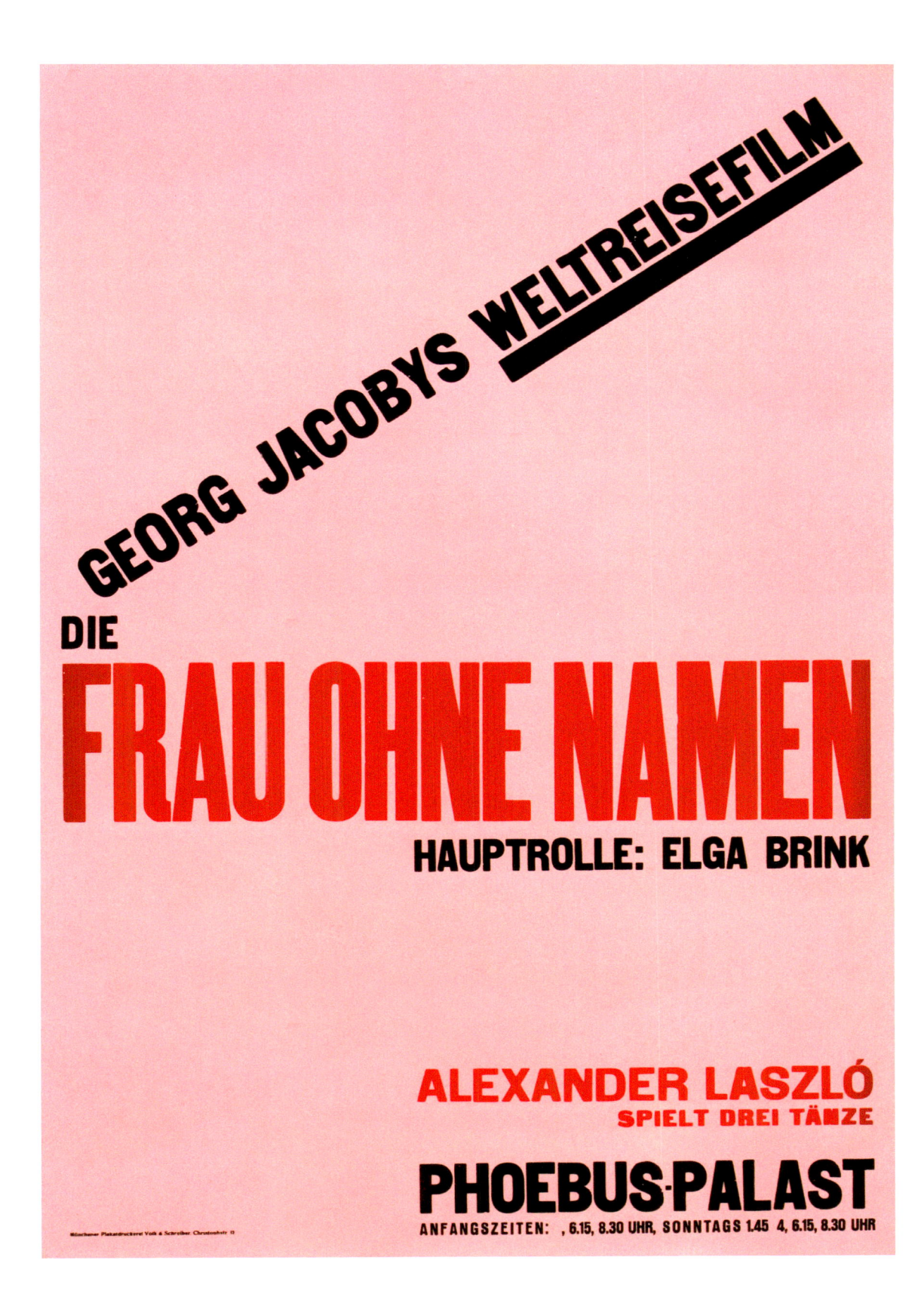

Film poster for *The Woman Without a Name*, 1927, letterpress on pink paper, 2 sheets, in pencil: "Tschichold febr 27," 124.5 × 86.3 cm, printer: Münchener Plakatdruckerei Volk & Schreiber, Munich, PC

Advertisement for *Ivan the Terrible* at the Phoebus-Palast cinema, published in *Münchner Neueste Nachrichten*, 1927

Ivan the Terrible, film poster, 1927, letterpress on pink paper, 2 sheets, "Jan Tschichold Muenchen Planegg," 124.5 x 83.5 cm, printer: Plakatdruckerei Volk & Schreiber, Munich, TE

PHOEBUS PALAST

ANFANGSZEITEN: 4 6:15 8:30
SONNTAGS: 1:45 4 6:15 8:30

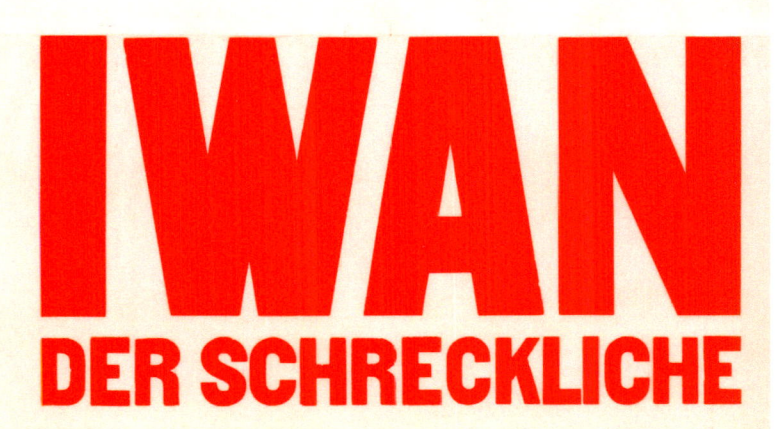

IWAN
DER SCHRECKLICHE

The notes of Johann (Hans) Popp (1872–1944), the director of the Berufsschule für Buchdrucker, of which the Meisterschule would become a part, made in a copy of *elementare typographie* that is preserved in the school archive, revealed that Tschichold's appointment as instructor at the Meisterschule was surrounded by politics. Popp speculated on whether Tschichold's theses had a political background. Obviously, in conservative Munich the last thing one needed was a leftist political agitator—particularly at a school that was being launched with a large donation of money from the authorities. Apparently these suspicions led to Tschichold being denied a permanent appointment for almost a year. This prevented him from receiving the German title *Professor*, which normally was automatically awarded to teachers with an above-average standing. Instead, Tschichold was, and remained, a *Studienrat* (lecturer). In any case, the political implications of his views on art must have been somewhat clear to Tschichold: he changed his name from Ivan Tschichold to Jan Tschichold. He accordingly informed his friend Werner Doede (ca. 1904–2000), a painter as well as a type and art historian, whom Tschichold had met in Leipzig in 1924, and who had also been the best man at his wedding, in a letter of June 5, 1926: "Regarding my goals, my work here is delightful, but the path to get there is a struggle …but Munich is a beautiful city. From now on Jan instead of Ivan, since Munich! Ivan is impossible here!"

In those years, Munich was the foremost city for the arts in Germany, rivaled only by Dresden. Founded in 1158, the city on the Isar River in southern Germany, close to the Alps, soon became the capital of the kingdom of Bavaria, which existed until 1918 as part of the German Empire. In the mid-1920s Munich had a population of around 750,000 and was growing rapidly with various urban expansions. For instance, between 1924 and 1929 a new neighborhood designed by the architect Bernhard Borst (1883–1963) was built along Dachauer Straße. Called the Borstei, it consisted of 774 dwellings in 77 buildings. In terms of design, the complex contrasted strongly with the Bauhaus concepts of the *Neues Bauen* (New Building). This innovative architecture was based on standardized dwellings built according to rigid principles and with modern materials, as had been done in Karlsruhe in the Dammerstock residential quarter, following the designs of Bauhaus architect Walter Gropius. Borst, on the contrary, designed houses with decorative elements in a traditional style, but with modern conveniences such as central heating and running water. It was here that the Tschicholds moved in December 1928.

With its favorable location, the city had become a railroad junction for central Europe. Its many breweries, which had flourished in and around the city for centuries, were also of economic importance. A newer industry was the Bayerische Motoren Werke AG (BMW), which in the 1920s was converting from the manufacture of airplanes to motorcycles and automobiles.

Die Sünde am Kinde (Sins Against the Child), film poster, 1927, letterpress on pink paper, 2 sheets. "Jan Tschichold Muenchen Planegg," 123.5 x 82.7 cm, printer: Plakatdruckerei Volk & Schreiber, Munich, TE

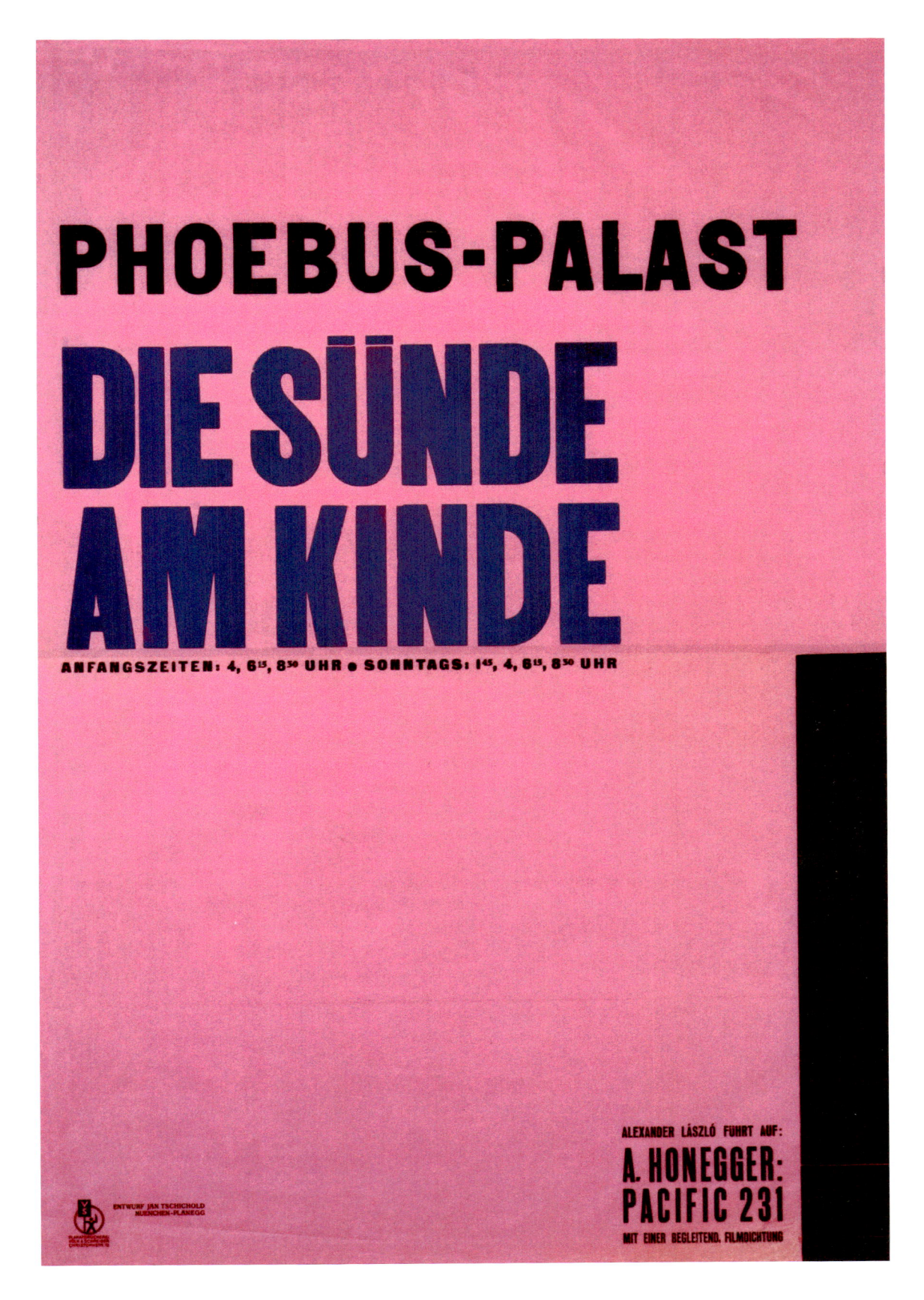

The Woman Without a Name, Part II, film poster, 1927, photographic print and letterpress on white coated paper with silver paper glued on, 1 sheet, "Jan Tschichold Planegg b. Mch," 124 x 86.8 cm, printer: Gebr. Obpacher AG, Munich, PC

Munich harbored its own university as well as many cultural institutions and theaters. In 1808 the Akademie der Bildenden Künste (Academy of Visual Arts) had been established. The Kunstverein (Art Society) followed in 1824, and the Kunstgewerbeverein (Arts and Crafts Society) in 1850. One of the arts training programs in Munich was the already mentioned Berufsschule für Buchdrucker, where on February 1, 1927, the Meisterschule für Deutschlands Buchdrucker was launched with Renner as its director. The Meisterschule was an initiative of the Deutscher Buchdruckerverein in Berlin and was supported by the city of Munich. The aim of the Meisterschule was "to train the full-time student on both theoretical and practical levels to run a print shop." It was not by chance that the Meisterschule should be located in Munich. It was, after all, the city of Alois Senefelder (1771–1834), the inventor of lithography, Georg Meisenbach (1841–1912), inventor of half-tone photo engraving, and Joseph Albert (1825–1886), photographer and inventor of the collotype.

The Meisterschule's curriculum consisted of composition, printing, technology of printing machines, stereotyping and electrotyping, production of printing blocks, flat-bed printing, gravure printing, bookbindery, calligraphy, color theory, and the history of printing. This program also had courses in economics and jurisprudence to provide the students with a solid education—not to forget "physical recreation by means of exercise and walking" either! Excursions were organized to interesting exhibitions such as the Werkbund show *Die Wohnung* (The Dwelling) in Stuttgart in 1927. The training lasted two years, divided into four semesters, and ended with a *Meisterprüfung* (examination for the master craftsman diploma). About thirty students from the German-speaking countries of Europe enrolled each year.

The work of the Meisterschule was publicized by contributions in professional magazines and by participation in professional exhibitions in Germany and other countries. For example, in 1928 the Gutenberg Museum in Mainz included a submission from the Meisterschule for the *Pressa* exhibition in Cologne, and in the same year the Meisterschule presented its work in Zurich. Furthermore, every year saw the publication of a portfolio with samples—unfortunately anonymous—of the production at the Meisterschule. These portfolios reveal the great influence of Trump and Tschichold on the work of their pupils.[3]

The vast majority of Munich's residents (about 80 percent) were Roman Catholics. Munich was the conservative opposite of the more cosmopolitan Berlin, the capital of the Empire, which lay in the northern, Protestant region of Germany. In contrast to Munich's *Gemütlichkeit* (coziness) stood the Prussian *Tüchtigkeit* (diligence). No year was complete without *Fasching* (carnival), *Salvator* and *Maibock* (regional beer specialties or brands), *Sommerfest* and *Oktoberfest* (annual festivals),

Schäfflertanz and *Metzgersprung* (local customs). Kurt Schwitters put it this way in 1928 at the annual convention of the Werkbund in Munich: "What does Munich stand for? A residential city? An artists' city? Bourgeois coziness? Bolshevism, as once upon a time in May? Or white sausages? All of these things, and affluence too."

An unsuccessful attempt at revolution had taken place in Munich in April and May 1919, with the brief installation of a Soviet-style republic, and the city was also the cradle of the NSDAP, receiving the distinction from Hitler of "*Hauptstadt der Bewegung*" (Capital of the Movement). It was there that Hitler had organized his failed putsch on November 9, 1923. On March 15, 1933, the NSDAP took over the government in the state of Bavaria, and Hitler was made an honorary citizen of the city. A great political purge followed.

Noble Blood, film poster, 1927, photomontage, photographic print, letterpress and silverprint on white coated paper, 1 sheet, NS, 119.5 x 85.5 cm, printer: Gebr. Obpacher AG, Munich, BPS/MGZ. A proof exists in the TE.

Kiki, film poster, 1927, letterpress on yellow paper, 2 sheets, "Tschichold München Pranckhstr 2 tel 57268," 124.3 x 84 cm, printer: Plakatdruckerei Volk & Schreiber, Munich, BPS/DNS/KB/MGZ/SMA

PHOEBUS-PALAST   The posters for the Phoebus-Palast cinema were Tschichold's first large commission and one in which he was given much latitude to experiment. In late 1926 the Phoebus-Palast was opened with great fanfare as a branch of the Berlin company Phoebus AG. It was the largest cinema in Germany at that time, with seating for 2,174 movie patrons. An orchestra of fifty musicians was available to accompany the films. (It would be some years yet before the arrival of the "talkies.") In a regular format, first a newsreel was screened, followed by a short opening film (generally a kind of comedy), then a musical interlude (an overture from an opera, or the pianist Alexander László with, for example, *Love's Dream* by Liszt), and finally the feature film. When they arrived, the visitors were handed a program detailing the sequence of the upcoming feature attractions. Although the interior design and façade were traditional in style, the director Michael Demmel opted for a modernist aura. For instance, in early 1927 Arthur Honegger's symphonic poem *Pacific 231* was performed as part of the pre-program. Together with the newspaper advertisements Tschichold's posters became the "calling card" for the Phoebus-Palast, and as early as February 27, 1927, the journal *Der Kinematograph* wrote, "It is the achievement of Mr. Demmel, the Director, that today the Phoebus-Palast, a mere two months after its opening, is generally recognized as an institution for the arts. It is difficult to imagine the physiognomy of today's Munich without it."

Tschichold seized the unique opportunity to create for the cinema what today would be called a corporate identity: posters, newspaper advertisements, and programs all formed a unity. Just as the posters stood out in the streets, the ads were prominent in the newspapers. This was vital exposure, since the illuminated advertising used by cinemas in other cities was forbidden in Munich.

In the short time between the announcement of the film and its screening (sometimes only a week), it was impractical to design a decorative poster, have it transferred to stone and then lithographed. By sheer necessity Tschichold worked from small sketches that he further developed on site at the printer. A proof of the poster for *Das edle Blut* (Noble Blood) has been preserved, demonstrating how proofs were corrected until a satisfactory result was achieved. Only if the film was announced well in advance, and if Tschichold received photographic material, could a negative be produced in time to print a photographic poster. In these situations, the design for the poster was often unrelated to the subject of the film. For example, a sketch made for a Buster Keaton film was adapted for the film *Laster der Menschheit* (Vices of Humanity), and a sketch for *Das Meer* (The Sea) was later used for *Die Hose* (The Pair of Trousers).

Prince Louis Ferdinand, film poster, 1927, photographic print, linocut, and letterpress on white coated paper, 1 sheet, "Jan Tschichold Planegg b. Mch," 118.5 x 83.7 cm, printer: Gebr. Obpacher AG, Munich, BPS/DNS/MGZ

Only in the type for *Der Anwalt des Herzens* (Advocate of the Heart) and *König Harlekin* (*The Magic Flame*) can a reference to the title be detected, very rare for Tschichold. Although he often combined different typefaces, no concessions were ever made regarding readability and expressive power. In some of his designs he implied the dynamics of film projection in a constructivist manner. The pattern of lines in *Die Frau ohne Namen. 2. Teil* (The Woman Without a Name, Part II) and *Laster der Menschheit* (Vices of Humanity), and the shaft of light in *Orient-Express* are good examples of this. These designs would have also been suitable for reuse: a different title with a different photograph would have yielded a new poster.

In the posters for the Phoebus-Palast, Photograph and text are forged into one perfect composition, unnecessary texts and ornaments are avoided, and the message is delivered in a most effective manner. Through a typographic pattern the eye is drawn from the photograph to the message. "In the case of the poster all decorative bias as well as everything that goes beyond the factual contents has to be rejected emphatically." Tschichold wrote in *Die neue Typographie*, referring to the type poster (*Typoplakat*) and to posters in general: "The poster, whether it is pictorial or typographical, has to be grasped in the moment of walking or driving past it. If, however, a longer text is necessary, then it has to astonish and attract attention.... Any ingredients betraying the signature of a particular artist contradict the essence of the poster."

In Germany, the most widely used occupational title was *Plakatmaler* (poster painter) rather than poster designer, the former term indicating a craft orientation. In an extensive account of the department of applied graphics at the Schule Reimann, an important private Berlin school for art and applied art education, the instructor Max Hertwig wrote in May 1927: "Apart from the pictorial poster, a new poster type focusing on area-based graphics and a rhythmic architecture has evolved in the last decade. This latter one receives special consideration in my curriculum.... A phenomenon parallel to this modern poster type manifests itself in the powerful contemporary stylistic trend of the New Objectivity. In this sense, much good has been achieved, particularly in the fields of architecture, the applied arts, and typography etc., with all sentimentality being discarded."

Tschichold soon commissioned Hilde Horn (née Hildegard Posse, 1897–1943), who had studied with Moholy-Nagy at the Bauhaus in Dessau, to design some of the advertisements to accompany his posters. Although Horn always signed her work, Tschichold did not sign the advertisements he designed himself. Much of the material could only be ascribed to him with certainty when a copy had been found in his archives on which he had written his name in pencil. Horn was one of a circle of close friends in Munich whom the Tschicholds saw frequently. Of Tschichold's many acquain-

PRINZ LOUIS FERDINAND

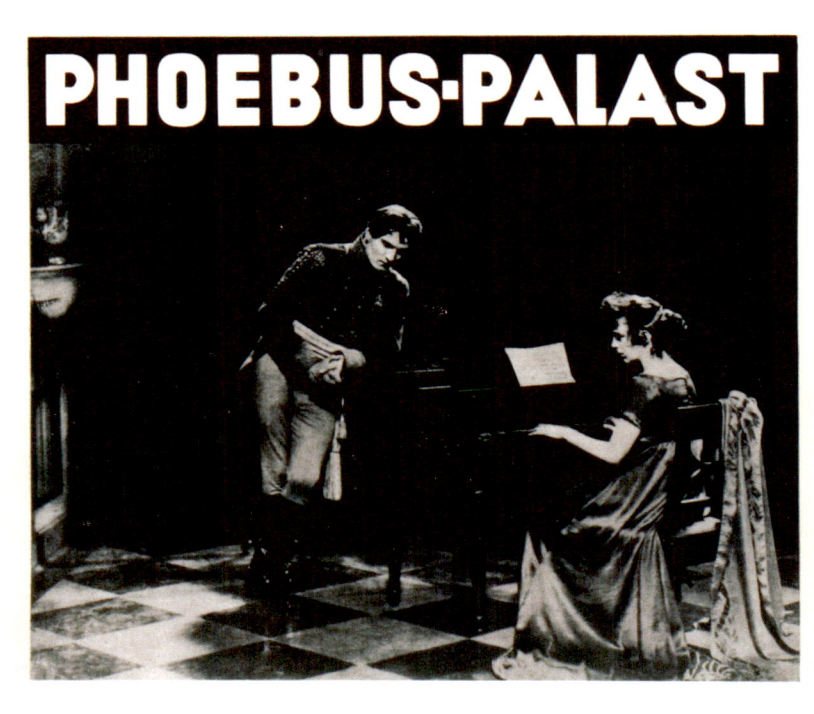

PHOEBUS-PALAST

ANFANGSZEITEN: 4 6:15 8:30
SONNTAGS: 1:45 4 6:15 8:30

ENTWURF: JAN TSCHICHOLD, PLANEGG B. MCH. • DRUCK: GEBR. OBPACHER A.G. MÜNCHEN

196

tances several others deserve mention: the German (later Swiss) designer and typographer Walter Cyliax (1899–1945), who as an instructor in Leipzig had once shared lodgings with Tschichold, and like him was a native of that city; the Swiss artists Hans (Jean) Arp (1886–1966) and his wife Sophie (née Täuber, 1889–1943); Otto Neurath (1882–1945), an Austrian philosopher and economist, inventor of pictograms, and a member of the Austrian Werkbund; the Dutch designer Peter Alma (1886–1969); the Germans Gerd Arntz (1900–1988) and Werner Graeff (1901–1978), photographer and member of De Stijl; Hans Richter (1888–1976), designer, publisher of the avant-garde journal G: *Zeitschrift für elementare Gestaltung*, and filmmaker; and of course Schwitters, with whom the Tschicholds maintained the warmest relations. Lucia (1894–1984, a Czech photographer) and László Moholy-Nagy often visited Munich, and Lissitzky and his wife would also pause there for a few days on their way from Russia to Switzerland to have Lissitzky's lung condition treated.

In addition to his work in typography, Tschichold assisted in organizing and designing exhibitions. He also actively collected the work of other progressive designers, both for his own pleasure and as illustrative material for his lessons, lectures, and publications. He became involved with *Graphische Werbekunst. Internationale Schau zeitgemäßer Reklame* (The Art of Graphic Advertising: An International Exhibition of Contemporary Publicity), which was held between August and October 1927 in the Städtische Kunsthalle (Municipal Art Gallery) in Mannheim. Tschichold not only designed the poster for this exhibition—which was also used as the cover of the catalog—but also made available his own work and items from his collection. The show placed considerable emphasis on contemporary design and especially on the application of photography. It was the first time that Tschichold's posters for the Phoebus-Palast were exhibited. *Laster der Menschheit* and *Die Frau ohne Namen. 2. Teil* were specifically mentioned in the catalog and shown in a separate gallery, side by side with works by Bayer, Dexel, Schlemmer, Burchartz, Schwitters, Albert Fuss (1889–1969), and Leistikow. All these posters may well have come from Tschichold's collection. In addition, there was a separate space with work by Bauhaus artists such as Baumeister, Bayer, Robert Michel (1897–1983), Moholy-Nagy, Alexander Schawinsky (1904–1979), Schlemmer, and Schmidt. These works evidently came from the collection of Adolf Behne, who was a great champion of the Bauhaus.

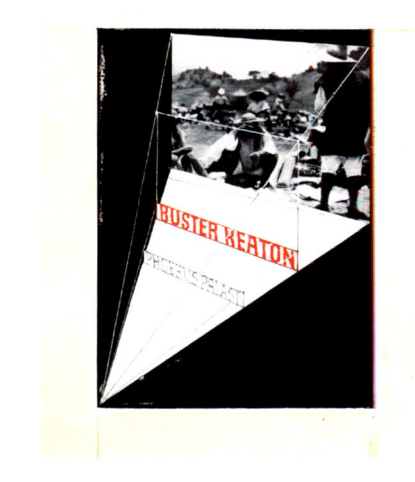

The series of posters for the Phoebus-Palast was interrupted by Tschichold's involvement in Mannheim. A preliminary sketch for the poster *Das Meer* was never finished, and a previous design for *Man spielt nicht mit der Liebe* (Don't Play with Love) was reused instead. Two subsequent posters are missing or have been lost, and the poster for *Danton* was designed by a certain Sametzki.

Vices of Humanity, film poster, 1927, photolithograph on white coated paper, 1 sheet, "Jan Tschichold, Planegg b. Mch," 119 x 84 cm, printer: F. Bruckmann AG, Munich, BPS/DNS/KB

Sketch for a Buster Keaton poster, 1927, photocollage and gouache, NS, 12 x 8.5 cm, TE

Again, apparently through Renner, who was a member of the board of the Münchner Bund, the Munich branch of the Werkbund, Tschichold worked on the exhibition *Das Bayerische Handwerk* (Bavarian Crafts). The Grafische Berufsschule was to have a section in the exhibition, and that was a wonderful opportunity to introduce the new Meisterschule. The exhibition took place from May to October 1927. Tschichold designed a poster for the lottery and provided advertising for the Phoebus-Palast to go on the back of the entrance tickets. However, Tschichold did not design the official poster for the exhibition. That was left in the hands of Glass, who in 1926 had won not only the first, but also the second prize in the poster competition. Although Tschichold's poster is not his most successful design, it contrasts remarkably with Glass's prizewinning but ultimately inferior work.

On January 26, 1928 Tschichold wrote to Zwart: "Due to the insolvency of Phoebusfilm I will cease to do posters for films." In a later letter he added: "This is a substantial loss for me and mainly so in terms of income." In fact, Phoebus AG had run into financial problems in late 1927, and the cinema in Munich was taken over by the Emelka film company.

A heavy schedule at the school and work on his book *Die neue Typographie* made it all the more difficult for Tschichold to produce other work. For some time he had planned to move to Paris after Easter 1928 (the date his book was to be published) because he was still not very happy in Munich. Since the Phoebus-Palast remained open, Carl Otto (C.O.) Müller (1901–70) was hired as his replacement to design the posters and advertisements.[4] The new series of Phoebus posters were executed more cheaply than Tschichold's. Linocuts printed in two colors on inferior paper, they had little to do with modern typography. Still, through their design bordering on the abstract and their use of color, they constituted an unusual series.

Buster Keaton in *The General*, film poster, 1927, photographic print and letterpress on white coated paper, 1 sheet, "Jan Tschichold Planegg b./mch," 120 x 84 cm, printer: F. Bruckmann AG, Munich, BPS/DNS/MGZ/MoMA/SMA

BUSTER KEATON
IN: ›DER GENERAL‹
PHOEBUS PALAST
ANFANGSZEITEN 4⁰⁰ 6¹⁵ 8³⁰
SONNTAGS 1⁴⁵ 4⁰⁰ 6¹⁵ 8³⁰
entwurf: tschichold planegg b/mch. ● druck: f. bruckmann a.g., münchen

NACHT DER LIEBE
MIT VILMA BANKY U. RONALD COLMAN

PHOEBUS
PALAST

ANFANG:
4⁰⁰ 6¹⁵ 8³⁰
SONNTAGS:
1⁴⁵ 4⁰⁰ 6¹⁵ 8³⁰

TSCHICHOLD

After his work for Phoebus, Tschichold became involved with the Volksverband für Filmkunst (People's Association for Film Art), the predecessor of the Münchner Liga für unabhängigen Film (Munich League for Independent Films), which in turn was connected with the Deutsche Filmliga (German Film League). As he wrote to Zwart on June 13, 1928, "Ever since this firm [Universum Film AG, the main film production company in Germany, which had been bought by the right wing media tycoon Alfred Hugenberg in 1927] has been completely taken over by nationalist circles, its productions have gone down the drain both artistically and intellectually. These conditions have deteriorated to such an extent, that we have witnessed the founding of 'People's Film Clubs' in some German cities; these are pure fighting organizations, trying to show artistically and socially valuable films instead of the ordinary dross. There is a similar group about to be founded in Munich. I myself am part of the preparatory committee."

A film league had previously been established in the Netherlands, with prominent members including Schuitema and Zwart. Zwart had organized the Internationale Tentoonstelling op Filmgebied (ITF; International Exhibition of the Film Industry) in The Hague in 1928, where, in addition to posters by Russian constructivists, considerable work by Tschichold was also seen. Zwart had asked Tschichold for addresses of designers of film posters, specifically including Hohlwein, and received this answer: "I cannot recall a single example of a good German film poster. This is why I am unable to provide you with names of artists who have worked in this field in any manner different from ours, but at least aesthetically successful. All film posters are of average standard, an extraordinarily low one at that. Merely in the case of the film *Metropolis* (one of the worst existing movies), I remember two somewhat acceptable posters by someone called Graul [Werner Graul, 1905–84; his design work included film posters for the Phoebus in Berlin]. I will try to find out his address." And in a later letter he wrote: "My efforts to retrieve the address of Graul (film posters) were, alas, unsuccessful. Theo Ballmer, who created the poster *One Hundred Years of Photography* has the following address: Basel, Hardstr. 26. Hohlwein is a representative of the pre-war poster in southern Germany.... These days his designs are rather poor and he keeps repeating himself. His posters for movies are not evocative of film at all. Nevertheless, his works ought to be shown. His address: Professor Ludwig Hohlwein, Munich, Gabelsbergerstraße 36."

Tschichold himself designed a poster for the Münchner Filmwochen (Munich Film Festival) in 1928 and the program for the same event in 1932. Further, he designed the posters for the films *Johanna von Orleans* (*The Passion of Joan of Arc*, Carl Dreyer, 1928) and *Hochzeitsmarsch* (*The Wedding March*, Erich von Stroheim, 1928). The poster for a lecture by the Russian film director Dziga Vertov (1896–1954) is a story of its own. Vertov was a good friend of Tschichold and one of the most out-

The Night of Love, film poster, 1927, photographic print, linocut, and letterpress, "Tschichold," 120 x 85 cm, printer: Kunst im Druck GmbH, Munich, BPS/DNS/DPM/MGZ spoken representatives of the new experimental film. His credo was "Show life as it is." Vertov spread his philosophy by giving lectures after the screening of his films and made at least two trips through Western Europe for that purpose in 1929 (Germany) and 1931 (Germany, the Netherlands, and Britain). The Ring neuer Werbegestalter and the film leagues in Germany and the Netherlands were all closely connected with each other.

The purely typographic posters formed, as it were, a second style. Tschichold enjoyed an unprecedented artistic freedom but in turn had to work rapidly on a limited budget. Apparently, he had to make several inexpensive typographic posters to give himself the luxury of one more expensive photographic design. The photo posters not only required a specially made negative—four-color offset printers were still rare at this time—but the printing required more accuracy and thus more time. Also, the process needed specially prepared and more expensive paper. To avoid having to print with thick ink, the paper was covered with a layer of white chalk that made it very ink-sensitive. Only in this way could a sharp print be obtained from the negative. In the typographic posters Tschichold generally combined large fields with bold color combinations to draw attention to the message. Particularly striking is his use of colored paper as the basis for his typographic posters, rendering them even more conspicuous on the streets.

For the filled shapes in his typographic posters, Tschichold followed Wijdeveld's example by fitting together pieces of typesetting material to create the desired forms. However, unlike Tschichold, the architect Wijdeveld used typesetting material to construct entire compositions from typographic elements. Others who created notable typographic posters were Bayer for the exhibition *Europäisches Kunstgewerbe* (European Arts and Crafts) in Leipzig (1927); Schwitters for the *Opel-Tag* (Open Day at the Opel Corporation, 1927); van Doesburg and Schwitters who created a handbill for Dada evenings in December 1922; the Dutch architect van Ravesteyn for the *Rekken* exhibition in 1925; Zwart for Laga rubber floors in 1923; and the Austrian De Stijl member Friedrich Kiesler (1890–1965) for the Vienna Theater Exhibition in 1924. It is not surprising that these designers were used as models in Tschichold's book *Die neue Typographie* (1928) and that he collected their work.

In May 1928 an exhibition of 100 drawings by Vincent van Gogh (1853–1890) was held in Munich. The exhibition had previously been in Berlin, and a committee of Munich residents was formed to raise money to bring the show to their own city. The exhibition took place at Briennerstraße 10 in the Graphisches Kabinett, which was a collaboration between Israel Ber Neumann (1887–1961) from New York and Günther Franke (1900–1976), director of the Munich gallery. Tschichold designed the poster for the exhibition, which was printed at the Meisterschule. Until his death in

Die 3 Niemandskinder (The Three Nobodies), film poster, 1927, letterpress on yellow-brown paper, 2 sheets, "tschichold, planegg," 126 x 86 cm, printer: Plakatdruckerei Volk & Schreiber, Munich, BPS/DNS

ENTFESSELTE ELEMENTE

MIT VILMA BANKY UND RONALD COLMAN

PHOEBUS PALAST

ANFANGSZEITEN:
4^{00} 6^{15} 8^{30}
SONNTAGS:
1^{45} 4^{00} 6^{15} 8^{30}

entwurf:
tschichold,
planegg

1976, Franke continued to organize ten exhibitions per year—even during the war years. Tschichold designed a large-format poster for at least six of the exhibitions at the Graphisches Kabinett,[6] as well as a small window poster for *Deutsche Landschaft in zeitgenössischen Zeichnungen und Aquarellen* (The German Landscape in Contemporary Drawings and Watercolors) in April 1929. Tschichold may well have designed more posters for Franke, but, with the exception of a poster announcing a 1929 slide show on the work of Emil Nolde (1867–1956), these have not been found. In addition, the Meisterschule—and apparently to a great extent Tschichold himself—produced designs for a number of the catalogs, such as one for an exhibition of the work of Alfred Kubin (1877–1959), held at the Graphisches Kabinett in November 1930. An important exhibition for Tschichold was undoubtedly *Plakate der Avantgarde* (Posters of the Avant-Garde), which took place in January and February 1930 and used material from his own collection.

Entfesselte Elemente (US title: *The Winning of Barbara Worth*), film poster, 1927, letterpress on yellow paper, 2 sheets, "tschichold, planegg," 125 x 85 cm, printer: Plakatdruckerei Volk & Schreiber, Munich, BPS/DNS/MGZ

The exhibition Das Internationale Plakat This event was organized on the initiative of the Deutsche Städte-Reklame GmbH (the Federal Association of Municipal Advertising Lobbyists) as the conclusion of the great Weltreklame-Kongress (World Advertising Congress) held in Berlin in the summer of 1929. As was customary, the Bavarian section of the Bund Deutscher Gebrauchsgraphiker (Association of German Functional Designers) had organized an internal poster competition, and, unsurprisingly, the winners were Glass and Zietara. Glass's poster was also printed on the cover of the catalog. It is interesting to observe the encounter between the two currents in graphic design in the catalog and the exhibition: Glass's catalog cover is immediately followed on the opening page by (or after a design by) Tschichold. In the accompanying text, Hermann Karl Frenzel (1882–1937), publisher of *Gebrauchsgraphik* and editor of a book on the posters of Hohlwein, wrote at length about the history of the poster, without mentioning the modernist, objective direction. In fact, his history does not go beyond Bernhard's *Sachplakat*. In the same catalog, Glass wrote: "Munich art, south German art, one thinks of the sun, of gaiety and of flights of the imagination. The pulse of life of an inexhaustible German tribe permeates the city, every fiber vibrates with grace and zest for life. This holds true in the art of posters. Whereas in northern Germany, abstract, frosty, and tectonic design prevails, in Munich there is spirit and good humor, warmth and vitality." Two posters by Tschichold were on display as well. His *Napoleon* hung next to a poster by Walter Schnackenberg (1880–1961), publicizing a dance performance by Peter Pathe and Maria Hagen (probably from 1919), and *Laster der Menschheit* (Vices of Humanity) was hung next to Hohlwein's poster *Der Stahlhelm und Du?* (Stahlhelm, and what about you?). Since Stahlhelm was a right-wing paramilitary group, a greater contrast is hardly imaginable. It is striking that the Batavier Line poster by Van der Leck and an entire wall of Russian constructivist posters, apparently all from Tschichold's collection, were shown. In *Gebrauchsgraphik* (VI-10, 1929) Frenzel included photographs of all the walls except for the wall with Tschichold's own posters. Frenzel, and many like him, had declared Tschichold, and the aesthetic direction for which he and the recently founded Ring neue Werbegestalter stood, to be anathema. By exhibiting his own collection in Franke's gallery, Tschichold demonstrated that work was being done other than that produced by Glass and Zietara. He included posters by Bayer, Burchartz, Dexel, Lissitzky, Moholy-Nagy, Schlemmer, Schuitema, Sutnar, Zwart, and others. These names are remembered, whereas Glass and Zietara are forgotten. The exhibition also traveled to Basel (Museum of Arts and Crafts, April 1930), Stuttgart (Schaller Art Gallery, summer 1930), Prague (Manes Exhibition Hall, November 1930), perhaps to Brno, and part of it may also have been shown in New York.

Das Meer (The Sea), film poster, 1927, letterpress, 2 sheets, "tschichold," ca. 120 x 85 cm, printer: Plakatdruckerei Volk & Schreiber, Munich, DNS/MKG/TA

BERGNER
JANNINGS
VEIDT

IN: NJU
EINE UNVERSTANDENE FRAU

PHOEBUS PALAST

ANFANGSZEITEN:	4:00	6:15	8:30
SONNTAGS:	1:45	4:00	6:15	8:30

entwurf: tschichold planegg b/mch. • druck: f. bruckmann a.g., münchen

With the closed system of poster competitions, as organized by the Bund Deutscher Gebrauchsgraphiker, in which prominent members such as Glass, Zietara, and Preetorius made up the juries, Tschichold and other likeminded designers had no chance from the outset of acquiring important commissions or winning the monetary prizes. That is surprising, since Glass and Zietara called themselves *Kunstmaler* (fine artists) and distanced themselves from typography.

Tschichold must have executed many more designs than the handful of posters and examples of letterheads that are known, since he noted them in his own books. In a 1945 after-dinner speech, he said: "From 1919 until now I have not only typographically arranged countless advertisements and other forms of printed matter, but also hundreds of book publications on a wide range of themes."

In January 1933 Tschichold submitted his resignation to the Munich Meisterschule to assume a teaching position at the Höhere Graphische Fachschule der Stadt Berlin where Trump had become director. However, after visiting Berlin, he changed his mind and decided that he would rather stay in Munich. As stated in the previous section, on March 15, 1933 Tschichold was arrested and imprisoned for six weeks, during which time he was dismissed from his teaching position. On May 10, 1933 the Nazis organized the first book-burning in Berlin, and it was soon clear that Tschichold's position in Germany had become untenable. On April 1, 1933 the Tschicholds exchanged their apartment in Voitstraße for a temporary address elsewhere in Munich. On July 28, 1933 they signed themselves out of the city register, and left Germany for good, moving to Basel, the city which would grant them Swiss citizenship in 1942 and where Tschichold would remain until his retirement.

On September 19, 1933, local officials informed the directors of the school that, "as part of the *Gleichschaltung* and political reorganization, communists, individuals without religious affiliation, and leading, politically prominent social democrats must not become members of the board of trustees." As a consequence of this measure, Renner was forced into retirement, although he retained his pension and the income from Futura.

In 1934 Trump returned from Berlin to become Renner's successor and would continue to be connected with the school until his retirement in 1953. Although Trump was decidedly no Nazi sympathizer, he alienated himself from Tschichold in Switzerland by sending him a letter with the closing formula "Heil Hitler,"[7] probably in an attempt to evade censorship. (However, there is no archival evidence of such a letter.)

Nju: eine unverstandene Frau (US title: *Husbands or Lovers*), film poster, 1927, photographic print, letterpress on white coated paper, 1 sheet, "Tschichold, Planegg b/mch," 120 x 83.8 cm, printer: F. Bruckmann AG, Munich, BPS/DNS/DPM/FMB

Hilde Horn remained in Munich until her death, working at the Mercedes-Benz showroom. Although travel abroad was severely restricted, Hilde was allowed to visit the Tschicholds in Switzerland with her son Peter Horn in 1938. She took the opportunity to give Tschichold a part of her private archive of avant-garde design, as keeping such material in Nazi Germany was very risky. Tschichold would stay in touch with the Horns until Hilde's death from tuberculosis in 1943.[8] Contacts with Herbert Bayer were broken off after 1933. Bayer stayed in Berlin until as late as 1938. "Fight against fascism," as Tschichold would write in 1934 to the Belgian artist Edouard Mesens (1903–71). Anyone who did not do that was a traitor in his eyes.

Much of the avant-garde art and design in Germany was destroyed by the Nazis or by the war they had begun. Of the total of 748 posters mentioned in the catalog of the *Plakate in München 1840–1940* exhibition, organized in 1976 by the Munich Stadtmuseum, only one is by Tschichold. That is how thoroughly the Nazis erased the past.[9] Fortunately, however, a large part of Tschichold's collection survived those years. Many books, including the Russian children's books and a large number of other works, were seized during the searches of his home in 1933, but since much of his collection was used for teaching, it was stored at the school on Pranckhstraße. In any case, Tschichold left Germany just in time to take along much of his collection, his own work, his Mondrian painting, and his Bauhaus furniture.

SWITZERLAND There was little extra work for Tschichold as a graphic designer, so he devoted himself to promoting new typefaces and typesetting technology, especially the Uhertype photo-typesetting machine, which had been introduced in 1925 but was having a bumpy ride commercially. With only a few exceptions, such as a 1934 brochure for Uhertype, there were no opportunities for him in Switzerland to use the precepts of *Die neue Typographie*. A significant part of Tschichold's graphic production consisted of "headlines for three Ciba journals." There was no opportunity to design commercial posters. The only commissions Tschichold received for posters came from the Gewerbeschule in Basel and the Gewerbemuseum connected to it. Tschichold was often involved with the preparations for exhibitions, so designing the poster and the accompanying catalog were obvious next steps.

Tschichold's 1937 poster *Konstruktivisten* (Constructivists) and *Der Berufsphotograph* (The Professional Photographer), designed a year later, constitute the close of Tschichold's poster oeuvre. These two posters stand apart from previous work because of their overtones of symbolism, an aspect absent in Tschichold's earlier creations. The sand-yellow circle, which Tschichold had used as early as 1927 for his own letterhead, became the setting sun in the *Konstruktivisten* poster. The

Der Bettelpoet (The Beloved Rogue), film poster, 1927, letterpress on pink paper, 2 sheets, "Tschichold," 117.5 x 84 cm, printer: Plakatdruckerei Volk & Schreiber, Munich, BPS/DNS

STÄDTISCHE
KUNSTHALLE
MANNHEIM
GRAPHISCHE
WERBEKUNST
INTERNATIONALE SCHAU
ZEITGEMÄSSER REKLAME
EINTRITT FREI
ENTW. JAN TSCHICHOLD, PLANEGG
VOM 7. AUGUST BIS 30. OKTOBER
LITHOGRAPHIE: GEBR. OBPACHER A.G., MÜNCHEN

sun would soon set entirely, and the work of the Constructivists would no longer be seen (at least not in Hitler's Europe). The poster powerfully alluded to the social and political realities in which these modern artists lived. Their work had been declared *entartet* (degenerate) in Germany, removed from museums, and in some cases even burned. Aside from the Museum of Modern Art in New York, there was little interest in them elsewhere in the world either. The opening of the *Konstruktivisten* exhibition, which also included Tschichold's Mondrian painting, occasioned a reunion of friends. There were also many who were absent, having fled to Britain or the United States. The *Berufsphotograph* poster presented a brighter image. The contrast between the negative portrait, rendered in black, and the stripe of color, creates associations with a dark raincloud and a rainbow, suggesting that after the rain comes the sunshine.

Graphische Werbekunst (Graphic Advertising Art), exhibition poster, 1927, offset lithograph, 86 x 63 cm, DNS/KB/MGZ/MKG

Late in 1938 Tschichold submitted two poster designs for the exhibition of the Ortsgruppe Basel of the Schweizerische Werkbund (Basel Chapter of the Swiss Werkbund), of which he had become a member. The themes under which he submitted his entries were *Simplicitas* (Simplicity), for the poster in the style of the New Typography, and *Klassik* (Classicism), for the poster in the traditional, symmetrical style. The winner was a design by the Swiss graphic designer Hermann Eidenbenz (1902–1993), with whom Tschichold was on good terms. After that, Tschichold would only occasionally design posters in the classic style.[10]

Tschichold began collecting mainly to provide illustrative material for his publications and lectures. Nothing indicates that he strove for completeness as a passionate collector would. In late 1929 and early 1930 he did, however, seek posters in a more focused way for his exhibition on posters of the avant-garde at the Graphisches Kabinett. For example, on January 21, 1930, Dexel wrote to Tschichold asking about ten of his posters (including some duplicates) that he had sent to Tschichold for his exhibition. Tschichold was allowed to keep the duplicates. Tschichold also asked Klutsis and Schwitters for posters. On June 25, 1930 Helma Schwitters wrote to Tschichold: "Kurt sends you two of his posters, for your collection of posters to be completed." Tschichold continued to collect after his move to Basel, including posters by Matter.

As early as the 1930s Tschichold was in touch with the Museum of Modern Art in New York regarding finding material for their collection. On June 4, 1938, in a letter to Beaumont Newhall, librarian at the Museum of Modern Art, he offered to obtain for them *Champs délicieux* by Man Ray (1922) and *Dlja Golossa* by El Lissitzky (1923). The museum also had work by Tschichold in its collection, as would appear from the exhibition "Cubism and Other Forms of Abstract Art" in 1936. In 1950, Tschichold sold the remains of his poster collection and other applied graphics to the museum through the mediation of architect Philip Johnson (1906–2005), founder of the museum's Department of Architecture and Design. Part of this acquisition was shown in 1977 in the exhibition "The Graphic Revolution 1915–1935." Previously the collection had already served as the basis for the 1968 exhibition "Word and Image." However, all of Tschichold's collection did not end up in New York. He sold or gave parts to the Gewerbemuseum in Basel (works by Schwitters, Trump, Klutsis, etc.) and to the Museum für Gestaltung (Museum for Design) in Zurich (works by Klutsis and apparently Cassandre, Carlu, and more). After his death, the Getty Institute in Los Angeles purchased much of his correspondence. He gave much of his own work to the museums in Basel and Zurich, and also to the Neue Sammlung in Munich.

Tschichold's poster designs rank among the finest in the history of graphic design. His background in typography permitted him to achieve preeminence with minimal means while consistently maintaining elegance and a maximum of expression.

Notes

1. A-D Gallery, 130 West 46th Street, Room 309, New York City.
2. Card from Dexel dated December 4, 1925. The letters from Lissitzky and Dexel are to be found in the Jan and Edith Tschichold Papers, Getty Institute, Los Angeles.
3. Christopher Burke, Paul Renner: *The Art of Typography*, London: Hyphen Press, 1998, p.59.
4. Müller was a fine artist (*Kunstmaler*) and had already designed film posters, evidently for the extra income, as so many painters did. There is preserved, for instance, a poster from about 1925 for *Das Milliardentestament* (The Testament of Billions), a film directed by Franz Seitz; the poster is signed "COM." Illustrated in: *The Golden Age of Hungarian Film Posters*, Ernst Gallery, Budapest 2004.
5. The poster is in the Bayerisches Hauptstaatsarchiv, Munich, Plakatsammlung 21959.
6. A number of these exhibitions were also presented at the Kestner-Gesellschaft in Hanover. The posters for the exhibitions were designed by Vordemberge-Gildewart.
7. According to Tschichold's heirs, the letter is in his archive.
8. For instance, Tschichold had a portfolio with work by Hilde Horn from the period between 1928 and 1936.
9. The Stadtmuseum, Munich, acquired a number of the series of posters by C.O. Müller that surfaced in California around 1985. Two of Müller's posters are also found in the Bayerisches Hauptstaatsarchiv, and the Neue Sammlung (Staatliches Museum für angewandte Kunst) has a Tschichold collection, which was apparently acquired from Tschichold's archive after World War II.
10. These include small window placards for Birkhäuser Verlag in Basel and for musical performances (collection of the Museum für Gestaltung, Zurich).

Gehetzte Frauen (Hated Women), film poster, 1927, photographic print, letterpress, 1 sheet, "Tschichold," 119.5 x 83.3 cm, printer: Plakatdruckerei Volk & Schreiber, Munich, DNS/MGZ

Piquedame (The Queen of Spades), rough design for a film poster, 1927, collage and gouache, NS, 13 x 10 cm, TE

Piquedame (The Queen of Spades), film poster, 1927, photographic print, letterpress on white coated paper, 1 sheet, "Tschichold," 118.4 x 83.5 cm, printer: F. Bruckmann AG, Munich, DNS/DPM/MGZ. The poster reproduced opposite is from the archive of Jan Tschichold; on it, the artist has changed the straight tail of the Q by hand into a rounded tail.

PIQUEDAME

MIT JENNY JUGO UND RUD. FORSTER

PHOEBUSPALAST

ANFANG: 4.00 6.15 8.30 SONNTAGS: 1.45 4.00 6.15 8.30

ENTWURF: TSCHICHOLD

218

Die Hose (The Pair of Trousers), film poster, 1927, photographic print, letterpress on white coated paper, 1 sheet, "Tschichold," 119.5 x 84 cm, printer: F. Bruckmann AG, Munich, DNS/KB/MoMA

Das Meer (The Sea), rough sketch for film poster, 1927, NS, 7.5 x 5 cm, TE

Cover of Phoebus-Palast cinema program, 1927. The logo, however, was not designed by Tschichold, but by Werner Graul.

Die Kameliendame (US title: *Camille*), film poster, 1927, photographic print, letterpress on white coated paper, 1 sheet, "Tschichold," 118.5 x 83.7 cm, printer: F. Bruckmann AG, Munich, DNS/DPM/MGZ/SMA

Orient-Express, film poster, 1927, photographic print, letterpress on white coated paper, 1 sheet, "Tschichold," 117.7 x 83.8 cm, printer: F. Bruckmann AG, Munich, DNS/DPM

LIL DAGOVER UND HEINRICH GEORGE IN:
ORIENT-EXPRESS
PHOEBUS PALAST
ANFANG 4 00 6 15 8 30
SONNTAGS 1 45 4 00 6 15 8 30
TSCHICHOLD
DRUCK F. BRUCKMANN A.-G. MÜNCHEN

CASANOVA
MIT IWAN MOSJUKIN
PHOEBUS-PALAST
ANFANG 400 615 830
SONNTAGS 145 400 615 830
TSCHICHOLD
DRUCK: F. BRUCKMANN A.G. MÜNCHEN

Casanova, film poster, 1927, photographic print, letterpress on white coated paper, 1 sheet, "Tschichold," 119.7 x 84.5 cm, printer: F. Bruckmann AG, Munich, BPS/DNS/FMA/SMA

Der Anwalt des Herzens (Advocate of the Heart), film poster, 1927, letterpress on orange paper, 2 sheets, "Tschichold," 119.4 x 83.3 cm, printer: Plakatdruckerei Volk & Schreiber, Munich, DNS/MGZ. The black bar next to the words "Phoebus-Palast" in the upper right corner is composed from 13 pieces of type!

Violantha, film poster, 1927, photographic print, linocut and letterpress, 2 sheets, "Tschichold," 120 x 83.6 cm, printer: Plakatdruckerei Volk & Schreiber, Munich, KB

König Harlekin (US title: *The Magic Flame*), film poster, 1927, photographic print, letterpress on white coated paper, 1 sheet, "Tschichold," 118.5 x 84 cm, printer: F. Bruckmann AG, Munich, DSM/PC

225

TSCHICHOLD

Napoleon, film poster, 1927,
photographic print, letterpress
on white coated paper, 1 sheet,
"Tschichold," 118.8 x 84 cm,
printer: F. Bruckmann AG, Munich,
BPS/KB/PME

Napoleon, rough sketch for film poster, 1927, collage, gouache and pencil, NS, 17.5 x 15.5 cm, TE

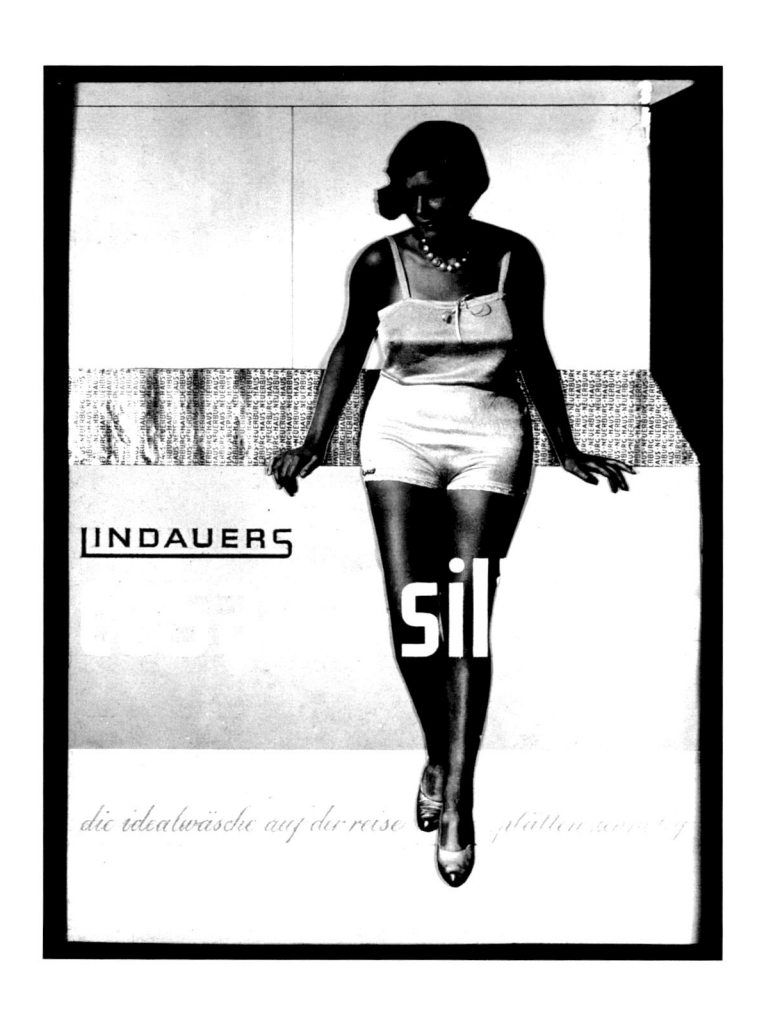

Lantern slide used by Jan Tschichold, ca. 1929

Advertising card for Lindauer's *Bellisana* underwear range, 1929, photolithograph, letterpress, printed in silver ink on cardboard, "Tschichold," 41.8 x 29.6 cm, printer: Gebr. Obpacher AG, Munich, HGM/MGZ

LINDAUERS
BELLISANA

fein
durchlässig
anschmiegend

Herren-Bekleidung

Anzüge **75.-**
Paletots **85.-**
Ulster **95.-**

BESTE QUALITÄTEN, durch eigene Anfertigung besonders gut und preiswert. Maßanfertigung unter Garantie tadellosen Sitzes

JOSEF KIESEL
Sendlingerstraße Nr. 9 (Ecke Sendlingertorplatz)

Poster for men's clothing, ca. 1927–1928, signed in pencil: "Tsch," 52.4 x 78 cm, TE

Van Gogh exhibition poster, 1928, letterpress on yellow paper, 2 sheets, NS, 109 x 83.7 cm, printer: Meisterschule für Deutschlands Buchdrucker, PC/TE

AUSSTELLUNG

VINCENT VAN GOGH

100 Handzeichnungen aus holländischem Privatbesitz

GRAPHISCHES KABINETT

Briennerstraße 10 am Wittelsbacher Palais
Geöffnet von 9-6, Sonntags von 9-1 Uhr

Emil Nolde exhibition poster, 1928, letterpress on pink paper, 2 sheets, "Tschichold," 83.1 x 119.5 cm, printer: Plakatdruckerei Volk & Schreiber, Munich, PS

Max Beckmann exhibition poster, 1928, letterpress on yellow paper, "Tschichold," 60 x 83.5 cm, printer: Plakatdruckerei Volk & Schreiber, Munich, DNS/KB

Four posters for Vincent Van Gogh exhibition, 1928, letterpress, two on yellow paper and two on red paper, "tschichold," each poster 60 x 84.5 cm, printer: Plakatdruckerei Volk & Schreiber, Munich, DNS/PC

AUSSTELLUNG VINCENT VAN
GOGH
UNBEKANNTE GEMAELDE
GRAPHISCHES KABINETT
BRIENNERSTRASSE 10
OFFEN: WERKTAGS 9-6
SONNTAGS 10-1

AUSSTELLUNG VINCENT VAN
GOGH
UNBEKANNTE GEMAELDE
GRAPHISCHES KABINETT
BRIENNERSTRASSE 10
OFFEN: WERKTAGS 9-6
SONNTAGS 10-1

dsiga werthoff

**einer der bedeutendsten jungen russischen filmgestalter
spricht über das thema**

was ist kino-auge?

2 mal in münchen: **samstag**, den **29.** juni 1929, 22⁴⁵ uhr
sonntag, den **30.** juni, 11 uhr vormittags
in den **rathaus-lichtspielen**, weinstr 8, tel 90464

bayerische landes-filmbühne und rathaus-lichtspiele

während des vortrags laufen streifen aus folgenden, in westeuropa noch unbekannten **filmen** werthoffs:
lenins wahrheit - der sechste teil der welt - das elfte jahr - kino-auge - der mann mit dem kinoapparat

karten von rm 1,50 bis rm 3,00

entwurf tschichold · druck b. heller, münchen

"Was ist Kino-Auge?," poster for a lecture by Dziga Vertov, 1929, letterpress, "tschichold," 54 x 79.5 cm, MB

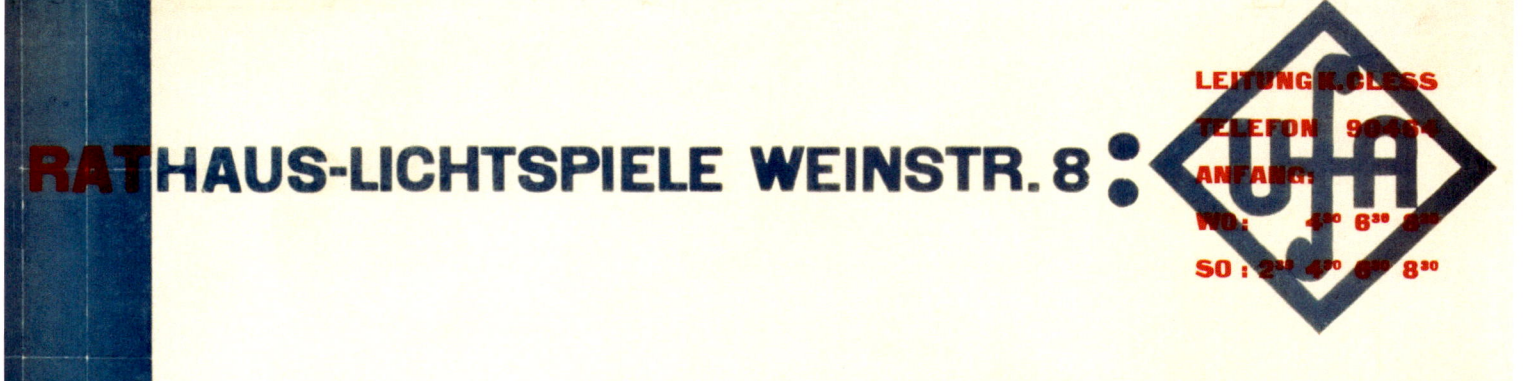

Johanna von Orleans (*The Passion of Joan of Arc*), theater poster, 1929, letterpress, "Tschichold," 60 x 84.4 cm, printer: Plakatdruckerei Volk & Schreiber, Munich, KB. The logo for the UFA was designed by Lucian Bernhard.

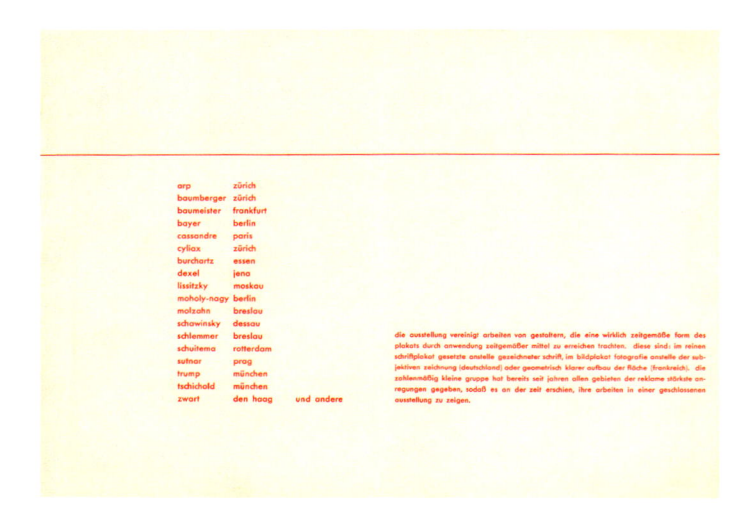

Four-page catalog for the *Plakate der Avantgarde* exhibition, 1930, typography by Jan Tschichold, letterpress, NS, 21 x 15 cm, TE

Plakate der Avantgarde (Posters of the Avant-Garde), exhibition poster, 1930, letterpress, "tsch," 42 x 59.7 cm, printer: Buchdruckerei Franz Eggert, Hessstr. 60, MoMA/PC

graphisches kabinett münchen

briennerstrasse 10   leitung guenther franke

buchdruckerei franz eggert, heßstr. 60

ausstellung der sammlung jan tschichold

plakate der avantgarde

arp	molzahn
baumeister	schawinsky
bayer	schlemmer
burchartz	schuitema
cassandre	sutnar
cyliax	trump
dexel	tschichold
lissitzky	zwart
moholy-nagy	und andere

tsch   24. januar bis 10. februar 1930   geöffnet 9–6, sonntags 10–1

Munich, Summer 1930, poster design by Jan Tschichold, most probably not executed, intended format: 124 x 88 cm, reproduced from *Arts et Métiers Graphiques*, Paris, no. 19, September 1930. On a copy of a different sketch, found in the TE, the following text appears in French: "The word 'Munich' is to be done in cobalt blue, the surface surrounding 'summer 1930' in silver, the writing in white, the photo and the line in black."

Poster design, 1929–1930, photocollage with opaque watercolor and pencil, and instructions for the printer, on the back of half a Bellisana showcard, NS, 29 x 21.5 cm, TE

Munich and Southern Bavaria, travel brochure, ca. 1929, photographic print and letterpress, NS, 22.8 x 14 cm, TE

München *und* **Südbayern**

vvm

Herausgegeben vom Verkehrsverband München und Südbayern

Rough design for exhibition poster for the Berufsschule and Meisterschule, 1931, photocollage, collage, gouache, and pencil, NS, 9 x 12.7 cm, TE

Exhibition poster for the Berufsschule and Meisterschule, 1931, photolithograph on white coated paper, "tschichold," 59.7 x 83.6 cm, photo: Eduard Wasow, printer: Hermann Sonntag & Co., Munich, BSA/HGM/KB/MGZ/TA

AUSSTELLUNG STÄDT. BERUFS- UND MEISTER- SCHULEN

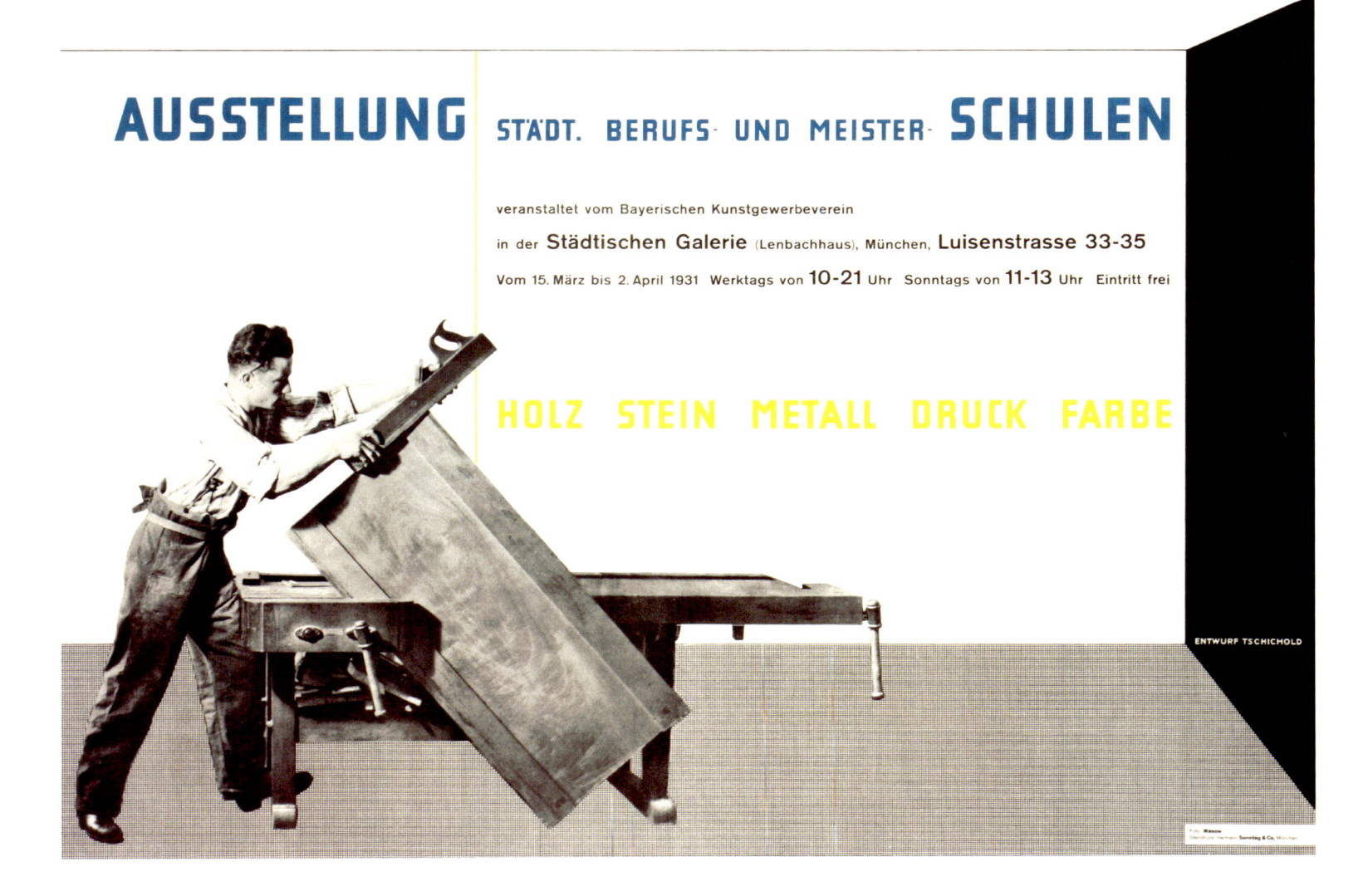

veranstaltet vom Bayerischen Kunstgewerbeverein

in der **Städtischen Galerie** (Lenbachhaus), München, **Luisenstrasse 33-35**

Vom 15. März bis 2. April 1931 Werktags von **10-21** Uhr Sonntags von **11-13** Uhr Eintritt frei

HOLZ STEIN METALL DRUCK FARBE

ENTWURF TSCHICHOLD

FESTIVALS of the Bavarian State Theatres Munich

July 18th to August 28th, 1932

Prince Regent Theatre: **Richard Wagner**
Residence Theatre: **W. A. Mozart**

followed by a Richard **Strauss** and Hans **Pfitzner** Week in the Prince Regent Theatre

Wagner-Mozart

Monday	July 18	Die Meistersinger	Monday	July 28	Die Meistersinger	Monday	Aug. 7	Die Meistersinger
Wednesday	July 20	Das Rheingold	Wednesday	July 29	Das Rheingold	Wednesday	Aug. 8	Das Rheingold
Thursday	July 21	Figaros Hochzeit	Thursday	July 30	Figaros Hochzeit	Thursday	Aug. 9	Figaros Hochzeit
Friday	July 22	Die Walküre	Friday	July 31	Die Walküre	Friday	Aug. 11	Die Walküre
Saturday	July 23	Die Zauberflöte	Saturday	Aug. 3	Die Zauberflöte	Saturday	Aug. 12	Die Zauberflöte
Sunday	July 24	Siegfried	Sunday	Aug. 4	Siegfried	Sunday	Aug. 13	Siegfried
Tuesday	July 26	Götterdämmerung	Tuesday	Aug. 5	Götterdämmerung	Tuesday	Aug. 14	Götterdämmerung
Wednesday	July 27	Don Giovanni	Wednesday	Aug. 6	Don Giovanni	Wednesday	Aug. 15	Don Giovanni

Monday	Aug. 16	Die Meistersinger
Wednesday	Aug. 18	Das Rheingold
Thursday	Aug. 19	Figaros Hochzeit
Friday	Aug. 20	Die Walküre
Saturday	Aug. 21	Die Zauberflöte
Sunday	Aug. 22	Siegfried

Richard Strauss

Monday	Aug. 23	Der Rosenkavalier
Wednesday	Aug. 24	Salome

Hans Pfitzner

Saturday	Aug. 27	Palestrina
Sunday	Aug. 28	Der arme Heinrich

Prices of admission
to Wagner Performances ...... RM 23,50 18,– 13,50
to Mozart Performances .... RM 33,50 18,– 13,50 7,30
to Strauss-Pfitzner Performances RM 14,50 9,– 4,50

→ Seats may be booked
at the Amtliches Bayrisches Reisebüro, 16 Promenadeplatz, Munich, or at the Tageskasse der Staatstheater, Max Joseph Platz, Munich

---

Design for a theater festival poster, 1932, collage, gouache, pen, NS, 60 x 79.5 cm, not executed, TE

Exhibition poster for the Gewerbemuseum, 1933, lithograph, NS, 128 x 90.3 cm, printer: Benno Schwabe & Co., Basel, BPS/TE

Schüleraufnahmen
der Allg. Gewerbeschule Basel
Wintersemester 1937-38

Montag, 18. Oktober 1937

9-12 **Lehrlinge der mechanisch-technischen Berufe**
Maschinen-Zeichner, Mechaniker und verwandte Berufe, Elektromechaniker, Elektroinstallateure usw.

14-16 **Lehrlinge der Ernährungs- und Bekleidungsgewerbe**
Bäcker, Konditoren, Köche, Coiffeure, Schneider, Schuhmacher, Sattler, Färber und Appreteure, Zahntechniker, Drogisten, Laboranten usw.

18-20 **Gehilfen der genannten Berufsgruppen**

Dienstag, 19. Oktober 1937

9-12 u. 14-16 **Lehrlinge der Baugewerbe**
Bauzeichner, Maurer, Gipser und Plattenleger, Zimmerleute, Schreiner, Wagner, Tapezierer, Schlosser, Schmiede, Bau- und Autospengler, Sanitär- und Heizungsinstallateure, Gärtner usw.

9-12 u. 14-16 **Lehrlinge der Kunstgewerbe**
Maler, Schriftsetzer, Buchdrucker, Buchbinder und Einrahmer, Lithographen, Photographen, Chemigraphen, Bildhauer, Goldschmiede, Graveure, Ziseleure, Schaufensterdekorateure, Stickerinnen, Blumenbinderinnen usw.

18-20 **Gehilfen der genannten Berufsgruppen**

9-12, 14-16 u. 18-20 **Aufnahmen in die Vorkurse, Fach- und Tagesklassen**
Vorkurse für graphische und textile Berufe, Vorkurse für Bauberufe
Allgemeine Zeichen- und Malklassen
Fachklassen für das Baufach und für Möbelschreiner
    für Graphik mit Photographie und Modezeichnen
    für Buchbinderei
    für Bildhauerei
    für Weben und Sticken
Fachschule für dekorative Malerei
Schweizerische Schlosserfachschule
Seminar für Zeichen-, Schreib- und Handarbeitslehrer

Unterrichtsbeginn: **Mittwoch, 20. Oktober 1937**
Für die Vorlehren (Sternengasse 18) und die Vorklassen (Rampe der Dreirosenbrücke) beginnt der Unterricht Montag, den 18. Oktober, vormittags 8 Uhr

Auskunft erteilt die Direktion der Allg. Gewerbeschule, Petersgraben 52

Poster listing admissions details for the Gewerbeschule, Basel, 1937, letterpress, NS, 127.5 x 90.8 cm, printer: Benno Schwabe & Co., Basel, TE

Chagall, exhibition poster, 1933, lithograph, "Jan Tschichold," 127 x 90.2 cm, printer: Benno Schwabe & Co., Basel, BPS/MGZ/MoMA/TA

Promotional postcard, ca. 1928, NS, 10.5 x 14.8 cm, TE

Constructivists, exhibition poster, 1937, letterpress, linocut with retouching (right 1 cm), "Jan Tschichold," 127.7 x 90.7 cm, printer: Benno Schwabe & Co., Basel, BPS/KB/MGZ/MoMA/SMA/TA. A smaller-format version, measuring 29.5 x 21 cm, is extant; in it, the circle is silkscreened.

● vom 16. januar bis 14. februar 1937

kunsthalle basel

konstruktivisten

van doesburg
domela
eggeling
gabo
kandinsky
lissitzky
moholy-nagy
mondrian
pevsner
taeuber
vantongerloo
vordemberge
u. a.

Overleaf:
Der Berufsphotograph (The Professional Photographer), exhibition poster, 1938, photographic print, rainbow print, and letterpress on white glossy paper, "jan tschichold swb," 63.4 x 90.7 cm, photo: Spreng, print: Schwitter AG, Basel, printer: Benno Schwabe & Co., Basel, BPS/LoC/MGZ/MoMA/SMA. Tschichold also designed the accompanying catalog.

unter mitarbeit des schweizerischen photographen-verbandes

gewerbemuseum basel **ausstellung**

der beruf

sphotograph sein werkzeug — seine arbeiten

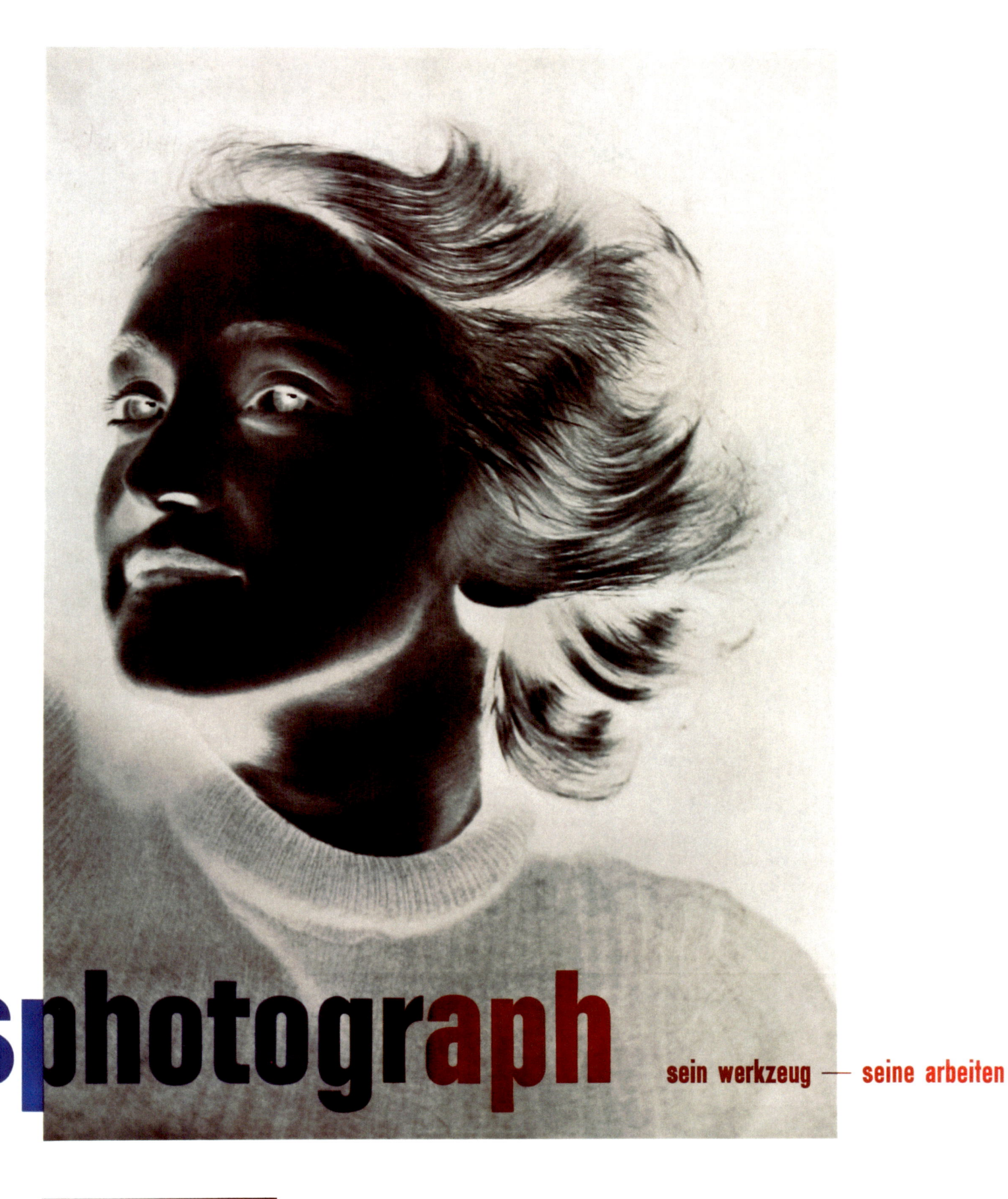

8. mai — 6. juni

werktags		14-19	
mittwochs		14-19	19-21
sonntags	10-12	14-19	

eintritt frei

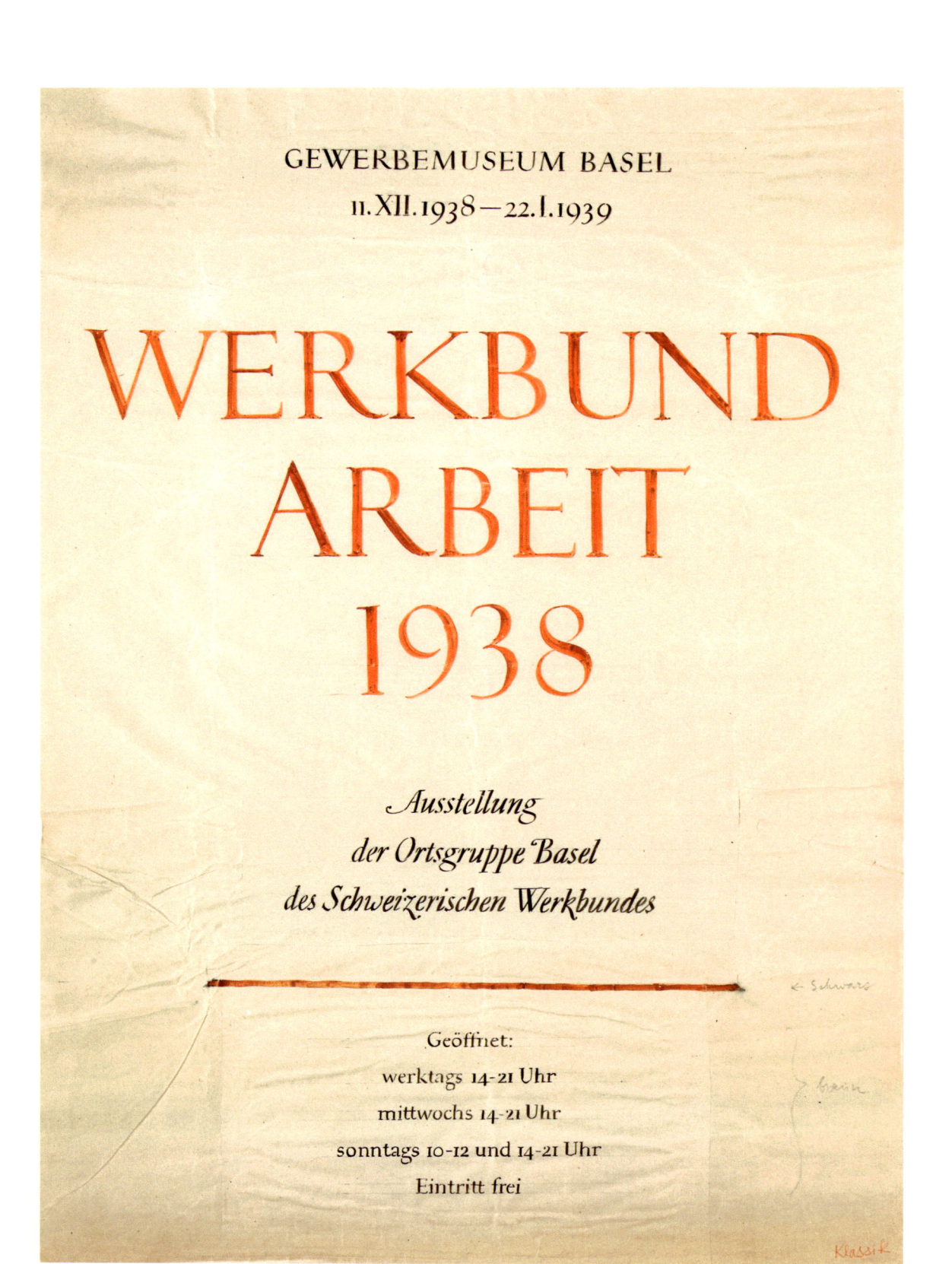

Poster design (not executed) for a Werkbund exhibition, 1938, gouache, ink, pencil, and collage on gray paper, NS, 125.8 x 89.8 cm, TE

Poster design (not executed) for a Werkbund exhibition, 1938, gouache, ink, pencil, and collage on gray paper, NS, 126.5 x 90.5 cm, TE

Poster for Basel Academy of Music, 1968, letterpress on light pink paper, "Jan Tschichold," 51.2 x 67.5 cm, PC

Poster for Basel Academy of Music, 1965, letterpress on blue paper, "Jan Tschichold," 51.5 x 68 cm, PC

Poster for Basel Academy of Music, 1973, letterpress on yellow paper, "Jan Tschichold," 51.5 x 68 cm, PC. Tschichold designed more posters of this type between 1965 and 1973.

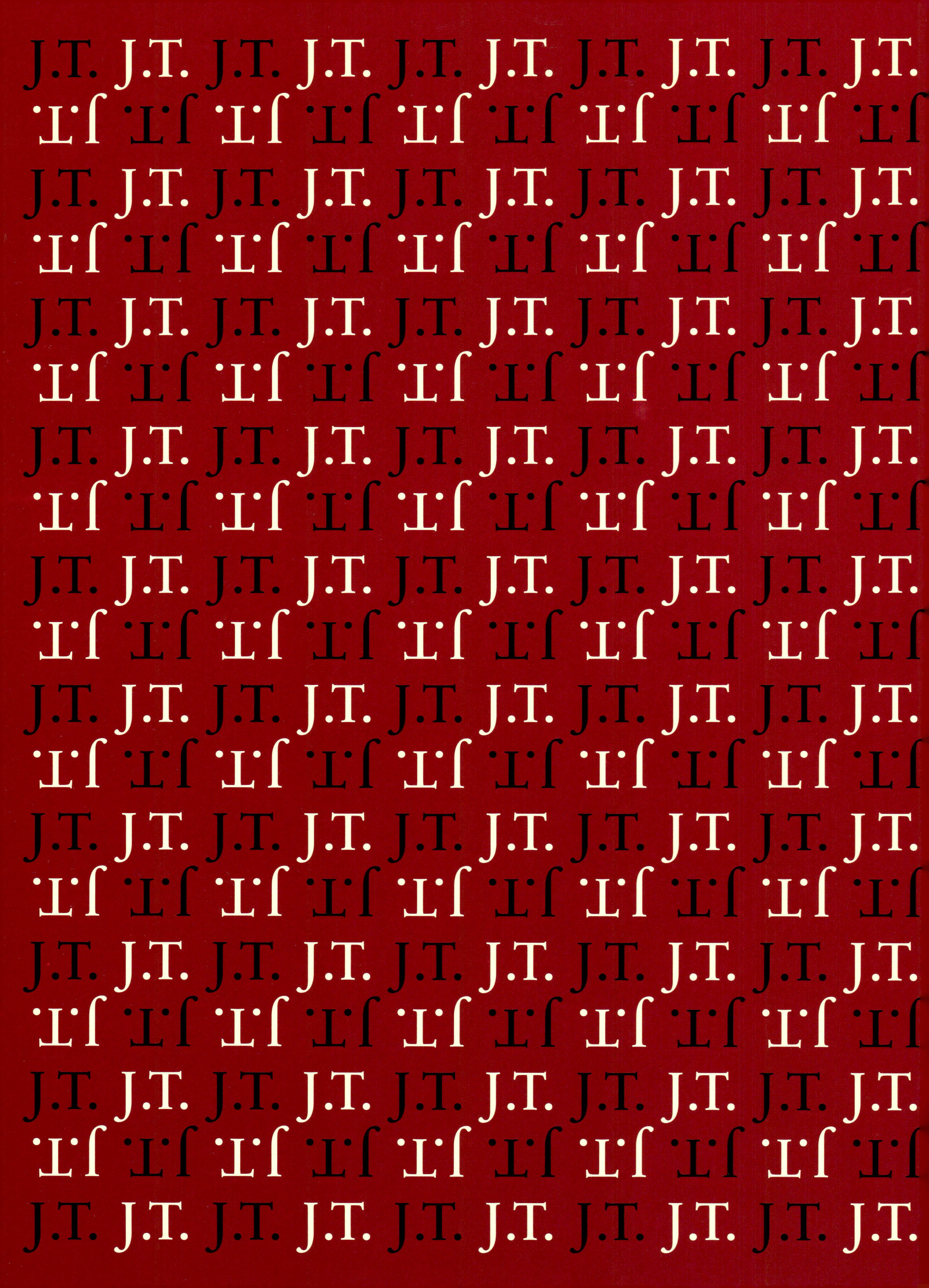

Resurgence of Classical Design

Richard B. Doubleday

Jan Tschichold (with his signature bow tie) with guests at Voitstraße 8/1, ca. 1931

Jan Tschichold at Penguin Books in London, ca. 1947
(photo: B. Heger)

J.T.

PENGUIN BOOKS

RESURGENCE OF CLASSICAL DESIGN

Hans Schmoller (left) and Jan Tschichold (right) attending the Alliance Graphique Internationale meeting in Mainz, 1966. Photo courtesy of Tanya Schmoller

A last visit with Kurt Schwitters, England, ca. 1947. Left to right: Mr. William (Bill) Pierce Jr., Edith Thomas, Kurt Schwitters, and Gwyneth Alban-Davies. Photo by Hilde Goldschmidt

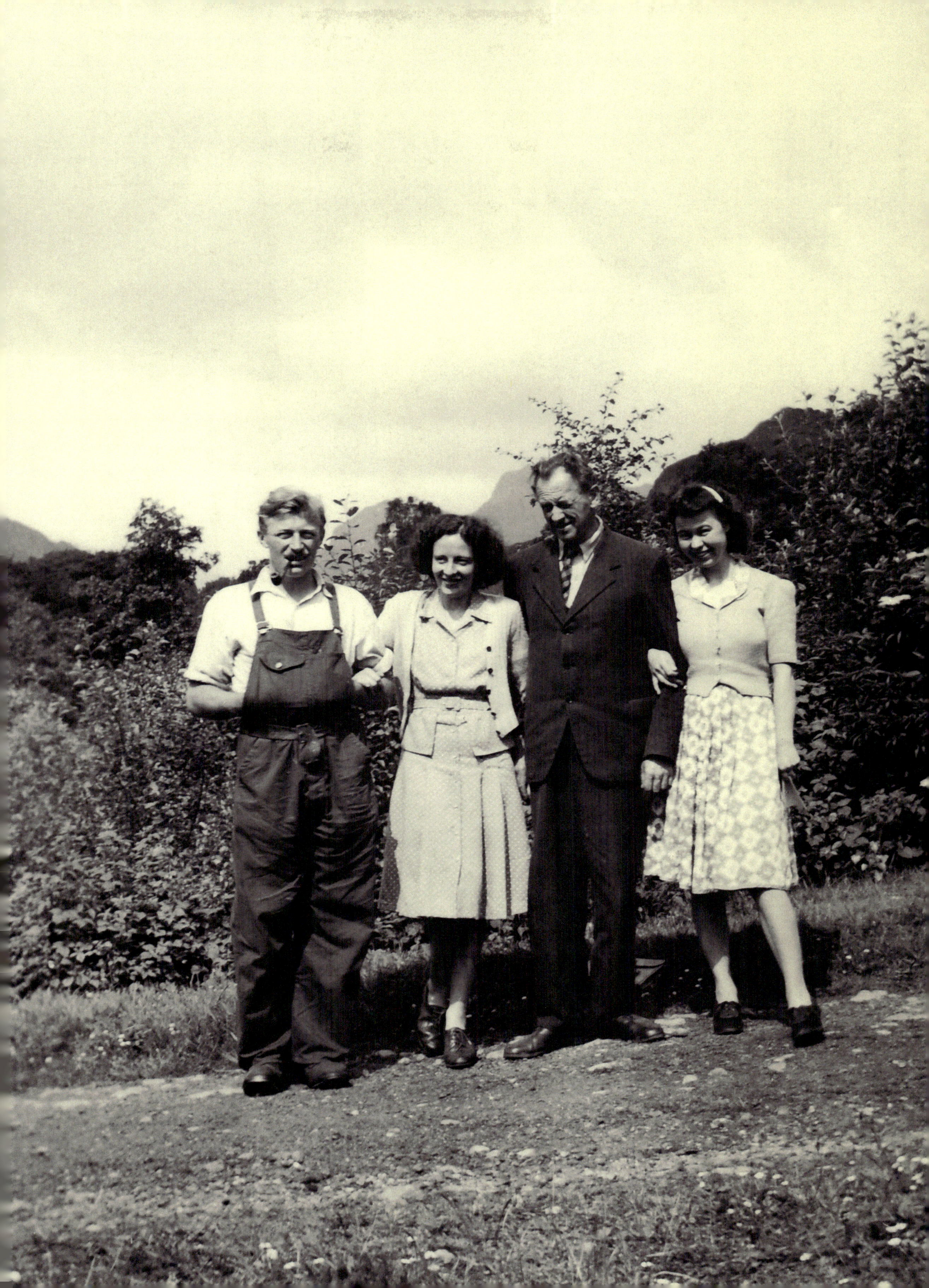

Resurgence of Classical Design

In the years following World War II, book publishers like Penguin sought the best typographic talent in Europe and offered designers unparalleled artistic freedom to develop a new set of typographic rules and standards for the mass production of books. When Penguin Books publisher Allen Lane hired Jan Tschichold in March 1947 to redesign its publications, he would have been surprised had he realized that his new designer would set the standard for all book design for years to come in Britain. Tschichold's demand for consistency and superior design and his successful management of the varied departments involved in the production process brought about significant change within the mass-market publishing industry. Most importantly, Tschichold helped to bring forth a resurgence of classical typography and book design.

Shortly after emigrating to Riehen, Switzerland, in 1933, Tschichold designed books for Basel publishing houses, principally Birkhäuser, Holbein-Verlag, and Benno Schwabe & Co. Tschichold's work at Benno Schwabe, particularly the typographic house rules he established and enforced there, foreshadowed the composition rules he would devise for Penguin. Likewise, the practical, symmetrical house style that Tschichold set for the 53-volume Birkhäuser Classics series was similar to his design approach at Penguin. Although produced for a mass market, Birkhäuser spared no expense on the production of its titles, using patterned papers and covers made of linen and leather. Tschichold's work on the Birkhäuser Classics established a house style using black and one color on unbleached paper, ornate patterns, and all uppercase typography with a thin rule separating the title from the publisher's name—elements that would be seen in titles produced later at Penguin.

Tschichold's styling of the Birkhäuser Classics caught the attention of Oliver Simon of the Curwen Press in England, who saw that Tschichold possessed the aptitude and skill for implementing superior typographical standards for an extensive readership. British publishers were beginning to recognize the importance of a book's appearance for marketing purposes, and thus the demand for skilled designers was increasing. Simon suggested to Lane that Tschichold would be the perfect designer for the challenging task of redesigning Penguins.

Homer, *The Odyssey*, 1943, jacket design by Jan Tschichold. Birkhäuser Classics series, Birkhäuser Verlag, Basel.

Luigi Da Porto: *The Tale of Romeo and Juliet*, 1944, cover design by Jan Tschichold, Sammlung Birkhäuser series. Tschichold designed this paper cover three years before his arrival at Penguin. The florid and intricately patterned paper may have derived from Tschichold's study of the French Rococo era as well as the geometric stylings of Giovanni Battista Palatino. This style would become an important recurring theme for many of the Penguin series. The small rectangular title plate is similar to Tschichold's design for the King Penguins, and the patterned paper effect is comparable to the Penguin Music Scores.

> No Teniendo cosa cierta del
> mundo ni de sus cosas hazemos ca
> sas costosas estando el huer
> co a la puerta. Se
> guimos a sathanas y a ti buen dios
> no tememos de contino
> te ofendemos con
> los bienes que nos das.
>
> A a b c d e f g h i k l m n o p q r
> ſ s t v u x y z ʒ.
>
> Ioannes de yciar scribebat.
> 1550
> .I.D.V.

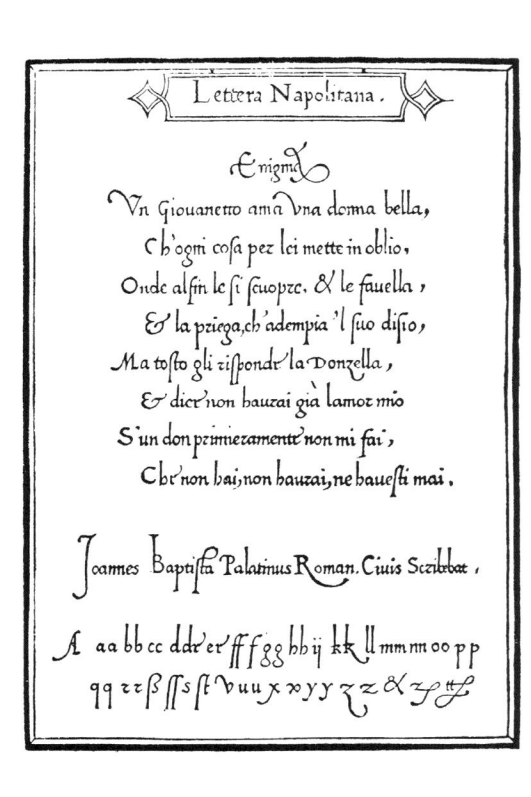

Lettera Napolitana.

Enigma

Vn Giouanetto ama vna donna bella,
Ch'ogni cosa per lei mette in oblio,
Onde alfin le si scuopre, & le fauella,
& la priega, ch'adempia'l suo disio,
Ma tosto gli risponde la Donzella,
& dice non haurai già l'amor mio
S'un don primieramente non mi fai,
Che non hai, non haurai, ne hauesti mai.

Ioannes Baptista Palatinus Roman. Ciuis Scribebat.

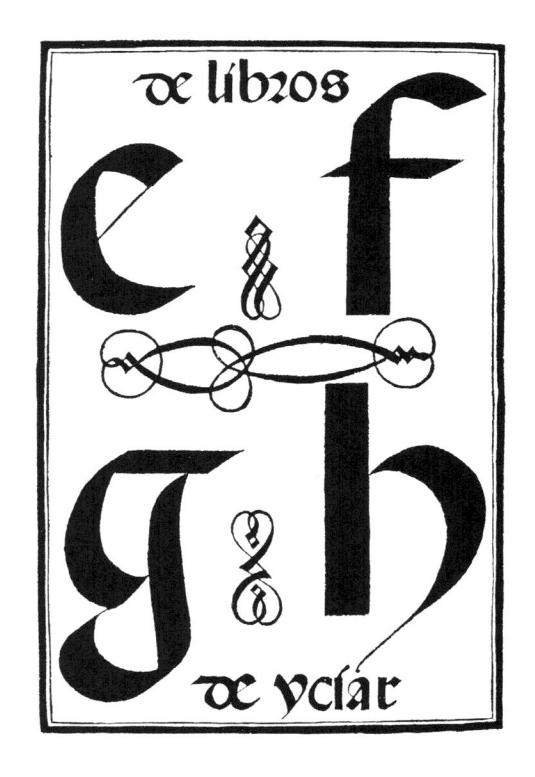

A aa bb cc dd er fff gg hh ij kk ll mm nn oo pp
qq rr ſſ s st vu u x x yy z & ʒ ſſ lb

de libros
e f
g h
de yciar

Resurgence of Classical Design

Tschichold's writings on typography and book design in Switzerland and Britain were informed by his early training and educational background and thus shaped by his classical roots. Tschichold spent time studying civilizations, typography, and the book arts in the Leipzig "Hall of Culture," in 1914, at the age of twelve. It was during this period that he studied Roman alphabets, calligraphy, illuminated manuscripts, the history and craftsmanship of written letters, and old type specimens. Tschichold had witnessed for the first time the work of Italian, Spanish, German, Swiss, Dutch, and French calligraphic masters such as Giovanni Battista Palatino, Lodovico Arrighi, Giovanni Antonio Tagliente, Juan de Yçiar, Johann Neudörffer, Urban Wyss, Jan van de Velde, and Pierre Simon Fournier le Jeune.

In 1916, during his studies at the Teacher Training College at Grimma, Tschichold realized that he wanted to become a type designer and was given permission by his parents to enroll at the Academy for the Graphic Arts and Book Production in Leipzig, where he learned bookbinding, calligraphy, etching, and engraving. Tschichold taught himself handlettering and calligraphy, examining the lettering in Edward Johnston's book *Writing & Illuminating & Lettering* and Rudolf von Larisch's book *Instruction in Ornamental Writing*. These self-taught calligraphy exercises increased Tschichold's knowledge and sensitivity to letterspacing, word spacing, and leading. Tschichold also enrolled for one year at the School of Arts and Crafts in Dresden, where he was mentored by the type designer and writing teacher Heinrich Wieynck. Tschichold was inspired by many of Wieynck's type designs—Mercedes Antiqua, Tranon, Woellmer Antiqua, Belvedere, and Kolumbus—which were based on the Italian Renaissance writing scripts.

Tschichold began to look at the Gothic revival lettering of Rudolph Koch's German scripts and embraced the handwritten style in his own type designs. During this time, he spent many hours studying the great type specimen book collection at the Master Printers Federation Library in Leipzig. The Italian Renaissance writing masters and reading-room resources impressed Tschichold, and firmly established his classical typographical roots, which would later inform his approach to book design.

In August 1923, at the age of twenty-one, Tschichold attended the first Weimar Bauhaus Exhibition, where he saw for the first time the graphic design work of Herbert Bayer and László Moholy-Nagy. Tschichold was particularly inspired by the asymmetrical layout in Moholy-Nagy's catalog for the exhibition. He soon embraced the design concepts of the Bauhaus and the Russian constructivists, which proved to be a significant departure from his classical roots. It is this asymmetrical repertoire that Tschichold is most noted for, but he drew away from it while in Switzerland and England.

Juan de Yçiar, script sample from *Arte subtilissima, por la qual se enseña a escrevir perfectamente*, Zaragoza, 1550. From illustrations in *L'Art pour tous*. This Spanish style is derivative of cursive.

Giovanni Battista Palatino, script sample from *Libro di Giambattista Palatino nel quale s'insegna a scrivere ogni sorte lettera*, Rome, 1544

Juan de Yçiar, script sample from *Arte subtilissima, por la qual se enseña a escrevir perfectamente*, Zaragoza, 1550. From illustrations in *L'Art pour tous*. From the Gothic period, the ornamental alphabet Redonda.

Urban Wyss, *Libellus valde doctus, elegans & utilis, multa & varia scribendarum literarum genera complectens*, Zurich, 1549

Tschichold met El Lissitzky shortly after the Bauhaus exhibition. He was deeply influenced by Lissitzky's work and followed Lissitzky's lead in treating typography as concrete and abstract contrasting shapes. In his original manifesto, *Die neue Typographie*, Tschichold advocated the New Typography for all forms of communication; the setting of type must always be asymmetrical, and sans serif typography (then called Grotesque), was the only type capable of expressing modern ideas. Tschichold came to abandon these rigid rules at Penguin. Although he had been a strong proponent of modern functional design, he changed his position based on a more realistic assessment of the requirements of book design for the Swiss publishers Birkhäuser, Holbein-Verlag, and Benno Schwabe.

Tschichold had first begun to pull away from the New Typography and the functionalist principles of the Bauhaus while designing books in Switzerland between 1933 and 1946. He realized then that symmetrical typographic treatments could fulfill the requirements of successful book design and that asymmetrical compositions were less appropriate for the great works of literature and for the desires of conservative Swiss publishing clients. In a letter dated January 31, 1946, to Rudolf Hostettler, editor-in-chief of *Typographische Monatsblätter*, Tschichold disclosed: "The position today is that neither symmetrical nor asymmetrical setting can be regarded as the 'ideal'; the typographer will move in one direction or the other according to his assignment."[1] He felt that a practicing book designer must serve and respect the given text. As he stated in a 1959 lecture at the Type Directors Club in New York: "Obeying good rules of composition and book design in the manner of traditional typography is not 'putting the clock back;' but an eccentric style of setting is almost always debatable."[2]

In April 1935, Tschichold's change of design direction became public when, in his article "The Design of Centered Typography" in *Typographische Monatsblätter* no. 4, he stated that centered typography was acceptable, and that typographic design was subject to the technical and aesthetic requirements and demands of book design. For example, he believed that title pages with short lines of text were more aesthetically appealing when centered, and symmetrical settings were easier for compositors.

Tschichold was particularly concerned with title pages, feeling that they had become a neglected area for book designers. He believed that the title page was important because it sets the tone and first impression for the reader and that it should convey the style of the written work. He studied examples of title pages from French typographic reference books of the 19th century, M. Brun's *Practical Manual of French Typography* (1825), and Henri Fournier's *Handbook of*

*Qui semel à ueritate deflexit, hic non maiore religione ad p̄-
iurium, quàm ad mendatium pauci consueuit. Et quæ pœ-
na à Dijs immortalibus periuro, hæc mendaci constituta e
Non enim ex pactione verborū, quibus jusiurandum cō-
prehendit, sed ex p̄fidia, ac malitia, p quam insidiæ tendūt
alicui, Dij immortales irasci, ác succensere consuetunt.*

A A B C D E F G J K L M N O P Q R

Tschichold's cover design for a Leipzig printer's New Year card, 1922. Originally in blue, green, red, and yellow. Based on Tschichold's examination of the calligraphy manuals of Ludovico Arrighi and Giovanni Antonio Tagliente, the two Italian Renaissance masters of scripts and chancery cursive. Note Tschichold's careful centered placement of exquisitely handdrawn calligraphy, the delicate symmetry of the flower motif and the inverted uppercase letters within the frame. This early design treatment is similar to Tschichold's cover designs many years later at Penguin.

Typography (1825). These practical handbooks covered the fine details of composition and presswork and served as references for Tschichold when he designed books for Birkhäuser, Holbein-Verlag, and Benno Schwabe. Tschichold applied the principles he learned from these books, following their examples regarding word spacing, typeface usage, type sizes, ornaments, and rules.

The challenging task at Penguin perfectly suited Tschichold as a designer. Penguin's invitation presented him with an opportunity to develop a new set of typographic rules, to put to use his knowledge gained from working with Swiss publishing houses, to exercise his typographic theories, and to apply his classical and historical knowledge of typography to the mass production of books.

By the time Tschichold arrived at Penguin in March 1947, paperbacks had become a popular form of mass media, and Penguin Books in particular provided the general public with a wide range of affordable literature. Penguin's designs, however, fell far short of their literary reputation as a result of the decline in the quantity and quality of paper during the war years. Penguin was now capable of returning to pre-war standards of design and book production. Before arriving at Penguin, Tschichold requested samples of Penguin books and soon realized that composition rules and standards were virtually nonexistent at the company, as the production department depended on sample pages and different sets of house rules supplied by Penguin's various printers. In addition, Old Style No. 2, Gill Sans, and Times New Roman were the only fonts being utilized throughout all the series. Tschichold's strategy to help educate employees unfamiliar with the design process was to provide explanatory notes and criticisms and circulated them to the editorial and production staff.

Tschichold decided to set a practical look for Penguin that would suit a large number of books and achieve balance, consistency, and legibility. In his view, adherence to the tenets of classic typography —legibility, a balance of type styles, wide margins, contrast, simplicity, and integrated rules and ornaments—was integral to a book's function. For example, he preferred classical typefaces for long pages of text, noting that: "Good typography has to be perfectly legible and is, as such, the result of intelligent planning. The classical typefaces such as Garamond, Janson, Baskerville, and Bell are undoubtedly the most legible."[3]

THE PENGUIN COMPOSITION RULES Once at Penguin, Tschichold circulated written comments and criticisms about existing Penguin designs to the editorial staff. He then developed the Penguin Composition Rules, with standardized formats and detailed typographic specifications addressing every last aspect of design and typesetting. These rules directed attention to text composition, indenting, punctuation marks, spelling, capitals, small capitals, italics, folios, figures, references, footnotes, make-up, and the printing of plays and poetry. The Penguin Composition Rules unified the design of all the Penguin series, while bringing a sense of harmony and economy to its publishing program.

Underlying the Penguin Composition Rules was the implementation of a grid system. The grids were unalterable instructions that set the foundation for the trimmed page area, the width and height of each book, the visual cover size, the type area on the cover and the spine, the position and the style of the spine label and lettering of book titles on the labels for all the Penguin series. The grid gave Tschichold the flexibility to create appropriate scale relationships between the type and dimensions of each book, to initiate a maximum area and correct imposition for a King Penguin plate, for example, to set the correct central placement and maximum depth for illustrations with a one-line caption, and to designate the most appropriate typeface to accurately reflect the content of the book.

After establishing these design standards, Tschichold had the responsibility of explaining it to the large group of Penguin Books compositors and printers, many of whom were less than enthusiastic at the intensified level of scrutiny and involvement in their work. Tschichold's presence was most clearly felt in the Penguin composing rooms, which he visited often in order to make exacting revisions to typographical arrangements and layouts. Tschichold stated: "Every day I had to wade through miles of corrections (often ten books daily). I had a rubber stamp made: 'Equalize letterspaces according to their visual value.' It was totally ignored; the hand compositors continued to space out the capitals on title pages (where optical spacing is essential) with spaces of equal thickness." [4] Despite initial resistance, Tschichold persisted, and after about a year he began to see improvements. He could then turn his full energies toward the individual book designs.

MONOTYPE TYPEFACES During the 1920s and 1930s the Monotype Corporation, under the direction of typographic consultant Stanley Morison, raised the standard of British publishing and printing by reviving a series of classical typefaces for machine composition. By the time Tschichold arrived at Penguin Books, the setting of type by machine had become an accepted practice by printers and publishers, as composition machines had become more proficient, and books composed and printed by mechanical means were considered equal to those created by hand. The revolution of mechanical production moved quickly through the printing trade as composition machines became more proficient.

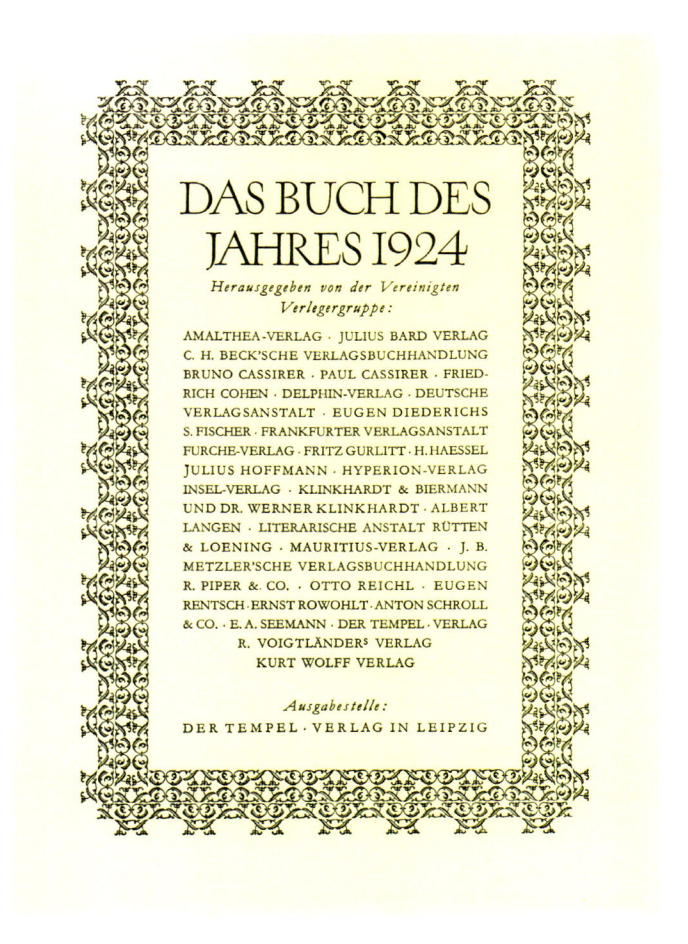

Cover drawn by Jan Tschichold for a Leipzig printer's leaflet, 1923. Based on Tschichold's study of the calligraphy books of Ludovico Arrighi and Giovanni Antonio Tagliente.

Design by Jan Tschichold for *Das Buch Des Jahres 1924*, 1924. Der Tempel, Leipzig. The centered typography and decorative border were forerunners to many of the Penguin covers and title pages, particularly the decorative border of the Penguin Poets series. The restrained typographic composition is based on Tschichold's study of Roman alphabets and ornate writing in illuminated manuscripts.

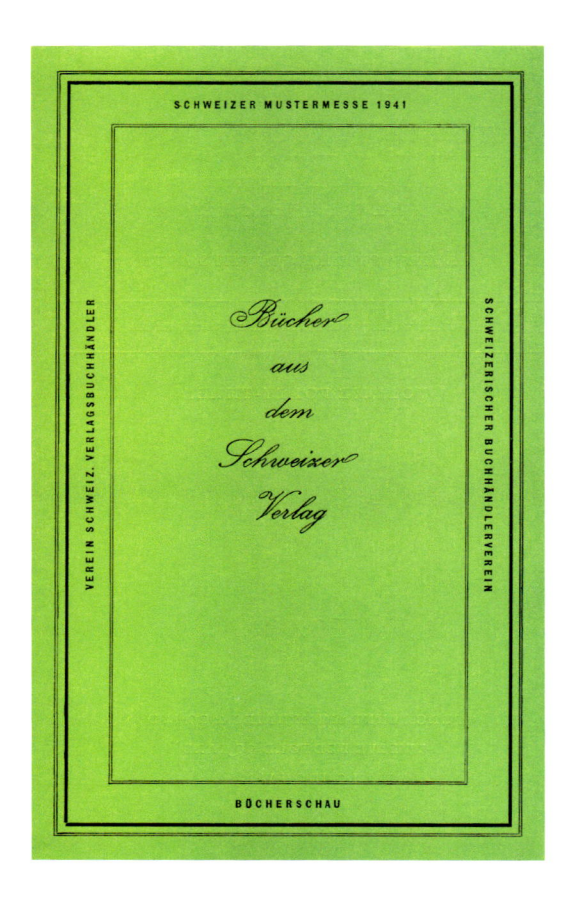

SCHWEIZER MUSTERMESSE 1941

*Bücher
aus
dem
Schweizer
Verlag*

VEREIN SCHWEIZ. VERLAGSBUCHHÄNDLER
SCHWEIZERISCHER BUCHHÄNDLERVEREIN

BÜCHERSCHAU

Shakespeares dramatische Werke

3

Julius Cäsar
Antonius und Cleopatra
Coriolanus

Birkhäuser-Klassiker

BEETHOVEN
Coriolan and Egmont
PENGUIN SCORES III · 2/6

Tschichold adopted the Monotype Corporation's most distinguished typefaces for Penguin Books, skillfully identifying the right face for every variety of book and choosing the font that would most appropriately suit the personality of the given text: for example, Garamond and Caslon Old Face with its distinctive oblique styling for the Penguin Musical Scores, Bembo for the Penguin Shakespeare series, and the elegant and slender Bell for many of the Penguin Poets.

THE PENGUIN SERIES   One of Tschichold's first design tasks was to refine the Penguin series covers. Penguin publisher Lane recognized The Albatross Library's effective use of design to establish a brand identity in the marketplace, and he wanted Penguin to do the same. Tschichold therefore modeled his cover designs after Albatross, using the golden section proportions $4^{3}/_{8}$ x $7^{1}/_{8}$ inches (11.1 x 18.1 cm), color-coding by genre, sans serif typographic covers, and the bird logo. Prevented by his publisher from completely redesigning the Penguin series due to brand loyalty, Tschichold did what he could to modify the existing "Penguin look"—the distinguishing orange horizontal top and bottom panels, originally developed by the imprint's first production editor, Edward Young.

Tschichold's first revision in 1948 was to introduce weights of Gill Sans for hierarchy and emphasis, and meticulous letter and word spacing for both the title and author's name. Tschichold introduced a less condensed, slightly more extended and overall cleaner looking version of Gill Sans by the Monotype Corporation. Tschichold commented on his design strategy: "I could only bring the earlier ugly proportions into a happier relationship."[5] For the second revision, Tschichold then redesigned the Penguin logo at the bottom center of the front jacket. He also reduced the point size of the typography and introduced an orange rule between the title and author's name. What he did retain was Penguin's characteristic color-coding by genre—orange for fiction, green for crime, blue for biography, burgundy for travel, yellow for miscellaneous, and gray for current affairs—and he continued Penguin's tradition of avoiding pictorial covers.

Tschichold's final revision of the Penguin cover, in 1949, was to modify the Penguin trademark. He improved the letterspacing and reduced its overall size for improved proportion. He decreased the weight of the orange rule between the title and author's name and also introduced two hairline rules running parallel along the orange horizontal top and bottom panels. These final revisions firmly established a standardized format, which unified the Penguin series.

Catalog cover for Schweizer Verlag, design by Jan Tschichold, 1941. Tschichold designed this cover six years before his tenure at Penguin. The arrangement of the type is comparable to the redesign of the Pelican series, with uppercase sans serif type inside a ruled border and a beautiful script font for the title.

William Shakespeare, *Julius Caesar, Antony and Cleopatra, Coriolanus*. Cover design by Jan Tschichold. Birkhäuser Classics series, 1943. Birkhäuser Verlag, Basel

Beethoven, *Coriolan and Egmont*, cover design by Jan Tschichold. Penguin Music Scores, no. SC 3, June 1949. $5^{1}/_{8}$" x $7^{3}/_{4}$" (13.0 x 19.7 cm). The distinguishing typographic features are Monotype Caslon Old Face and Garamond. The decorative Curwen Press patterned paper is by the German designer Elizabeth Friedlander.

Penguin Composition Rules

TEXT COMPOSITION

All text composition should be as closely word-spaced as possible. As a rule, the spacing should be about a middle space or the thickness of an 'i' in the type size used.

Wide spaces should be strictly avoided. Words may be freely broken whenever necessary to avoid wide spacing, as breaking words is less harmful to the appearance of the page than too much space between words.

All major punctuation marks – full point, colon, and semicolon – should be followed by the same spacing as is used throughout the rest of the line.

INDENTING OF PARAGRAPHS

The indent of the paragraph should be the em of the fount body.

Omit indents in the first line of the first paragraph of any text and at the beginning of a new section that comes under a sub-heading. It is not necessary to set the first word in small capitals, but if this is done for any reason, the word should be letter-spaced in the same way as the running title.

If a chapter is divided into several parts without headings, these parts should be divided not only by an additional space, but always by one or more asterisks of the fount body. As a rule, one asterisk is sufficient. Without them it is impossible to see whether a part ends at the bottom of a page or not. Even when the last line of such a part ends the page, there will always be space for an asterisk in the bottom margin.

PUNCTUATION MARKS AND SPELLING

If this can be done on the keyboard, put thin spaces before question marks, exclamation marks, colons, and semicolons.

Between initials and names, as in G. B. Shaw and after all abbreviations where a full point is used, use a smaller (fixed) space than between the other words in the line.

Instead of em rules without spaces, use en rules preceded and followed by the word space of the line, as in the third paragraph above.

Marks of omission should consist of three full points. These should be set without any spaces, but be preceded and followed by word spaces.

Use full points sparingly, and omit after these abbreviations: Mr, Mrs, Messrs, Dr, St, WC2, 8vo, and others containing the last letter of the abbreviated word.

Use single quotes for a first quotation and double quotes for quotations within quotations. If there is still another quotation within the second, return to single quotes. Punctuation belonging to a quotation comes within the quotes, otherwise outside.

Opening quotes should be followed by a hairspace except before A and J. Closing quotes should be preceded by a hairspace except after a comma or a full point. If this cannot be done on the keyboard, omit these hairspaces, but try to get the necessary attachment.

When long extracts are set in small type do not use quotes.

Use parentheses ( ) for explanation and interpolations; brackets [ ] for notes.

For all other queries on spelling, consult the *Rules for Compositors and Readers at the University Press, Oxford*, or Collins's *Authors' and Printers' Dictionary*.

CAPITALS, SMALL CAPITALS, AND ITALICS

Words in capitals must always be letter-spaced. The spacing of the capitals in lines of importance should be very carefully optically equalized. The word spaces in lines either of capitals or small capitals should not exceed an en quad.

All display lines set in the same fount should be given the same spacing throughout the book.

Use small capitals for running headlines and in contents pages. They must always be slightly letter-spaced to make words legible.

Running headlines, unless otherwise stated, should consist of the title of the book on the left-hand page, and the contents of the chapter on the right.

Italics are to be used for emphasis, for foreign words and phrases, and for the titles of books, newspapers, and plays which appear in the text. In such cases the definite article 'The' should be printed in roman, unless it is part of the title itself.

In bibliographical and related matter, as a rule, authors' names should be given in small capitals with capitals, and the titles in italics.

FIGURES

Do not mix old style text composition with modern face figures. Either hanging or ranging figures may be used if they are cut in the fount used for the text.

In text matter, numbers under 100 should be composed in letters. Use figures when the matter consists of a sequence of stated

quantities, particulars of age, &c. In dates use the fewest possible figures, 1946–7, not 1946–1947. Divide by an en rule without spaces.

REFERENCES AND FOOTNOTES

The reference to a footnote may be given by an asterisk of the fount body, if there are only a few footnotes in the book, and not more than one per page. But if there are two or more footnotes per page, use superior fraction figures preceded by a thin space.

Do not use modern face fraction figures in any old style fount. Either hanging or ranging fraction figures may be used provided that they are in harmony with the face used for the text. For books composed in any old face letter, we recommend Monotype Superior Figures F627, to be cast on the size two points below the size of the face used.

Footnotes should be set two points smaller than the text. Indent the first line of these with the same number of points as the paragraphs in the text matter. Use equal leading between all lines of footnotes, use the same leading as in the text matter, and put 1–2 point lead underneath the last line in order to get register with the normal lines.

For the numbering of footnotes use normal figures followed by a full point and an en quad. These figures may run either throughout the chapter, or even through the whole book, according to the special instructions given by the typographer.

FOLIOS

These should, as a rule, be set in the same size and face as the text, and in arabic numerals.

Pagination should begin with the first leaf in the book, but the first folio actually appearing is that on the verso of the first page of the text.

When there is preliminary matter whose extent is unknown at the time of making up the text into pages, it is necessary to use lower-case roman numerals, numbered from the first page of the first sheet. The first actually appearing cannot be definitely stated, but may be on the acknowledgements page, or at latest on the second page of the preface. In this case, the first arabic folio to appear will be '2' on the verso of the first text page.

Folios for any text matter at the end of the book, such as index &c., should continue the arabic numbering of the text pages.

THE PRINTING OF PLAYS

The same rules should apply to the printing of plays as to the printing of prose. Names of characters should be set in capitals

and small capitals. The text following is indented. Stage directions should be in italics, enclosed in square brackets. The headline should include the number of the act and the scene.

THE PRINTING OF POETRY

For printing poetry use type of a smaller size than would be used for prose. All composition should be leaded and the words evenly spaced with middle spaces. The titles should be centred on the measure, not on the first line. The beginning of each poem may be treated as a chapter opening, with small capitals, &c.

Extra leading, especially between verses of irregular length, may often be misleading, as it is impossible to see whether the verse ends at the bottom of the page or not. The safest way of recognizing the poet's intention is to indent the first line of every new verse, after which leading is not really necessary. Therefore, the first line of the second and following verses should be indented, unless the poet has indicated a shape not allowing for indentations.

MAKE-UP

Books should, with certain exceptions, be made up in the following order:

I. Preliminary pages: 1, half title; 2, frontispiece; 3, title; 4, Imprint or date of publication; 5, dedication; 6, acknowledgements; 7, contents; 8, list of illustrations; 9, list of abbreviations; 10, preface; 11, introduction; 12, errata.

II. The text of the book.

III. Additional matter: 1. appendix; 2. author's notes; 3. glossary; 4. bibliography; 5. index.

The above should each begin on a right-hand page, imprint and frontispiece excepted. As a rule, chapter headings should be dropped a few lines.

The preliminary pages should be set in the same face and style as the book itself. Avoid bold faces.

The index should be set in two or more columns and in type two points smaller than the text. The first word of each letter of the alphabet should be set in small capitals with capitals.

Jan Tschichold

The Penguin Composition Rules devised by Jan Tschichold, 1947. Some designers of Tschichold's generation had accomplished the implementation of house design rules before Tschichold joined Penguin: Alvin Lustig at New Directions in the United States; Stanley Morison at Victor Gollancz in the UK; and Giovanni Mardersteig at The Albatross Library in Germany.

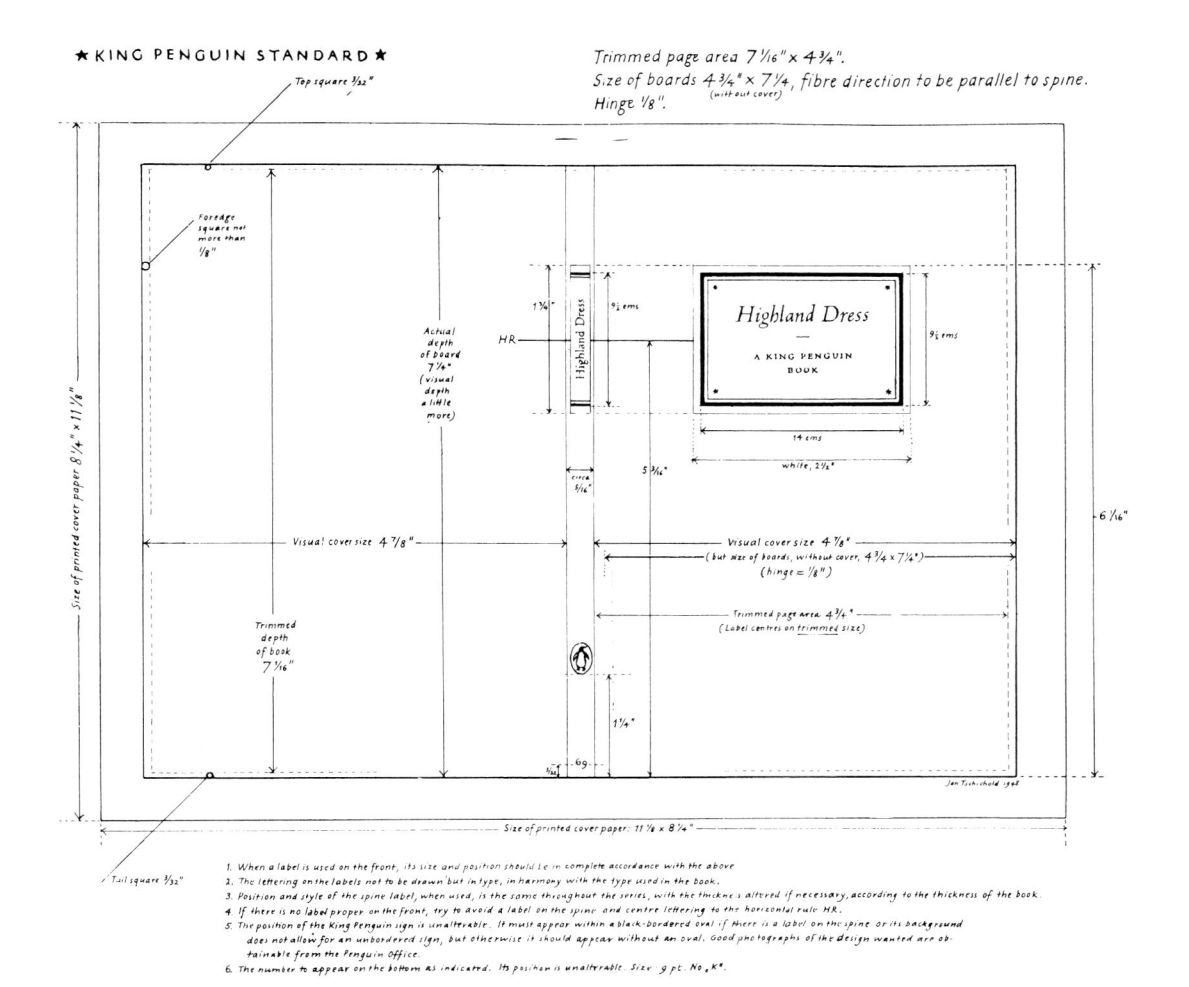

Standard instructions or 'grid' for King Penguin covers, as applied to *Highland Dress* by John Piper. A King Penguin Book, no. K 46, 1948. 4³/₄″ x 7¹/₁₆″ (11.9 x 17.9 cm). King Penguin series cover drawn and devised by Jan Tschichold.

King Penguin maximum area and correct imposition for any King Penguin plate. Design by Jan Tschichold, 1948. 4³/₄″ x 7¹/₁₆″ (11.9 x 17.9 cm).

A DOUBLE VOLUME

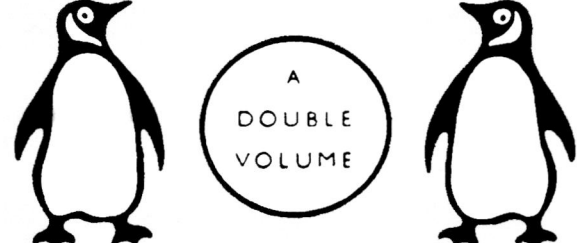

Penguin logos, 1947. Tschichold redrew the Penguin symbol which was originally designed by Edward Young in 1935, as well as the Pelican and Puffin.

Rough sketches of the Penguin logo by Jan Tschichold, 1947

RESURGENCE OF CLASSICAL DESIGN

THE KING PENGUIN SERIES The King Penguin series, which covered art, science, leisure, and world history, was Penguin's first series to be printed in color and in hardcover. With improvements in color printing, particularly for small-scale color reproductions such as wood engravings, drawings, and prints, Penguin began producing color plates and pictorial covers as attractive collector's items for the general reader. Tschichold decided that the overall redesign of the King Penguins would emulate the prominent and much admired Insel-Verlag picture books from Germany. Each book numbered approximately 64 pages, with an equal distribution of text and images. The appearance was classic and elegant. They were slightly smaller in format, at a size of $4^{3}/_{4}$ x $7^{1}/_{16}$ inches (11.9 x 17.9 cm), and sold at twice the price because they were more expensive to produce than paperback Penguins. For King Penguins, Tschichold used unusual classic typefaces, including Centaur, Pastonchi, Poliphilus, Scotch Roman, Lutetia, and Walbaum. Often these typeface choices were dictated by their suitability to the books' subject matter and the type of paper they were to be printed on.

Of particular note in the King Penguin series is *A Book of Scripts* by Alfred Fairbank. Tschichold adapted the cover design from a page in *Arte Subtilissima*, a classic work on calligraphy and engraving by the 16th-century Spanish master calligrapher Juan de Yçiar, one of Tschichold's early influences. Tschichold was concerned with achieving the highest-quality reproduction, particularly when it involved calligraphy and fine lettering. Another production problem was that the most desirable originals at hand had been printed from broken-down woodblocks. For *A Book of Scripts*, Tschichold utilized his early training as a calligrapher by drawing the roman capitals with a pen and brush by hand on the front and back cover panels, carefully restoring them to their original shapes. The National Book League in England recognized this title as one of the best-designed books of 1949.

THE PENGUIN CLASSICS Penguin Classics were launched in January 1946, as a new series of translations of Greek, French, and Latin classics, including such titles as *Old Goriot, Crime and Punishment*, and *The Odyssey*. These titles appealed to the many serious readers looking for foreign literature translated into English. Within seven months of joining Penguin, Tschichold redesigned the following two volumes within the Penguin Classics series: Dante's *The Divine Comedy I* and Virgil's *The Pastoral Poems*.

The original Penguin Classics cover design was disordered, and its elements did not complement each other. For the redesign of the Penguin Classics series, Tschichold reintroduced the common monochromatic color-coding system around the frame. He also added a thick patterned rule just within the frame, which gave the series a classic and appealing personality. The illustrated engravings and roundels appearing on the covers and throughout the interior spreads were commissioned

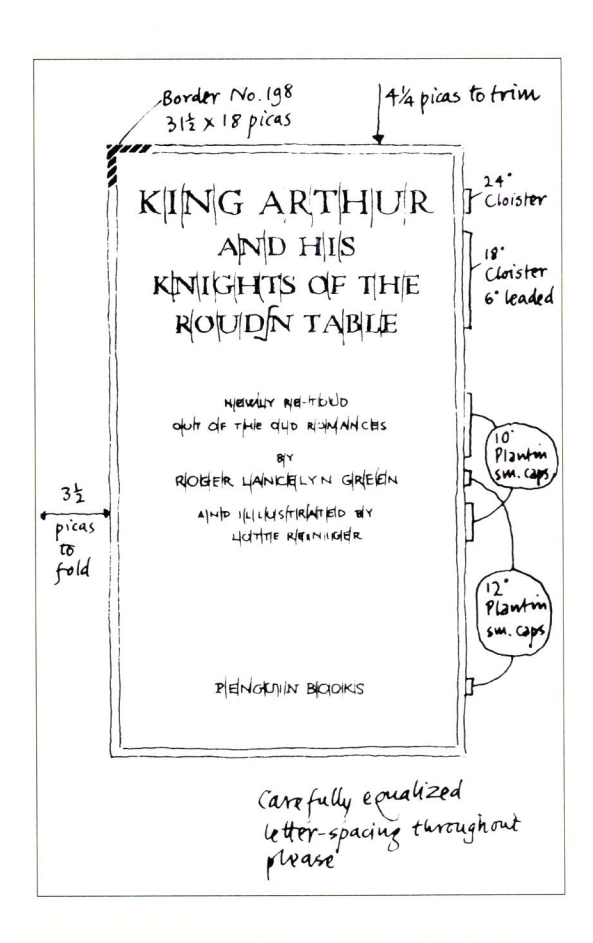

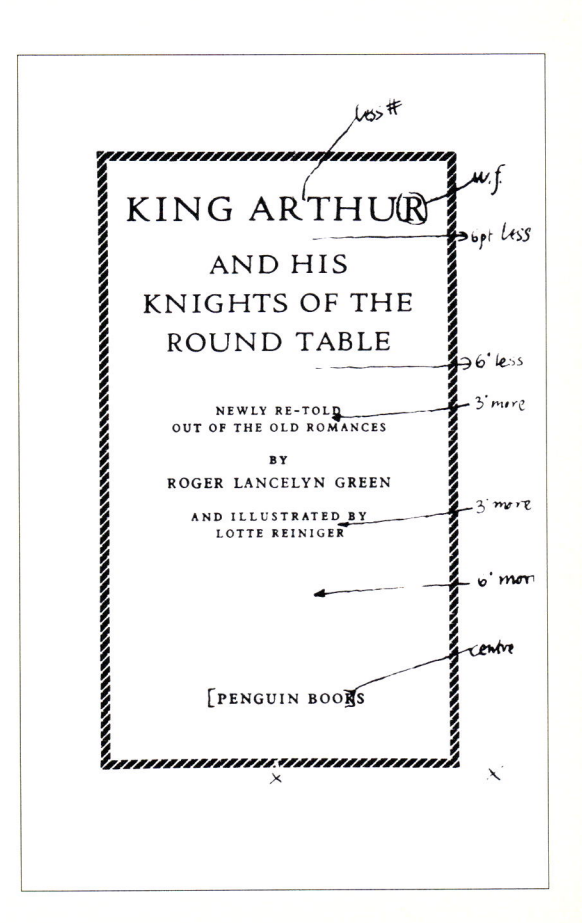

Roger Lancelyn Green, *King Arthur and His Knights of the Round Table*, illustrations by Lotte Reiniger. A Puffin Story Book, no. PS 73, May 1953. 4³⁄₈″ x 7¹⁄₈″ (11.1 x 18.1 cm). Title page instructions by Jan Tschichold. This handdrawn and marked-up title page shows Tschichold's attention to details such as word and letterspacing, placements, and font preferences. The title is to be set in Monotype Cloister and the smaller type is to be set in Monotype Plantin Light.

Roger Lancelyn Green, *King Arthur and His Knights of the Round Table*. Typeset title page with instructions by Jan Tschichold. Tschichold's annotations request adjustments to letterspacing and leading before the final stage.

Roger Lancelyn Green, *King Arthur and His Knights of the Round Table*. Final title page design by Jan Tschichold. The design incorporates Tschichold's final modifications. Note the subtle change to the frame from the previous revision, as it more closely resembles the geometric forms in the cover illustration.

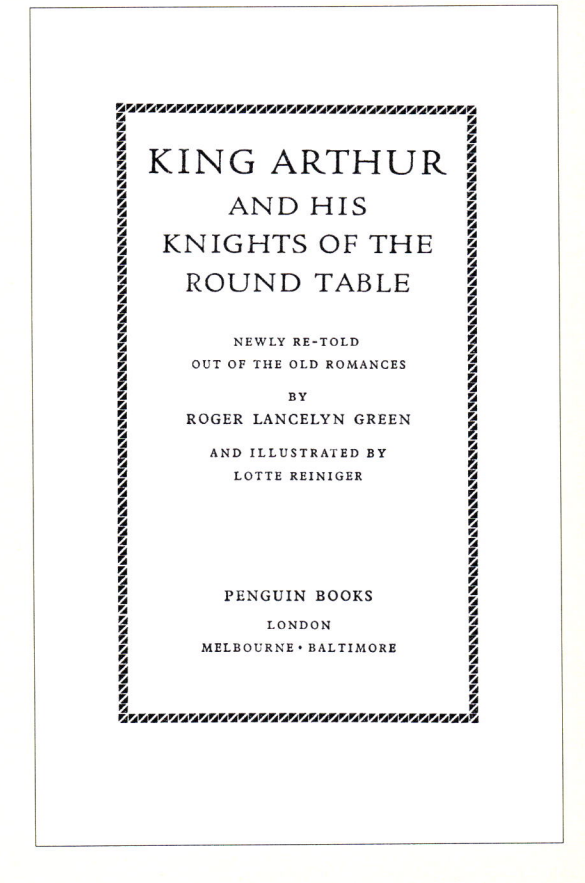

MENDELSSOHN
Overtures: A Midsummer Night's Dream & Fingal's Cave
PENGUIN SCORES 5 · 2/6

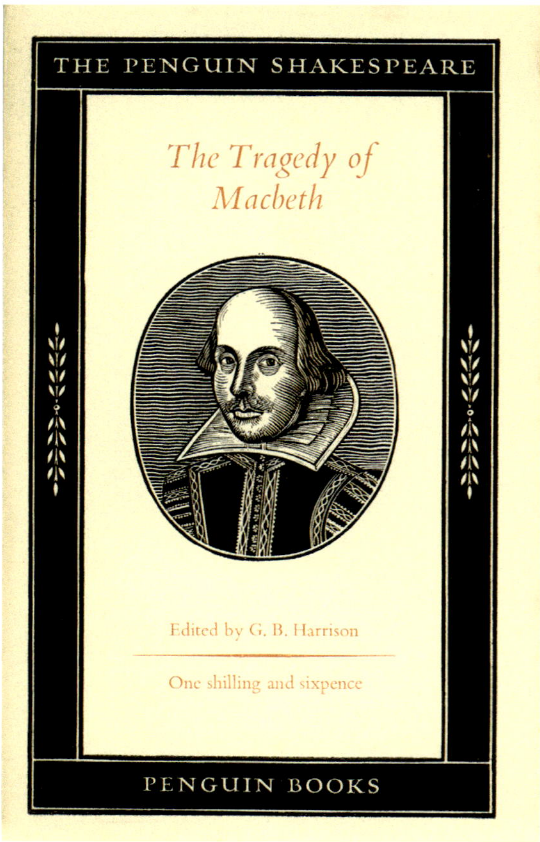
THE PENGUIN SHAKESPEARE
The Tragedy of Macbeth
Edited by G. B. Harrison
One shilling and sixpence
PENGUIN BOOKS

by prominent English designers and artists such as Elizabeth Friedlander and Berthold Wolpe. The roundels were iconic representations of the characters in the story, adding personality and a finishing touch to the design. Tschichold employed the classic typographic features of Monotype Perpetua for many of the covers within the Penguin Classics range. For the chapter headings and body text, he mixed various weights of Monotype Bembo and Monotype Centaur Titling. The results were stunning, unique, and yet classical.

One notable masterpiece from the series of Penguin Classics is Tschichold's book design for *The Transformations of Lucius,* otherwise known as *The Golden Ass,* first published as a paperback in 1950, shortly after Tschichold left Penguin. Penguin issued its own hardback version, a 298-page, 2,000-issue deluxe limited edition the following year. The book's detail included beige cloth with gilded stamped lettering on a vellum spine, with vellum tips, also referred to as French corners, finished by hand to reinforce the spine and binding and minimize damage while handling. For the lettering on the spine, Tschichold created handdrawn cursive lettering in a decorative and graceful script. He added two rules of different weights for visual support within the spine. The book was protected with a tan dustwrap and fitted inside a two-color card stock slipcase. Tschichold set the two-color card stock slipcase in all caps Monotype Perpetua in three distinctive typographic groupings. What makes this design unique is the harmony and clarity achieved by Tschichold's centered arrangements, typographic groupings, and relationships.

BACK TO SWITZERLAND Tschichold resolved to return to Switzerland in December 1949, this decision being influenced by a feeling that his work at Penguin was complete, coupled with the substantial drop in the value of sterling. His last task was recommending his compatriot Hans Schmoller from the Curwen Press as his successor.

Tschichold's only design assistant, Erik Ellegaard Frederiksen, left Penguin on the same day as his mentor, but returned to Penguin in February 1950 to help with Schmoller's transition into his new job. The tradition of typographic excellence in book design continued at Penguin Books under Schmoller. As Penguin's production director, Schmoller maintained and built upon the design standards and composition rules implemented by Tschichold. During his twenty-five-year tenure, he carefully modified and adapted the composition rules to reflect the continuous technological developments in the publishing and printing industry. Tschichold commented on his successor by saying: "I am also glad that my work is being well taken care of by H. P. Schmoller, a first-class book designer, and its fundamental lines can now hardly be altered."[6]

Felix Mendelssohn, *Overtures: A Midsummer Night's Dream & Fingal's Cave.* Series cover design by Jan Tschichold. Penguin Music Scores, no. SC 5, May 1950. $5^{1}/_{8}"$ x $7^{3}/_{4}"$ (13.0 x 19.7 cm). The typefaces used are Monotype Caslon Old Face and Garamond. The decorative Curwen Press patterned paper is by the German designer Elizabeth Friedlander.

William Shakespeare, *The Tragedy of Macbeth*, edited by G.B. Harrison, design by Jan Tschichold. The engraved portrait is by Reynolds Stone. Penguin Shakespeare, no. B 12, this edition first published 1937, reprinted 1940, revised and enlarged 1950. $4^{3}/_{8}"$ x $7^{1}/_{8}"$ (11.1 x 18.1 cm). The type is set in Monotype Bembo, one of Tschichold's favorites for classic works. Tschichold created the frame for this series using a scraperboard and a pin. He succeeded in drawing the frame to the correct proportions on his first attempt.

Adherence to his design principles allowed Tschichold to concentrate on the character of each book and to add his personal aesthetic touch. Tschichold's tenure at Penguin, during which he designed or prepared for press 500 books—sometimes one per day—was a significant chapter in his career. He could claim to be the first typographer to successfully design and manage, on such a wide-ranging scale—book series, editors, compositors, binders, and printers—the mass production of books for a publishing firm. Upon his return to Switzerland, Tschichold continued to write on typography and carry on his approach to classical typography and book design, similar to his tenure at Penguin, for different Swiss and German publishers and the large pharmaceutical company of F. Hoffmann-La Roche & Co. Late in his career, he reflected on his experience and efforts at Penguin Books by saying: "I could be proud of the million Penguin books for whose typography I was responsible. Beside them, the two or three luxurious books I have designed are of no importance. We do not need pretentious books for the wealthy, we need more really well-made ordinary books." [7]

Notes

1. "Letter written by Jan Tschichold to Rudolf Hostettler." 31 January 1946. Translation by Ruari McLean from *Jan Tschichold: Typographer*. Boston: David R. Godine, 1975: pp. 153–155.

2. Jan Tschichold, "Jan Tschichold's lecture to the Typography USA seminar sponsored by The Type Directors Club, New York on 18 April 1959." *Print* XVIII, no. 1, 1964: pp. 16–17.

3. Jan Tschichold, "Glaube und Wirklichkeit (Belief and Reality)," *Schweizer Graphische Mitteilungen*, June 1946: pp. 233–42.

4. Jan Tschichold, "Mein Reform der Penguin Books," *Schweizer Graphische Mitteilungen*, no. 6, 1950. Translation by Ruari McLean from *Jan Tschichold: Typographer*. Boston: David R. Godine, 1975: p. 145.

5. "Letter to Ruari McLean." *British Printer* May 12 1975: p. 1.

6. Jan Tschichold, "Mein Reform der Penguin Books," *Schweizer Graphische Mitteilungen*, no. 6, 1950. Translation by Ruari McLean from *Jan Tschichold: Typographer*. Boston: David R. Godine, 1975: p. 147.

7. Jost Hochuli, *Jan Tschichold, Typographer and Type Designer, 1902–1974*, trans. Ruari McLean, W.A. Kelly, and Bernard Wolpe. Edinburgh: National Library of Scotland, 1982: p. 35.

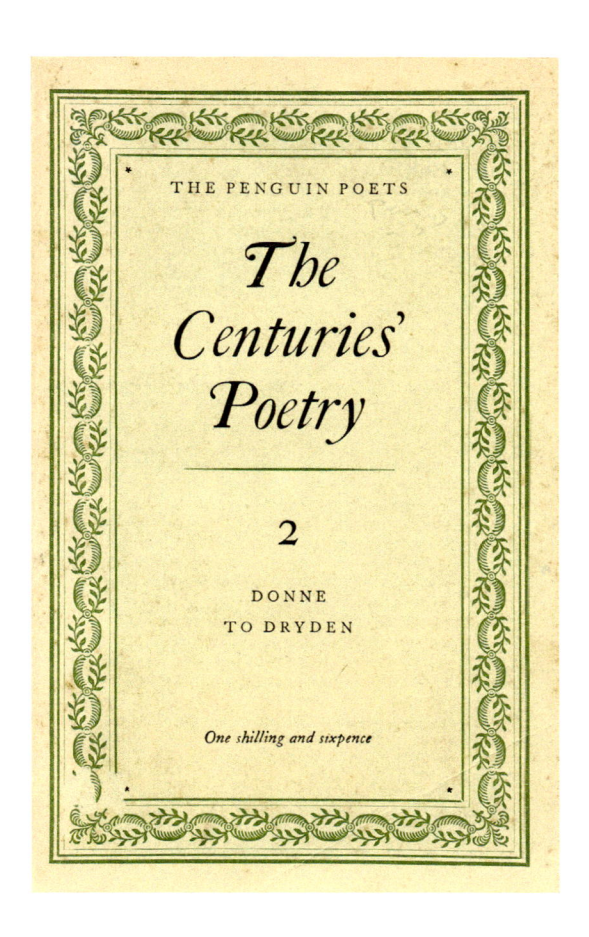

The Centuries' Poetry, vol. 2: Donne to Dryden, edited by D. Kilham Roberts, cover series design by Jan Tschichold. The Penguin Poets, no. D 7, September 1949. 4³/₈" x 7¹/₈" (11.1 x 18.1 cm). The sole typographic component is the beautiful Monotype italic Bell.

Sinclair Lewis, *Mantrap*, design by Giovanni Mardersteig, 1935. The Albatross series. 4³/₈" x 7¹/₈" (11.1 x 18.1 cm). Giovanni Mardersteig, lead typographer at the Albatross Library, was the first designer within a publishing firm to establish house design rules based on the golden section. He also used high-quality paper, an illustrated albatross for the colophon, sans serif typography, color-coding to distinguish the genre of each volume, and standardized cover patterns. Allen Lane, who understood the importance of design as an instrumental marketing tool, often stated that he was trying to emulate the Albatross series in the early Penguin titles.

283

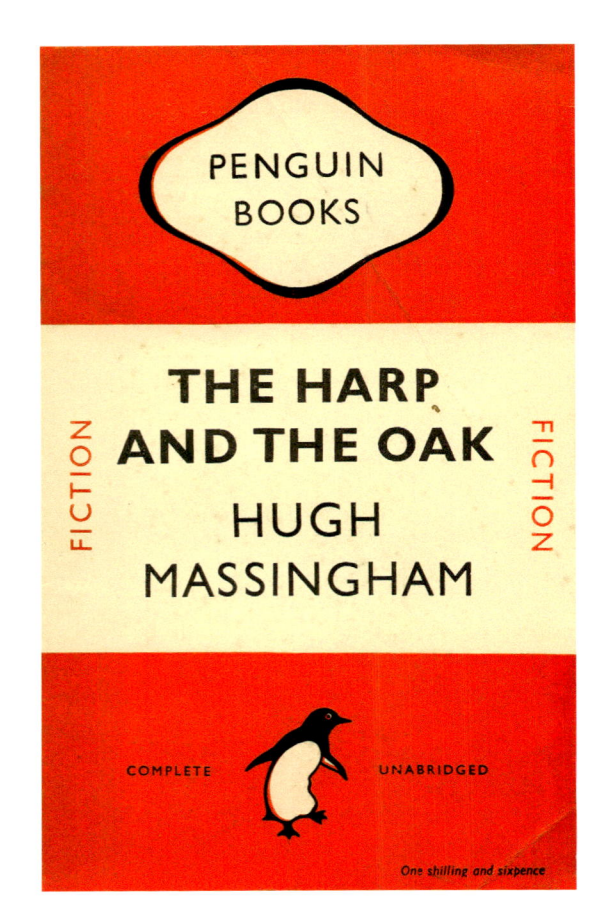

Saki (H.H. Munro), *When William Came*. Penguin Books, no. 331, first published March 1941. 4³/₈″ x 7¹/₈″ (11.1 x 18.1 cm). This was the Penguin cover as Tschichold found it upon his arrival in 1947. This original cover was designed by Edward Young, Penguin's first production editor, who created a distinctive paperback brand.

Hugh Massingham, *The Harp and the Oak*, cover design by Jan Tschichold. Penguin Books, no. 622, September 1948. 4³/₈″ x 7¹/₈″ (11.1 x 18.1 cm). Tschichold's first revision of the Penguin cover, keeping the original Penguin logo.

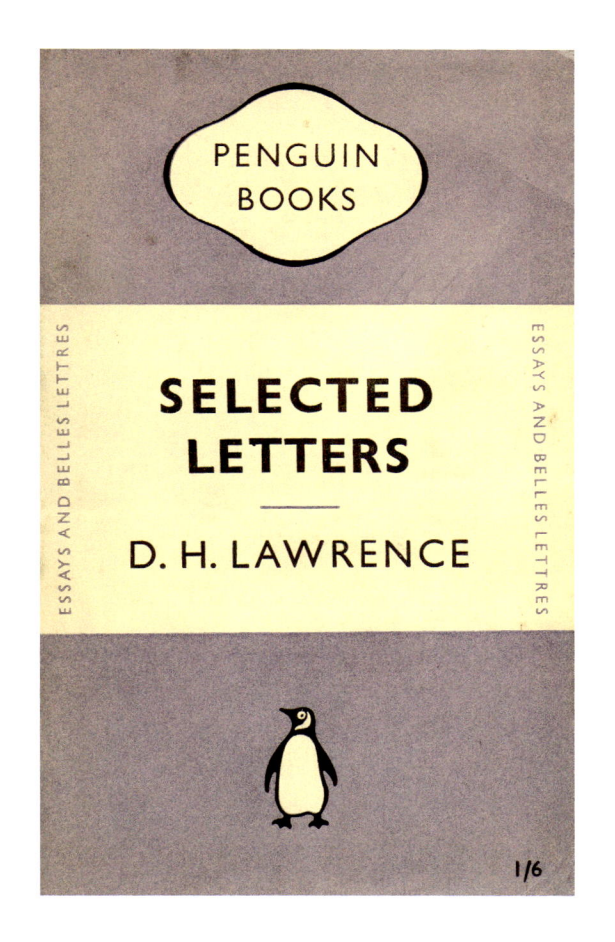

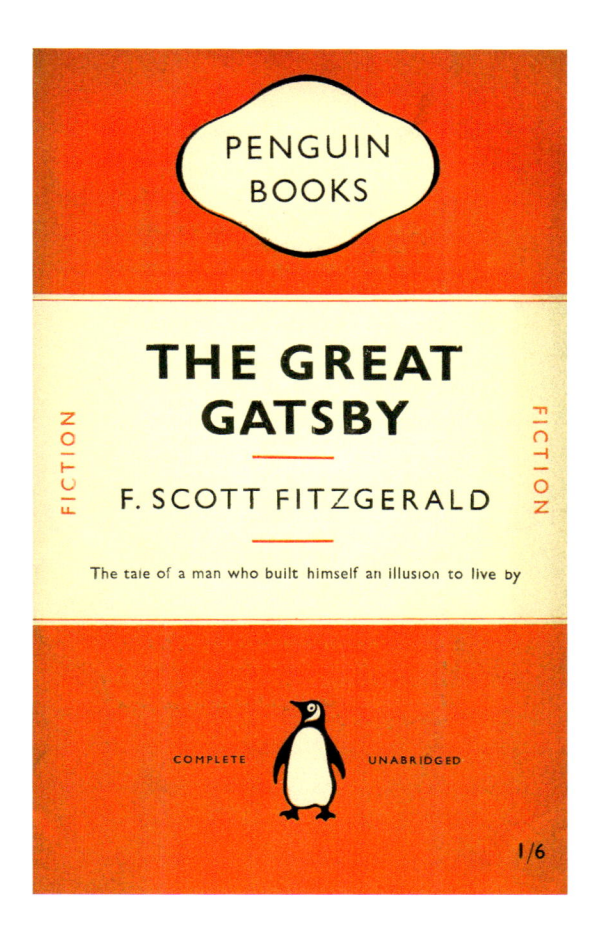

D.H. Lawrence, *Selected Letters*, cover design by Jan Tschichold. Penguin Books, no. 759, March 1950. 4³⁄₈″ x 7¹⁄₈″ (11.1 x 18.1 cm). Tschichold's second revision of the Penguin cover with the new Penguin logo.

F. Scott Fitzgerald, *The Great Gatsby*, cover design by Jan Tschichold. Penguin no. 746, January 1950. 4³⁄₈″ x 7¹⁄₈″ (11.1 x 18.1 cm). Tschichold's subtle variation of the Penguin cover. Modifications included a smaller point size for the author's name and the introduction of a descriptive line about the book.

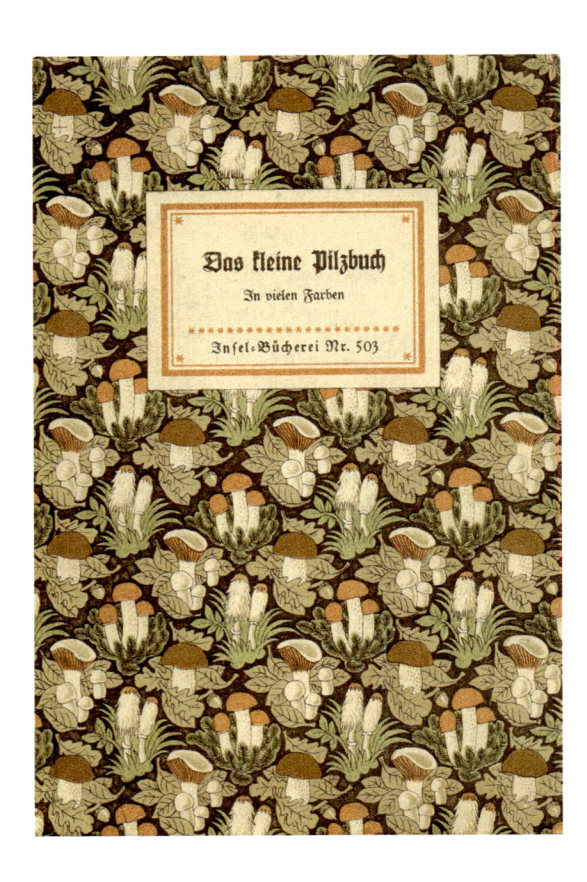

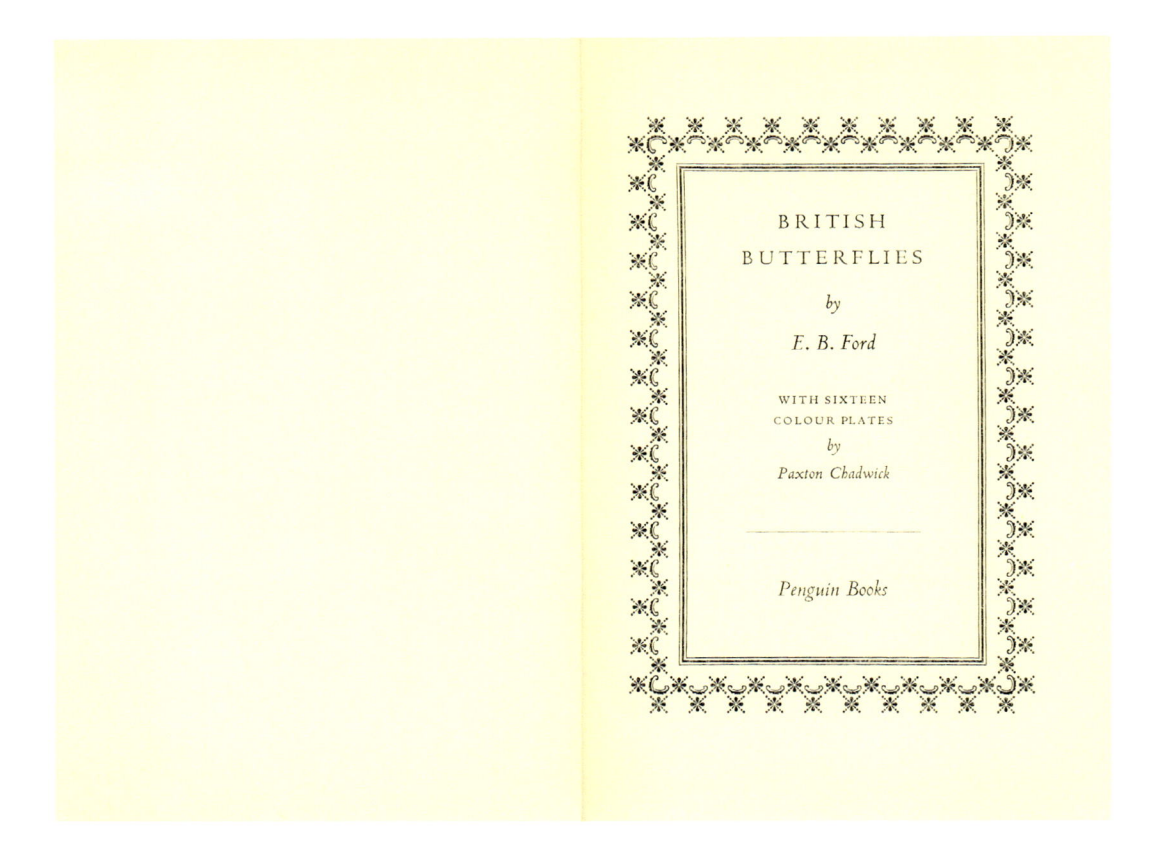

E. B. Ford, *British Butterflies*, with sixteen color plates and cover illustrations by Paxton Chadwick. Series design by Jan Tschichold. A King Penguin Book, no. K 41, October 1951. 4¾″ x 7¹⁄₁₆″ (11.9 x 17.9 cm)

Willi Harwerth, *Das Kleine Pilzbuch* (The Little Fungi Book). Insel-Verlag no. 503, Leipzig, 1937. 4¾″ x 7¹⁄₁₆″ (11.9 x 17.9 cm). The title is in Fraktur (blackletter type), the German manuscript style that was invented by Leonard Wagner. The format of the Insel-Verlag illustrated books was later used by Tschichold for the King Penguin series, particularly, the patterned covers and the title plate with its distinctive ruled border and delicate fleurons.

E. B. Ford, *British Butterflies*, title page design by Jan Tschichold. A King Penguin Book, no. K 41, October 1951. 4¾″ x 7¹⁄₁₆″ (11.9 x 17.9 cm)

Christian Barman, *Early British Railways*, page spread design by Jan Tschichold. A King Penguin Book, no. K 56, May 1950. 4¾″ x 7¹/₁₆″ (11.9 x 17.9 cm)

Christian Barman, *Early British Railways*, cover design by Jan Tschichold. A King Penguin Book, no. K 56, May 1950. 4¾″ x 7¹/₁₆″ (11.9 x 17.9 cm). The typography on this cover uses the classic Monotype Scotch Roman italic.

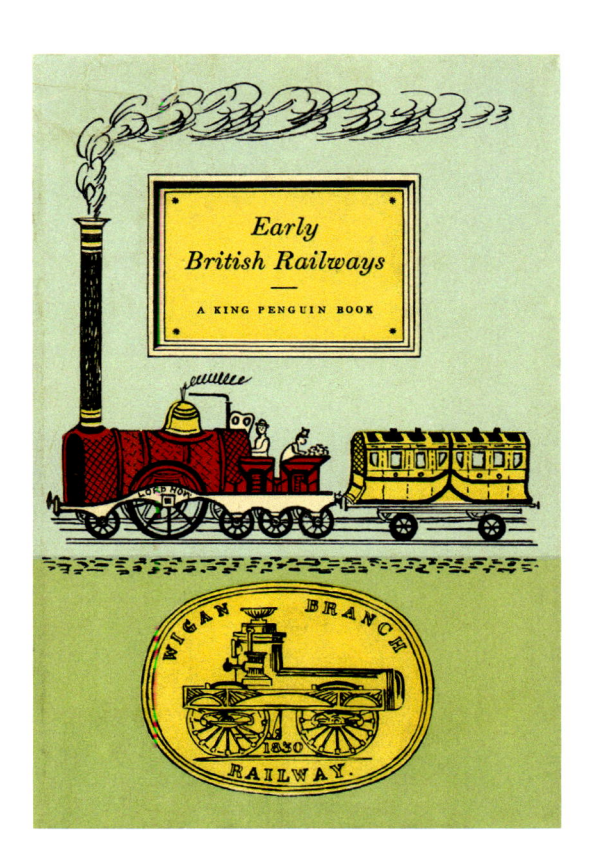

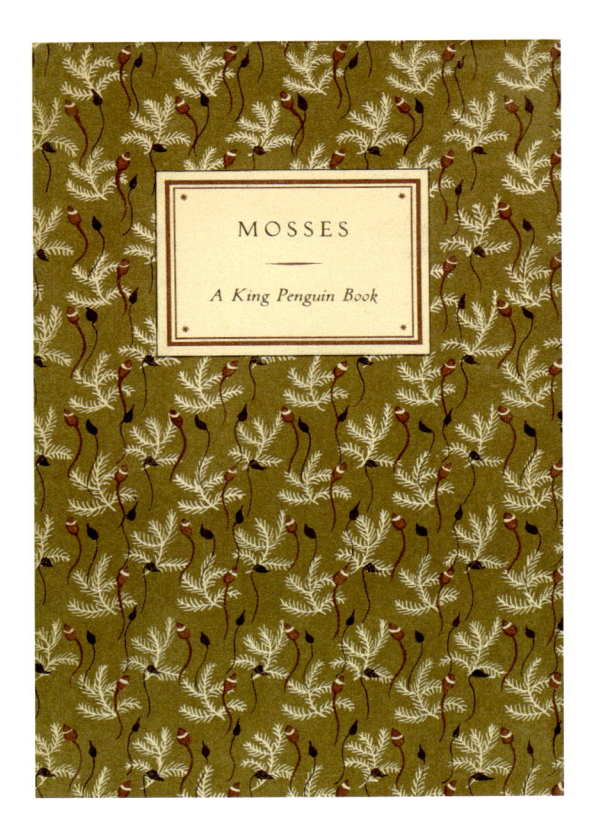

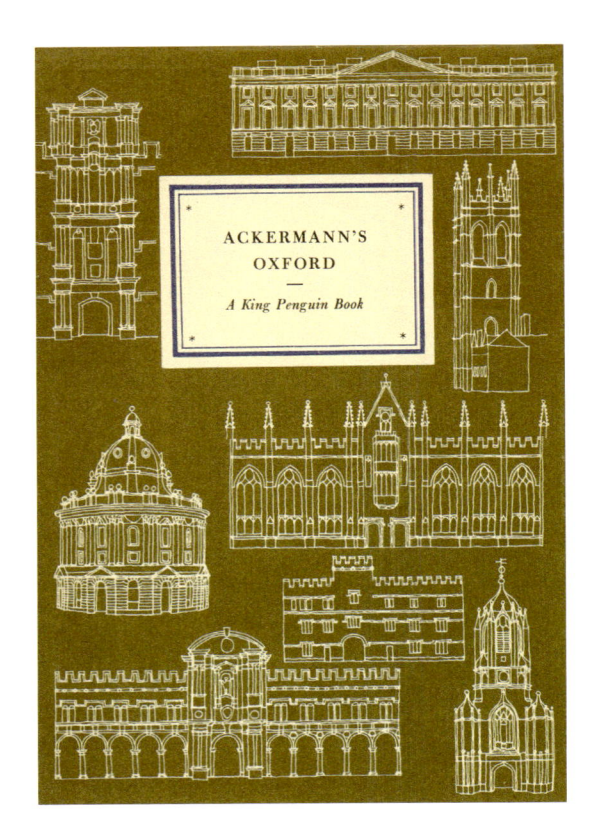

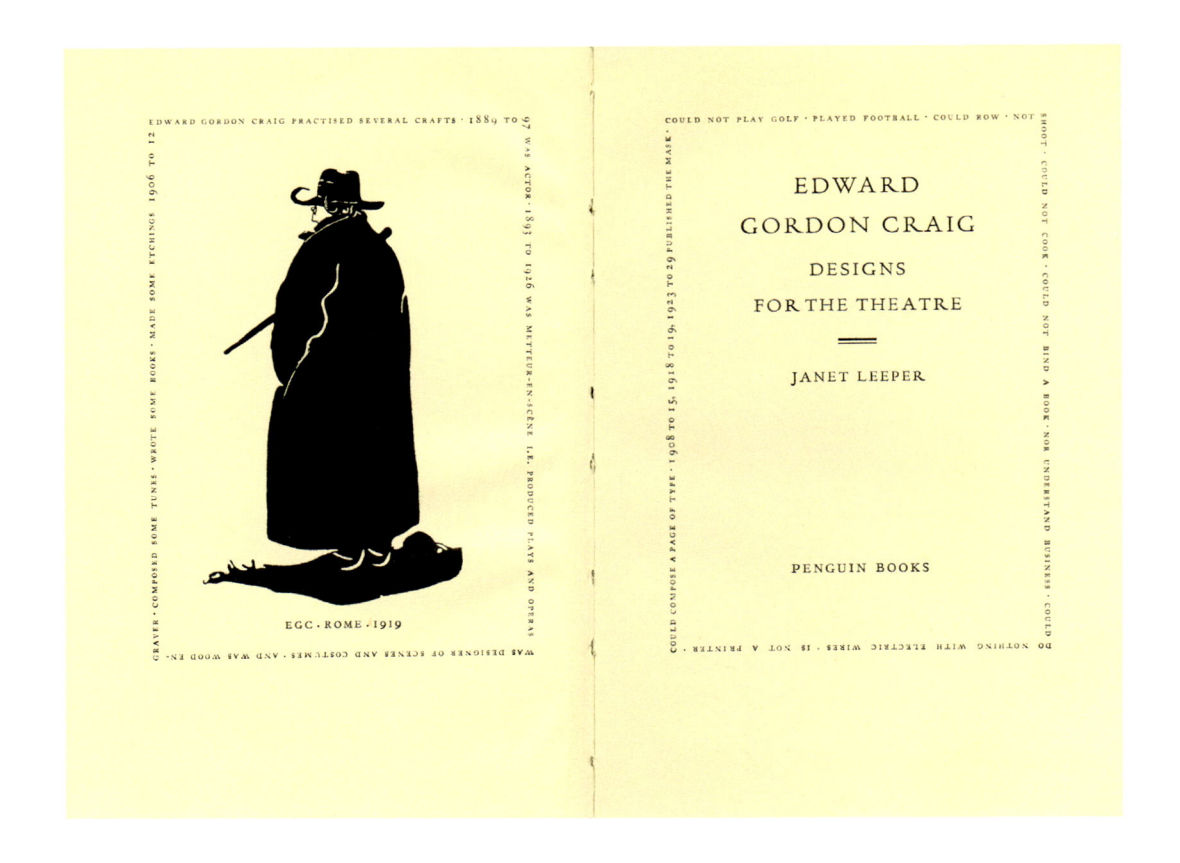

Paul W. Richards, *A Book of Mosses*, with 16 plates from Johannes Hedwig's *Descriptio Muscorum*; cover design by Jan Tschichold. A King Penguin Book, no. K 57, July 1950. 4¾" x 7¹⁄₁₆" (11.9 x 17.9 cm)

H. M. Colvin, *Ackermann's Oxford*, a selection of plates from Rudolph Ackermann's *A History of the University of Oxford, its Colleges, Halls, and Public Buildings*, 1814, and James Ingram's *Memorials of Oxford* 1837; cover design by Jan Tschichold. A King Penguin Book, no. K 69, March 1954. 4¾" x 7¹⁄₁₆" (11.9 x 17.9 cm)

Janet Leeper, *Edward Gordon Craig: Designs for the Theatre*, title page design by Jan Tschichold. A King Penguin Book, no. K 40, October 1948. 4¾" x 7¹⁄₁₆" (11.9 x 17.9 cm). The type is set in Monotype Poliphilus.

Alfred Fairbank, *A Book of Scripts*, cover design by Jan Tschichold. A King Penguin Book, no. K 48, November 1949. 4¾″ x 7¹/₁₆″ (11.9 x 17.9 cm). Adapted from a page in *Arte Subtilissima* (1547), a classic work on calligraphy and engraving by the 16th-century Spanish master calligrapher, Juan de Yçiar of Zaragoza. The National Book League of England recognized this title as one of the best-designed books of 1949.

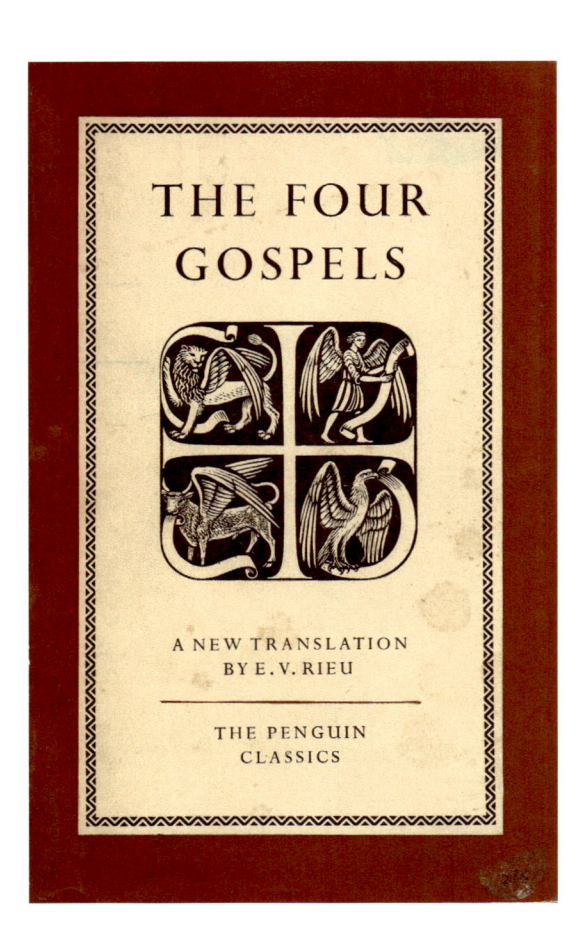

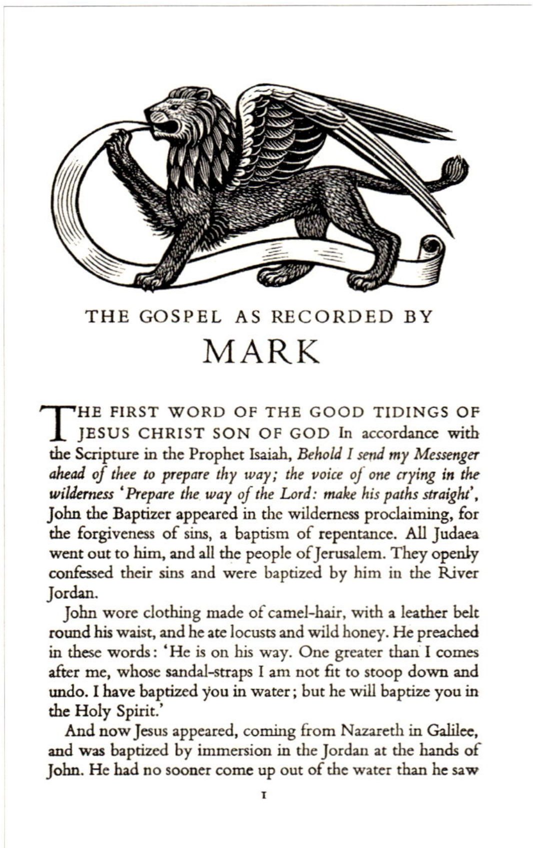

The Four Gospels, translation by E. V. Rieu. Cover design by Jan Tschichold. Penguin Classics, no. L 32, November 1952. 4³/₈″ x 7¹/₈″ (11.1 x 18.1 cm). The woodcut design is by Reynolds Stone. The typography is Monotype Perpetua, set in uppercase throughout.

The Four Gospels, translation by E. V. Rieu. Chapter page design by Jan Tschichold. Penguin Classics, no. L 32, November 1952. 4³/₈″ x 7¹/₈″ (11.1 x 18.1 cm). The woodcut illustrations for each chapter are by Reynolds Stone. Monotype Bembo is combined with Monotype Centaur Titling.

Nikolaus Pevsner, *The Buildings of England: Middlesex*, cover design by Hans Schmoller. Buildings of England, no. BE 3, October, 1951. 4³/₈″ x 7¹/₈″ (11.1 x 18.1 cm). Tschichold's design influence is visible in Schmoller's choice of typography and centered styling. The white horizontal band technique can be traced back through several of the Penguin covers to the earliest Penguin fiction titles. The significant design modification on this cover is the thick band of white behind the word "Middlesex," for emphasis. A slender white frame around the edge of the book creates a window-like effect. The subtle detailing in the form of a rhythmical Monotype border replicates the delicate edging of the building's architectural detail. The typography is carefully positioned and set in uppercase Monotype Perpetua. The word "Middlesex" is set in Monotype Bell. Schmoller adorns the cover with a circular illustrated architectural roundel to promote individual character.

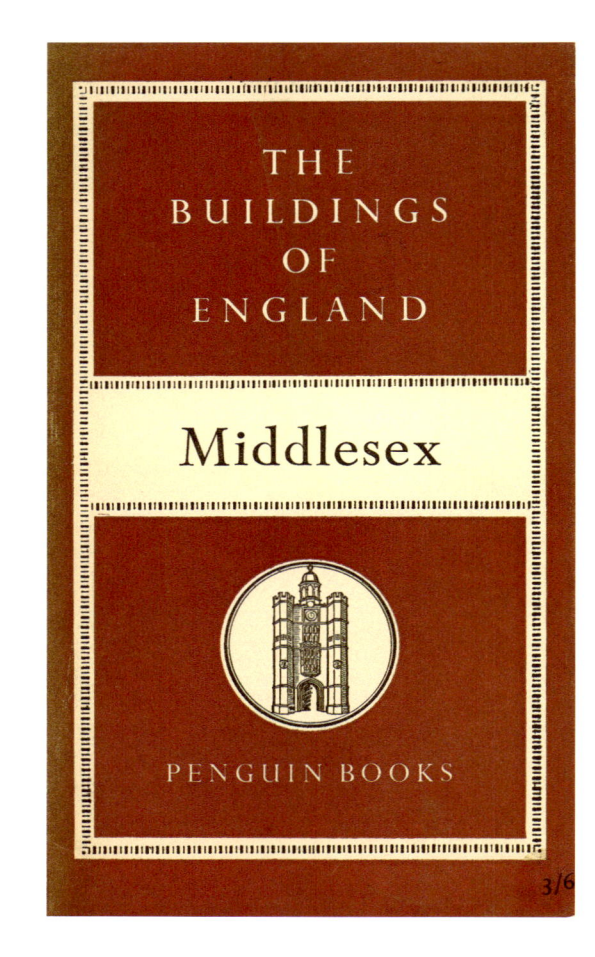

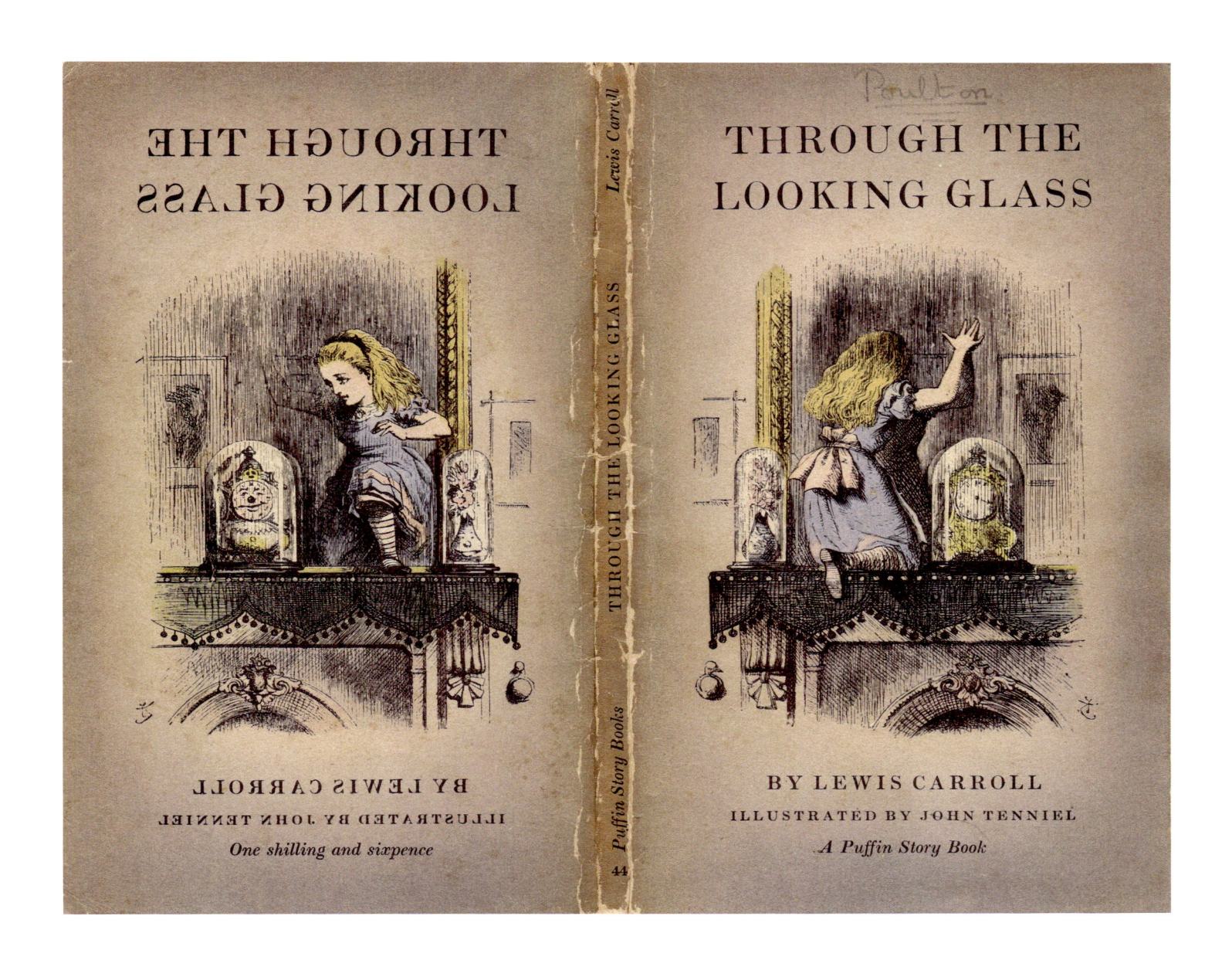

Lewis Carroll, *Through the Looking Glass*, front and back cover design by Jan Tschichold. A Puffin Story Book, no. PS 44, October 1948. 4³⁄₈″ x 7¹⁄₈″ (11.1 x 18.1 cm). The typeface on this cover is Monotype Scotch Roman.

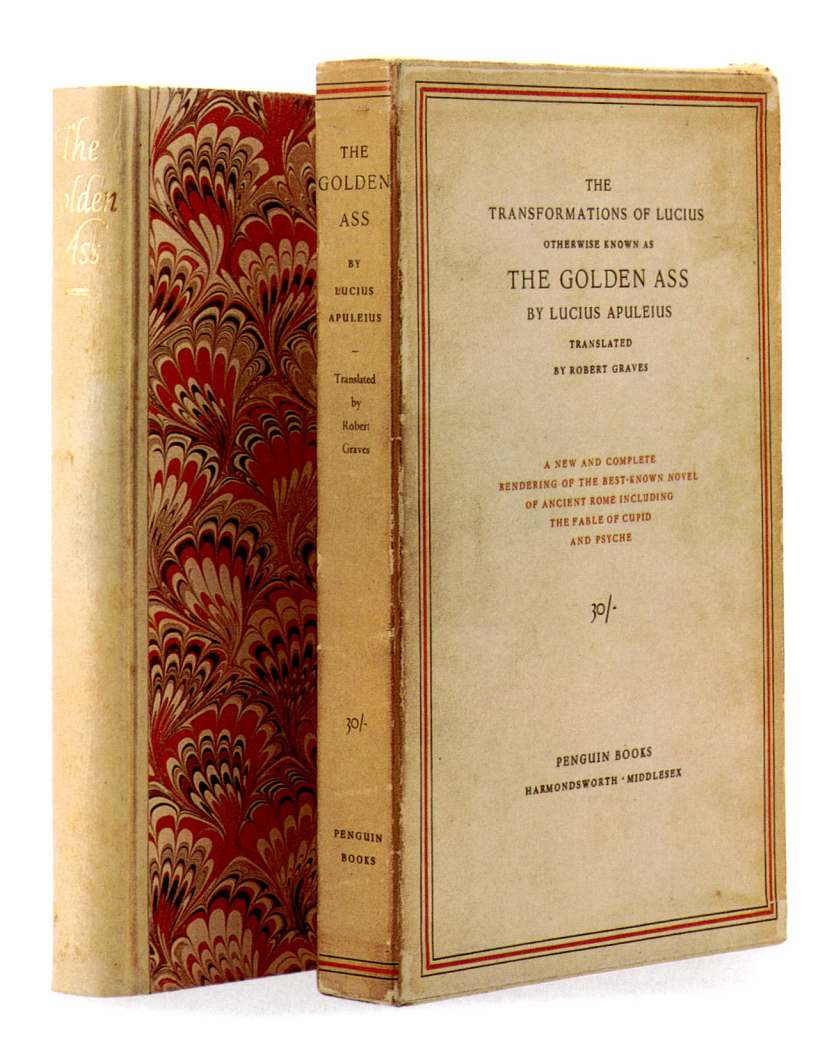

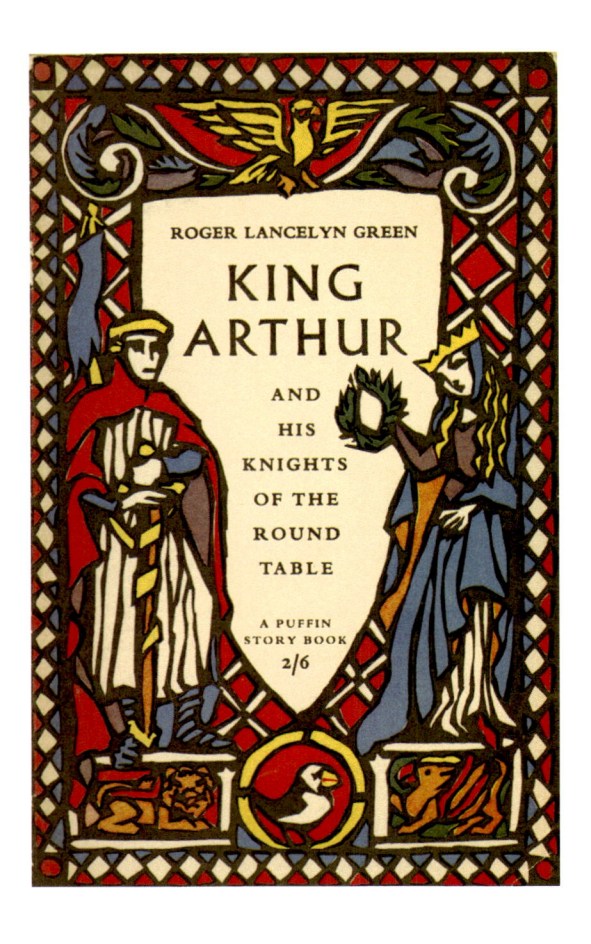

Lucius Apuleius, *The Transformation of Lucius, Otherwise Known As The Golden Ass*, translated by Robert Graves, design by Jan Tschichold. Penguin Classics, no. Q 13, December 1951. 4³/₈″ x 7¹/₈″ (11.1 x 18.1 cm). Photo courtesy of Yoshihiro Yamada, from *Idea*, no. 321, *Works of Jan Tschichold 1902–74*.

Roger Lancelyn Green, *King Arthur and his Knights of the Round Table*, illustrations by Lotte Reiniger, cover design by Jan Tschichold. A Puffin Story Book, no. PS 73, May 1953. 4³/₈″ x 7¹/₈″ (11.1 x 18.1 cm). A woodblock effect gives this cover a distinct personality. The artist Lotte Reiniger cut the illustrations out of thin black paper. The delicate cutouts are mounted on transparent paper, and a set of much smaller pictures were made for the book. The shape and weight of the uppercase typography compliments the illustration style.

Penguins Progress, Penguin's house magazine, no. 5, 1948. Cover design by Jan Tschichold, 4¾″ x 7⅛″ (11.1 x 18.1 cm)

Penguins Progress, Penguin's house magazine, no. 8, 1949. Cover design by Jan Tschichold, 4¾″ x 7⅛″ (11.1 x 18.1 cm). Tschichold chooses a beautiful handdrawn letter 'P' set in Monotype Felix Titling with a drop shadow combined with an intricate spiral motif, imitating the initials of the manuscript book. The title is composed from Monotype Centaur.

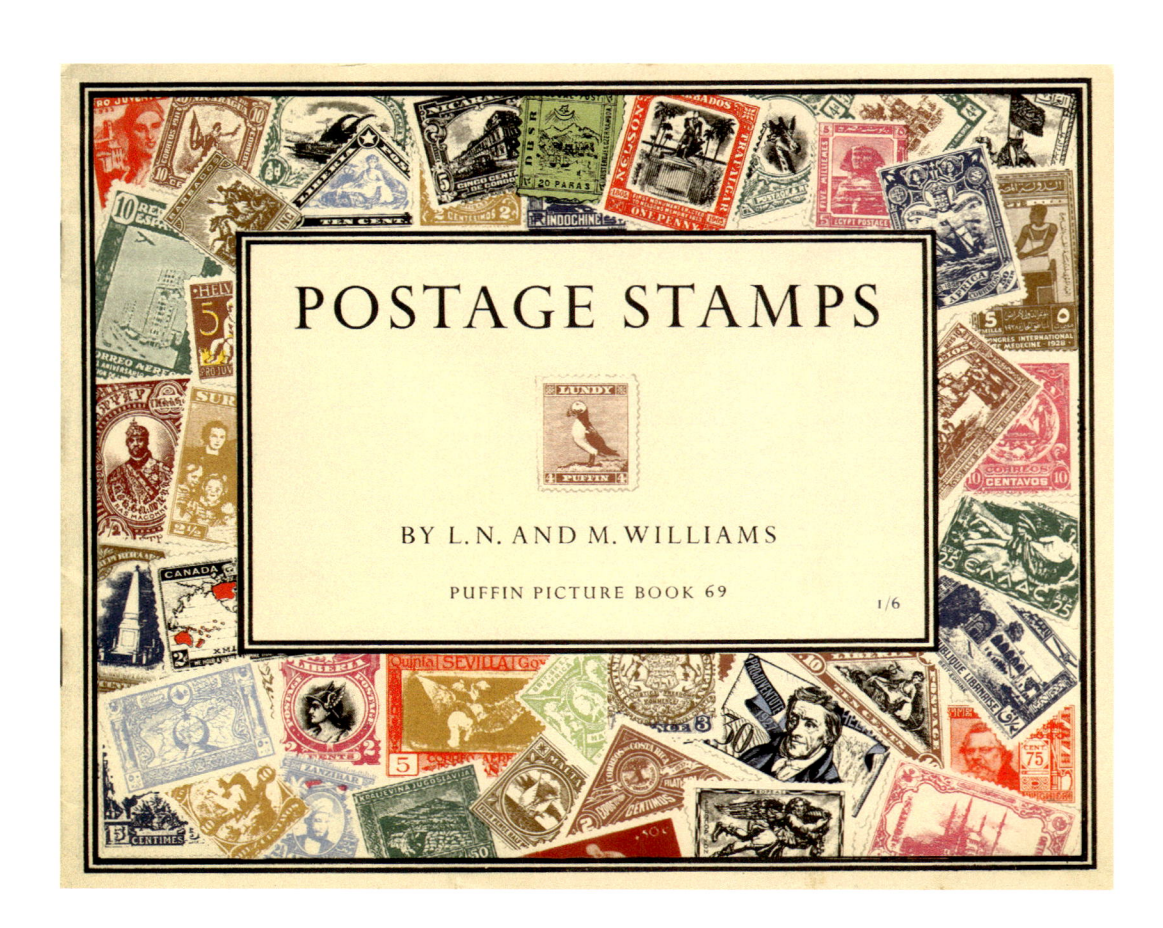

L. N. & M. Williams *Postage Stamps*, cover design by Jan Tschichold. Puffin Picture Book, no. PP 69, first published, April 1950. 8¾″ x 7⅛″ (20.9 x 18.1 cm). The uppercase title, author's name and book number are carefully positioned within the illustrated collage of stamps. Tschichold cleverly chooses a Lundy Puffin stamp, to add a whimsical accent to the overall design. In 1946, Ruari McLean was hired by Lane to manage the production of the Puffin Picture Books' children's series.

L. N. & M. Williams *Postage Stamps*, page spread design by Jan Tschichold. Puffin Picture Book, no. PP 69, first published, April 1950. 8¾" x 7⅛" (20.9 x 18.1 cm). Tschichold's use of a grid becomes visible with the placement and structure of the postage stamps. The body text has been set with left and right justification to simulate a rectangular shape—a subtle way of visually integrating the body text and stamps.

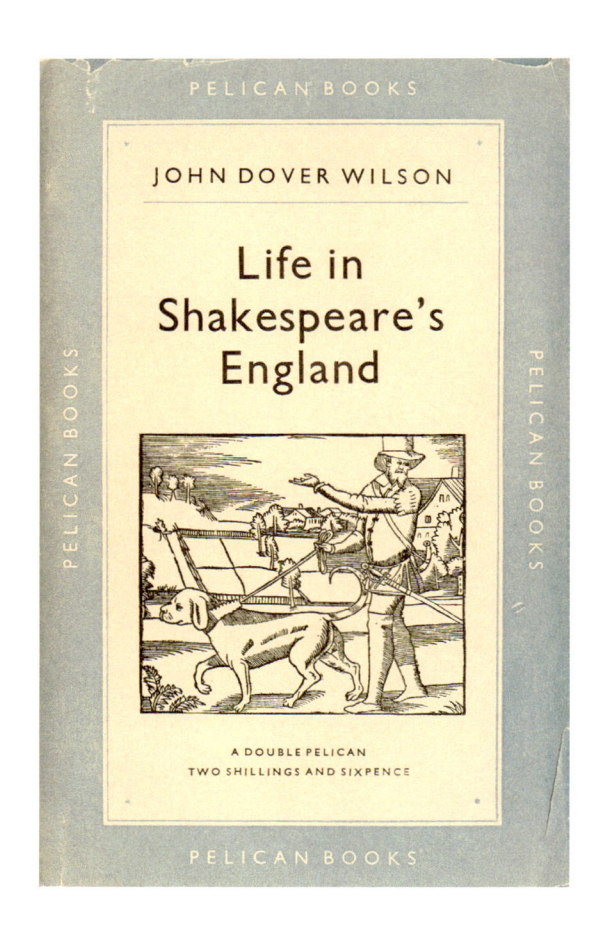

John Dover Wilson, *Life in Shakespeare's England*, jacket redesign by Jan Tschichold. Pelican Books, no. A 143, first published August 1944. 4³/₈″ x 7¹/₈″ (11.1 x 18.1 cm). Monotype Gill Sans is used throughout. For the Pelican jackets, Tschichold introduced a pale aqua frame with inverted uppercase typography, creating a dynamic contrast to the typography within the white panel.

John Dover Wilson, *Life in Shakespeare's England*, jacket redesign by Jan Tschichold. Pelican Books, no. A 143, revised design, 1949. 4³/₈″ x 7¹/₈″ (11.1 x 18.1 cm). Some of the covers within the redesigned Pelican series maintained the original three horizontal bands. Eventually, these covers were replaced with the new Pelican jacket design with the introduction of a white rectangular window and surrounding pale aqua blue border with improved fonts and letterspacing.

Science News 14, edited by
J. L. Crammer, cover design by Jan
Tschichold. Penguin periodicals,
no. SN 14, December 1949. 4¾"
x 7¹⁄₁₆" (11.9 x 17.9 cm)

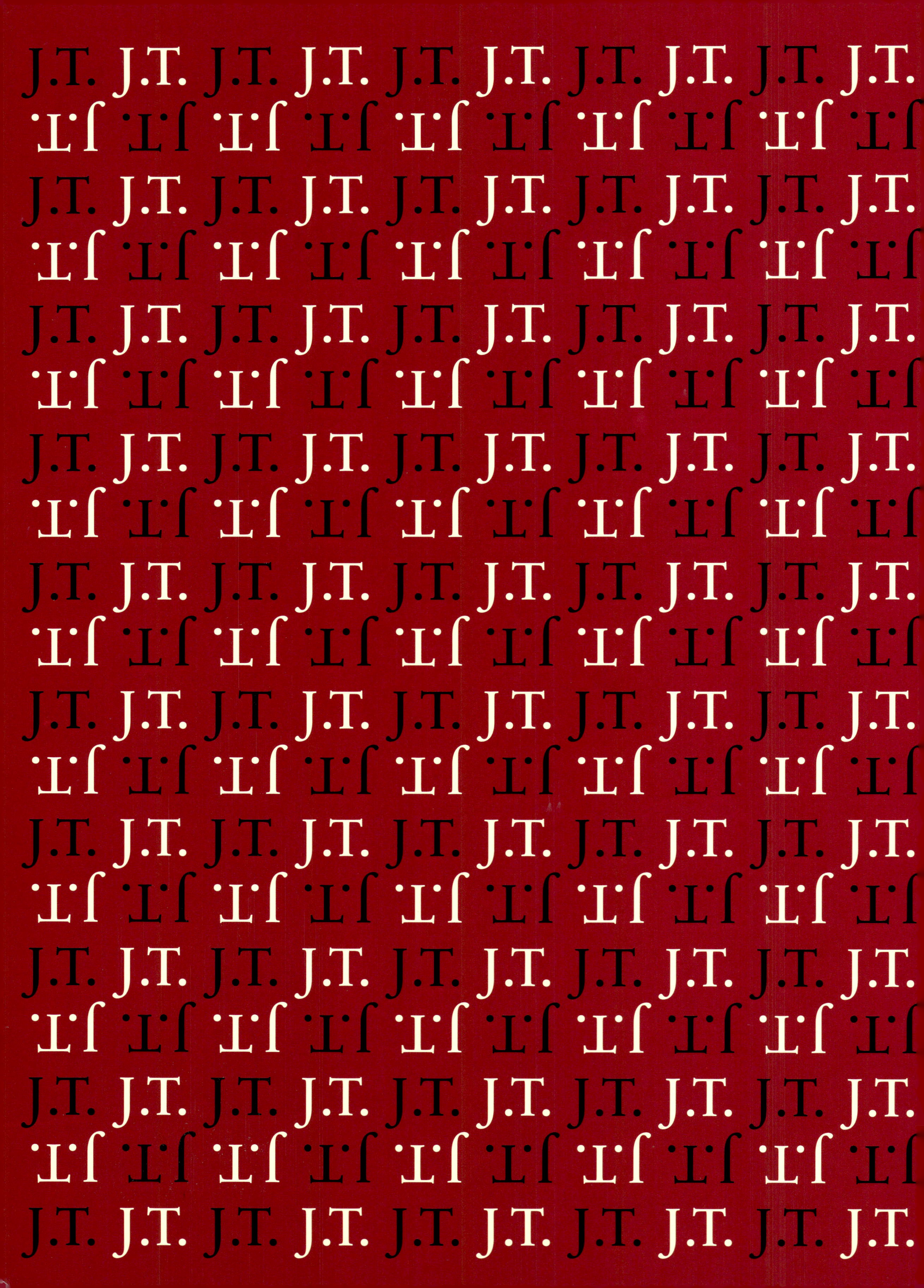

Perfectly Legible and Readable

Hans Reichardt & Cees W. de Jong

Jan Tschichold, ca. 1926
(photo: Kurt Schwitters)

Jan Tschichold in Basel, ca. 1934

J.T.

Perfectly Legible and Readable

Eighty years after the publication of *Die neue Typographie*, in which Jan Tschichold promoted the use of sans serif typefaces and the importance of photography, the question of the degree to which his ideas still have any influence remains. "In the light of my present knowledge, it was a juvenile opinion to consider the sans serif as the most suitable or even the most contemporary typeface. A typeface has first to be legible, nay, readable, and a sans serif is certainly not the most legible typeface when set in quantity, let alone readable. …The classic typefaces such as Garamond, Janson, Baskerville, and Bell are undoubtedly the most legible." Jan Tschichold returned to the traditional, symmetrical typography he had so vehemently rejected a decade earlier.

Legibility was vitally important to Jan Tschichold. A typeface had to be comprehensible and clear to everyone. He had previously attempted to achieve this with sans serif letters. Over the years, however, he came to the conclusion that, as is clear from the quote, the classic typefaces were more suitable for this purpose. While, in the past, he had resisted anything that was not sans serif, he ultimately returned to traditional, symmetrical typography. Tschichold's major principle had always been the legibility of the face, but his idea of legibility had changed in the course of time. As far back as the 1950s, Jan Tschichold was commissioned to design a Renaissance Antiqua in the style of Garamond, at that time under the working title of T-Antiqua. It had to be suitable for not only handsetting but also the Linotype setting machine. Due to various circumstances (capacity problems and the priority of developing Helvetica, for example), finishing the face was postponed further and further. There was also a demand from the printing industry for the design of a font that could be used for not only handsetting and Linotype, but also Monotype setting machines, with equal spacing in 6–12 points. This was no problem for handsetting or the Linotype setting machine; after all, D. Stempel AG had been supplying the Linotype matrices since 1900 and a large number of typefaces were already being manufactured to these requirements.

"And so Tschichold's heritage lives on in the digital age, proving that he is amongst the greatest typographic designers ever, his influence still being visible in the world of typography to this day."

Jean-François Porchez

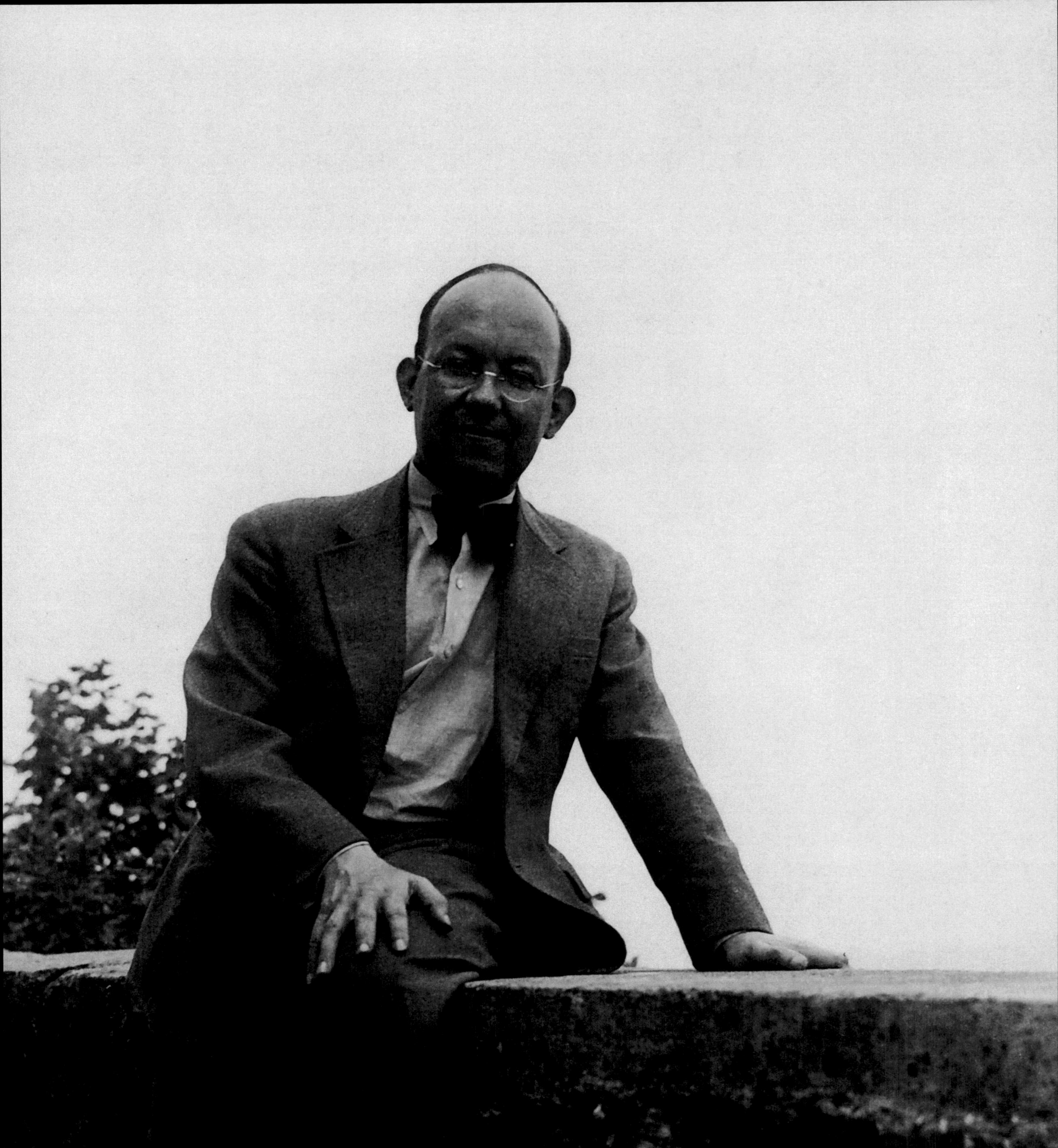

For Monotype, however, the fonts had to be produced in an 18-unit system, which necessitated a great deal of trial and testing, but which also made adapted letterforms possible. It was therefore not until the 1967 DRUPA exhibition that the font could be presented to the profession. This was the fair that heralded the end of the lead era. Sabon-Antiqua, named after the typographer Jacques Sabon (1535–1580), came too late to fulfill the objective of developing a typeface commonly usable in all setting systems. It was, nevertheless, a success and was even expanded, years later, with a semi-bold, italic face.

Many years later, the technical limitations of lead having been eliminated, Linotype asked the French typographer Jean-François Porchez to refine Sabon for the 21st century. The result was Sabon Next, which was published in 2002.

Jan Tschichold in Switzerland,
ca. 1938

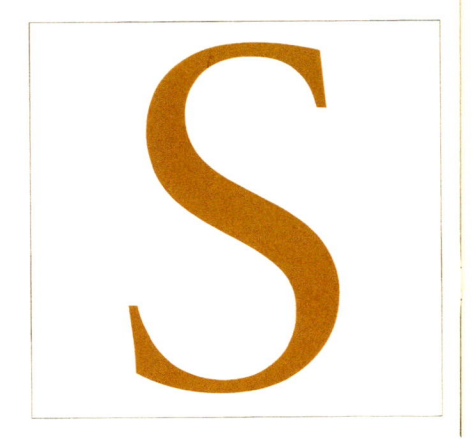

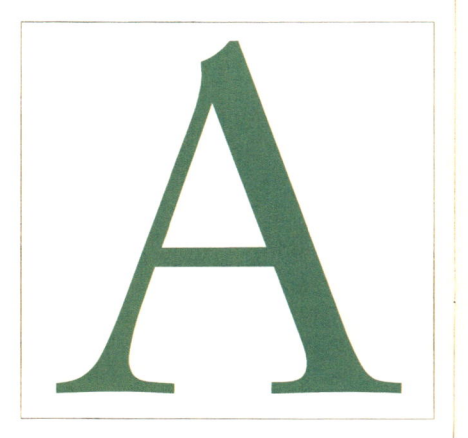

Cover and pages from type specimen of Sabon, 1967. design by Jan Tschichold, 22 x 21 cm, issued by Linotype, Bad Homburg

Warum eine Schrift im Stil der Renaissance-Antiqua?

Eine Renaissance-Antiqua im Stile Garamonds oder eine Barock-Antiqua im Stile Baskervilles standen am Ende der vorausgegangenen Überlegungen. Die Entscheidung fiel schließlich auf eine Schrift im Charakter der historischen Garamondtype. Diese formvollendete klassische Schrift steht im fünften Jahrhundert ihrer Bewährung und hat an Aktualität nichts eingebüßt. Ihr hoher Grad an Lesbarkeit ist unübertroffen. Darüber hinaus ist sie den zahlreichen technischen Bedingungen gewachsen, die an eine vielseitig verwendbare Schrift zu stellen sind. Dank robuster Strichverhältnisse bewahrt sie ihre Deutlichkeit und ihren Charakter bei allen Druckverfahren, den unterschiedlichsten Papiersorten und bei den heute üblichen hohen Druckgeschwindigkeiten. Gleichwertige ästhetische, funktionelle und technische Eignung sowie die Beliebtheit und Verbreitung der Garamond-Varianten führten dazu, einen Schriftentwurf im Renaissance-Charakter zugrunde zu legen.

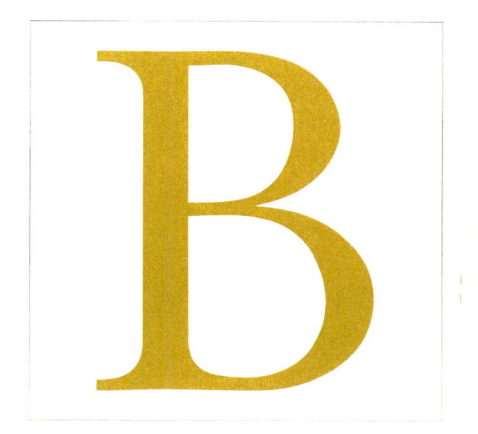

Warum wurde Jan Tschichold mit dem Entwurf der Schrift beauftragt?

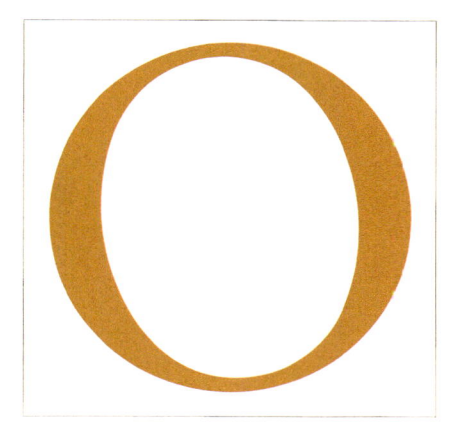

Nur ein erfahrener Typograph und Schriftkenner von Rang konnte mit einer so bedeutenden und schwierigen Aufgabe betraut werden. Die Wahl fiel auf Jan Tschichold, der sich bei der Entwurfsarbeit auf reiche Kenntnisse und ein gründliches Quellenstudium historischer Schriften – in besonderem Maße der Garamondtypen – stützen konnte. Das gesamte Schaffen Tschicholds weist ihn darüber hinaus als feinsinnigen Buchgestalter und Typographen aus. In Anerkennung seines Werkes erhielt er im Jahre 1954 die Goldmedaille des American Institute of Graphic Arts, und die Royal Society of Arts in London verlieh ihm 1965 die Würde eines Honorary Royal Designer for Industry. Beim Entwurf der Sabon kam Tschichold auch zustatten, daß er mit den Besonderheiten aller drei Setzverfahren gut vertraut ist. Die meisterhaften Zeichnungen und der Ausfall der gesamten Schrift zeigen Tschicholds schriftkundiges Wissen und seine Form- und Stilsicherheit bis in die feinsten Details. In der Sabon-Antiqua hat seine jahrzehntelange Beschäftigung mit der Schrift ihre Krönung gefunden. Schon heute liegen Urteile von hervorragenden Schriftkennern des In- und Auslandes vor, die dieser Schrift eine große Zukunft voraussagen.

Warum erhielt die Schrift den Namen Sabon-Antiqua?

Jakob Sabon war ein aus Lyon stammender Stempelschneider und Schriftgießer, als dessen geistige Lehrmeister Garamond und Granjon gelten können. Um 1554 oder 1557 kam er nach Frankfurt am Main, wo er für die Witwe des Druckers und Schriftgießers Christian Egenolff arbeitete. Um 1565 war er vorübergehend in der Schriftgießerei des berühmten Druckers und Verlegers Christophe Plantin in Antwerpen tätig. Nach Deutschland zurückgekehrt, heiratete er im Jahre 1571 die Enkelin Christian Egenolffs und erwarb die Frankfurter Bürgerrechte. Nach der Erbteilung des Egenolffschen Unternehmens wurde er Besitzer der Schriftgießerei. Durch den Erwerb von Stempeln oder Abschlägen der berühmten Antiqua-Garnitur Claude Garamonds wurde Sabon zum deutschen Wegbereiter für eine bis zum heutigen Tage unübertroffene Schrift. Dieses Verdienst und sein nicht geringerer eigener Beitrag als Stempelschneider zum Schriftschaffen seiner Zeit waren Anlaß, daß die drei Frankfurter Firmen ihrer neuen ›harmonisierten‹ Schrift den Namen Sabon-Antiqua gaben.

307

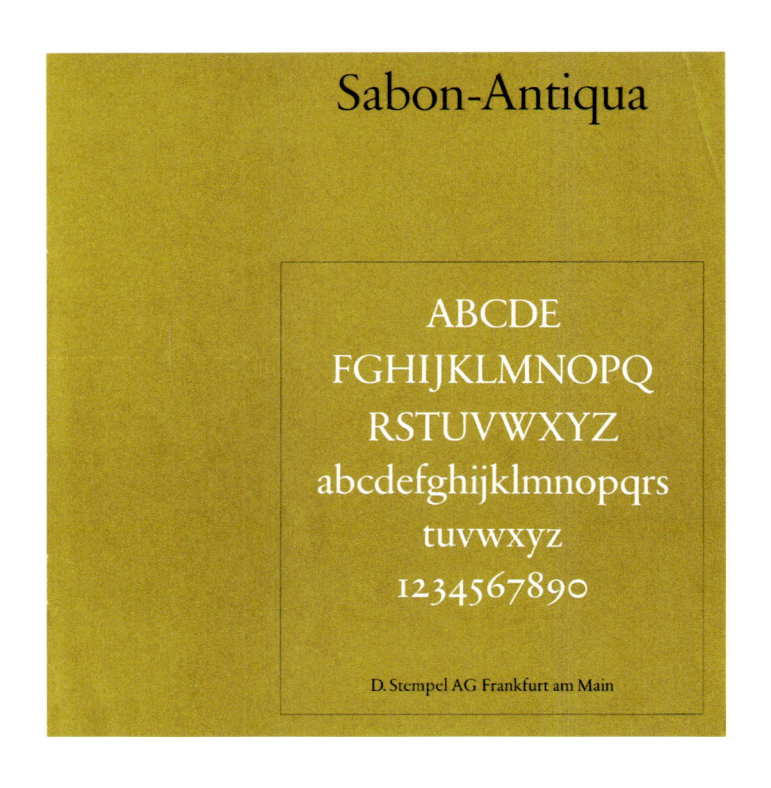

L'art de faire d'un livre un tout harmonieux n'a jamais atteint un niveau aussi élevé qu'à l'époque de l'invention de l'imprimerie. Ce que Gutenberg et ses compagnons ont gravé, fondu, composé et imprimé en respectant la plus pure tradition des écritures gothiques n'a été dépassé en force et en harmonie par aucun de leurs

Die heutige Typographie verlangt moderne Akzidenz- und Werkschriften
Ruderwettkämpfe der traditionsreichen Universitäten Oxford und Cambridge
Ausstellung im Haus des Goldschmiedehandwerks in Hanau am Main

The art of bookproducing was never on a higher level than at the time of the invention of printing. The power and harmony

Internationales Automobilrennen auf der Solitude
Ausstellung deutscher Expressionisten in Düsseldorf

Histoire littéraire de la Suisse romande

Medieval scripts in a modern style

Klavierkonzert von Bach

Cover and pages from a type specimen of Sabon-Antiqua, 1967, 29.7 x 20 cm, issued by Linotype, Bad Homburg

Sabon-Antiqua

*Een nieuwe letter
in drie zetmethodes
identiek*

De Sabon-Antiqua is een opmerkelijk novum in de geschiedenis van de gegoten letter. De Sabon-Antiqua is ontstaan door de vraag uit de praktijk naar een letter, die bij beide zetmachinesystemen, dus in machinale regel- en losse letter produktie, en bovendien als handletter volkomen gelijk is. Na jarenlange voorbereiding werd in samenwerking tussen Linotype GmbH, Monotype GmbH en D. Stempel AG de letter verwezenlijkt in 3 garnituren, die bij de verschillende zetmethodes in de corpsen 6 t/m 12 pt in vorm, beeldgrootte en zetbreedte volkomen identiek zijn. Aan een uit de Sabon gezette tekst kan men niet zien volgens welke methode deze gezet is. Daardoor is het voor het eerst mogelijk bij een bepaald zetwerk drie zetmethodes toe te passen, ze te kombineren of waar nodig van het ene systeem over te gaan op het andere. Deze voordelen maken de nieuwe letter tot een ideaal type voor onze tijd, waarin men bij de zetselverwerving streeft naar rationalisatie.

De Sabon-Antiqua is ontstaan naar ontwerpen van de befaamde Zwitserse typograaf en letterdeskundige Jan Tschichold. Gebaseerd op het historische Garamond type vertegenwoordigt hij het ware karakter van de klassieke Antiqua, die zich reeds vijf eeuwen onverminderd handhaaft en aan aktualiteit nog niets heeft ingeboet. Duidelijk en zichzelf niet aan de lezer opdringend voldoet de Sabon, zoals de klassieke Antiqua, aan de voornaamste eis die men aan een letter stellen moet, nl. door goede leesbaarheid het oog prettig aan te doen.

De naam ontleent de letter aan de lettergieter en graveur Jakob Sabon, een tijdgenoot van Garamond. Hij kwam uit Lyon en heeft lange tijd in Frankfort/Main gewerkt bij de Lettergieterij Egenolff, waarvan hij later eigenaar werd.

Bij D. Stempel AG zijn naast de handletter in de corpsen 6 t/m 12 pt van alle drie garnituren, ook reeds de corpsen 14 t/m 48 pt van de Sabon-Antiqua verkrijgbaar. De grote corpsen van de kursief en halfvet zijn in voorbereiding.

Sabon-Antikva

*En ny stil,
identisk i tre
sättningsförfaranden*

Sabon-Antikva är en remarkabel nyhet i stilgjutningens historia. Den har uppstått ur ett behov av ett typsnitt som är identiskt för de båda sättmaskinsförfarandena med såväl hela rader som lösa typer och även för handsats. Under många år har ett gemensamt utvecklingsarbete skett hos de tre företagen Linotype, Monotype och Stempel. Det svåra arbetet är nu slutfört och tre garnityr har framställts, vilka för de olika sättningsförfarandena överensstämmer helt beträffande form, bildstorlek och bokstavsbredd i graderna 6–12 pt. Om man betraktar en satsbild framställd med Sabon, kan man inte avgöra med vilket sättningsförfarande den framställts. Nu är det för första gången möjligt att använda alla tre sättningsförfarandena på en gång och vid behov kombinera dem efter respektive arbetes fordringar. Dessa fördelar gör att denna nya stil är ett idealiskt typsnitt i vår tids rationaliseringssträvanden.

Sabon-Antikvans upphovsman är Jan Tschichold, den erfarne och erkände schweiziske typografen och stilkännaren. Med utgångspunkt från det historiska Garamond-snittet speglar Sabon den klassiska antikvan, som i fem århundraden varit omtyckt och inte förlorat i aktualitet. Klar och enkel förenar Sabon-Antikva alla anspråk på en hög grad av läsbarhet med en utomordentlig estetisk verkan.

Namnet på den nya stilen kommer från en av Garamonds samtida, formgivaren och stilgjutaren Jakob Sabon. Han härstammade från Lyon och arbetade länge i Frankfurt am Main hos Egenolffsch's stilgjuteri vars ägare han så småningom blev genom ingifte.

Från D. Stempel AG kan man i dag förutom handstil i graderna 6–12 pt i alla tre garnityren även få den raka Sabon-Antikvan i graderna 14–48 pt. De större graderna i kursiv och rak halvfet är under förberedande.

D. STEMPEL AG
6 FRANKFURT AM MAIN 70
POSTFACH 701160
TELEFON (611) 610391
TELEX 411003 lino d

50X1076 Printed in Germany

Sabon-Antiqua

ABCDEFGHIJKLMNO

ABCDEFGHIJKLMNOPQRSTUVWXYZ
abcdefghijklmnopqrstuvwxyzß ch ck ff fi fl ft &
ÄÁÀÂÃÅÆÇËÉÈÊĞÏÍÌÎİÑÖÓÒÔØÕŒŞÜÚÙÛ
äáàâåãæçëéèêğïíìîijñöóòôøõœşşüúùû
1234567890 £$ 1234567890
.,:;-!?·"()[]*†§%/„"" ‹›«»¡¿—

PQRSTUVWXYZ&abcd

ABCDEFGHIJKLMNOPQRSTUVWXYZ
abcdefghijklmnopqrstuvwxyzß ch ck ff fi fl ft &
ÄÁÀÂÃÅÆÇËÉÈÊĞÏÍÌÎİÑÖÓÒÔØÕŒŞÜÚÙÛ
äáàâåãæçëéèêğïíìîijñöóòôøõœşşüúùû
1234567890 £$ 1234567890
.,:;-!?·"()[]†§%/„"" ‹›«»¡¿—*

efghiklmnopqrsßtuvwxyz

ABCDEFGHIJKLMNOPQRSTUVWXYZ
abcdefghijklmnopqrstuvwxyzß ch ck ff fi fl ft &
ÄÁÀÂÃÅÆÇËÉÈÊĞÏÍÌÎİÑÖÓÒÔØÕŒŞÜÚÙÛ
äáàâåãæçëéèêğïíìîijñöóòôøõœşşüúùû
1234567890 £$ 1234567890
.,:;-!?·"()[]*†§%/„"" ‹›«»¡¿—

$£12345678901234567890

Sabon-Antiqua

*Un caractère nouveau
identique dans les 3 procédés
de composition*

Le Sabon-Antiqua est une nouveauté marquante dans l'histoire du caractère. Il a été créé d'après les désirs et les besoins de l'imprimerie suivant un type de caractères qui convient aux deux systèmes de machines à composer, à savoir, composition mécanique de lignes blocs, composition lettre par lettre, et composition manuelle. Après de nombreuses années de recherches communes, les trois sociétés Linotype GmbH, Monotype GmbH et D. Stempel AG ont solutionné un difficile problème et créé trois séries dans les corps 6 à 12 absolument identiques, que ce soit par la forme, la grosseur, ou la largeur du caractère. Une composition en Sabon ne peut être différenciée quel que soit le procédé utilisé. De ce fait et pour la première fois, il est possible, en cours de composition, d'utiliser les 3 procédés, de les combiner comme désiré, ou même, suivant les besoins, de passer d'un procédé à l'autre. Par ses avantages et à une époque ou l'on recherche la rationalisation dans la composition, ce caractère est vraiment idéal pour notre temps.

Le Sabon-Antiqua est né d'après les esquisses de Jan Tschichold, un excellent typographe suisse bien connu. Basé sur le type Garamond historique, il personnifie en fait le romain classique, lequel, au Ve siècle, était très apprécié et qui n'a pas perdu de sa personnalité à ce jour. Clair et discret comme celui-là il accomplit la tâche difficile de rendre la lecture agréable à l'œil par sa lisibilité.

Ce nouveau caractère a hérité du nom de Jakob Sabon, fondeur et créateur, contemporain de Garamond. Originaire de Lyon, il a travaillé longtemps à Francfort s/Main dans la Fonderie Egenolff de laquelle il devint propriétaire à la suite d'une alliance.

Chez Stempel AG à part les corps 6 à 12 dans les 3 séries, vous pouvez aussi obtenir les corps 14 à 18 romain. Ces mêmes corps, en italique et romain demi-gras, sont en préparation.

Sabon-Antiqua

*Un nuovo carattere
identico
nei tre metodi di composizione*

La serie Sabon-Antiqua è una delle più recenti novità nella produzione di caratteri da stampa. La serie Sabon-Antiqua è nata dal desiderio e dalla necessità pratica di offrire un carattere sempre identico sia per i vari sistemi di composizione meccanica (linotipica, monotipica), sia per la composizione a mano. Dopo molti anni di lavoro le Società Linotype GmbH, Setzmaschinen-Fabrik Monotype e D. Stempel AG, sono riuscite a realizzare questo carattere nei corpi dal 6 al 12, per matrici linotipiche, matrici monotipiche e caratteri mobili, con assoluta uniformità di disegno, occhio e sviluppo. Un testo in carattere Sabon-Antiqua, non lascia capire in che modo sia stato composto. E' stato reso così possibile per la prima volta, l'uso contemporaneo per uno stesso testo, di tutti e tre i sistemi di composizione. In considerazione delle odierne necessità della grafica, questa nuova serie è veramente il carattere ideale per la composizione.

La Sabon-Antiqua è stata creata su studi e disegni di Jan Tschichold, noto e esperto tipografo svizzero. Infatti questa serie basandosi sull'antico tipo Garamond incorpora anche elementi della classica serie Antiqua del V° secolo, carattere questo che sino ad oggi non ha perso di attualità.

Chiara ed insuperabile come le sue antenate, la Serie Sabon-Antiqua assolve in pieno il suo compito di carattere classico, ma moderno, offrendo una grande leggibilità ed una riposante lettura. Il nome di questo nuovo carattere è quello di un grande disegnatore e fusore della Stempel, Jakob Sabon originario di Lione, contemporaneo di Garamond, che lavorò per lungo tempo a Francoforte sul Meno nella fonderia di caratteri Egenolff, di cui in seguito ne divenne il proprietario.

La Ditta D. Stempel AG oltre che ai corpi da 6 a 12 della serie Sabon-Antiqua, avverte che può fornire i caratteri a mano dal corpo 14 al corpo 48 delle tre serie di Antiqua. I corpi superiori al corpo 48 «Corsivo» e «Neretto» Antiqua, sono in preparazione.

Sabon-Antiqua

*En ny skrift
identisk
for alle tre satsmetoder*

Sabon-Antiqua er en bemærkelsesværdig nyskabelse inden for skriftstøbningens historie. Den opstod ud fra praktiske krav og ønsket om en skrift, som skulle være identisk for begge sættemaskin-systemer – altså maskinelt fremstillet liniesats og enkeltbogstavsats – såvel som håndsats. Efter et årelangt, fælles udviklingsarbejde mellem de tre selskaber: Linotype GmbH, sættemaskinfabrikken Monotype GmbH og firmaet D. Stempel AG blev denne vanskelige opgave løst og skriften fremstillet i tre garniturer, som er nøje overensstemmende i form, billedstørrelse og skriftvidde inden for de forskællige satsmetoder i graderne fra 6 til 12 punkt. Det kan ikke ses på et satsbillede i Sabon, hvilken satsmetode der er anvendt. Derved er det for første gang blevet muligt at anvende alle tre satsmetoder ved siden af hinanden i samme satsarbejde, at kunne kombinere disse efter ønske, eller at skifte over fra den ene metode til de andre, alt efter krav og formål. Disse fordele gør den nye skrift til den ideelle moderne skrift, især med henblik på nutidens rationaliseringsbestræbelser inden for satsfremstillingen.

Sabon-Antiqua blev skabt efter udkast af Jan Tschichold, den kendte og erfarne svejtsiske grafiker og en skriftkender af rang. Baseret på den historiske Garamond-skrift virkeliggør den en formfuldendt stil i den klassiske antikva, som i fem århundreder har bevaret sin værdi og ikke mistet noget i aktualitet. Klar og saglig som disse skrifter opfylder Sabon-Antiqua den krævende mission at virke velgørende på øjet ved sin gode læselighed.

Den nye skrift fik navnet efter stempel-skæreren og skriftstøberen Jakob Sabon, en af Garamond's jævnaldrende. Han stammede fra Lyon, men arbejdede i mange år i Frankfurt am Main i det Egenolff'ske skriftstøberi, som han gennem sit ægteskab senere overtog som ejer.

Firmaet D. Stempel AG kan allerede nu levere håndsatsen i graderne 6-12 punkt i alle tre garniturer og desuden alle graderne 14-48 punkt i Antiquagarnituret. De store grader i kursiv og halvfed er under forberedelse.

Sabon-Antiqua

*En ny skrift som er
identisk
i alle tre satsmetoder*

Sabon-Antiqua er en nyhet i skriftstøpingens historie som en har all grunn til å merke seg. Ønsket og kravet om en skrift som var identisk både i Monotype, Linotype og håndsats fikk tre ledende firmaer til å gå inn for oppgaven. Det er Linotype GmbH, Monotype Gesellschaft mbH og D. Stempel AG (alle i Frankfurt) som etter årelangt samarbeid kunne by trykkeriene en skrift som fra 6 til 12 punkt stemmer helt overens i alle satsmetoder, både i form og størrelse. Det er ikke mulig å se hvilken satsmetode som er benyttet med denne skriften, slik at en kan kombinere alle tre satsmetoder som det best passer i trykkeriets produksjon, til de forskjelligste behov og arbeider. Denne fordel gjør at dagens rasjonaliseringsbestrebelser tilfredsstilles fullt ut, og skriften kan med full rett betegnes som en av vår tids ideelle skrifter.

Sabon-Antiqua er tegnet etter forslag av den berømte sveitsiske skriftkjenner Jan Tschichold. Den baserer seg på den historiske Garamond-type, som gjennom fire århundrer har bevart sin aktualitet. Det beror på at den foruten sin klassiske skjønnhet også er en utmerket leseskrift.

Den nye skriften er oppkalt etter stempelskjæreren og skriftstøperen Sabon, som levde i Lyon på Garamonds tid og senere overtok Egenolffs skriftstøperi i Frankfurt.

D. Stempel AG leverer håndsatsskriftene til alle garnityrer fra 6 til 12 punkt, såvel som de større gradene i antikva. De større gradene i kursiv og halvfet er under forberedelse.

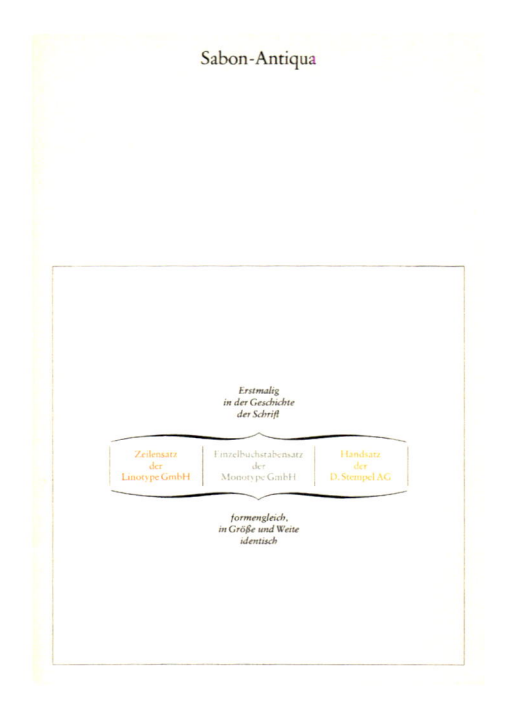

Cover and pages from a Typerello type specimen of Sabon-Antiqua, 1967, 21 x 10 cm, issued by Linotype, Bad Homburg

Die Maßstäbe für Schönheit und Zweckmäßigkeit einer Drucktype wurden vor Jahrhunderten gesetzt und haben bis zum heutigen Tage ihre Gültigkeit behalten. Aus der bewußten Besinnung auf die hohe Schriftkultur der Renaissance ist die Sabon-Antiqua entstanden. Sie verkörpert in Maß und Form den klassischen Typus der Antiqua, entwickelt für die vielfältigen Satz- und Druckaufgaben unserer Zeit und verwirklicht mit den Mitteln und Möglichkeiten heutiger Schriftschneide- und Gießtechniken. Klar und unaufdringlich im Ausdruck erfüllt sie die anspruchsvolle Aufgabe, durch einen hohen Grad an Lesbarkeit dem Auge wohlzutun. Neu und einmalig ist die Identität in drei Setzverfahren bei den kleinen Graden: Linotype-Satz und Monotype-Satz stimmen mit dem Handsatz überein. Das erweitert die Einsatzmöglichkeit dieser Schrift und erhöht ihren Gebrauchswert. Schon heute kann man der Sabon-Antiqua eine große Zukunft voraussagen.

Sabon-Antiqua

Sabon Antiqua

ABCDEFGHIJKLMNOPQ
RSTUVWXYZÄÖÜ
abcdefghijklmnopqrstuvwxyz
ßchckffffifflft&äöü
1234567890 1234567890
.,:;-!?'()[]*†‹›«»„"/£$

Sabon Kursiv

Eine neue Schrift

Nach Entwürfen
von Jan Tschichold

D. Stempel AG

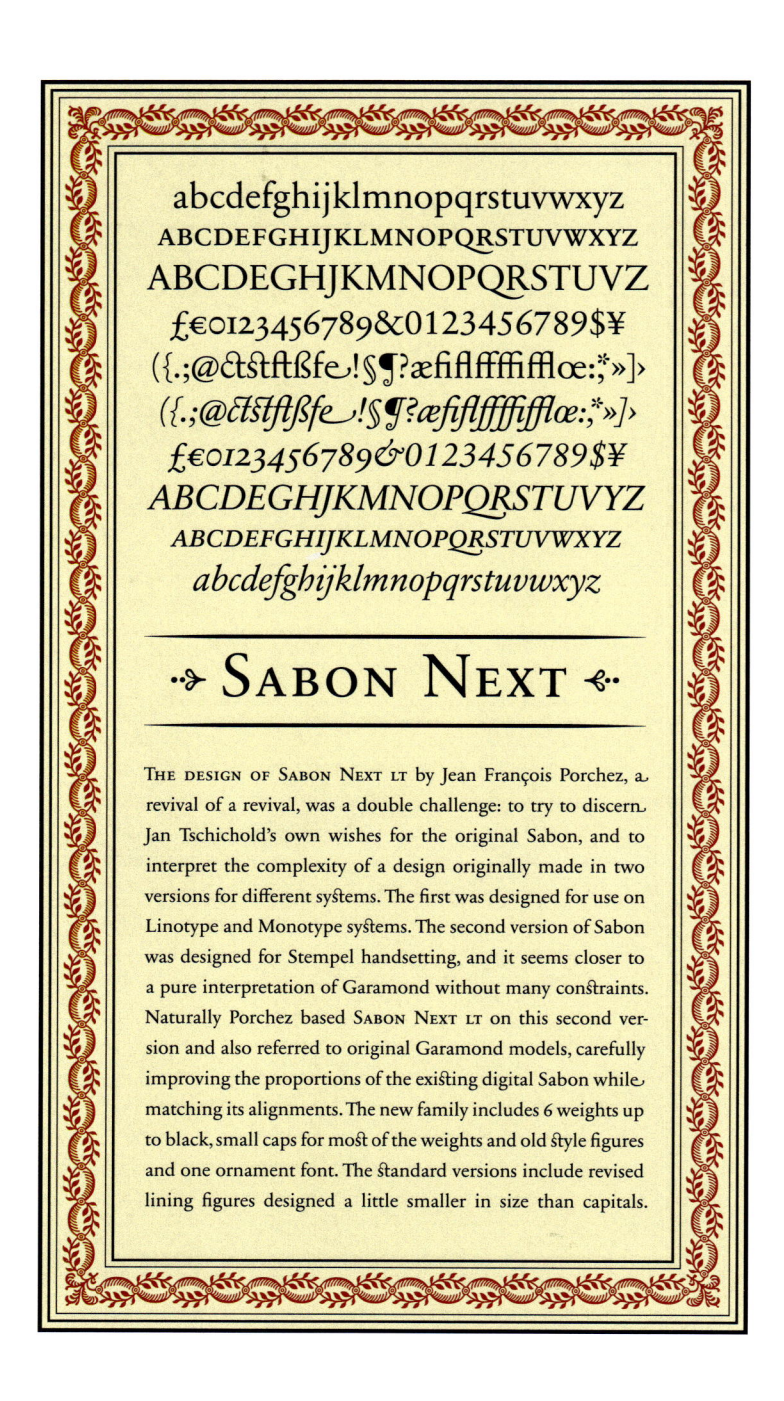

abcdefghijklmnopqrstuvwxyz
ABCDEFGHIJKLMNOPQRSTUVWXYZ
ABCDEGHJKMNOPQRSTUVZ
£€0123456789&0123456789$¥
({.;@ctstftßfe⸗!§¶?æfiflffffifflœ:;*»]›
({.;@ctstftßfe⸗!§¶?æfiflffffifflœ:;*»]›
£€0123456789&0123456789$¥
ABCDEGHJKMNOPQRSTUVYZ
ABCDEFGHIJKLMNOPQRSTUVWXYZ
abcdefghijklmnopqrstuvwxyz

⸎ SABON NEXT ⸏

THE DESIGN OF SABON NEXT LT by Jean François Porchez, a revival of a revival, was a double challenge: to try to discern Jan Tschichold's own wishes for the original Sabon, and to interpret the complexity of a design originally made in two versions for different systems. The first was designed for use on Linotype and Monotype systems. The second version of Sabon was designed for Stempel handsetting, and it seems closer to a pure interpretation of Garamond without many constraints. Naturally Porchez based SABON NEXT LT on this second version and also referred to original Garamond models, carefully improving the proportions of the existing digital Sabon while matching its alignments. The new family includes 6 weights up to black, small caps for most of the weights and old style figures and one ornament font. The standard versions include revised lining figures designed a little smaller in size than capitals.

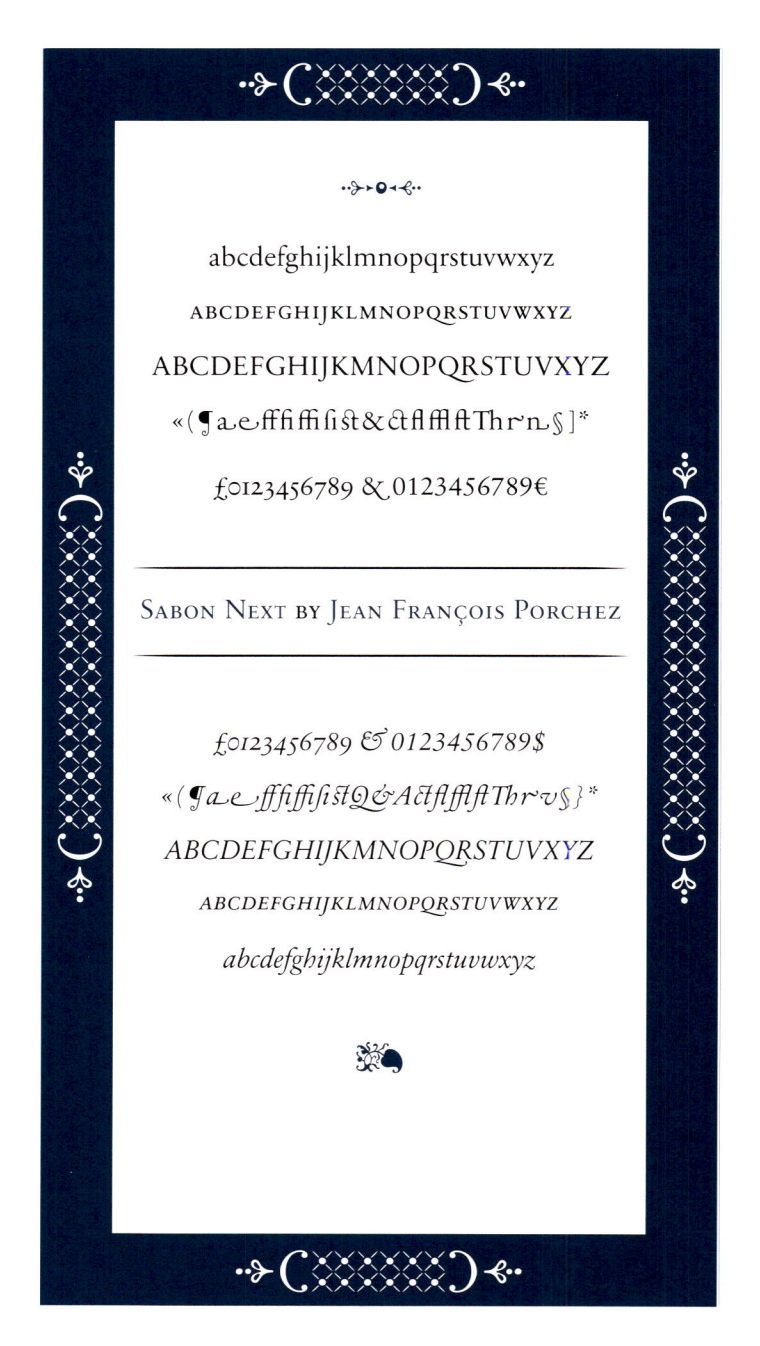

---

abcdefghijklmnopqrstuvwxyz
ABCDEFGHIJKLMNOPQRSTUVWXYZ
ABCDEFGHIJKMNOPQRSTUVXYZ
«(¶æffffiffist&ctflfflftThrn§]*
£0123456789 & 0123456789€

SABON NEXT BY JEAN FRANÇOIS PORCHEZ

£0123456789 & 0123456789$
«(¶æffffifisiſtQ&ActflfflftThrv§}*
ABCDEFGHIJKMNOPQRSTUVXYZ
ABCDEFGHIJKLMNOPQRSTUVWXYZ
abcdefghijklmnopqrstuvwxyz

Jean-François Porchez's design of Linotype Sabon Next, a revival of a revival, was a double challenge: to discern Jan Tschichold's own wishes concerning the original Sabon and to interpret the complexity of a design originally made in two versions for different systems.

The first version of Sabon was designed for use on Linotype and Monotype systems, whereas the second was designed for Stempel handsetting and seems closer to a pure interpretation of Garamond. Naturally, Porchez based Linotype Sabon Next on this second version and also referred to original Garamond models, carefully improving the proportions of the existing digital Sabon while matching its alignments.

The new family includes 6 weights up to black. Small caps are available for most of the weights and the family has Old Style Figures and one Ornament font. The standard versions include revised lining figures designed a little smaller than the capitals.

Sabon Antiqua

669-1

& &

& &

Sabon Next LT

Sabon
Next

Sabon Next LT Regular

A B C D
E F G H
I J K L M
N O P Q

RSTUV
WXYZ
12345
67890

SABON NEXT LT REGULAR

abcdefg
hijklm
nopqrst
uvwxyz

«(ɡaeff
fi ffi fi st &
ctſt ſm ft Th
r n ſ]*

Sabon Next LT Regular Small Caps

A B C D
E F G H
I J K L M
N O P Q

RSTUV
WXYZ
1 2 3 4 5
6 7 8 9 0

Sabon Next LT Regular Small Caps

ABCDEF
GHIJKLM
NOPQRS
TUVWXYZ

« (¶ FF FI

FFI Æ & FL

FFL §] *

Sabon Next LT Regular Italic

A B C D

E F G H I

J K L M N

O P Q R S

TUVW

XYZ

12345

67890

Sabon Next LT Regular Italic

*a b c d e f g
h i j k l m
n o p q r s t
u v w x y z*

« (ꝙ a e ﬀ ﬁ ﬀﬁ ſi ﬄ ſl ſt & et ſl ſſl ﬅ T h r n §] *

Sabon Next LT Italic Small Caps

A B C D

E F G H

I J K L M

N O P Q

RSTUV
WXYZ
12345
67890

Sabon Next LT Italic Small Caps

ABCDEF

GHIJKLM

NOPQRST

UVWXYZ

«(¶ FF FI
FFI Æ & FL
FFL §]*

Sabon Next LT Bold

A B C D
E F G H
I J K L M
N O P Q

RSTUV
WXYZ
12345
67890

Sabon Next LT Bold

abcdefg
hijklm
nopqrst
uvwxyz

«(Ɠae
ff fi ffi fi ſt
& ɛt fl ffl ft
Th r n §]*

Sabon Next LT Black

A B C D
E F G H
I J K L M
N O P Q

RSTUV
WXYZ
12345
67890

Sabon Next LT Black

abcdefg
hijklm
nopqrst
uvwxyz

«(ȷ a e
ff fi ffi ffi fi st
& ꝛ ſl ſm ſt
Th r n §]*

Sabon Next LT

A B C D E F G H I J K L M N O P Q
R S T U V W X Y Z
a b c d e f g h i j k l m n o p q r s t
u v w x y z ß ff fi fl &
1 2 3 4 5 6 7 8 9 0
(. , - : ; ! ? ' ' * { [% ~)

Sabon Next LT Regular

A B C D E F G H I J K L M N O P Q
R S T U V W X Y Z
A B C D E F G H I J K L M N O P Q R S T
U V W X Y Z SS FF FI FL &
1 2 3 4 5 6 7 8 9 0
(. , - : ; ! ? ' ' * { [% ~)

Sabon Next LT Regular Small Caps

A B C D E F G H I J K L M N O P Q
R S T U V W X Y Z
a b c d e f g h i j k l m n o p q r s t u v
w x y z ß ff fi fl &
1 2 3 4 5 6 7 8 9 0
*(. , - : ; ! ? ' ' * { [% ~)*

Sabon Next LT Italic

A B C D E F G H I J K L M N O P Q
R S T U V W X Y Z
A B C D E F G H I J K L M N O P Q R S T
U V W X Y Z SS FF FI FL &
1 2 3 4 5 6 7 8 9 0
*(. , - : ; ! ? ' ' * { [% ~)*

Sabon Next LT Italic Small Caps

J.T. J.T. J.T. J.T. J.T. J.T. J.T. J.T. J.T. J.T.

J.T. J.T. J.T. J.T. J.T. J.T. J.T. J.T. J.T. J.T.

J.T. J.T. J.T. J.T. J.T. J.T. J.T. J.T. J.T. J.T.

J.T. J.T. J.T. J.T. J.T. J.T. J.T. J.T. J.T. J.T.

J.T. J.T. J.T. J.T. J.T. J.T. J.T. J.T. J.T. J.T.

J.T. J.T. J.T. J.T. J.T. J.T. J.T. J.T. J.T. J.T.

J.T. J.T. J.T. J.T. J.T. J.T. J.T. J.T. J.T. J.T.

J.T. J.T. J.T. J.T. J.T. J.T. J.T. J.T. J.T. J.T.

J.T. J.T. J.T. J.T. J.T. J.T. J.T. J.T. J.T. J.T.

J.T. J.T. J.T. J.T. J.T. J.T. J.T. J.T. J.T. J.T.

Index of names

Albers, Josef 32
Albert, Joseph 189
Alma, Peter 197
Arntz, Gerd 197
Arp, Hans (Jean) 197
Arp, Sophie (Täuber) 197

Ballmer, Theo 201
Baumberger, Otto 36
Baumeister, Willi 9, 19, 33, 39, 49, 55
Bayer, Herbert 8, 10, 32, 36, 40, 44, 55, 160, 173, 197, 202, 206, 210, 265
Beall, Lester 160
Beckmann, Max 84, 86, 233
Behne, Adolf 36, 197
Behrens, Peter 170, 172, 176
Bernhard, Lucian (Kahn, Emil) 170, 206, 237
Biermann, Aenne 17, 48, 84, 108
Bill, Max 10, 32, 63
Borst, Bernhard 186
Breuer, Marcel 31
Brinton, Christian 165
Brodovitch, Alexey 64, 165
Burchartz, Max 9, 18, 36, 48, 55, 67, 91, 197, 206

Carlu, Jean 48, 160, 214
Cassandre, Alphonse Mouron 32, 48, 59, 165, 173, 214, 346
Cyliax, Walter 197

Delitsch, Hermann 8, 28
Demmel, Michael 193
Dexel, Walter 9, 18, 32, 48, 55, 67, 197, 206, 213, 214

Doede, Werner 186
Doesburg, Theo van 10, 32, 35, 36, 39, 55, 67, 160, 202
Domela, César 9, 18, 48
Doubleday, Richard B. 6, 67, 255
Dreyer, Carl 201
Eidenbenz, Hermann 213

Franke, Günter 202, 205, 206, 346, 348
Frenzel, Hermann Karl 206
Fuss, Albert 197

Galpern, Lasar 40, 166, 168
Gebs (Gebhart, Max) 181
Ginsburger, Roger 56
Glass, Franz Paul 170, 181, 198, 206, 209
Goebbels, Joseph 10, 21, 64
Gogh, Vincent van 84, 202, 230, 234
Goldschmidt, Hilde 260
Graeff, Werner 47, 55, 158, 197, 345
Graul, Werner 201, 219
Gropius, Walter 31, 35, 39, 180, 186

Hagen, Maria 206
Heartfield, John (Herzfeld, Helmut) 55, 173, 181
Hertwig, Max 194
Hindenburg, Paul von 169
Hitler, Adolf 64, 169, 191, 209, 213
Hohlwein, Ludwig 170, 181, 201, 206
Honegger, Arthur 193

Horn, Hilde (Hildegard Posse) 21, 48, 50, 53, 78, 79, 160, 194, 210, 214

Johnson, Philip 214
Johnston, Edward 8, 28, 265

Kandinsky, Wassily 31
Kassák, Lajos 55
Keaton, Buster 182, 193, 198, 197
Kepes, Gyorgy 160
Kienzle, Hermann 11, 60
Kiesler, Friedrich 202
Klemke, Werner 165, 345
Klutsis, Gustav 32, 173 181, 213, 214
Kogan, M. 84
Kramer, Maria Mathilda Edith 8, 166
Kubin, Alfred 84, 205

Larisch, Rudolf von 8, 28, 265
László, Alexander 193
Leck, Bart van der 173, 208
Leistikow, Hans 9, 18, 55, 197
Liebknecht, Karl 169
Link, Liselotte Christine Frederieke 166
Lissitzky, El 9, 31, 32, 36, 39, 55, 67. 90, 156, 160. 181, 197, 206, 213, 214, 346
Lissitzky-Kuppers, Sophie 156, 346
Luxemburg, Rosa 169

Macke, August 84
Malevich, Kazimir 31, 32
Marinetti, Filippo Tommaso 43, 83

Matsumoto, Ruki 160
Matter, Herbert 160, 165, 213, 346
McKnight Kauffer, Edward 160
McLean, Ruari 11, 40, 60, 67, 165, 282, 294, 346
Meisenbach, Georg 189
Mesens, Edouard 210
Michel, Robert 9, 18, 197
Mies van der Rohe, Ludwig 31, 31/32
Moholy-Nagy, László 9, 11, 18, 31, 106, 108, 161, 197, 265
Molzahn, Johannes 36, 55
Mondrian, Piet 9, 32, 48, 60, 160, 210, 213, 347
Morison Stanley 11, 21, 270, 274, 345
Morris, William 44
Mueller, Otto 84
Müller, Carl Otto 160, 198, 214

Neumann, Israel Ber 202
Neurath, Otto 197
Newhall, Beaumont 213
Nicholson, Ben 32
Nolde, Emil 84, 205, 232

Pankok, Otto 84
Pathe, Peter 206
Pierce, William (Bill) 260
Popp, Johan (Hans) 186
Porchez, Jean-François 303, 305, 312
Porstmann, Walter 98
Preetorius, Emil 170, 209

Rand, Paul 32, 64, 67, 160

343

Ravesteyn, Sybold van 48, 202
Ray, Man 21, 32, 63, 213
Reichel, Hans 84
Renner, Paul 8, 9, 11, 18, 44, 47, 55, 60. 67, 170, 178, 181, 189, 198, 209, 214, 345
Richter, Hans 47, 55, 158, 197, 346
Rodchenko, Alexander 31, 32, 160
Roh, Franz 47, 48, 78, 346
Röhl, Karl Peter 35, 39

———

Sametzki 160, 197
Schawinsky, Alexander 197
Schlemmer, Oskar 31, 32, 39, 107, 173, 197, 206
Schmidt, Joost 173, 197
Schnackenberg, Walter 206
Schuitema, Paul 9, 18, 32, 55, 56, 173, 201, 206
Schwabe, Benno 11, 60, 135, 136, 139, 140, 142, 245, 246, 247, 248, 249, 262, 266, 269, 346
Schwitters, Helma 213
Schwitters, Kurt 9, 14, 18, 32, 36, 44, 55, 56, 67, 78, 158, 181, 190, 197, 202, 213, 214, 260, 300
Senefelder, Alois 189
Seuphor, Michel 48
Stenberg, Georgii 173
Stenberg, Vladimir 173
Stroheim, Erich von 201, 344
Sutnar, Ladislav 32, 67, 160, 165, 206, 346

———

Teige, Karel 10, 55
Thälmann, Ernst 169
Thomas, Edith 260

Tiemann, Walter 8, 28
Trump, Georg 8, 9, 10, 18, 47, 48, 55, 59, 181, 189, 209, 214, 345
Tschichold, Edith 14, 24, 59, 60, 67, 166, 181, 214
Tschichold, Peter 9, 24, 27
Tzschichhold, Franz 8

———

Vertov, Dziga 201, 202, 236
Virl, Hermann 181
Vordemberge-Gildewart, Friedrich 9, 18, 32, 48, 60, 214, 345

———

Wasow, Eduard 24, 74, 79, 86, 156, 242
Westermayer, Konrad 84
Wieynck, Heinrich 8, 265
Wijdeveld, Hendrikus Theodorus 32, 202
Wilhelm II 169

———

Zapff, Maria 8
Zietara, Valentin 170, 206, 209
Zwart, Piet 9, 18, 31, 32, 43, 48, 55, 56, 67, 173, 198, 201, 202, 206, 346

Selected Literature & Source List

A MORE COMPREHENSIVE LIST OF WORKS BY AND ABOUT
JAN TSCHICHOLD IS INCLUDED IN:

Leben und Werk des Typographen Jan Tschichold, with an introduction by Werner Klemke. Dresden: Verlag der Kunst, 1977

OTHER SOURCES CONSULTED:

Atterbury, Rowley S. *The Contributors: Being the Paper Talk Delivered to the Wynkyn de Worde Society at Stationers' Hall on 16th May 1974.* Westerham, Kent: Westerham Press, 1974

Antin, Charles. "The Penguin *Golden Ass*, Jan Tschichold's Masterpiece." *Antiquarian Bookman*, 1 June 1998: pp. 1465–1466

Aynsley, Jeremy. *Graphic Design in Germany 1890–1945*. London: Thames & Hudson; Los Angeles: University of California Press, 2000

Bartram, Alan. *Making Books. Design in British Publishing Since 1945.* London: The British Library; New Castle, DE: Oak Knoll Press, 1999

bauhaus. drucksachen, typographie, reklame. Düsseldorf: Marzona, 1984

Beiträge zur Grafik und Buchgestaltung. 200-Jahr-Feier der Hochschule für Grafik und Buchkunst Leipzig. Leipzig: Hochschule für Grafik und Buchkunst, 1964

Bringhurst, Robert, and Hadeler, Hajo. *The Form of the Book: Essays on the Morality of Good Design.* London: Lund Humphries, 1991

Brockmann, Josef Müller. *A History of Visual Communication.* New York: Hastings House, 1971

Broos, Kees. *Mondriaan, De Stijl en De Nieuwe Typografie*. Amsterdam/The Hague: Uitgeverij De Buitenkant, 1994

Burbidge, P. G., and Gray, L. A. "Penguin Panorama: A historical and typographical study of the publications of Penguin Books, in honour of their twenty-first birthday." *Printing Review*, no. 72, 1956: pp. 5–30

Burke, Christopher. *Paul Renner: The Art of Typography.* London: Hyphen Press, 1998

Burke, Christopher. *Active Literature: Jan Tschichold and New Typography.* London: Hyphen Press, 2007

Caflisch, Max. *Die Schriften von Renner, Tschichold und Trump*. Munich: TGM-Bibliothek, 1991

Carrington, Noel. "A Century for Puffin Picture Books." *Penrose Annual: A Review of the Graphic Arts*, vol. 51, 1957: pp. 62–64

Cinamon, Gerald, ed. "Hans Schmoller Typographer, His Life and Work." *The Monotype Recorder*, no. 6, April 1987

Commercial Art and Industry, monthly, London: The Studio Ltd, 1929–1934

Der Bücherkreis, quarterlies, 1930–1932

De Reclame, officieel organ van het genootschap voor reclame, The Hague, October 1931

Die Form, Monatsschrift für gestaltende Arbeit. Berlin: Verlag Hermann Reckendorf, 1926–1933

Die Reklame, Zeitschrift des Vereins Deutscher Reklamefachleute, Berlin: Francken & Lang, 1926, June issue

Die Zwanziger Jahre des Deutschen Werkbunds, Frankfurt: Anabas Verlag, 1982

Doubleday, Richard B. "Bird in Hand." *Print*, May–June 2005: pp. 68–75

Doubleday, Richard B. "Jan Tschichold at Penguin Books, A Resurgence of Classical Book Design." *Baseline International Typographics Magazine* no. 49, 2006: pp. 13–20

Doubleday, Richard B. *Jan Tschichold, Designer: The Penguin Years.* New Castle, DE: Oak Knoll Press; London: Lund Humphries/Ashgate Publishing, 2006

Doubleday, Richard B. "Jan Tschichold at Penguin Books, A Resurgence of Classical Book Design." *Idea International Graphic Art and Typography Magazine*, no. 321, 2007: pp. 99–122

Dreyfus, John. "The impact of Stanley Morison." *Penrose Annual: A Review of the Graphic Arts*, vol. 62, 1969: pp. 94–111

Droste, Magdalena. *bauhaus-archiv*. Cologne: Taschen, 1990

Droste, Magdalena. *Bauhaus 1919–1933.* Berlin: Bauhaus-Archiv Museum für Gestaltung; Cologne: Taschen, 1998

Ehmcke, Fritz Hellmut. *Schrift: ihre Gestaltung und Entwicklung in neuerer Zeit*. Hanover: Günther Wagner, 1925

Graeff, Werner. *Es kommt der neue Fotograf!* Berlin: Verlag Hermann Reckendorf, 1929

Feather, John. *A History of British Publishing.* London: Routledge, Taylor & Francis Group, 1988

Fifty Penguin Years: published on the occasion of Penguin Books' fiftieth anniversary. Harmondsworth: Penguin Books, 1985

Flower, Desmond. *The Paperback: Its Past, Present and Future.* London: Arborfield Productions, 1959

Frederiksen, Ellegaard Erik. *The Typography of Penguin Books*, trans. K. B. Almlund. London: Penguin Collectors' Society, 2004

Friedrich Vordemberge-Gildewart, Typographie und Werbegestaltung, exhibition catalog. Wiesbaden: Landesmuseum, 1990

Gebrauchsgraphik, Monatschrift zur Förderung der Reklamekunst/International Advertising Art. Berlin: Phönix Verlag, 1925–1940

Gefesselter Blick. Stuttgart: Verlag Dr. Zaugg & Co., 1930

Graphische Berufsschule, "Schulmitteilungen" (in-house newsletter), Munich, 1926–1933

Graphische Revue. Eine Zeitschrift für das Buchgewerbe, Vienna: Graphische Gesellschaft, 1928, no. 1; 1930, no. 5

Gottschall, Edward M. *Typographic Communications Today*. Cambridge, MA: The MIT Press, 1989

Hare, Steve. *Penguin Portrait: Allen Lane and the Penguin Editors 1935–1970*. Harmondsworth: Penguin Books, 1995

Herbert Matter: Foto-Grafiker, Sehformen der Zeit. Zurich: Schweizerische Stiftung für die Photographie; Baden: Verlag Lars Müller, 1995

Hochuli, Jost. *Jan Tschichold, Typographer and Type Designer, 1902–1974*, trans. Ruari McLean, W. A. Kelly and Bernard Wolpe. Edinburgh: National Library of Scotland, 1982: p. 35

Hochuli, Jost and Kinross, Robin. *Designing Books: Practice and Theory*. London: Hyphen Press, 1996

Hommage à Günther Franke, exhibition catalog. Munich: Museum Villa Stuck, 1983

Jan and Edith Tschichold Papers, Getty Institute, Los Angeles,

Jan Tschichold: Schriften 1925–1974, edition in two volumes, Berlin: Brinkmann und Bose, 1991

Jan Tschichold: Typograph und Schriftentwerfer 1902–1974, exhibition catalog. Zurich: Kunstgewerbemuseum, 1976

J.T. Johannes Tzschichhold Iwan Tschichold Jan Tschichold. Munich: Typographische Gesellschaft, 1976

Käufer, Josef, ed. *Fünfundzwanzig Jahre Meisterschule für Deutschlands Buchdrucker München 1927/1952*, Munich, 1952

Kurt Schwitters, Typographie und Werbegestaltung, exhibition catalog. Wiesbaden: Landesmuseum, 1990

Ladislav Sutnar Papers, Cooper-Hewitt Museum, New York City

Ladislav Sutnar—Prague—New York—design in action, exhibition catalog. Prague: Museum of Decorative Arts/Argo Publishers, 2003

Lamb, Lynton. "Penguins Books: Style and Mass Production." *Penrose Annual: A Review of the Graphic Arts*, vol. 46, 1952: pp. 39–42

Lane, Allen. "Penguins and Pelicans." *Penrose Annual: A Review of the Graphic Arts*, vol. 40, 1938: pp. 41–44

Lane, Allen. *Penguins Progress 1935–1960*, published on the occasion of the Silver Jubilee of Penguin Books. Harmondsworth: Penguin Books, 1960

Le Coultre, Martijn F. and Purvis, Alston W. *Jan Tschichold: Posters of the Avantgarde*. Basel: Birkhäuser Verlag; Laren: V+K Projects, 2007

Lerch-Stumpf, Monika, ed. *Für ein Zehnerl ins Paradies, Münchner Kinogeschichte 1896–1945*. Munich: Dölling und Galitz Verlag GmbH, 2004

Lissitzky-Küppers, Sophie. *El Lissitzky: Life, Letters, Texts*, trans. Helene Aldwinckle and Mary Whittall. London: Thames & Hudson, 1968

McLean, Ruari. *How Typography Happens*. New Castle, DE: Oak Knoll Press; London: The British Library, 2000

McLean, Ruari. *Jan Tschichold: Typographer*. Boston: David R. Godine; London: Lund Humphries, 1975

McLean, Ruari. *True To Type: A Typographical Autobiography*. New Castle, DE: Oak Knoll Press; London: Werner Shaw, 2000

Meggs, Philip B. *A History of Graphic Design*, 3rd ed. New York: John Wiley & Sons, 1998

Melis, Urban von. *Die Buchgemeinschaften in der Weimarer Republik*. Stuttgart: Anton Hiersemann, 2002

Münchner Moderne. Kunst und Architektur der zwanziger Jahre. Munich/Berlin: Deutscher Kunstverlag, 2002

Münchner Neueste Nachrichten, 1926–1928; Günther Franke Estate, Bayerische Staatsbibliothek, Munich

New Poster: International Exposition of Design in Outdoor Advertising, Philadelphia: The Franklin Institute, 1937

Newton, Eric. "The King Penguins." *Penrose Annual: A Review of the Graphic Arts*, vol. 43, 1949

Offset-, Buch- und Werbekunst, Leipzig: Offset-Verlag, 1926, no. 7

Paris-Berlin 1900–1933, exhibition catalog. Paris: Centre Georges Pompidou; Munich: Prestel-Verlag, 1979

"The Penguin Look and Monotype Faces." *Penrose Annual: A Review of the Graphic Arts*, vol. 51, 1957

Penguins: A Retrospect: 1935–1951. Harmondsworth: Penguin Books, 1951

Piet Mondrian, catalogue raisonné (catalog of complete works). New York: Harry N. Abrams, 1998

Piet Zwart Papers, Getty Institute, Los Angeles

Plakate in München 1840–1940, exhibition catalog. Munich: Münchner Stadtmuseum, 1975–76

Powers, Alan. *Front Cover: Great Book Jacket and Cover Design*. London: Octopus, 2001

"Publicité, présenté par A.M. Cassandre," from *L'Art international d'aujourd'hui*. Paris: Éditions d'Art Charles Moreau, 1929

Richter, Hans. *Filmgegner von heute—Filmfreunde von morgen*. Berlin: Verlag Hermann Reckendorf, 1929

Ring neue Werbegestalter, Die Amsterdamer Ausstellung 1931, exhibition catalog. Wiesbaden: Landesmuseum, 1990

Roh, Franz and Tschichold, Jan. *Foto-Auge: 76 Fotos der Zeit.* Stuttgart: Wedekind, 1929

Schmoller, Hans. "Reprints: Aldine and After." *Penrose Annual: A Review of the Graphic Arts*, vol. 47, 1953: pp. 35–38

Schmoller, Hans. *Two Titans: Mardersteig and Tschichold, A Study in Contrasts.* London: British Library; New York: The Typophiles, 1990

Schubert, Walter F. *Die Deutsche Werbe-Graphik.* Berlin: Verlag Francken & Lang GmbH, 1927

Simon, Oliver. "Mass Production and the Art of the Book." *Penguins Progress*, no. 5, 1947: pp. 18–20

Spencer, Herbert. "Penguins on the March." *Typographica*, no. 5, June 1962

"Style and Legibility: The Penguin Composition Rules." *Print in Britain*, no. 6, 1953: pp. 165–169

Süddeutscher Graphischer Anzeiger, Schnitzler, Munich, 1930, no. 8

Taylor, John. "A checklist of Penrose articles 1895–1968." *Penrose Annual: A Review of the Graphic Arts*, vol. 62, 1969: pp. 253–292

Tschichold, Jan. *Asymmetric Typography.* Basel: Benno Schwabe, 1935; reprint: New York: Reinhold Publishing, 1967

Tschichold, Jan. *Designing Books.* New York: Wittenborn, Schultz, 1951

Tschichold, Jan. "Die neue Typographie." *Print* vol. 18, no. 1 1964

Tschichold, Jan. *Die neue Typographie*, facsimile of the 1928 edition. Berlin: Brinkman & Bose, 1987

Tschichold, Jan. "Glaube und Wirklichkeit (Belief and Reality)." *Schweizer Graphische Mitteilungen*, June 1946: pp. 233–42

Tschichold, Jan. "Jan Tschichold lecture to the Typography USA seminar sponsored by the Type Director's Club, New York on 18 April 1959." *Print*, XVIII, no. 1 1964: pp. 16–17

Tschichold, Jan. *Leben und Werk des Typographen.* Dresden: Verlag der Kunst, 1977

Tschichold, Jan. "Mein Reform der Penguin Books." *Schweizer Graphische Mitteilungen*, no. 6, 1950; English trans. Ruari McLean, in *Jan Tschichold: Typographer.* Boston: David R. Godine, 1975

Tschichold, Jan. "On mass-producing the classics." *Signature*, no. 3, 1947

Tschichold, Jan. "On mass-producing the classics." *Print*, no. 1, 18 April 1959

Tschichold, Jan. "Von schlechter und guter Typographie." *Publicité et Arts Graphiques.* Geneva: Maurice Collet éditeur, 1944–45

Typographische Mitteilungen, Sonderheft: elementare typographie, October 1925; reprint: Mainz: Verlag H. Schmidt, 1986

Vytvarné snahy, revue mensuelle artistique des arts décoratifs et de l'éducation artistique, Prague, 1928

Wem gehört die Welt, exhibition catalog. Berlin: Neue Gesellschaft für Bildende Kunst, 1977

Williams, William Emrys. *The Penguin Story MCMXXXV–MCMLVI.* Harmondsworth: Penguin Books, 1956

Word and Image, Posters from the Collection of the Museum of Modern Art, exhibition catalog. New York: MoMA, 1968

Illustration Credits

Bayerische Staatsbibliothek, Günther Franke Estate, Munich
Bayerische Staatsbibliothek, Munich
Bayerisches Hauptstaatsarchiv, Munich
Basler Plakatsammlung, Basel
Estate of Jan Tschichold, Switzerland and Leipzig, Germany
Kunstbibliothek, Staatliche Museen zu Berlin – Preußischer Kulturbesitz, Berlin
Municipal Archive, Munich (Education Authority)
Museum für Gestaltung, Zurich
Museum für Kunst und Gewerbe, Hamburg
Private collections
Penguin Books Ltd.